POCKET
THAI
DICTIONARY

Thai–English
English–Thai

REVISED AND EXPANDED

Compiled by Scot Barmé and Pensi Najaithong
Updated and revised by Jintana Rattanakhemakorn

PERIPLUS

Published by Periplus Editions (HK) Ltd.

www.periplus.com

Copyright © 2017 Periplus Editions (HK) Ltd.

ISBN: 978-0-7946-0783-8

Printed in China

Distributed by:

Japan
Tuttle Publishing
Yaekari Building, 3rd Floor, 5-4-12 Osaki
Shinagawa-ku, Tokyo 141 0032
Tel: (81) 3 5437-0171
Fax: (81) 3 5437-0755
sales@tuttle.co.jp
www.tuttle.co.jp

North America, Latin America & Europe
Tuttle Publishing
364 Innovation Drive
North Clarendon, VT 05759-9436 U.S.A.
Tel: 1 (802) 773-8930
Fax: 1 (802) 773-6993
info@tuttlepublishing.com
www.tuttlepublishing.com

Asia Pacific
Berkeley Books Pte Ltd
61 Tai Seng Avenue #02-12
Singapore 534167
Tel: (65) 6280 1330
Fax: (65) 6280 6290
inquiries@periplus.com.sg
www.periplus.com

20 19 18 17
6 5 4 3 2 1
1710RR

Contents

Introduction

This Pocket Thai Dictionary gives entries that are based on everyday colloquial Thai although more 'polite' or 'formal' ones are also included, where appropriate. To ensure that you are aware of these distinctions both 'colloquial' and 'formal' entries are clearly indicated, as is the case with various idioms and slang terms listed.

In compiling this work we have done our best to include the most commonly used Thai words. It should be emphasized, however, that in a book of such limited scope, it has been impossible to provide a totally comprehensive listing of vocabulary items. Even so we believe that this dictionary will meet the needs of users who would like to develop a proficiency in the language and a better understanding of a distinctively different socio-cultural world.

To help you get a better sense of how different Thai words function there are also a number of specific examples of usage provided. Merely providing lists of words and their Thai or English equivalents does not really give the user enough to work with if they are interested in moving beyond a rudimentary, and often unsatisfactory, level of communication.

Numerous examples of how the particular meanings of Thai words/expressions are formed are also provided. These examples are given in parentheses and appear as follows: (literally, 'word A'-'word B' and so on). A case in point is the way the Thai word for 'river' is formed. In English "river" is a single word. In Thai, however, "river"—**mâeh-náam** แม่น้ำ—is a combination of two distinct and completely different words. The first of these is **mâeh**, or "mother," and the second is **náam**, or "water." In other words "river" in Thai is literally "mother"-"water" (or "mother of water(s)"). Similarly, the English word "tear(s)" (i.e. the tears of someone crying) in Thai is **náam-taa** (literally, "water"-"eye[s]") น้ำตา, the word **taa** here meaning "eye(s)."

From examining the examples provided in the English-Thai section of the dictionary you should be able to not only extend your vocabulary and improve your facility with the language, but also develop a better understanding of the type of English typically spoken by many Thai people. Regardless of your language background it is natural to use your mother tongue as a type of template when speaking another language. That is until you begin to make a serious effort to understand the underlying nature of the language you are trying to learn and develop a fuller sense of it in its own terms.

The basics of Thai might be considered simple enough for you to quickly pick up the language, especially when compared to some European languages, for example:

1. Words are not modified or conjugated for tense, person, posses-
    sion, number (singular/plural), gender, or subject-verb agreement.

2. Determiners such as "a, an, or the" are not used.

Hence many Thai speakers of English speak in what is usually referred
to as 'broken English' (or 'Tinglish' as some would have it)—this being
strongly influenced by their native Thai language template. And, obvi-
ously, non-Thais do much the same thing when speaking Thai.

Here it should be mentioned that there are a significant, and ever increasing, number of English words in Thai, many concerned with tech-
nological advances and innovation. At the same time there is also a
growing body of 'non' technical words and expressions that have been
incorporated into Thai. Such instances are clearly indicated by the in-
clusion of the marker (from English) next to such entries. Inevitably,
English borrowings into Thai have been 'Thai-ified' and, at times, are not
immediately clear or comprehensible to the native English speaker. In
all cases an attempt has been made to provide a usable form of pronunciation for these various English 'loan' words.

A final note: In addition to 'polite,' 'formal,' 'colloquial' terms and a smat-
tering of widely used 'idioms,' a number of common crude, vulgar words
are included and clearly marked. These particular entries are for the
benefit of the curious reader—a form of FYI, as it were. However, it is
strongly advised that you avoid using any such words until you have
gained a good level of familiarity with Thai society and the way Thai
people interact. Under no circumstances experiment using such language with strangers as the consequences of doing so could, poten-
tially, be very unpleasant.

General overview of some key aspects of Thai

In one very basic sense Thai is like English—it has an alphabet. Thai
words, like those in English, are composed of particular combinations of
letters—both consonants and vowels. In the Thai case, however, different vowels are written before, above, below or after consonants, or a
combination of these positions. And in a very small number of cases, the
vowel sound, while the same as other written forms, is not written at all;
rather it is 'inherent' and has to be learned.

Thai has its own distinctive script which is similar to the closely related
language of neighboring Laos. Thai, like Lao, is written without spaces
between the words. In written Thai, however, spaces do occur between
what we might loosely call 'grouped associated ideas.'

It should be emphasized that there is no ideal way of writing – that is
romanizing or transliterating—Thai words in English. There are a number
of 'systems' for romanizing Thai and, regrettably, none of them (including that used in this dictionary) is ideal. In fact, at times, some of the sys-

tems used to romanize Thai words are rather unhelpful when it comes to getting the pronunciation correct. For example, you may have seen the common, polite everyday greeting for "hello" **sàwàt dii** written as **sawasdii/dee** or **sawas dii/dee**. There is no issue with the **dii/dee** which simply sounds like the English letter 'd'. As for the **sawas** what has occurred is that the writer has employed one of the romanization systems which adhere strictly to the actual Thai spelling. In written Thai, the final 's' in **sawas** is indeed spelled with an 's' letter, but what needs to be understood is that when 's' (and in Thai there are a number of different letters representing 's') appears at the end of a syllable or word it is pronounced as a 't' sound (although some consider this to be closer to a 'd'—hence you will sometimes see **sawad dii/dee**, or, for the popular noodle dish, **pad/phad thai** rather than the more accurate **phàt thai**—the word **phàt** actually sounding closer to the English golfing term "putt"). In a following section all of the syllable-final consonant sounds in Thai are provided.

In summary, while Thai and English share many of the same sounds there are a number of instances where there are no comparable sounds between the two languages. Hence it is a good idea, whenever possible, to ask a Thai friend or acquaintance to look at a particular word or phrase in the Thai script provided and help you with your pronunciation.

Romanized Thai

English pronunciation is often very confusing to non-native speakers as individual letters do not correspond to a single unchanging sound. Take the vowel sound 'e', for example, which is pronounced in a number of ways. Consider the 'e' sounds in the following: "mother," "women," "they," "he," and so on. Thai pronunciation, by contrast, is much more 'phonetic,' that is, vowels and consonants have but one sound which does not change in different words as is the case in English.

Consonants

The majority of Thai consonants are similar to those in English, although there are a number of important differences. The consonants listed below are in the 'initial' position, that is, at the beginning of a word.

Romanized letters	Sounds like	as in
k	g	"s<u>k</u>in"
kh	k	"<u>k</u>ing"
*ng	ng	"si<u>ng</u>ing"
j	j	"<u>j</u>et"
ch	ch	"<u>ch</u>at"

Romanized letters	Sounds like	as in
d	d	"<u>d</u>o"
t	t	"s<u>t</u>op"
th	t	"<u>t</u>ime"
n	n	"<u>n</u>ame"
b	b	"<u>b</u>ar"
p	p	"s<u>p</u>a"
ph	p	"<u>p</u>ass"
f	f	"<u>f</u>ar"
m	m	"<u>m</u>e"
y	y	"<u>y</u>ou"
r	r	"<u>r</u>at"
l	l	"<u>l</u>ove"
w	w	"<u>w</u>ine"
s	s	"<u>s</u>ee"
o	o	"<u>o</u>n"

*Note: The English sound 'ng' only occurs (with a slight exception—see below) in the syllable-final position of a word, as in "sing," "bring," etc. However, 'ng' occurs both at the beginning and end of Thai words and syllables. The closest comparable English sound to the syllable initial 'ng' in Thai is the sound that occurs at the beginning of the second syllable of words such as "singer" (i.e. sing-nging), or "wringer" (i.e. wring-nging). You may find it useful to practice pronouncing the 'ng' sound at the beginning of various Thai words by trying the following: say "sing," "sing," "singing, singing," then "nging, nging."

Syllable-final Consonant Sounds

In Thai only eight consonant sounds occur in the syllable-final position. These eight sounds can be divided into two groups—stops and sonorants. Stops are sounds whose pronunciation ends abruptly, while sonorants are sounds whose pronunciation can be sustained for some time. For example, the 't' in "hot" is a stop while the 'n' in "bin" is a sonorant. It is possible to sustain the 'n' in "bin" for a long time—"binnnnn....," but the 't' in "hot" has a short, sharp sound which brings the pronunciation of that word to a sudden stop once it has been spoken.

The eight final consonant sounds in Thai are:

Stops	Comparable English Sound
k	si<u>ck</u>
t	fla<u>t</u>
p	si<u>p</u>

Sonorants	Comparable English Sound
ng	wi<u>ng</u>
n	bi<u>n</u>
m	ja<u>m</u>
y	jo<u>y</u>
w	no<u>w</u>

Syllable-initial Consonant Clusters

Only a relatively small number of consonant clusters (i.e. two or more consonants together) occur in Thai, compared to English. All Thai consonant clusters occur in syllable-initial position. No consonant clusters occur at the end of Thai words. The consonant clusters are as follows:

kr, kl, kw, khr, khl, khw, tr, pr, pl, phr, phl.

Also '**fr**' and '**fl**' which only occur in English loan words.

'R' and 'L' sounds in Thai

The pronunciation of 'r' and 'l' sounds in Thai varies according to the speech style or register. In the formal style 'r' and 'l' are usually pronounced quite clearly and distinctly. However, in casual and informal conversation, 'r' and 'l' both tend to be pronounced as 'l' in the syllable-initial position. In consonant clusters in informal Thai 'r' is often replaced by 'l' and sometimes both 'r' and 'l' sounds are omitted altogether from consonant clusters. Note that the change of 'r' sound to 'l' in casual spoken Thai does not alter the tones of words, which remain unchanged. Compare the following examples:

Formal style pronunciation	Informal style pronunciation
khráp (Male polite particle)	**kháp**
plaa (a fish)	**paa**
ruai (to be rich)	**luai** (luu-ay)
à-rai (What?)	**à-lai**
krà-thá (a pan)	**kà-thá**

Vowels

In Thai there are both 'long' and 'short' vowels. This distinction between long and short vowels is very important. In the short form used in this dictionary the following are written the same as in English, but the sound is very short:

Short vowels	Sounds like
a	a as in "<u>a</u>h"
e	e as in "l<u>e</u>t"
i	i as in "h<u>i</u>t"
o	o as in "<u>o</u>h!"
u	u as in "p<u>u</u>t"

As for the 'long' vowels, they are written as follows:

Long vowels	Sounds like
aa	ar as in "f<u>ar</u>"
eh	ey as in "he<u>y</u>"
ii	ee as in "fr<u>ee</u>"
oh	o as in "g<u>o</u>ld"
uu	oo as in "g<u>oo</u>d"
am	um as in "dr<u>um</u>"
ai	ai as in "Th<u>ai</u>"
ao	ow as in "c<u>ow</u>"

The following vowel sounds have both a 'long' and a 'short' form. However, in the instances below the 'short' form is not as abrupt as in the selection of vowels listed above, yet there is a clear distinction between 'long' and 'short' vowel sound which is best demonstrated by a native speaker with good, clear enunciation.

Long/short vowels	Sounds like
ae	air as in "p<u>ai</u>r"
aw	aw as in "l<u>aw</u>"

Long/short vowels	Sounds like
oeh	er as in "h<u>er</u>"
ia	ea as in "n<u>ea</u>r"
iu	ew as in "n<u>ew</u>"
oi	oy as in "b<u>oy</u>"
ua	our as in "t<u>our</u>"
ueh	on as in "pris<u>on</u>" (longer)
uea	ure as in "c<u>ure</u>" (longer)

Tones

Thai is a 'tonal' language, which means variations in tone or pitch determine the meaning of a word. Thus the assistance of a native Thai speaker to help you approximate the correct tones would be invaluable.

Some people find the idea of 'tones' particularly daunting but, in fact, tones in Central Thai (the name of the official language in Thailand) are not as impenetrable as these individuals imagine. Indeed, there are a relatively small number of words where it is vital to get the tone absolutely correct to be understood (for example, see the entries for 'near' and 'far'). These days with a large and growing number of foreigners visiting Thailand, Thais are becoming accustomed to non-native speakers 'mangling' their language to one degree or another when trying to speak it. So often meaning can be conveyed, partially through context, even if one's tones are slightly off kilter. To say this is not to reduce the significance of tones, for ultimately they are crucial; rather it is to encourage you, the learner, to use the language as much as you can and develop your confidence, and hopefully your interest, so as to help you move on to another level.

Thai has five tones: mid, low, falling, high and rising. In the system of romanization used in this dictionary the mid-tone is unmarked. The other tones are represented by the following symbols written above the relevant syllable (in the case of words with a number of syllables) or the word if it is monosyllabic: low tone ` ; falling tone ^ ; high tone ´ ; and rising tone ˇ .

Here are some examples of the tones with words given in romanized form – their English meaning and in Thai script. Try having a Thai friend or acquaintance pronounce the words written in Thai to get some idea of the differences in tone, then practice saying them yourself.

Tone Level	Tone symbol	Example	Meaning
mid	No mark	**mai** ไมล์	a mile (from English)
low	`	**mài** ใหม่	new
falling	^	**mâi** ไม่	No/not
high	´	**mái** ไม้	wood
rising	ˇ	**mǎi** ไหม	silk

In closing it should be pointed out that many of the words in this dictionary with two or more syllables have hyphens included to help you with your pronunciation. Here, for example, is the word for the month of August: **sǐng-hǎa-khom**.

We wish you 'Good luck' on your journey into the Thai language or, as the Thais would say, โชคดี **'Choke dee'**.*

---

* While this particular rendering of Thai might cause some to laugh, make jokes or bad puns it's very close to what the Thai for 'Good luck' actually sounds like.

List of Abbreviations

AUX V	Auxiliary verb
ADJ	Adjective
ADV	Adverb
CONJ	Conjunction
EXCL	Exclamation
EXP	Expression
FEM	Feminine
INTERJ	Interjection
MASC	Masculine
N	Noun
NUM	Numeral
PHR	Phrase
PREP	Preposition
V	Verb
VI	Verb, intransitive
VT	Verb, transitive

Thai–English

A

aa N อา aunt or uncle (i.e. a younger sister or brother of one's father)

aa-chîip N อาชีพ occupation, profession, career

aa-hǎn N อาหาร food

aa-hǎn cháo N อาหารเช้า breakfast, morning meal

aa-hǎn jeh (pronounced similar to 'jay') N อาหารเจ Chinese vegetarian food, vegan food

aa-hǎn klaang wan N อาหารกลางวัน/อาหารเที่ยง lunch, midday meal

aa-hǎn tháleh N อาหารทะเล seafood

aa-hǎn wâang N อาหารว่าง an entrée/starter/hors d'oeuvres

aa-hǎn yen N อาหารเย็น dinner, evening meal

aai (long vowel) ADJ อาย to be shy, embarrassed

aa-jaan N อาจารย์ teacher (usually with degree), university lecturer

aa-jian N อาเจียน (POLITE) to vomit; (COLLOQUIAL) ûak อ้วก throw up/puke/spew

aa-kaan N อาการ (physical) condition/symptom

aa-kàat N อากาศ weather, air

àan V อ่าน to read

àan lên V อ่านเล่น to read for pleasure

àan mâi àwk ADJ อ่านไม่ออก illegible

àan nǎng sǔe V อ่านหนังสือ to read

àang àap náam N อ่างอาบน้ำ a bath(tub)

àang láang nâa N อ่างล้างหน้า wash basin

àao N อ่าว a bay, gulf (as in the 'Gulf of Thailand' àao thai อ่าวไทย)

âao อ้าว (COLLOQUIAL) an exclamation meaning something like 'Oh!', 'huh!', 'eh!'

àap náam V อาบน้ำ to bathe, take a bath, take a shower, to have a wash

àap náam fàk bua V อาบน้ำฝักบัว to have a shower

aarom N อารมณ์ emotion, mood, temper

aa-rom-khǎn N อารมณ์ขัน humor

àat AUX V อาจ may, might

àat jà AUX V อาจจะ could, might, may; perhaps, maybe, possibly

àat (jà) pen pai dâi PHR อาจ(จะ)เป็นไปได้ (that) could well be possible

aa-thít N อาทิตย์ a week

aa-thít-nâa N อาทิตย์หน้า next week

aa-thít-níi N อาทิตย์นี้ this week

aa-thít thîi-láew N อาทิตย์ที่แล้ว last week

àat-yaa-kawn N อาชญากร (FORMAL) criminal, (COLLOQUIAL) phûu ráai ผู้ร้าย 'evil doer'/'baddie'

aa-wút N อาวุธ a weapon (general term), arms

aa-yú N อายุ age

aa-yú mâak/sǔung aa-yú ADJ อายุมาก/สูงอายุ aged, to be (very) old

aa-yú nói ADJ อายุน้อย young (in age)

aa-yú thâo rài PHR อายุเท่าไร how old (are you/is she/it)? (NOTE: the pronoun – 'you/she/he' etc. – comes before the question tag)

à-dìit ADJ อดีต (the) past, former (e.g. prime minister/husband)

ae N (pronounced like 'air') แอร์ air (conditioning)

àep V แอบ to hide

áeppôen N (from English) แอปเปิล apple

ai (short vowel) V ไอ to cough

âi N ไอ้ a derogatory title used with first names of men and also for insult

ai náam N ไอน้ำ steam

ai-oh-diin N ไอโอดีน iodine

ai-sà-kriim N (commonly pronounced something like 'ai-tim' – from English) ไอศกรีม ice cream

ai-sĭa N ไอเสีย exhaust fumes

à-kà-tanyuu N อกตัญญู to be ungrateful, thankless

à-khá-tì N อคติ bias, prejudice

àk-sǎwn N อักษร letter (in alphabet)

àk-sèp VT อักเสบ become inflamed; a response of body tissues to infection

à-lài N อะไหล่ spare part (of machine), replacement part(s)

am V อำ to hide, conceal

à-mátà ADJ อมตะ to be immortal (Note: also commonly used in the sense of something being 'classic' – as in a 'classic song' etc.)

à-meh-rí-kaa N อเมริกา America

à-meh-rí-kan N อเมริกัน an American; from America

amnâat N, V อำนาจ authority, to have power

amphoeh N (pronounced similar to 'am-pur') อำเภอ an administrative district (often written in English as 'amphoe')

an N (pronounced like 'un') อัน universal classifier (i.e. counting word) for things when the specific classifier for the item is unknown – e.g. may be used in the case of such things as hamburgers, spectacles, etc.

à-naa-jaan ADJ อนาจาร lewd/immoral act or conduct

à-na-khót N อนาคต the future

an-dàp N อันดับ series, order, rank

à-naa-mai N อนามัย hygiene

ang-krìt N อังกฤษ England, English

ang-khaan N อังคาร Tuesday

à-ngùn N องุ่น grapes

àn nǎi อันไหน which one?

an-tàraai N, ADJ อันตราย danger; to be dangerous; peril, harm; dangerous

à-nú-baan N อนุบาล kindergarten

à-númát V (FORMAL) อนุมัติ to approve/consent, e.g. of a building, or a tender (for a project) etc.

à-núrák V อนุรักษ์ to preserve/conserve, e.g. an old building/historical site etc.

ànú-sǎa-wárii N อนุสาวรีย์ a monument

à-nú-sǎ-wárii chai N อนุสาวรีย์ชัยฯ (COLLOQUIAL – slightly shortened version of the formal full name) the Victory monument in Bangkok, commemorating the Thai armed forces and temporary gains of territory in WW II

à-nú-sǎ-wárii prà-chaa-thíp-pàtai N อนุสาวรีย์ประชาธิปไตย the Democracy Monument in Bangkok commemorating the establishment of a representative form of politics after the overthrow of the Absolute Monarchy in 1932

à-nú-yâat V อนุญาต to let, allow, permit

àn-yá-má-nii N อัญมณี precious stones

ao V เอา to take, receive or accept (something from someone)

ao àwk V เอาออก to take out, remove

ao cháná เอาชนะ to defeat/beat (someone/something)

ao ìik láew (COLLOQUIAL) เอาอีกแล้ว Not again!/Here we go again/(they're) at it again

ao jai V เอาใจ to please someone, make (someone) happy, to go along with (someone)

ao jai sài V เอาใจใส่ to pay attention (to), take an interest (in), be conscientious, put one's mind to something

ao jing (COLLOQUIAL) เอาจริง serious (i.e. to do something seriously/not kidding around)

ao kan V (COLLOQUIAL/SLANG) เอากัน to have sex/to mate/to screw

ao lá (COLLOQUIAL) เอาละ OK then, now then

ao loei (COLLOQUIAL) เอาเลย go for it!

ao maa V เอามา to bring

ao măi (colloquial question form used for offering something to someone) เอาไหม Do you want it?

ao pai v เอาไป to take (away)

ao prìap v เอาเปรียบ to take advantage of (someone else), to exploit (someone)

ao tàeh jai tua ehng ADJ, v เอาแต่ใจตัวเอง to be self-centered/self-indulgent; think of one's own interests rather than anyone else's

ao tua râwt IDIOM (COLLOQUIAL) เอาตัวรอด to save one's own skin, to get out of a predicament

àp ADJ อับ stale, musty

àp-aai ADJ อับอาย shameful

à-páatméhn N (from English) อพาร์ตเมนต์ apartment

à-phai v อภัย to pardon/forgive (When used in speech as in to 'forgive' someone you say hâi à-phai ให้อภัย)

àrai อะไร (question word generally used at the end of a sentence) what?

àrai ìik อะไรอีก (is there) anything else?

àrai kan (COLLOQUIAL) อะไรกัน 'what's going on?', 'what's up?'

àrai kâw dâi (COLLOQUIAL) อะไรก็ได้ anything at all/anything is OK, e.g. in response to the question 'what would you like to eat? – 'anything at all/anything would be OK'

àrai ná (COLLOQUIAL) อะไรนะ pardon me? what did you say?

àròi ADJ อร่อย to be delicious, tasty

à-sù-jì N อสุจิ sperm, semen

àt v อัด to compress, pack tight, press

àt-chàriya N อัจฉริยะ a genius, prodigy, master (of some art or skill)

àt dii wii dii v อัดดีวีดี to record a DVD

àt sĭang v อัดเสียง to record (music/a voice/a sound)

àthí-baai v อธิบาย to explain

à-thí-kaan-baw-dii N อธิการบดี president (for college)

àt-traa N อัตรา rate

àt-traa lâeh plìan N อัตราแลกเปลี่ยน rate of exchange for foreign currency

à-wá-kâat N อวกาศ space (i.e. outer space)

à-wai-yá-wá N อวัยวะ organ (of the body)

àwk PREP ออก out

àwk jàak v ออกจาก to leave, depart

àwk kamlang kaai v (pronounced something like 'ork gum-lung guy') ออกกำลังกาย to exercise

àwk pai v ออกไป to go out, leave, exit; also used when someone (in a room/house) is angry and orders/commands another person to 'get out!'

àwk sĭang v ออกเสียง to pronounce (a word), also – to vote (in an election)

âwm v อ้อม to go around, make a detour

àwn ADJ อ่อน soft, tender, mild (not strong), weak, feeble

àwn aeh ADJ อ่อนแอ to be weak/to feel weak

àwn wawn v อ้อนวอน to plead/beg

àwn yohn ADJ อ่อนโยน to be gentle (behavior)/graceful/gracefully

áwp-fít N (from English) ออฟฟิศ office

áwt-sà-treh-lia N ออสเตรเลีย Australia

B

bàa N บ่า shoulder

bâa ADJ บ้า to be insane, crazy: (COLLOQUIAL) âi bâa ไอ้บ้า 'You must be mad/out of your mind', 'You jerk/dickhead'

bâa-bâa baw-baw ADJ (COLLOQUIAL) บ้าๆ บอๆ odd, crazy

baa N (from English) บาร์ a bar (serving drinks)

baa bii khiu N (from English) บาร์บีคิว barbeque

baa daan N บาดาล underground region

B

bâa kaam v บ้ากาม to crave sex

bàai n บ่าย afternoon, from midday until 4 p.m. – generally referred to as **tawn bàai** ตอนบ่าย

bàai bìang v บ่ายเบี่ยง to be evasive, equivocate, dodge (e.g. answering a question)

baan v บาน to bloom

baan n บาน classifier for doors, windows, mirrors

bâan n บ้าน home, house: (COLLOQUIAL) klàp bâan กลับบ้าน to go home/return home; phûean bâan (literally, 'friend'-'house') เพื่อนบ้าน neighbor

bâan nâwk n (COLLOQUIAL) บ้านนอก the country, rural, up-country, the sticks

bâang ADJ, ADV บ้าง some, partly, somewhat: e.g. phǒm khǎw bâang ผมขอบ้าง can I (male speaking) have some?

baang ADJ บาง some: e.g. baang khon บางคน some people; baang khráng บางครั้ง some time(s); baang hàeng บางแห่ง some places; baang yàang บางอย่าง some things

baang ADJ บาง to be thin (of objects)

bàap n บาป sin, moral wrongdoing

bàat n บาท Baht (Thai currency) IDIOM (COLLOQUIAL) mâi tem bàat ไม่เต็มบาท to be mad/not the full quid (Baht)/a few screws loose

bàat v บาด to cut/slice/wound; bàat jèp บาดเจ็บ to be injured/wounded; bàat jai บาดใจ to be hurt, for one's feelings to be hurt; bàat phláeh บาด แผล a wound/cut/laceration (NOTE: a very loud or deafening noise, e.g. deafening music is bàat hǔu บาดหู; also to be intolerable/offensive to the eyes/dazzling bàat taa บาดตา)

bàat n บาตร the alms or begging bowl of a Buddhist monk (NOTE: to make an offering of food to a monk by placing food in his bowl is to tàk bàat ตักบาตร)

bàat lǔang n บาทหลวง a priest (from any one of the Christian denominations)

báas-két-bawn n (from English) บาสเกตบอล basketball

bàat-thá-yák n บาดทะยัก tetanus

baehn ADJ แบน to be flat (e.g. a flat tire/tyre)

baehn v, n (from English) แบน to ban; a ban

bàehp n แบบ design/style/kind/pattern (for tailoring) (NOTE: a female model is nang bàehp นางแบบ while a male model is naai bàehp นายแบบ)

bàehp fawm n (from English 'form') แบบฟอร์ม a form (a document with blanks for filling in with information)

bàehp fùek hàt n แบบฝึกหัด exercise (school work)

bàehp níi ADV แบบนี้ (COLLOQUIAL) (do it) like this (NOTE: to elicit the response 'like this' – you could ask the following question 'how do you do it?' **bàehp nǎi** แบบไหน)

bàeng v แบ่ง to divide/share/separate

báeng n (taken from 'bank' in English) แบ๊งค์ banknote

bàet-toeh-rîi n (from English) แบตเตอรี่ battery (NOTE: in colloquial speech this is commonly just bàet แบต)

bàet min tán n (from English) แบดมินตัน badminton

bai n (from English) ไบ bisexual

bai n ใบ classifier for round and hollow objects, e.g. fruit, eggs

bâi n ใบ้ dumb (unable to speak)

bai à-nú-yâat n ใบอนุญาต a permit/form giving approval (e.g. to build a house)/a licence

bai khàp khìi n ใบขับขี่ a driver's licence (for a car, truck, or motorbike)

bai mái n ใบไม้ a leaf, leaves

bai pliu n ใบปลิว leaflet

bai kòeht n ใบเกิด birth certificate

bai sà-màk n ใบสมัคร application form

bai sàng N ใบสั่ง order (placed for food, goods); a ticket (fine)/police summons

bai sàng yaa N ใบสั่งยา a prescription

bai sèt N ใบเสร็จ a receipt

bai yàa N ใบหย่า divorce certificate

bam-bàt V (pronounced 'bum-but') บำบัด to treat/cure/alleviate/relieve (a condition) (NOTE: physiotheraphy is kaai-yá-phâap bam-bàt กายภาพบำบัด)

bà-mìi N บะหมี่ egg noodles

bam-naan N (pronounced 'bum-narn') บำนาญ a pension

bam nèt N บำเหน็จ reward, remuneration

bam rung V บำรุง to improve, maintain

banchii N บัญชี an account (e.g. a bank account) (NOTE: to open a bank account is pòeht banchii เปิดบัญชี)

bandai N บันได steps, stairs, a ladder

bandai lûean N บันไดเลื่อน an escalator

ban dìt N บัณฑิต university graduate, scholar

bang V บัง to block the view

bâng fai N บั้งไฟ skyrocket (commonly fired during certain festivals in NE Thailand)

bang-kà-loh N (from English) บังกะโล lodge, bungalow (guest house)

bangkháp V บังคับ to force, compel

bang-oehn ADV บังเอิญ accidentally, by accident, by chance, unexpectedly (e.g. to meet someone by accident)

banjù V บรรจุ to load (up), pack (a suitcase)

banphá-burùt N บรรพบุรุษ ancestor(s)

ban-thoehng ADJ บันเทิง joyful, entertained

banthúek N, V บันทึก a note/memorandum; to note, record (e.g. minutes of a meeting, etc.)

banthúek khàaw prajam wan N บันทึกประจำวัน diary, journal

banyaai V บรรยาย to lecture, describe

ban-yaa-kàat N บรรยากาศ climate, atmosphere, ambience

bao ADJ เบา to be light (not heavy) (NOTE: to do something gently/softly – e.g. a massage/to speak – is bao-bao เบา ๆ)

bâo taa N เบ้าตา eye-socket

bao wǎan N เบาหวาน diabetes

bàt N (pronounced like the word 'but') บัตร a card/ticket/coupon (NOTE: an identity card – held by all adult Thai citizens – is bàt prà-chaachon บัตรประชาชน; also widely used in Thailand – name card/business card naam bàt นามบัตร)

bàt eh-thii-em N บัตรเอทีเอ็ม ATM card

bàt choehn N บัตรเชิญ invitation card

bàt khreh dìt N บัตรเครดิต credit card

bèhng VT เบ่ง to swell, expand

bàw N เบาะ cushion/padded seat (in car etc.)

bàw náam baa-daan N บ่อน้ำบาดาล a well (for water)

bàwk V บอก to tell; let someone know

bàwk khàwp khun บอกขอบคุณ to say thank you

bàwk láew V (COLLOQUIAL) บอกแล้ว (I) told you already, (I) told you so

bàwk mâi thùuk (COLLOQUIAL) บอกไม่ถูก (I) can't say, (I) can't put my finger on it

bàwk sĭa jai V บอกเสียใจ to say sorry

baw-khǎw-sǎw N บ.ข.ส. bus terminal

bàwp bang ADJ บอบบาง frail, thin, breakable, fragile

bawm N (from English) บอมบ์ bomb (also commonly used following the troubles in the three southernmost provinces on Thailand's east coast: khaa bawm คาร์บอมบ์ car bomb)

bawn N (from English) บอล a ball, (COLLOQUIAL) the game of football (soccer)

bàwn N บ่อน place for gambling (the full expression for 'a gambling den' is bàwn kaan phá-nan บ่อนการพนัน)

B

bâwng kanchaa N บ้องกัญชา a bong (water pipe) for smoking marihuana

bawrí-jàak v บริจาค to donate, give to charity

bawrí-kaan N, v บริการ service; to give service

bawrí-sàt N บริษัท company, firm

bawrí-sùt ADJ บริสุทธิ์ to be pure, innocent – also used to refer to a virgin

bawrí-wehn N บริเวณ vicinity, area

bàwt ADJ บอด to be blind; khon taa bàwt (literally 'person'-'eye[s]'-'blind') คนตาบอด a blind person

bàwt sǐi ADJ บอดสี to be color blind (literally, 'blind'-'color')

bèt N เบ็ด a fish hook

beung N บึง a swamp/marsh

bêung ADJ บึ้ง serious, solemn

bia N (from English) เบียร์ beer

biat v เบียด to squeeze in

biang v เบี่ยง to turn, turn aside

bîao ADJ เบี้ยว crooked, deformed

bì-daa N บิดา (FORMAL) father

bìip v บีบ to squeeze, compress

bìip trae v บีบแตร to honk

bìip khaw v บีบคอ to strangle

bin N (from English) บิล (the) bill

bin v บิน to fly

bin-thá-bàat v บิณฑบาต to go about with an alms bowl to receive food

bìt v บิด to twist, N บิด dysentery

bòk N บก land (as opposed to sea), terrestrial

bláek-meh v (from English) แบล็ก เมล์ to blackmail

boeh N (from the English word 'number' and pronounced 'ber') เบอร์ (most commonly used to refer to telephone numbers and sometimes numbers of lottery tickets; also used when selecting a particular young woman in a massage parlor or a dancer in a go-go bar – these women generally wear 'numbers' when working)

bòehk v เบิก to withdraw (money), requisition (funds)

boh N โบว์ bow (ribbon)

bòhk mueh v โบกมือ to wave a hand/ hands

boh-lîng N โบลิ่ง bowling

boh-nút N (from English) โบนัส a bonus

bohraan ADJ โบราณ ancient, antique, old-fashioned

bòht N โบสถ์ a place of worship but of a non-Buddhist variety: e.g. a Christian church bòht fàràng โบสถ์ฝรั่ง; a synagogue bòht yiu โบสถ์ยิว

bòi ADV, ADJ บ่อย often; frequent

bon PREP บน on, at

bòn v บ่น to complain

bòt v บด to grind

bòt bàat N บทบาท a role (e.g. in a movie/in real life)

bòt khwaam N บทความ an article (e.g. in a newspaper)

bòt rian N บทเรียน a lesson (i.e. in a classroom/in real life)

bòt sǒnthá-naa N (FORMAL) บทสนทนา conversation

bòt sùat mon N บทสวดมนต์ a prayer

bráwkkohlîi N (from English) บรอกโคลี broccoli

brèhk N, v (from English) เบรก a brake (in a car); to brake (while driving) (NOTE: the same word is also used for the English word 'break' as in to 'have a break' [while working])

bua N บัว lotus (flower), water lily

bùak PREP, v บวก plus; to add

buam ADJ บวม to be swollen

bûan v บ้วน to spit out; náam yaa bûan pàak น้ำยาบ้วนปาก mouthwash (e.g. Listerine)

bùat v บวช to be ordained, enter the (Buddhist) monkhood (the full expression being bùat phrá บวชพระ)

bùea v เบื่อ to be bored, be tired of, fed up (with), cannot stand (someone or something)

bûeang tôn ADJ เบื้องต้น introductory/ elementary/primary (e.g. level of learning); initially/at the outset

6

bùkkhá-lík N บุคลิก character/personality

bùp V บุบ to pound lightly

bun N บุญ Buddhist concept of merit (for the afterlife)

bun khun N บุญคุณ a favor, kindness, sense of indebtedness to someone else for their kindness or support. A very significant aspect of Thai culture.

burìi N บุหรี่ cigarette

bù-rùt-prai-sà-nii N บุรุษไปรษณีย์ postman

bùt N บุตร (pronounced similar to 'put' but with a 'b' rather than a 'p', and a low tone) child/children/offspring (NOTE: an adopted child is **bùt bun-tham** บุตรบุญธรรม)

buu-chaa V บูชา to worship/revere/venerate

buum N บูม boom

bùut ADJ บูด to be rancid/sour/spoiled (of food) (NOTE: to be sullen-looking/sour-faced is **nâa bùut** หน้าบูด)

CH

NOTE: all the entries here begin with 'ch'—this being a sound found both in English and Thai. As for the single English letter 'c' (pronounced as 'see') – this is represented by other letters and in other ways with the system of romanization used in this dictionary

chaa N ชา tea; ADJ also to be numb, without sensation

cháa ADJ ช้า to be slow; **cháa-cháa** ADV ช้า ๆ (e.g. drive/speak) slowly

chǎai V ฉาย to shine a light (NOTE: **chǎai nǎng** V ฉายหนัง is to screen/show a movie/film)

chaai ADJ, N ชาย male, masculine (general term and only for humans); N edge, rim, border

chaai daehn N ชายแดน border (between countries)

chaai hàat N ชายหาด beach

chaai thá leh N ชายทะเล seashore

chaam N ชาม a bowl

cháang N ช้าง an elephant

châang N ช่าง a tradesperson, skilled person (a few examples are included in the following entries)

châang prá-paa N ช่างประปา plumber

châang fai-fáa N ช่างไฟฟ้า an electrician (NOTE: the word **fai-fáa** ไฟฟ้า means 'electricity/electrical')

châang khrûeang N ช่างเครื่อง mechanic

châang mái N ช่างไม้ carpenter (NOTE: the word **mái** ไม้ means 'wood')

cháang náam N ช้างน้ำ hippopotamus (nowadays the abbreviated English form 'hippo' is commonly used in Thailand: **híppo** ฮิปโป)

châang phâap N ช่างภาพ photographer, camera man

châang tàt phǒm N ช่างตัดผม barber

chaan mueang N ชานเมือง outskirts, environs of a city

châat N ชาติ nation, country

chá-baa N ชบา hibiscus

chà-bàp ฉบับ classifier for counting newspapers, letters, and documents

chàe ADJ แฉะ swampy, wet

chǎeh V แฉ to reveal, disclose, expose

chaem pehn N (from English) แชมเปญ champagne

châeng V แช่ง to curse

châeh khǎeng V แช่แข็ง to freeze; to be frozen

chá-nii N ชะนี gibbon

chái ใช้ to use, utilize

châi ใช่ yes (NOTE: one of numerous ways 'yes' is expressed in Thai)

chái dâi (COLLOQUIAL) ใช้ได้ It's usable/it works; also valid

chái jàai V ใช้จ่าย to spend money, to expend

chái mâi dâi ADJ (COLLOQUIAL) ใช้ไม่ได้ no good, unusable, out of order

CH

chái mòt v ใช้หมด to use up

chái nîi v ใช้หนี้ to pay off a debt, repay

chái weh-laa v ใช้เวลา to spend time

chai yoh PHR ไชโย hooray, cheers!

chák v ชัก to have convulsions, pull, jerk

chák cháa v ชักช้า to hesitate ADV, ADJ slowly, sluggish

chák chuan v ชักชวน to invite, persuade, induce (someone to do something)

chák wâaw v ชักว่าว to fly a kite; (SLANG) to masturbate, jerk off

chà-làak N ฉลาก label, lot (as a ticket in a lottery)

chà-lǎam N ฉลาม shark

chà-làat ADJ ฉลาด astute, bright, smart, intelligent

chà-lǎwng v ฉลอง to celebrate (e.g. on passing an exam)

chà-lìa v เฉลี่ย to average (numbers), divide equally

chà-lěoi v เฉลย to solve (a problem or puzzle), give an answer

chà-lǒem v เฉลิม to celebrate (e.g. the King's birthday)

chá-law v ชลอ to slow down

chàm ADJ ฉ่ำ juicy, wet, damp, moist, humid

chám ADJ ช้ำ to be bruised

chamnaan v ชำนาญ to be highly skilled at something, have expertise

chamrút ADJ ชำรุด to be damaged

chan ADJ ชัน to be steep (e.g. a hill)

chán N ชั้น a layer, level, story (of a building); class, category

chán bon N ชั้นบน upstairs, upper story, upper layer, upper shelf

chán lâang N ชั้นล่าง downstairs, lower story, lower layer, lower shelf

chán mát-thá-yom N ชั้นมัธยม secondary grades, junior/high school

chán nam ADJ ชั้นนำ leading, outstanding

chán prà-thǒm N ชั้นประถม elementary grades, grade school level

chǎn PRON (INFORMAL/INTIMATE) ฉัน I, me v to eat (only for monk)

chá-ná v ชนะ to win, beat, defeat, be victorious

chang v ชัง to hate, detest

châng v ชั่ง to weigh (something)

châng man PHR (COLLOQUIAL) ช่างมัน 'Who cares!', 'Forget it!', 'To hell with it!'

chá-nít N ชนิด type, sort

chánít nǎi ชนิดไหน, (or more commonly) bàehp nǎi แบบไหน what kind of?

chà-nòht N โฉนด land titles, property

châo v เช่า to hire, rent

chǎo v เฉา to wilt, wither, shrivel up

cháo N เช้า morning

cháo mûehd N เช้ามืด dusk

cháo trùu N เช้าตรู่ dawn, very early in the morning

chaow bâan N ชาวบ้าน villager(s) (also general term for 'common people' whether in cities, towns, or villages)

chaow prá-mong N ชาวประมง fisherman

chaow indohnii-sia N ชาวอินโดนีเซีย Indonesian person/people

chaow khàměhn N ชาวเขมร Cambodian person/people

chaow khǎo N ชาวเขา hill tribe(s)

chaow maa-lehsia N ชาวมาเลเซีย Malaysian person/people

chaow naa N ชาวนา a farmer, someone who works the land (rice growers etc.)

chaow phà-mâa N ชาวพม่า Burmese person/people

chaow phúehn mueang N ชาวพื้นเมือง indigenous person/people

chaow phút N ชาวพุทธ Buddhist(s)

chaow râi N ชาวไร่ intercropping farmer

chaow sǔan N ชาวสวน gardener

chaow thai N ชาวไทย Thai people

chaow tàang prathêht N ชาวต่างประเทศ a foreigner/foreigners

CH

chaow ta-wan tòk N ชาวตะวันตก a westerner

chaow wîat-naam N ชาวเวียดนาม Vietnamese person/people

chaow yîipùn N ชาวญี่ปุ่น Japanese person/people

chà-pháw ADV เฉพาะ only, exclusively for

chá-raa ADJ (FORMAL) ชรา old, aged (of people)

chát ADJ, ADV ชัด clear; clearly (e.g. the image on a television screen; to speak clearly or fluently)

chát jehn ADJ ชัดเจน to be distinct (a view, the meaning of what is said, the way someone speaks), very clear

cháw N ช่อ cluster, bunch (fruit, flowers)

cháw dàwk mái N ช่อดอกไม้ bouquet

cháwk N ชอล์ก chalk

cháwk ADJ ช็อค shocked

cháwk-koh-láet N (from English) ช็อกโกแลต chocolate

cháwn N ช้อน spoon

cháwn chaa N ช้อนชา teaspoon

cháwn tó N ช้อนโต๊ะ tablespoon

châwng N ช่อง hole, aperture, slot, space, gap (also used when referring to a television channel – e.g. Channel 7 is **châwng jèt** ช่องเจ็ด)

châwng khâehp N ช่องแคบ strait (i.e. Straits of Gibraltar), narrow channel

châwng khlâwt N (polite medical term) ช่องคลอด vagina

châwng tháwng N ช่องท้อง abdomen

châwng wâang N ช่องว่าง a gap, a vacant space

châwp V ชอบ to be fond of; like, be pleased by

châwp jai ADJ ชอบใจ pleased with, happy, amused

cháwp-pîng N, V (from English) ช้อปปิ้ง shopping; to shop

châwp mâak kwàa V ชอบมากกว่า to prefer

chék N, V เช็ค a (bank/travellers') cheque/check (also used in the English sense of 'to check something to see if it is OK/functioning' etc.)

chên ADV เช่น for example …, such as

chên khoei เช่นเคย as usual, as before (e.g. he's doing it again, as usual)

chên nán เช่นนั้น like that, in that way/manner

chét V เช็ด to wipe

chia V เชียร์ (from English) to cheer

chǐang ADJ เฉียง oblique, aslant, deflected, inclined, diagonal

chìao V เฉียว swoop down upon, snatch, snatch away suddenly, pass swiftly

chîao ADJ เชี่ยว strong, swift, rapid (of current of water)

chîao chaan ADJ เชี่ยวชาญ to be skilled, experienced, expert

chìat V เฉียด to pass too close, very close, just miss, almost graze

chíi V ชี้ to point (at, to)

chìi V (COLLOQUIAL) ฉี่ to urinate, pee

chíi tua V ชี้ตัว to identify, point at (a person)

chíi jaeng V ชี้แจง to explain

chíi níu V ชี้นิ้ว to give orders (i.e. point the finger ordering someone to do this, that and the other)

chìk V ฉีก to tear, rip

chìit V ฉีด to inject: **chìit yaa** ฉีดยา to give an injection of liquid medicine

chìit sà-preh V ฉีดสเปรย์ to spray

chìit wák-siin V ฉีดวัคซีน to vaccinate, perform a vaccination N ชีววิทยา biology

chii-wít N ชีวิต life

chii-wít chii-waa ADJ (COLLOQUIAL) ชีวิตชีวา to be lively, vibrant, full of life

chim V ชิม to taste or sample something

chin ADJ ชิน to be accustomed (to)/used to/familiar (with)

chín N ชิ้น piece, section, morsel, slice

chìng N ฉิ่ง cymbal

ching cháa N ชิงช้า swing

chít ADJ ชิด close, near, nearby

9

chòk v ฉก to snatch, grab, strike (as a snake)

choehn v (pronounced like 'churn') เชิญ to invite (formally); please (go ahead)

chóeht N (from English) เชิ้ต shirt with collar

choei ADJ (COLLOQUIAL) เชย to be outdated, old fashioned, not with it

chŏei ADJ เฉย to be impartial, indifferent, uninterested in (commonly reduplicated when spoken: chŏei-chŏei เฉยๆ)

choeh-rîi N เชอรี่ cherry

chohey v โชย to blow gently (wind)

chôhk ADJ โชก soaking wet

chôhk N โชค luck

chôhk dii โชคดี good luck! To be lucky

chôhk dii thîi… ADV โชคดีที่ fortunately

chôhk ráai ADV โชคร้าย unluck(il)y, unfortunately

chók v ชก to punch, strike

chók muay N ชกมวย boxing (Western style), fighting

chom v ชม to admire, compliment, praise

chom wiu v ชมวิว to view, look at

chomphuu N ชมพู pink (color) (for a list of the most common colors see the entry under sĭi สี which means 'color')

chomphûu N ชมพู่ rose apple (fruit)

chom-rom N ชมรม gathering, meeting club

chon v ชน to collide with/bump into, crash into

chong v ชง to infuse, steep in

chong chaa v ชงชา to make (a cup/pot of) tea

chon klùm nói N ชนกลุ่มน้อย ethnic group, minority group

chonná-bòt N (FORMAL) ชนบท (COLLOQUIAL) **bâan nâwk** N บ้านนอก countryside, rural area

chót chái v ชดใช้ to reimburse, repay, compensate

chót choei v ชดเชย to compensate (for damage to property, etc.), indemnify

chûa ADJ ชั่ว bad, vile, wicked

chûa khànà N ชั่วขณะ a moment, an instant

chûa khraow ADJ ชั่วคราว to be temporary

chûa mohng N ชั่วโมง an hour; classifier for counting hours

chûai v ช่วย to assist, help; please (request for help: e.g. 'can you please give me that glass')

chûai chii wít v ช่วยชีวิต to rescue

chûai dûai ช่วยด้วย help! (there's a fire/there's been an accident)

chûai lŭea v ช่วยเหลือ to rescue

chûai oh kàat v ฉวยโอกาส to seize the opportunity

chûai tua ehng v ช่วยตัวเอง to help oneself, masturbate

chuan v ชวน to invite (ask along)

chûea v เชื่อ to believe

chûea fang v เชื่อฟัง to obey

chûea jai v เชื่อใจ to trust

chúea raa N เชื้อรา fungus, mould/mold

chúea rôhk N เชื้อโรค germs, infection (often simply chúea เชื้อ)

chûeak N เชือก rope, string, cord

chûea mân v เชื่อมั่น to believe firmly

chûeang ADJ เชื่อง to be tame (animal)

chûea thŭe v เชื่อถือ to have trust

chùeay ADJ, ADV เฉื่อย slow; steadily but gently, lazily (of a breeze blowing)

chûeh N ชื่อ name

chûeh dang ADJ ชื่อดัง famous

chûeh jing N ชื่อจริง first name, personal name

chûeh lên N ชื่อเล่น nickname

chúehn ADJ ชื้น damp, humid

chûeh sĭang N ชื่อเสียง fame, reputation

chûi ADJ (COLLOQUIAL) ชุ่ย crappy, lousy; done in a careless, slipshod way

chùk chŏehn N ฉุกเฉิน emergency

chum chon N ชุมชน N assemblage of people, community

chum num V ชุมนุม to gather together, congregate

chŭn ADJ ฉุน to be pungent (odor); to be angry

chúp V ชุบ to soak; to plate (metal)

chút N ชุด set (of clothes, furniture, etc.)

chút chán nai N ชุดชั้นใน underwear (more typically used to refer to female underwear)

chút nawn N ชุดนอน nightclothes, pajamas

chút wâai náam N ชุดว่ายน้ำ swimming costume, swimsuit

chúu N ชู้ adulterer, lover (usually refer to extramarital relations)

D

dàa V ด่า to curse, scold or berate; to tell someone off; to swear at

dâai N ด้าย thread (e.g. cotton thread)

dâan N ด้าน side (e.g. the back side of a house, the other side of an object, etc.), direction

dâan ADJ ด้าน to be hard/calloused, rough to the touch; also matte finish, dull, not shiny (NOTE: **nâa dâan** หน้าด้าน is thick skinned, shameless, brazen)

dâan khwăa N ด้านขวา on the right side

dâan nâa N ด้านหน้า front, in the front

dâan nâwk N ด้านนอก outside

dâan sáai N ด้านซ้าย on the left side

dàan trùat khâo mueang N ด่านตรวจเข้าเมือง immigration office

dàap N ดาบ sword

daa-raa N ดารา movie/TV star

dàat fáa N ดาดฟ้า deck

daehng N แดง red (for a list of the most common colors see the entry under **sǐi** สี which means 'color')

dàeht N แดด sunlight, sunshine (NOTE: **àab dàeht** V อาบแดด is to sunbake,

sunbathe)

dàeht àwk ADJ แดดออก to be sunny

dâi V ได้ to obtain, get, be able to, can; get to, gain (**dâi** is an important 'function' word in Thai. For example, 'can you?' (**dâi mái** ได้ไหม) questions are formed in this way: 'name of activity' + 'can you?' – **ao rót maa dâi mái** เอารถมาได้ไหม 'Can you bring the car?' To simply answer yes is **dâi** ได้; to answer no is **mâi dâi** ไม่ได้.)

dâi prìap V ได้เปรียบ to have an advantage

dâi dii V ได้ดี to make good, do well

dâi kam-rai V ได้กำไร to profit

dâi phǒn ได้ผล to be effective, get results

dâi ráp V ได้รับ to get, receive

dâi ráp à-nú-yâat V ได้รับอนุญาต to be allowed to, be given permission

dâi ráp bàat jèp V ได้รับบาดเจ็บ to be injured

dâi thîi V ได้ที่ to get the upper hand, not excessive or extreme

dâi yin V ได้ยิน to hear

dam N ดำ black, a dark hue (for a list of the most common colors see the entry under **sǐi** สี which means 'color')

dam náam V ดำน้ำ to dive

dâam N ด้าม handle, classifier for pens

dan V (pronounced like 'dun') ดัน to push, shove

dang ADJ (pronounced like 'dung') ดัง to be loud (sound); also to be famous

dâng doehm ADJ ดั้งเดิม traditional, original

dâng jà-mùuk N ดั้งจมูก bridge of the nose

dang nán CONJ (FORMAL) ดังนั้น so, therefore

dao V เดา to guess, speculate

daow N ดาว star

daow hăang N ดาวหาง comet

daow thiam N ดาวเทียม satellite

daow tòk N ดาวตก shooting star, meteor

dàp V ดับ to go out (fire, candle), extinguish; (SLANG) to die/be killed

dàp fai V ดับไฟ to put out a fire

dàt V (pronounced like 'dut') ดัด to bend; to shape; to straighten out

dàt phŏm V ดัดผม to perm hair

dàwk ดอก classifier for flowers, incense, arrows

dàwk bîa N ดอกเบี้ย interest (money)

dàwk bua N ดอกบัว lotus, water lily

dàwk kà-làm N ดอกกะหล่ำ cauliflower

dàwk mái N ดอกไม้ flower

dàwk mái fai N ดอกไม้ไฟ fireworks

dáwktoeh N (from English) ด็อกเตอร์ Doctor (PhD)

dawn N (pronounced like 'don') (COLLOQUIAL) ดอล dollar

dawn-lâa N (from English) ดอลลาร์ dollar

dawng ADJ (pronounced like 'dong') ดอง pickled, preserved (fruit, vegetables)

dèk N เด็ก child (young person; also commonly used to refer to adults who are in very junior, or lowly, positions in an organization)

dèk àwn N เด็กอ่อน infant, baby, a small child

dèk chaai N เด็กชาย boy

dék kamphráa N เด็กกำพร้า an orphan

dèk nák-rian N เด็กนักเรียน schoolchild(ren)

dèk phûu-yĭng N เด็กผู้หญิง girl

dèk wát N เด็กวัด temple boy

dèn ADJ เด่น prominent, conspicuous

dèt ADJ เด็ด decisive, resolute, bold ADV really, quite

dèt khàat ADV เด็ดขาด absolutely, strictly, definitely

dĭao ADV เดี๋ยว for a moment, just a moment

diao ADJ เดียว single, one, only (NOTE: khon diao N คนเดียว is 'alone', 'by oneself'; 'single person')

diao kan เดียวกัน the same – as in khon diao kan คนเดียวกัน 'the same person'

dĭao níi ADV เดี๋ยวนี้ right now, now

dĭao níi ehng ADV เดี๋ยวนี้เอง just now

dìchăn PRON, FEM (FORMAL) ดิฉัน I

dîi N (COLLOQUIAL) ดี้ (feminine) lesbian (from the English word 'lady')

dii ADJ ดี fine (okay), good, nice, well

dii jai ADJ ดีใจ glad, happy

dii khûen V ดีขึ้น to improve, get better

dii kwàa ADV, ADJ ดีกว่า better, better than

dii mâak ADJ ดีมาก well done! very good

dii thîi sùt ADJ ดีที่สุด (the) best

dii wii dii N (from English) ดีวีดี DVD

dìit V ดีด to flick, pluck, flip

dík N (COLLOQUIAL – from English 'dictionary') ดิค dictionary

din N ดิน earth, soil, ground

din phǎo N ดินเผา porcelain, china

dîn ron V ดิ้นรน to struggle

din-sǎw N ดินสอ pencil

ding ADJ ดิ่ง vertical, righteous

dìp ADJ ดิบ raw, uncooked, unripe, rare (as with a steak)

doehm ADJ เดิม former, previous, old, original

doehn V เดิน to walk

doehn lên V เดินเล่น to go for a stroll; to walk for leisure

doehn maa ADJ เดินมา on foot (coming); **doehn pai** ADJ เดินไป on foot (going)

doehn-pàa V เดินป่า to hike

doehn pai dâi N เดินไปได้ (within) walking distance

doehn ruea V เดินเรือ to operate/sail a vessel/ship/boat

doehn thaang V เดินทาง to travel, take a trip

doehn thaang dohy plàwt phai ná (POLITE EXPRESSION) เดินทางโดยปลอดภัยนะ Have a safe trip

dohn V, PASSIVE (pronounced as in

'Methadone') โดน e.g. dohn rót chon โดนรถชน to be hit by a car, to be punished, to get it in the neck (NOTE: dohn dii v (COLLOQUIAL) โดนดี to cop it, to get what one is asking for)

dòht v โดด to jump, leap, spring, bound

doi N ดอย hill, mountain, peak (used in the North of Thailand)

dohy PREP โดย by (author, artist); by way of, by means of

dohy bang-oehn ADV โดยบังเอิญ accidentally, by chance

dohy chà-phá-w ADV โดยเฉพาะ particularly, especially

dohy mâi mii ADV โดยไม่มี without

dohy mâi tâng-jai ADV โดยไม่ตั้งใจ by chance, not intentionally

dohy pà-kà-tì ADV โดยปกติ normally, usually

dohy rótfai โดยรถไฟ (to go/be transported) by rail, by train

dohy sîn choehng ADV โดยสิ้นเชิง completely (thoroughly)

dohy thûa pai ADV โดยทั่วไป in general, generally

dohy trong ADV โดยตรง directly

dòk ADJ ดก abundant, plentiful

dom v ดม to smell, inhale, sniff

don-trii N ดนตรี music

dù ADJ ดุ fierce, vicious (e.g. a vicious dog) v to blame, find fault with, censure

dù ráai ADJ ดุร้าย ferocious, pugnacious, wild

dûai PREP ด้วย as well, with, by, too, also

dûai kan ADV ด้วยกัน together

dûai khwaam praat-thànǎa dii (FORMAL) ด้วยความปรารถนาดี best wishes

duai khwaam sǐa jai (FORMAL) ด้วยความเสียใจ with regret(s), regrettably

dûai khwaam wǎng (FORMAL) ด้วยความหวัง hopefully

dûai khwaam yindii (FORMAL) ด้วยความยินดี with pleasure

dûai mueh PREP ด้วยมือ by hand

dûai tua-ehng ADV ด้วยตัวเอง by oneself

dûai wí-thii (FORMAL) ด้วยวิธี...by means of, using the method of

dùan ADJ ด่วน to be urgent, pressing, express (e.g. as in express bus)

dûan v ด้วน to cut, cut off, be cut off, amputated, cut short

duang N ดวง fortune, luck

duang aa-thít N ดวงอาทิตย์ sun

duang jan N ดวงจันทร์ (the) moon

duean N เดือน month

duean nâa N เดือนหน้า next month

duean níi N เดือนนี้ this month

duean thîi láew N เดือนที่แล้ว last month

dùeat v เดือด to reach the boiling point, rage at

dùeat ráwn ADJ เดือดร้อน to be in trouble, in a fix, distressed

dûeh ADJ ดื้อ stubborn, obstinate, headstrong

dùehm v ดื่ม to drink

dùek ADV ดึก late at night

dueng v ดึง to pull

dueng ao wái v ดึงเอาไว้ (pull up) to restrain; to tighten (a rope etc.) up

dueng dùut v ดึงดูด to attract

duu v ดู to look at, see, watch (TV, movie)

duu àwk v ดูออก to be able to see through (someone or something), to understand, to be able to tell

duu duang v ดูดวง to look at one's horoscope N fortune telling

duu laeh v ดูแล to take care of, look after

duu lên v ดูเล่น to look at something for fun (to pass time)

duu mǎw v (COLLOQUIAL) (mǎw is pronounced 'more' with a rising tone) ดูหมอ to have your fortune told/read, see a fortune teller

duu mǔean ดูเหมือน to seem (e.g. as if something was going to happen), look as if

D

duu mǔeankan N ดูเหมือนกัน to look the same

duu sí (COLLOQUIAL) ดูซิ look!

duu thùuk v ดูถูก to look down on someone, insult, disparage

dùut ดูด to suck, absorb, soak up

E

eh-chia N เอเชีย Asia

eh-ds N เอดส์ AIDS (the fuller form is rôhk eh-ds (literally, 'disease' + 'AIDS') โรคเอดส์)

eh-yêhn N (from English) เอเย่นต์ agent, agency

èhk-kàchon ADJ เอกชน private (company/sector)

èhk-kà-phâap N เอกภาพ unity, solidarity

èhk-kà-râat ADJ เอกราช (of a state, nation) independent, free sovereign

èhk-kà-sǎan N เอกสาร document(s), printed material, records

éhk-sà-reh v, N (from English) เอ็กซเรย์ X-ray

ehn v เอน to lean, recline

ehng N เอง self (NOTE: tua ehng ตัวเอง is 'myself')

ehn lǎng v เอนหลัง to lean back

eh-o N เอว waist

en N เอ็น tendon, sinew, gut

en-duu v เอ็นดู to adore, like very much

èt v เอ็ด (COLLOQUIAL) to scold

F

fǎa N ฝา lid, cover, (internal) wall

fǎa chii N ฝาชี cover placed over a dish of food

fǎa fàet N ฝาแฝด twins

fàa v ฝ่า to go against, violate, disobey

fàa N ฝ่า palm (of the hand), sole (of the foot)

fàa tháo N ฝ่าเท้า sole (of the foot)

fâa ADJ ฝ้า clouded (like a cloudy film of the surface of something), scum, blemish; pen fâa เป็นฝ้า to have freckles

fáa N ฟ้า sky, light blue color (for a list of the most common colors see the entry under sǐi สี which means 'color')

fáa lâep N ฟ้าแลบ lightning

fáa phàa N ฟ้าผ่า lightning

fǎa phànǎng N ฝาผนัง wall (of a room or building)

fáa ráwng N ฟ้าร้อง thunder

fàat ADJ ฝาด astringent (in taste)

fâat v ฟาด to strike, slap, hit hard

fâai N ฝ้าย cotton

fàai N ฝ่าย side, group, party

fàai diaow N ฝ่ายเดียว one (party, side)

fàai trong khâam ฝ่ายตรงข้าม opponent(s), (the) opposition (in politics etc.)

fàak v ฝาก to leave behind for safekeeping, deposit, entrust to someone, leave with

fàak ngoehn v ฝากเงิน to deposit money (in the bank)

fàak krà-pǎo v ฝากกระเป๋า to leave luggage

fàak krà-pǎo dâi mái ฝากกระเป๋า ได้ไหม May I leave my luggage?

faam N (from English 'farm', pronounced similar to the English) ฟาร์ม farm

fǎan v ฝาน to slice, cut thin

faang N ฟาง straw

fae-chân N (from English) แฟชั่น fashion (i.e. the latest fashion, etc.)

faen N แฟน boy/girlfriend, fan (admirer) (NOTE: also commonly used to refer to a husband or wife)

fǎeng v แฝง to hide, conceal

fâem N แฟ้ม file, folder

fáek N (from English) แฟกซ์ fax (message or machine)

fàet ADJ แฝด twin, double, coupled, paired (NOTE: fǎa fàet N ฝาแฝด is 'twins')

fǎi N ไฝ mole, beauty spot

fai N ไฟ fire; light (lamp)

fai chǎai N ไฟฉาย flashlight, torch

fai chǽek N ไฟแช็ค cigarette lighter

fai fáa ADJ, N ไฟฟ้า electric; electricity

fai mâi V ไฟไหม้ to be on fire

fai nâa N ไฟหน้า headlight

fai tháai N ไฟท้าย taillight

fàk N ฝัก pod, hull, case, sheath, scabbard

fák V ฟัก to hatch

fàk N ฝักบัว shower (head)

fák thawng N (pronounced 'fuck tong') ฟักทอง pumpkin

fan N (pronounced like 'fun') ฟัน tooth, teeth

fǎn V, N (pronounced like 'fun' with a rising tone) ฝัน to dream; a dream

fǎn klaang wan N ฝันกลางวัน to daydream

fǎn ráai N ฝันร้าย a nightmare

fǎn thǔeng V ฝันถึง to dream about (somebody)

fang V ฟัง to listen, hear

fǎng V ฝัง to bury, implant

fàng N ฝั่ง bank (river), shore

fang phlehng V ฟังเพลง to listen to music

fang yùu V ฟังอยู่ (to be) listening (the use of yùu อยู่ after a verb indicates the present continuous tense – '...ing')

fâo V เฝ้า to watch over, tend, take care of, keep watch

fâo duu V เฝ้าดู to keep an eye on, keep watch (over, on)

fâo rá-wang V เฝ้าระวัง to guard against, be on the alert/lookout (for)

fàràng N ฝรั่ง caucasian, westerner; guava (fruit)

fàràngsèht N ฝรั่งเศส France, French

fàw V, ADJ ฝ่อ wither, dry out; abortive

fawng N ฟอง foam, bubbles, froth, lather; a classifier for eggs

fáwng V ฟ้อง to sue, file legal proceedings, accuse, complain to someone about somebody else

fawng náam N ฟองน้ำ a sponge

fáwng ráwng V ฟ้องร้อง to sue, bring charges against

frii ADJ (from English) ฟรี free

fǐi N ฝี boil, pustule, abscess (NOTE: plùuk fǐi ปลูกฝี is 'to vaccinate')

fǐi-dàat N ฝีดาษ smallpox

fǐi mueh N ฝีมือ workmanship, craftsmanship, handiwork, skill; fǐi pàak N ฝีปาก verbal skill/gift of the gab

fǐi thâo N ฝีเท้า speed of foot

fílíppin N ฟิลิปปินส์ the Philippines

fim N ฟิล์ม film (for camera; or the tinted film on a car windscreen)

fǐn N ฝิ่น opium

fíu N (from English) ฟิวส์ fuse

fláet N (from English) แฟลต flat, apartment

fláet N (from English) แฟลช flash (camera)

flúk N (from English) ฟลุ๊ค fluke, a lucky chance

fók chám ADJ ฟกช้ำ bruised, swollen

foeh-ní-jôeh N (from English – pronounced like 'fer-ni-jer') เฟอร์นิเจอร์ furniture

fǒi N ฝอย shreds, fibers, droplets, trivial details; V (COLLOQUIAL) to brag

fǒn N ฝน rain (NOTE: nâa fǒn หน้าฝน is the 'rainy season' – generally from late May/early June to the end of October)

fǒn láeng N ฝนแล้ง drought

fǒn tòk V ฝนตก to rain, be raining, it is raining

fùeak N เฝือก cast or split (e.g. for a broken arm/leg)

fueang N เฟือง gearwheel

fúehn V ฟื้น to recover, regain consciousness, come to (after fainting)

fǔehn V ฝืน to disobey, contrary to, do something against (the law, one's will, etc.)

fùeht ADJ ฝืด tight, stuck, difficult to move

fùek V ฝึก to practice, drill/train

F

fùek hàt/fùek sáwm v ฝึกหัด/ฝึกซ้อม to train

fuen N ฟืน firewood

fûm-fueay N, ADJ ฟุ่มเฟือย luxury; luxurious, extravagant, unnecessary

fùn N ฝุ่น dust

fút N ฟุต foot (length)

fút bawn N ฟุตบอล (COLLOQUIAL) bawn บอล soccer/football

fuu v ฟู (COLLOQUIAL) to become fluffy

fûuk N ฟูก mattress

fǔung N ฝูง a crowd, group, herd, flock, pack

fǔung nók N ฝูงนก a flock of birds

fǔung plaa N ฝูงปลา a school of fish

H

hâa NUM ห้า five

hàa N ห่า cholera demon/spirit held responsible for plagues; (SLANG – rude) âi hàa ไอ้ห่า shit, damn, bastard

hǎa v หา to look for, look up (find in book), search for

hǎa kin v (COLLOQUIAL) หากิน to make a living

hǎa maa dâi v หามาได้ to earn

hǎa mâi joeh v (COLLOQUIAL) หาไม่เจอ cannot find (something)

hǎa ngoehn v (COLLOQUIAL) หาเงิน to make (some) money, to make a living

hǎa rûeang v (COLLOQUIAL) หาเรื่อง to look for trouble; be abrasive, provocative

hâa sip NUM ห้าสิบ fifty

hǎa wâa v หาว่า to accuse (someone of doing something)

hǎa yâak ADJ หายาก rare (scarce)

háad dis N (from English) ฮาร์ดดิสก์ hard disk

hǎai v หาย to be lost, to disappear ADJ to be missing

hǎai jai v หายใจ to breathe; hǎai jai àwk v หายใจออก to breathe out; hǎai jai khâo v หายใจเข้า to breathe in

hǎai pai v หายไป to disappear, vanish

hǎai wai wai หายไว ๆ get well soon!

hǎam v หาม to carry, bear

hàam ADJ ห่าม almost ripe (fruit)

hâam v ห้าม to forbid, be forbidden

hàan N ห่าน goose

hǎan v หาร to divide

hǎan dûai v หารด้วย divided by (e.g. 4 hǎan dûai 4 = 1 (4 ÷ 4 = 1))

hǎang N หาง tail

hǎang-pia N หางเปีย pigtail

hàang ADJ ห่าง to be apart/distant from

hâang sàp-phá-sǐnkháa N ห้างสรรพสินค้า (COLLOQUIAL) hâang ห้าง department store

hàap v หาบ to carry a pole across one's shoulder

hàat N หาด beach

hǎe N แห fishing net

haehm N (from English) แฮม ham

hâehng ADJ แห้ง to be dry

hâehng láehng ADJ, N แห้งแล้ง dry (weather), drought

hàeng N แห่ง of; classifier for places

hâi v ให้ to give; to, for; to allow, have something done (A very important 'functional' word in Thai. Here are a couple of examples [space limitations make it impossible to go into greater detail about the broad range of uses of hâi ให้]: To have something done: hâi khǎo ao rót maa ให้เขาเอารถมา – 'have him/get him to bring the car (along)'; To do something for somebody: khǎo súeh yean hâi faehn เขาซื้อยีนให้แฟน 'he brought a pair of jeans for his girlfriend'. In the first example the meaning of hâi ให้ is rendered by the word 'have'; in the second example it is the equivalent of the English word 'for'.)

hâi aa-hǎan v ให้อาหาร to feed (the dog)

hâi àphai v ให้อภัย to forgive

hâi châo v ให้เช่า to rent out

hâi kaan v ให้การ to plead (in court)

hâi khuehn v ให้คืน, (or simply) khuehn v คืน to return, give back

hâi thaan v ให้ทาน to give alms

hâi yuehm v ให้ยืม to lend

hàk ADJ หัก to break/fracture (e.g. of bones); also to deduct (money owed etc.)

hàk lăng v (COLLOQUIAL) หักหลัง to double-cross, betray

hăm N (SLANG; Isaan dialect) หำ balls (gonads)

hàn v หั่น to cut up, slice

hăn v หัน to turn

hăn klàp v หันกลับ to turn back

hăn lăng v หันหลัง turn around

hăn nâa v หันหน้า to face, turn one's head, turn the face toward a direction

hăn phuang-maa-lai v หันพวงมาลัย to steer (to turn the steering wheel – 'steering wheel' is phuang-maa-lai พวงมาลัย)

hanlŏh (from the English greeting) ฮัลโหล hello! (used on the phone)

hào v เห่า to bark

hăo N เหา louse, lice

hăow v หาว to yawn

hàt N (pronounced 'hut' with a low tone) หัด measles; hàt yur rá man หัดเยอรมัน German measles

hàt v หัด to drill, practice

heh-lí-kháwp-tôeh N เฮลิคอปเตอร์ helicopter

hĕow N เหว gorge, chasm, abyss

heh-roh-iin N (from English) เฮโรอีน heroin

hàw v (pronounced 'hor') ห่อ to wrap (up a parcel, etc.)

hàw khăwng N ห่อของ package

hăw duu daaw N หอดูดาว observatory

hăw khoi N หอคอย tower

hăw phák N หอพัก dormitory, hostel

hăwm ADJ หอม to be sweet-smelling, fragrant, aromatic

hăwm v หอม to kiss (the old Thai way of kissing is more like nuzzling or sniffing of one another's cheeks,

i.e. face cheeks)

hăwm yài N หอมใหญ่ onion (or hŭa hăwm หัวหอม)

hâwng N ห้อง room (in house, hotel)

hâwng khăai tŭa N ห้องขายตั๋ว ticket office

hâwng khăai tŭa yùu thîi năi ห้องขายตั๋วอยู่ที่ไหน Where is the ticket office?

hâwng kèp khăwng N ห้องเก็บของ storeroom

hâwng khrua N ห้องครัว kitchen

hâwng kong N ฮ่องกง Hong Kong

hâwng náam N ห้องน้ำ toilet (bathroom), lavatory

hâwng nâng lên N ห้องนั่งเล่น sitting room, living room, lounge (room)

hâwng nawn N ห้องนอน bedroom

hâwng ráp khàek N ห้องรับแขก living room

hâwng rian N ห้องเรียน classroom

hâwng sà-mùt N ห้องสมุด library

hâwng tâi din N ห้องใต้ดิน basement

hâwng thŏhng N ห้องโถง hall (as in 'assembly hall')

hàwp v หอบ to pant, breathe heavily

hèht-kaan N เหตุการณ์ happening, incident, event

hèht phŏn N เหตุผล reason

hĕn v เห็น to see, regard, to think (used to give opinion in reporting speech, e.g. 'I think that'); hĕn dûai v เห็นด้วย to agree

hĕn jai ADJ เห็นใจ to be sympathetic, understand someone's position

hĕn kàeh tua ADJ เห็นแก่ตัว to be selfish

hĕn pen phá-yaan v เห็นเป็นพยาน to witness (something)

hèp N เห็บ tick, wood tick, hail

hèt N เห็ด mushroom(s)

hĭi N (COLLOQUIAL, EXTREMELY RUDE) หี vagina (or, more accurately, 'cunt')

hìip N หีบ chest (box)

hìmá N หิมะ snow

hìmá tòk v หิมะตก to snow, snowing

hǐn N หิน rock, stone

hin duu N ฮินดู Hindu

hǐn pà-kaa-rang N หินประการัง coral (commonly simply pà-kaa-rang ประการัง)

hǐn puun N หินปูน limestone, tartar

hǐu, hǐu-khâow ADJ หิว, หิวข้าว to be hungry

hîu V หิ้ว to carry

hǐu náam V หิวน้ำ to be thirsty

hòht, hòht-ráai ADJ โหด, โหดร้าย cruel, wild, brutal, ruthless

hǒi N หอย mollusc/oyster/clam

hôi V ห้อย to hang, be suspended

hǒi naang rom N หอยนางรม a type of large, fleshy oyster

hǒi thâak N หอยทาก snail (or simply thâak ทาก)

hòk หก six

hòk V หก to spill (liquid)

hòk lóm V หกล้ม to fall over, take a tumble, (or, more simply, lóm ล้ม)

hòk sìp NUM หกสิบ sixty

hǒng N หงส์ a swan

hòt V หด to shrink

hǔa N หัว head, top

hǔa boh-raan ADJ หัวโบราณ to be old-fashioned, conservative

hǔa-dûe ADJ หัวดื้อ stubborn

hǔa jai N หัวใจ heart

hǔa jai waai N หัวใจวาย a heart attack

hǔa kào ADJ หัวเก่า conservative, old-fashioned

hǔa khǎeng ADJ หัวแข็ง obstinate, stubborn, headstrong

hǔa khào N หัวเข่า knee

hǔa khâw N หัวข้อ subject, topic, heading

hǔa láan ADJ หัวล้าน bald

hǔa mâe mueh N หัวแม่มือ thumb

hǔa nâa N หัวหน้า chief, leader, head, boss

hǔa nom N หัวนม nipple(s)

hǔa sǎi ADJ (COLLOQUIAL) หัวใส bright, shrewd

hùai ADJ (COLLOQUIAL/SLANG) ห่วย lousy, crappy, crummy, (SLANG) suck

hǔai N หวย underground lottery

hûan V, ADJ ห้วน to be brusque; curt, uncouth (talk or speech)

hǔan V หวน to turn back

hǔang V หวง to be jealous (of), possessive (of things), unwilling to part with something

hùang ADJ ห่วง to be anxious, concerned/worried (about)

hǔa ráw V หัวเราะ to laugh

hǔa ráw yáw V หัวเราะเยาะ to laugh at

hǔa sà-mǎwng N หัวสมอง brain concussion

hǔeng V หึง to be jealous (commonly of a sexual nature)

hùn N หุ่น dummy, mannequin, also the shape/appearance of someone's figure (NOTE: 'robot' is hùn yon หุ่นยนต์)

hûn N หุ้น share, stock (as traded on the stock market)

hûn sùan N หุ้นส่วน partner (in business)

hǔng V หุง to cook (rice)

hùp khǎo N หุบเขา valley

hùp pàak V หุบปาก to close the mouth, (COLLOQUIAL) shut up!

hǔu N หู ear(s)

hǔu fang N หูฟัง headset, headphone, earphone

hǔu nùak ADJ หูหนวก (to be) deaf

hǔu tueng ADJ หูตึง hard of hearing

hùut N หูด wart

I

iang V เอียง to bend, slant, incline

ii PRON อี (derogatory) title used with the first names of women, bound element in names of birds and animals

ii-kaa N อีกา crow

ìik ADV ... อีก again

ìik ADV อีก... another (different); else, more

ìik an nùeng อีกอันหนึ่ง (Can I have) another one

ìik khon nùeng (COLLOQUIAL) อีกคนหนึ่ง another person, one more person

ìik khráng nùeng (COLLOQUIAL) อีกครั้ง หนึ่ง again, one more time

ìik mâi naan (COLLOQUIAL) อีกไม่นาน soon

ìik sàk nòi (COLLOQUIAL) อีกสักหน่อย (Could I have) a little more

ii-sùk-ii-sǎi N อีสุกอีใส chicken pox

ìik yàang nùeng IDIOM อีกอย่างหนึ่ง by the way, another thing

ii-meh N (from English) อีเมล์ email (message)

ii-sǎan N อีสาน the northeastern region of Thailand – commonly written in English as Isaan, Isarn

i-lék-thrawnìk ADJ (from English) อิเล็กทรอนิก electronic

ìm V อิ่ม to be full, eaten one's fill, had enough

india N อินเดีย India

indohniisia N อินโดนีเซีย Indonesia (colloquially Indonesia is often referred to as in-doh อินโด)

ing V อิง to lean on/against

in-sii N อินทรี eagle ADJ อินทรีย์ organic

in-toeh-nét N (from English) อินเทอร์เน็ต Internet (or simply nèt เน็ต)

ìt N อิฐ brick, a brick

ì-taa-lii N อิตาลี Italy, Italian

ìtchǎa N, V อิจฉา envy; to be jealous of

it-sà-laam N (alternative pronunciation 'islaam') อิสลาม Islam

ìt-sà-rà ADJ อิสระ to be free, independent

ìt-sà-rà-phâap N อิสรภาพ freedom

ìt-thí-phon N อิทธิพล influence

J

jà AUX V จะ shall, will; future indicator

jàa N จ่า leader, head, chief

jâa ADJ จ้า bright (light), intense, glaring

jàai V จ่าย to pay; jàai láew จ่ายแล้ว (for a bill that has been) paid

jàai tà-làat V จ่ายตลาด to buy the groceries, go to shop at the market

jàai yaa V จ่ายยา to give medicine

jàak PREP จาก of, from

jàak kan V จากกัน to separate (from one another)

jàak pai V จากไป to depart, go away from a place

jaam V จาม to sneeze

jaan N จาน a plate/dish

jaang V, ADJ จาง to fade; faded, dilute

jâang V จ้าง to hire

jàehk V แจก to hand out, distribute

jaeh-kan N แจกัน a vase (for flowers)

jâehng V แจ้ง to inform, notify; jâehng khwaam แจ้งความ to report (to the police)

jáekkêt N (from English) แจ็คเก็ต a jacket, coat

jà-tù-ràt N จตุรัส square

jai N ใจ heart, mind

jai àwn ADJ ใจอ่อน yielding, soft-hearted, easily influenced, easily touched

jai bàap ADJ ใจบาป sinful

jai bun ADJ ใจบุญ pious, charitable

jai chúen ADJ ใจชื้น relieved

jai dam ADJ ใจดำ merciless, mean

jai diao ADJ ใจเดียว faithful

jai dii ADJ ใจดี to be kind, good (of people)

jai hǎi ADJ ใจหาย shocked, stunned with fear

jai khǎeng ADJ ใจแข็ง unyielding

jai khâep ADJ ใจแคบ selfish, narrow-minded

jai klâa ADJ ใจกล้า brave, bold

jai kwâang ADJ ใจกว้าง to be generous, broad-minded, magnanimous

jai loi ADJ ใจลอย absent-minded

jai ngâai ADJ ใจง่าย cheap (women), easy to get

jai ráai ADJ ใจร้าย malicious

jai ráwn ADJ ใจร้อน impatient, impetuous, hasty

jai sàn ADJ ใจสั่น frightened

jai tàek ADJ ใจแตก spoiled, self-indulgent and unrestrained

jai yen ADJ ใจเย็น calm, cool-hearted, steady, imperturbable

jàk-kà-jàn N จักจั่น cicada

ják-kà-jǐi ADJ จักจี้ ticklish

jàk-krà-phát N จักรพรรดิ emperor

jàk-krà-waan N จักรวาล universe

jàk-krà-yaan N จักรยาน bicycle

jàk-krà-yaan-yon N (FORMAL) จักรยานยนต์ motorcycle, (COLLOQUIAL) maw-toeh-sai มอเตอร์ไซค์ (from English)

jàk yép phâa N จักรเย็บผ้า sewing machine

jam V (pronounced like 'jum' in 'jump') จำ to remember, retain

jam dâi V จำได้ to remember, recognize

jam jai V จำใจ to force/be forced to do something

jam jeh ADJ จำเจ tiresome, monotonous, repetitious

jam kàt V จำกัด to limit, define

jam lawng V จำลอง to imitate, copy, reproduce, model

jam leoy N จำเลย defendant

jam nam V จำนำ to pawn, mortgage

jam nawng V จำนอง to mortgage

jam-nuan N จำนวน amount

jam-pen ADJ จำเป็น to be necessary V to need

jà-mùuk N จมูก nose

jang ADV (COLLOQUIAL) จัง very (used as an intensifier, e.g. 'very beautiful' sǔai jang สวยจัง)

jang-wà N จังหวะ rhythm

jang-wàt N (pronounced something like 'jung-what') จังหวัด a province (regional administrative unit)

jâo N เจ้านาย master

jâo bàow N เจ้าบ่าว bridegroom/groom

jâo chaai N เจ้าชาย prince

jâo chúu N เจ้าชู้ philanderer

jâo khǎwng N เจ้าของ owner

jâo nâa thîi N เจ้าหน้าที่ official, bureaucrat, public servant, authority (person in charge)

jâo nîi N เจ้าหนี้ creditor

jâo phâap N เจ้าภาพ host (of a party, wedding, etc.)

jâo sǎow N เจ้าสาว bride

jâo ying N เจ้าหญิง princess

jàp V จับ to capture, arrest, catch, grab

jà-raa-jawn N จราจร traffic

jà-rùat N จรวด rocket

jàt V (pronounced like the English word 'jut' as in 'to jut out') จัด to arrange (e.g. furniture); also used as an intensifier: e.g. extreme, intense – ráwn jàt ร้อนจัด intense/extreme heat

jàt hâi rîap rói V จัดให้เรียบร้อย to tidy up

jàt-kaan V จัดการ to manage, organize, sort out, deal with

jàt tó V จัดโต๊ะ to lay or set a table

jaw N (pronounced like the English word 'jaw') จอ screen, monitor (of television/computer)

jàw ruu V เจาะรู to make a hole

jawn-jàt N จรจัด homeless wanderer, vagebond

jawng V จอง to reserve, book (seats, tickets), i.e. khǎw jawng tǔa pai... sǎwng thîi nâng ขอจองตั๋วไป...สองที่ นั่ง I'd like to reserve two seats to ...

jâwng V จ้อง to gaze at, stare

jawng hǎwng ADJ จองหอง unduly proud, haughty

jàwt V จอด to stop (a vehicle), i.e. rót jàwt thîi...mái? รถจอดที่...ไหม Does this train/bus stop at?; jàwt thîi...dâi mái? จอดที่...ได้ไหม Could you please stop at...?

jàwt rót V จอดรถ to park a vehicle

jeh N (pronounced similar to 'jay') เจ vegetarian; kin jeh กินเจ to eat vegetarian food

jéng ADJ (COLLOQUIAL) เจ๊ง (of an object – e.g. a mobile phone) to be broken, worn out, kaput; (for a business) to go broke/bankrupt

jěng (COLLOQUIAL) เจ๋ง 'that's cool, great, awesome'

jèp ADJ เจ็บ to be sore, hurt (injured)

jèp mâak ADJ เจ็บมาก to be very painful

jèt NUM เจ็ด seven

jèt sìp NUM เจ็ดสิบ seventy

jiin N (pronounced like the English word 'jean(s)') จีน China, Chinese

jiin klaang N จีนกลาง Mainland China; also used to refer to Mandarin Chinese (language)

jìip V (pronounced like 'jeep' with a low tone) จีบ to flirt with someone, court, try to chat up someone

jîm V จิ้ม to dip in, pick

jîm N จิ๋ม (COLLOQUIAL) vagina

jing ADJ จริง to be true, real

jing jai ADJ จริงใจ sincere, honest

jing jang ADJ จริงจัง serious

jing-jing ADV จริง ๆ really, truly, indeed!

jing-jôh N จิงโจ้ kangaroo

jîng-jòk N จิ้งจก house lizard

jîng-rìit N จิ้งหรีด cricket (insect)

jing rŭeh INTERJ จริงหรือ Really? Is that so? (used to express surprise)

jìp V จิบ sip

joeh V (pronounced like 'jer' in 'jerk') เจอ to meet, find

jîi V จี้ to poke, tickle, point at/out, prod, exhort N pendant of a necklace

jóhk N โจ๊ก joke; rice porridge

johm tii V โจมตี to attack (in a war)

john N โจร robber

john sà-làt N โจรสลัด pirate

jom V จม to sink or drown

jom náam V จมน้ำ to drown

jon ADJ จน to be poor

jon krà-thâng CONJ จนกระทั่ง until

jong jai V จงใจ to intend

jòp V จบ to end (finish)

jòt V จด to take note, jot down

jòt-măai N จดหมาย letter; mail

jòt-măai-long thàbian N จดหมายลงทะเบียน registered letter/mail

jàw V เจาะ to drill, make a hole

juan ADV จวน almost

juea jaang ADJ เจือจาง thin (of liquids)

jùeht ADJ จืด bland, tasteless

jueng CONJ จึง (FORMAL – more written than spoken language) consequently, therefore

jùk N จุก topknot, stopper (of bottle), cork

jùt N จุด point, dot

jùt fai V จุดไฟ to light a fire

jùt-jùt ADJ จุด ๆ spotted (pattern)

jùt-măai plaai thaang N จุดหมายปลายทาง destination

jùt mûng măai N จุดมุ่งหมาย purpose

jùt rôehm tôn N จุดเริ่มต้น origin, starting point

jûu-jîi ADJ จู้จี้ fussy

jùu-johm V จู่โจม to attack, rush

juung V จูง to tow, drag

jùup V, N จูบ kiss

K

NOTE: This letter should not be confused with the English 'k' sound. In this case 'k' is pronounced like 'g' in 'gun', or like the 'k' in the word 'skin'

kà V กะ to estimate (the price), guess N a shift – as in a shift at work (i.e. the night shift)

kaa-faeh N (pronounced 'gar-fey') กาแฟ coffee

kaa kii ADJ กากี khakhi (color)

kaai-yá-kam N กายกรรม gymnastics

kaam N กาม sexual desire

kâam N ก้าม claw, pincer (of crab)

kaam-má-rôhk N กามโรค venereal disease

kaam-má-thêhp N กามเทพ Cupid, Eros

kaan N การ the action/task/business of...

kaan bâan N การบ้าน homework

kaan bàat jèp N การบาดเจ็บ injury

kaan bin N การบิน flying, aviation

kaan chûay lŭea N การช่วยเหลือ aid, assistance

K

kaan doehn thaang N การเดินทาง trip, journey

kaan hâi àphai N การให้อภัย forgiveness, mercy

kaan kàw sâang N การก่อสร้าง building, construction

kaan khàeng khǎn N การแข่งขัน competition, a race of game

kaan lûeak tâng N การเลือกตั้ง election

kaan mueang N การเมือง politics

kaan ngoehn N การเงิน finance

kaan prá chum N การประชุม meeting, conference

kaan rák sǎa N การรักษา care, maintenance, remedy

kaan thûut N การทูต diplomacy

kaan pàtìbàt ngaan N การปฏิบัติงาน performance (of work)

kaan pàtìsèht N การปฏิเสธ refusal

kaan phát-thà-naa N การพัฒนา development

kaan sà-daehng N การแสดง a display, a show, a performance

kaan sǐa sàlà N การเสียสละ sacrifice

kaan sùek-sǎa N การศึกษา education

kaan tàwp sànǎwng N การตอบสนอง reaction, response

kaan thák thaai N การทักทาย greetings

kaan tham aa-hǎan N การทำอาหาร cooking, cuisine

kaan thòk panhǎa N การถกปัญหา discussion (of issues)

kaan thót sàwp N การทดสอบ test, examination

kaang V กาง to spread out, stretch out, hang out

kâang N ก้าง fishbone

kaang-kehng N กางเกง trousers, pants

kaang-kehng khǎa sân N กางเกงขาสั้น shorts (short trousers)

kaangkehng nai N กางเกงใน underpants, panties

kaa-tuun N (from English) การ์ตูน cartoon

kà-bòt N กบฏ rebel, rebellion

kà-laa N กะลา hard shell coconut

kà-laa-sǐi N กะลาสี sailor, seaman

kà-lá-manng N กะละมัง enameled bowl or basin

kà-làm dàwk N กะหล่ำดอก cauliflower

kà-làm plii N กะหล่ำปลี cabbage

kà lòhk N กะโหลก skull, hard shell of the coconut

kà ràt N กะรัต carat

kà rìang N กะเหรี่ยง Karen tribe

kà-rìi N กะหรี่ (COLLOQUAIL) curry, female prostitute

kà-tan-yuu ADJ กตัญญู grateful

kà-tì-kaa N กติกา rule (in sports)

kà-rá kà-daa-khom N กรกฎาคม July

kà-sèht-trà-kam N เกษตรกรรม agriculture

kà-thí N กะทิ coconut cream/milk

kà-wii N กวี poet

kà-thoey N กะเทย a transvestite, also referred to by the English term 'ladyboy'

kàe N แกะ sheep

kâe kháen V แก้แค้น to take revenge

kâe khǎi V แก้ไข to correct, mend, revise, resolve

kàe sàlàk V แกะสลัก to carve

kaeh PRON (COLLOQUIAL, INFORMAL) แก you, he, she, they

kàeh ADJ แก่ old (of persons), strong (coffee)

kâeh V แก้ to fix (repair); to loosen, untie; to amend, revise, correct

kàeh dàet ADJ (COLLOQUIAL) แก่แดด to be cheeky, a whipper snapper, smart arse kid

kâeh hâi thùuk V แก้ให้ถูก to correct

kàeh kwàa ADJ แก่กว่า to be older, elder

kâeh panhǎa V แก้ปัญหา to solve (a problem)

kâeh phâa V แก้ผ้า to get undressed, take off clothing, be naked

kàeh tua V แก้ตัว to get old, grow old

kâeh tua V แก้ตัว to make excuses,

K

find an excuse/make up for one's losses/failures

kâehm N แก้ม cheek(s)

kaehng N แกง curry

kaehng jùet N แกงจืด mild soup/plain soup

kaehng phèt N แกงเผ็ด hot curry

káet N (from English) แก๊ส gas (e.g. cooking gas)

kâew N แก้ว glass (for drinking)

kâew hŭu N แก้วหู eardrum

kài N (pronounced similar to 'guy') ไก่ chicken

kái N (from English) ไกด์ a guide

kài nguang N ไก่งวง turkey

kài yâang N ไก่ย่าง BBQ or grilled chicken

kàk khăng V กักขัง to confine, restrict, detain

kam N (pronounced like 'gum') กรรม karma

kam dao N กำเดา nosebleed

kam kuam N กำกวม ambiguous

kam lai N กำไล bracelet, bangle

kamjàt V (pronounced 'gum-jut') กำจัด to rid, get rid of

kamlang AUX (pronounced 'gum-lung') กำลัง to be presently doing N strength, power, (armed) force

kamlang doehn thaang V กำลังเดินทาง on the way, in the process of travelling

kam-má-kaan N กรรมการ committee, judge (competition)

kam-má-phan ADJ (pronounced 'gum-màpun') กรรมพันธุ์ hereditary, congenital, genetic

kam-má-thăn N กำมะถัน sulfur

kam-má-yìi N กำมะหยี่ velvet

kam mueh V กำมือ to clench the fist

kamnan N (pronounced 'gum none') กำนัน sub-district headman, chief of sub-district (tambon)

kam-nòt N กำหนด schedule, program

kam-nòt-kaan N กำหนดการ schedule, program

kam pân N กำปั้น fist

kam-phaehng N กำแพง (stone or brick) wall (of a yard or town)

kam-phuu-chaa N กัมพูชา Cambodia

kamrai N กำไร profit

kan ADV กัน together, mutually V to prevent

kân V กั้น to cut off, shut off, bar

kan thòe กันเถอะ let's (e.g. go) (used at the end of a sentence to urge the other party to do something)

kan-chaa N (pronounced 'gun jar') กัญชา marihuana, hemp, grass, dope, pot, weed

kan chon N กันชน bumper

kan daan ADJ กันดาร barren, arid, lacking

kang hăn N กังหัน windmill

kankrai N กรรไกร scissors

kang won N กังวล worry

kan-yaa-yon N กันยายน September

kao V เกา to scratch lightly

kào ADJ เก่า old (of things)

kâo NUM เก้า nine

kâo îi N เก้าอี้ chair

kâo sìp NUM เก้าสิบ ninety

kaolĭi nŭea N เกาหลีเหนือ North Korea

kaolĭi tâi N เกาหลีใต้ South Korea

kaow N กาว glue

kôw V ก้าว to step

kôw nâa V ก้าวหน้า to advance, go forward

kôw ráow ADJ ก้าวร้าว aggressive, disrespectful

kàp CONJ กับ and PREP with

kàp dàk N กับดัก trap, snare

kàp tan N กัปตัน captain

kàp khâow N (COLLOQUIAL) กับข้าว the food eaten with rice (e.g. curry/vegetables/soup, etc.)

kàp klâem N กับแกล้ม hors d'oeuvres, entrée, a light meal

kà-phrao N กะเพรา sweet basil

kà-phríp V กะพริบ to blink (flash on and off); **kà-phríp-taa** กะพริบตา eyes blinking

kàpì

kàpì N กะปิ fish paste

kàrú-naa กรุณา please ... (a very polite, formal means of asking for something); kindness, mercy

kàt V (pronounced like 'gut' with a low tone) กัด to bite

kàt fan V กัดฟัน to gnash one's teeth

kàt kan V (COLLOQUIAL) กัดกัน to be at odds with another person, to snipe at

kàw N เกาะ island V to cling to

kâw ADV (pronounced 'gor') ก็ also, too, either (used to add an agreeing thought); **kâw loei** CONJ ก็เลย then, so

kàw sâang V ก่อสร้าง to construct

kàw tâng V ก่อตั้ง to establish, set up

káwf N (from English) กอล์ฟ golf

káwk N ก๊อก, ก๊อกน้ำ tap, faucet

kàwn ADV ก่อน first, earlier, before

kâwn N ก้อน lump; classifier for lump-like objects, cube (e.g. sugar)

kàwn níi ADV ก่อนนี้ earlier, before this, previously

kawng N กอง troop, force, pile, heap

kawng tháp N กองทัพ troops, the military, the army (in particular)

kawng-tháp aa-kàat N กองทัพอากาศ air force

kawng-tháp-bòk N กองทัพบก army, military land forces

kawng-tháp-ruea N กองทัพเรือ navy, naval forces

kaw-rá-nii N กรณี a case (e.g. a legal case), a particular instance (NOTE: (COLLOQUIAL) khûu kaw-rá-nii คู่กรณี the other party in an accident/incident)

kàwt V กอด to embrace, hug

ké N เก๊ะ a drawer (in a table etc.)

kéh ADJ เก๊ fake

kěh ADJ เก๋ to be with it, stylish, chic

keh N (pronounced 'gay') (from English) เกย์ gay, homosexual

kehm N (from English) เกม match, game

kèng ADJ เก่ง clever, smart, good at something (also used colloquially to mean 'a lot': e.g. kin kèng กินเก่ง 'to eat a lot'; nawn kèng นอนเก่ง 'to sleep a lot')

kèp V เก็บ to save, collect, accumulate, keep, pick up

kèp khǎwng V เก็บของ to gather things together, pack (luggage)

kèp kòt V (COLLOQUIAL) เก็บกด to suppress (one's true feelings)

kèp-ngoehn V เก็บเงิน to save money, check the bill

kèp tó V เก็บโต๊ะ to clear the table (e.g. after dinner)

kèp tua V เก็บตัว to avoid others, keep to oneself, shun society

kia N (from English) เกียร์ gear

kíao N เกี๊ยว small Chinese dumpling or wonton

kìao V เกี่ยว to cut (with sickle), harvest, reap, to pertain (to), be related (to) (often used in a negative sense/statement, e.g. 'It's got nothing to do with it/He's got nothing to do with it', etc. mâi kìao ไม่เกี่ยว)

kìao kàp PREP เกี่ยวกับ about, regarding, concerning

kìao khâwng V เกี่ยวข้อง to involve, in connection with

kíao náam N เกี๊ยวน้ำ wonton soup

kìat N เกียรติ honour, dignity

kìat-tì-yót N เกียรติยศ honor, prestige

kìi... กี่ how many...?: kìi chûa mohng กี่ชั่วโมง how many hours (e.g. will it take to clean the house)?

kii-laa N กีฬา sport(s)

kìi mohng láew (EXPRESSION) กี่โมงแล้ว what's the time?

kiit khwǎang V กีดขวาง to hinder, obstruct

kiitâa N (from English) กีตาร์ guitar

kì-loh(kram) N (COLLOQUIAL – kiloh) กิโล(กรัม) kilogram

kì-loh(méht) N (COLLOQUIAL – kiloh) กิโล(เมตร) kilometer

kin V กิน to eat (SLANG) to be corrupt, take bribes

kin aa-hǎan cháo V กินอาหารเช้า to

eat breakfast

kin jeh v กินเจ to be vegetarian

kin jù v กินจุ to eat a lot (until you're stuffed)

kin khâow v กินข้าว to eat (breakfast, lunch, dinner, a meal; the expression itself means literally, 'eat'-'rice')

kíp N กิ๊บ hairclip

kìng mái N (pronounced ging [low tone]-mai [high tone]) กิ่งไม้ the branch of a tree

kíng-kàa N กิ้งก่า tree lizard

kíng-kue N กิ้งกือ millipede

kìt-jà-kam N กิจกรรม activity

klâa hăan ADJ กล้าหาญ to be brave, daring

klaai pen v กลายเป็น to become (e.g. friends)

klâam núea N กล้ามเนื้อ muscle(s)

klaang N กลาง in the middle, center

klaang khuehn N กลางคืน night

klaang mueang N กลางเมือง city/ town center

klaang wan N กลางวัน day/daytime

klâehng v แกล้ง to pretend, tease someone (maliciously), annoy (deliberately, intentionally)

klâi ADJ ใกล้ near, nearby, close to

klai ADJ (with a mid tone and a longer sounding vowel than the word for 'near' klâi ใกล้) ไกล to be far away, distant, a long way

klâi wehlaa ใกล้เวลา almost time (e.g. to go), to approach (in time)

klàn v กลั่น to distill, extract

klân v กลั้น to suppress, hold back, restrain, inhibit, refrain from

klàow hăa v กล่าวหา to accuse

klàow kham praa-săi v (FORMAL) กล่าว คำปราศรัย to make (give) a speech

klàow thŭeng v (FORMAL) กล่าวถึง to mention

klàp v กลับ to return (e.g. home), turn over (e.g. a steak on a BBQ pit)

klàp bâan v กลับบ้าน to return home, go back home

klàp jai v กลับใจ to have a change of heart, turn over a new leaf, be re- formed

klàp khâang ADJ กลับข้าง to be inside out, be on back to front

klàp maa v กลับมา to come back (to where you began from)

klàp pai v กลับไป to return (to where you began from)

klèt N เกล็ด scale, flake, tuck, dart

klawng N กลอง a drum

klâwng N กล้อง, กล้องถ่ายรูป a cam- era; also pipe

klâwng sàwng thaang klai N กล้องส่องทางไกล binoculars

klawn N กลอน bolt, latch, a kind of Thai verse form

klàwng N กล่อง box

klàwng krà-dàat N กล่องกระดาษ cardboard box

klìat v เกลียด to hate

klìn N กลิ่น odor, a smell

klîng v กลิ้ง to roll, slide

klom ADJ กลม round (shape)

klua v กลัว to be afraid, fear

klua phǐi v กลัวผี to be afraid of ghosts

klua taai v กลัวตาย to be afraid of death/dying

klûai N กล้วย banana

klûai mái N กล้วยไม้ orchid(s)

klueah N เกลือ salt

kluehn v กลืน to swallow

klùm N กลุ่ม group

klûm jai ADJ กลุ้มใจ to be depressed, glum

koehn ADV เกิน to exceed, surpass

koehn pai ADV, ADJ เกินไป too... (e.g. expensive, small, big, etc.); exces- sive

kòeht v (pronounced like 'gurt/girt') เกิด to be born

kòeht àrai khûen (COLLOQUIAL) เกิดอะไร ขึ้น what happened?

kòeht khûen v เกิดขึ้น to happen, oc- cur, come about

koh-dang N โกดัง warehouse

K

koh-hòk v (pronounced 'go hok') โกหก to lie

koh-kôh N (from English) โกโก้ cocoa

kohn v โกน to shave

kohng v โกง to cheat

kôi N ก้อย the little finger, pinky

kôm v ก้ม to bend down, stoop, bow

kôn N ก้น bottom, buttocks

kongsŭn N, ADJ กงสุล consul; consular

kòp N กบ a frog

kòt N กฎ rule, regulation, law

kòt v กด to press

kòt krìng v กดกริ่ง to ring (door bell)

kòtmăi N กฎหมาย laws, legislation

kraam N กราม jaw

kràap v กราบ to postrate oneself (as a sign of respect), (in some contexts this could be) to grovel

krà-buai N กระบวย ladle, dipper

krà-buan kaan N กระบวนการ a movement (e.g. for human rights), a process

krà-daan N กระดาน board, plank

krà-daan prà-kàat N กระดานประกาศ signboard, bulletin board

krà-dàat N กระดาษ paper

krà-dàat khăeng N กระดาษแข็ง cardboard (literally 'paper'-'hard/stiff')

krà-dàat thít-chûu N (from English) กระดาษทิชชู่ tissue paper, toilet paper

krà-dàat saai N กระดาษทราย sandpaper

krà-dìng N กระดิ่ง bell, doorbell

krà-dòht v กระโดด to jump

krà-tìk N กระติก thermos bottle

krà-tùk v กระตุก to jerk

krà-tûn v กระตุ้น to encourage, stimulate

krà-dum N กระดุม button

krà-dùuk N กระดูก bone(s)

krà-dùuk săn lăng N กระดูกสันหลัง the spine/backbone

krà-jaai sĭang v กระจายเสียง to broadcast

krà-jàwk ADJ (SLANG) กระจอก piddling, petty, of no significance, crap

krà-jòk N กระจก glass (material), the windshield of a car, a mirror

kram N กรัม gram

krà-păo N กระเป๋า a bag, a pocket in a garment

krà-păo doehn thaang N กระเป๋าเดินทาง (or kra-păo sûea phâa N กระเป๋าเสื้อผ้า) a suitcase

krà-păo ngoehn N กระเป๋าเงิน, or (MORE COLLOQUIAL) krà-păo tang กระเป๋าตังค์ a purse/wallet

krà-păo thŭe N กระเป๋าถือ handbag

krà-păo tham ngaan N กระเป๋าทำงาน briefcase

krà-păwng N กระป๋อง a can, tin

krà-phŏm PRON, MASC (FORMAL) กระผม I, me

krà-phàw aa-hăan N กระเพาะอาหาร stomach

krà-phàw pàt-săa-wá N กระเพาะปัสสาวะ urinary bladder

krà-râwk N กระรอก squirrel

krà-prohng N กระโปรง a skirt

krà-pùk N กระปุก (a smallish) receptacle or box (e.g. for ointment, jewelry, etc.)

krà-săe N กระแส current, flow, stream (of river, sea); a trend/vogue

krà-săeh fai-fáa N กระแสไฟฟ้า electric current

krà-săeh náam N กระแสน้ำ current of water

krà-sàwp N กระสอบ sack, bag

krà-sìp v กระซิบ to whisper

krà-suang N กระทรวง (government) ministry

krà-sŭn N กระสุน a bullet

krà-tàai N กระต่าย rabbit

krà-thá N กระทะ a wok/Chinese-style frying pan for making stir-fried dishes

krà-thăang N กระถาง flowerpot

krà-thâwm N กระท่อม hut, shack, cottage

krà-thiam N กระเทียม garlic

krà-thong N กระทง basket, small banana leaf receptacle, an integral part of the Loi/Loy (which means 'float') Krathong ลอยกระทง Festival that marks the end of the rainy season

kràwk (baehp) fawm v กรอก(แบบ) ฟอร์ม to fill out a form

krawng v กรอง to filter, strain

kràwp ADJ กรอบ crisp, brittle

kràwp N กรอบ a frame, (within the) confines/limitations (of); **kràwp rûup** กรอบรูป a (picture) frame

krùat N กรวด pebble

krehng-jai N, V เกรงใจ a key Thai concept which means something like a fear of imposing on someone else; to be thought of, in Thai culture, as considerate

kreng ADJ, V เกร็ง tense, stiffened; to flex a muscle

kròht v โกรธ to be upset, cross, angry

krom N กรม (a government) department, e.g. krom tam-rùat กรมตำรวจ the police department

kron v กรน to snore

krong N กรง cage

kròt N กรด acid (not LSD)

krung N กรุง city

krung-thêhp N กรุงเทพฯ Bangkok (literally 'City of Angels')

kŭai tĭao N ก๋วยเตี๋ยว noodles

kŭai tĭao náam N ก๋วยเตี๋ยวน้ำ noodle soup

kuan v กวน to bother, annoy, disturb (someone)

kuan jai ADJ กวนใจ to bother, disturb, be irritating

kùeap ADV เกือบ almost, nearly

kùlàap N กุหลาบ a rose (bush/flower)

kum-phaaphan N กุมภาพันธ์ February

kûng N กุ้ง shrimp, prawn: kûng mang-kawn (literally, 'prawn'-'dragon') กุ้งมังกร lobster

kun-jaeh N กุญแจ key (to room)

kunjaeh mueh N กุญแจมือ handcuffs

kuu N กู I, me (impolite)

kûu v กู้ to borrow (money), take a loan

kwàa ADJ กว่า over, more, more than (NOTE: this word is used to make comparisons in Thai – dii kwàa ดีกว่า better; yài kwàa ใหญ่กว่า bigger; phaehng kwàa แพงกว่า more expensive (than…))

kwaang N กวาง dear

kwâang ADJ กว้าง broad, spacious, wide

kwàat v กวาด to sweep

kwàeng v แกว่ง to swing

KH

NOTE: like the English sound 'k'

khâ ค่ะ female polite particle (when answering a question or making a statement)

khá คะ female polite particle (when asking a question)

khá-ná-baw-dii N คณบดี Dean of Faculty

khàa N ข่า galangal (spice used in Thai cooking)

khăa N ขา leg(s)

khâa v ฆ่า to kill, murder

khăa àwn N ขาอ่อน thigh

khâa N ค่า value (cost)

khâa baw-rí-kaan N ค่าบริการ service fee/charge

khâa baw-rí-kaan e-thii-em thâo-rài N ค่าบริการเอทีเอ็มเท่าไร What is the fee for using the ATM machine?

khâa chái jàai N ค่าใช้จ่าย expenses

khâa dohy-săan N ค่าโดยสาร fare (for a bus, plane trip)

khâa jâang N ค่าจ้าง wage(s)

khăa prà-jam N ขาประจำ a regular customer

khâa pràp N ค่าปรับ a fine (for infringement)

khâa râat-chákaan N ข้าราชการ government official(s), bureaucrat(s), public servant(s)

khâa rót N ค่ารถ fare (for bus/taxi)

khâa tham-niam

khâa tham-niam N ค่าธรรมเนียม fee (for official service)

khâa tŭa N ค่าตั๋ว fare (for transportation ticket)

khâa-tŭa chán-nùeng/chán-săwng thâo-rài ค่าตั๋ว ชั้นหนึ่ง/ชั้นสอง เท่าไร How much is a first class/second class train?

khâa-tŭa thîaw-diaw/pai-klàp thâo-rài ค่าตั๋ว เที่ยวเดียว/ไปกลับ เท่าไร How much is a single/return ticket?

khăai V ขาย for sale, sell

khăai láew V ขายแล้ว to be sold

khăai mòt láew ADJ, V ขายหมดแล้ว sold out, to have sold the lot

khâam PREP, V ข้าม across, to cross, go over

khâam thà-nŏn V ข้ามถนน to cross the road

kháan V ค้าน to oppose, be opposed to

khâang N ข้าง side

khâang bon N, ADJ ข้างบน upstairs

khaang N คาง chin

khâang-khâang PREP ข้าง ๆ next to, beside

kháang khuehn V ค้างคืน to stay overnight

khâang lâang N, ADJ ข้างล่าง below, downstairs

khâang lăng PREP ข้างหลัง in the rear of, behind

khâang nâa N, ADJ ข้างหน้า front, in the front

khâang nai N, ADJ ข้างใน inside

khâang nâwk N, ADJ ข้างนอก outside

khâang tâi PREP, N, ADJ ข้างใต้ at the bottom (base), underneath

khàat V ขาด to lack; to break (e.g. a rope) N lack of ADJ to be lacking, be insufficient, be torn

khàat mòt ADJ ขาดหมด (completely) worn out (e.g. of clothes)

khàat pai ADJ ขาดไป to be missing (absent)

khàat thun V ขาดทุน to lose money (on an investment), take a loss

khâat wâa... V คาดว่า to expect that.. (e.g. he'll arrive tomorrow)

khà-buan N ขบวน a procession

khâe ADV แค่ just, only, merely, e.g. (COLLOQUIAL) khâe níi แค่นี้ 'just this much'; khâe năi แค่ไหน 'to what degree' or 'how much' (e.g. do you love her?)

khàehk N แขก guest, a person of swarthy complexion – in Thailand commonly used to refer to people from the Indian subcontinent and the Middle East

khàehk phûu mii kìat N แขกผู้มีเกียรติ guest of honour

khăehn N แขน arm(s)

khaeh-na-daa N แคนาดา Canada

khâehp ADJ แคบ narrow

khaeh-rawt N (from English) แครอต carrot

khàeng V แข่ง to compete in a race

khăeng raehng ADJ แข็งแรง to be strong

kháep suun N (from English) แคปซูล capsule (medicine/vitamins)

khài N ไข่ egg

khâi N ไข้ fever

khài daehng N ไข่แดง egg yolk

khài dao N ไข่ดาว a fried egg

khài jiao N ไข่เจียว an omelette

khài khon N ไข่คน scrambled eggs

khài lùak N ไข่ลวก soft boiled egg

khâi lûeat àwk N ไข้เลือดออก dengue fever

khăi man N ไขมัน fat (body fat), grease

khài múk N ไข่มุก pearl(s)

khài múk thiam N ไข่มุกเทียม cultured pearl(s)

khài tôm N ไข่ต้ม hard boiled egg(s)

khâi wàt yài N ไข้หวัดใหญ่ flu, influenza

khăm ADJ (pronounced like 'come' with a rising tone) ขำ to be funny, amusing

kham N คำ word(s)

kham choehn N คำเชิญ an invitation

KH

kham dàa N คำด่า abuse, blame; a swear word

kham mueang N คำเมือง the dialect spoken in the northern part of Thailand

kham náe-nam N คำแนะนำ advice, suggestion

kham praa-săi N คำปราศรัย a speech

kham ráwng thúk N คำร้องทุกข์ a complaint

kham sàng N คำสั่ง order, command

kham sàp N คำศัพท์ vocabulary

kham tàwp N คำตอบ answer, response

kham thăam N คำถาม question

kham tuean N คำเตือน warning

kham yók yâwng N คำยกย่อง (words of) praise

khàmĕhn N เขมร Cambodia

khamnuan V คำนวณ to calculate

khà-mohy V ขโมย to steal N a thief, thieves

khà-mùat khíu V ขมวดคิ้ว to frown

khà-mùk khà-mŭa ADJ ขมุกขมัว overcast (weather)

khan ADJ คัน to be itchy N classifier for counting vehicles, umbrellas, spoons and forks

khân N ขั้น stage, grade, step, rank

khăn N ขัน dipping bowl (used when bathing in the old-style Thai manner)

khà-nà níi ADV ขณะนี้ at present, at this moment

khà-nàat N ขนาด size

khànŏm N ขนม sweets, dessert, snacks

khànŏm khéhk N ขนมเค้ก cake

khànŏm-pang N (pang pronounced like 'pung') ขนมปัง bread

khànŏm-pang kràwp N ขนมปังกรอบ a cracker (biscuit)

khà-nŏm wăan N ขนมหวาน confectionery, dessert

khà-nŭn N ขนุน jackfruit

khăo N เขา mountain

khăo PRON เขา she, her, he, him, they, them

khàow N เข่า knee

khâo V เข้า to enter, go in

khâo hăa V เข้าหา to approach

khâo in-ter-nèt V เข้าอินเตอร์เน็ต access to the internet

khâo kan V เข้ากัน (COLLOQUIAL) to get on well together, get on (with)

khâo-jai V เข้าใจ to understand

khâo-jai phìt V เข้าใจผิด to misunderstand

khâo khâang V (COLLOQUIAL) เข้าข้าง to take sides (with someone)

khâo khiu V เข้าคิว to queue, line up (khiu คิว from English)

khâo maa V เข้ามา come in

khâo rûam V เข้าร่วม to join in, attend, participate

khàow N ข่าว news, report

khăow ADJ ขาว white (for a list of the most common colors see the entry under sĭi สี which means 'color')

khâow N ข้าว rice; khâow klâwng ข้าวกล้อง brown rice/unpolished rice; khâow phàt ข้าวผัด fried rice; khâow nĭao ข้าวเหนียว sticky rice

khâow kaehng N ข้าวแกง rice and curry, (COLLOQUIAL) (Thai) food

khâow klâwng N ข้าวกล้อง brown rice, unpolished rice

khâow lăam N ข้าวหลาม a Thai sweetmeat – glutinous rice with coconut milk roasted in a section of bamboo

khàow lueh N ข่าวลือ a rumor

khâow nĭao N ข้าวเหนียว sticky or glutinous rice

khâow phôht N ข้าวโพด corn

khâow săa-lii N ข้าวสาลี wheat

khâow săn N ข้าวสาร rice (uncooked)

khâow sŭai N ข้าวสวย rice (cooked)

khàow yài N ข่าวใหญ่ a big/significant news story

kháp ADJ คับ to be tight (fitting)

khàp V ขับ to drive a vehicle

khát kháan V คัดค้าน to protest, object

khàt ngao V ขัดเงา to polish

kháw V เคาะ to knock

29

KH

khǎw v ขอ to ask for, request (informally), apply for permission, please

khǎw..... ขอ...คะ/ครับ I'd like to.../ May I ... please?

khâw N (pronounced like 'khor' with a falling tone) ข้อ joint (in the body), articulation; also clause, section, provision, question/point(s) (as in 'there are a number of questions/ points to be addressed')

khaw N คอ neck

khâw bòk-phrâwng N ข้อบกพร่อง defect

khaw hǒi N คอหอย throat

khâw khwaam N ข้อความ message

khâw mueh N ข้อมือ wrist

khâw muun N ข้อมูล information, data

khâw ráwng v ขอร้อง to request (formally)

khâw sà-daehng khwaam yin-dii dûai (FORMULAIC EXPRESSION) ขอแสดงความยินดีด้วย congratulations!

khâw sà-nǒeh N ข้อเสนอ a (FORMAL) proposal

khaw sǎw ABBREV ค.ศ. *anno domini* – the Christian Era

khâw sàwk N ข้อศอก elbow

khǎw thaang nòi ขอทางหน่อย excuse me! (can I get past)

khâw tháo N ข้อเท้า ankle

khâw thét jing N ข้อเท็จจริง fact

khǎw thôht v ขอโทษ to apologize; sorry!, excuse me!

khâw tòk-long N ข้อตกลง an agreement

khǎw yuehm v ขอยืม to borrow

khawm-phiu-tôeh N คอมพิวเตอร์, (COLLOQUIAL) khawm คอม computer

kháwn N ค้อน hammer

kháwn khâang ADV ค่อนข้าง rather, fairly

khǎwng N ของ thing(s), belongings

khǎwng v ของ to belong to, indicates the possessive – "of"

khǎwng chán PRON ของฉัน my, mine

khǎwng hǎai N ของหาย lost property

khǎwng kào N ของเก่า antiques

khǎwng khǎo PRON ของเขา his, hers, their, theirs

khǎwng khwǎn N ของขวัญ a present (gift)

khǎwng kin N ของกิน edibles, things to eat

khǎwng lên N ของเล่น toy(s)

khǎwng plawm N ของปลอม a copy, a fake, pirated merchandise

khǎwng rao PRON ของเรา our, ours

khǎwng sùan tua N ของส่วนตัว one's own personal possession(s)

khǎwng thiam ADJ ของเทียม synthetic, artificial

khǎwng thîi ra-lúek N ของที่ระลึก souvenir

khǎwng wǎan N (COLLOQUIAL) ของหวาน a sweet, dessert

khàwp N ขอบ border, edge

khàwp khun ขอบคุณ to thank, thank you

khà-yà N ขยะ garbage, rubbish

khà-yǎn ADJ ขยัน to be hardworking, diligent

khà-yào v เขย่า to shake (something)

khem ADJ เค็ม salty (to the taste)

khêm ADJ เข้ม intense, strong, concentrated

khěm N เข็ม a needle

khêm khǎeng ADJ เข้มแข็ง strong, unyielding; industrious, assiduous

khěm khàt N เข็มขัด belt

khêm khôn ADJ เข้มข้น concentrated (liquid), sharp taste, flavorful

khèt N เขต boundary, frontier, zone, district

khèt v เข็ด (COLLOQUIAL) to have learned one's lesson, chastened, dare not do something again

khǐan v เขียน to write, to draw

khîan v เฆี่ยน to whip

khǐan jòt-mǎai v เขียนจดหมาย to correspond (write letters)

khǐan tàwp v เขียนตอบ to reply (in writing)

khǐang N เขียง a chopping board

KH

khĭao ADJ เขียว green (for a list of the most common colors see the entry under sĭi สี which means 'color')

khĭao V เคี้ยว to chew

khìi V ขี่ to ride (a motorbike/horse)

khìi jàk-krá-yaan V ขี่จักรยาน to ride a bike

khîi N ขี้ feces, excrement (shit – although the Thai word is in no way rude or coarse as is the English term)

khîi aai ADJ ขี้อาย given to shyness (actually 'extremely shy')

khîi-bawt N (from English) คีย์บอร์ด keyboard (of computer)

khîi kìat ADJ ขี้เกียจ to be lazy

khîi mao N, ADJ ขี้เมา a drunkard

khîi nĭao ADJ ขี้เหนียว to be stingy

khîi phûeng N ขี้ผึ้ง wax

khîi yaa N ขี้ยา a junkie, drug addict

khiim N คีม pliers

khĭng N ขิง ginger

khít V คิด to think, have an opinion

khít dàwk bîa V คิดดอกเบี้ย to charge interest (on a loan etc.), or simply khít dàwk คิดดอก

khít mâak ADJ (COLLOQUIAL) คิดมาก to be anxious/overly sensitive/to worry incessantly

khít mâi thŭeng ADJ คิดไม่ถึง (to be) unexpected; to assume something wouldn't happen

khít tang V (COLLOQUIAL) คิดตังค์ to ask for the bill in a downmarket restaurant or eatery on the street

khít thŭeng V คิดถึง to miss (e.g. a loved one)

khiu N (from English – although in practice the concept generally has little meaning in Thailand) คิว queue, line

khíu N คิ้ว eyebrow

khláai ADJ คล้าย to be similar, analogous

khlâwng ADJ คล่อง to be fluent (in a language), to do something physical well

khlawng N (often written in English as 'klong') คลอง canal, watercourse, channel

khlâwt lûuk V คลอดลูก to give birth (to a child)

khlohn N โคลน mud, slush

khlûean thîi V เคลื่อนที่ to move

khlûehn N คลื่น a wave (in the sea)

khlùi N ขลุ่ย flute

khlum V คลุม to cover

khlum khruea ADJ คลุมเครือ to be vague, ambiguous

khoei ADV เคย ever – used to ask questions in the form 'have you ever…?' To respond 'yes (I have)' the answer can simply be khoei เคย. As for a negative response ('I have never…') the answer is simply mâi khoei ไม่เคย

khŏei N เขย male in-law (son-in-law, brother-in-law)

khoei pai V เคยไป to have been to somewhere before

khoei tham V เคยทำ to have done something before

khoei tua V (COLLOQUIAL) เคยตัว to be habitual; used to doing something (e.g. going to bed very late etc.)

khohm fai N โคมไฟ lamp

khóhng ADJ โค้ง curved, convex

khóhng N โค้ง a curve, a bend in the road

khoi V คอย to wait for

khôi ADV ค่อย gradually, little by little

khôi yang chûa V ค่อยยังชั่ว to get better from an illness, to be on the mend

khŏm ADJ ขม bitter (taste)

khom ADJ คม to be sharp (of knives, razors, etc.)

khŏn N ขน body hair

khôn ADJ ข้น thick (of liquids), to be condensed (e.g. condensed milk)

khon N คน person, people; classifier for people

khon à-meh-rí-kan N คนอเมริกัน American (person)

khon áwt-sà-treh-lia N คนออสเตรเลีย Australian (person)

KH

khon bâa N คนบ้า a lunatic, mad person

khon chái N คนใช้ a servant

khon diao ADJ คนเดียว on one's own, alone; single (only one), sole

khon fâo ráan N คนเฝ้าร้าน shopkeeper

khon jiin N (pronounced 'jean') คนจีน Chinese (person)

khon jon N คนจน a poor person, someone who is poor

khon kao-lǐi N คนเกาหลี a Korean (person)

khon khâi N คนไข้ a patient, a sick person

khon khàp N คนขับ driver

khon khîi kohng N คนขี้โกง a cheat, a dishonest/crooked person

khon lao N คนลาว a Laotian person

khón phóp V ค้นพบ to discover, find out; **khon plàehk nâa** N คนแปลกหน้า a stranger

khǒn sàt N ขนสัตว์ wool

khon sòehp N คนเสิร์ฟ waiter, waitress

khon thîi... คนที่ the one/person who...

khong ADV คง probably, possibly

khóp V คบ to associate (with), socialize

khòp khǎn ADJ ขบขัน to be humorous

khrai PRON ใคร who? whom

khrai kâw dâi ใครก็ได้ anybody at all, anyone, e.g. in response to a question such as: 'who can go into the park?' (answer) khrai kâw dâi ใครก็ได้ anybody at all/anyone

khráng N ครั้ง time; classifier for times, occasions – e.g. to say 'five times' is the number 5 (hâa) followed by khráng ครั้ง

khráng kàwn ADV ครั้งก่อน (kàwn pronounced 'gorn' with a low tone) previously, before; the last time

khráng khraaw ADV ครั้งคราว occasionally, from time to time

khráng râehk ADV ครั้งแรก the first time

khrao N (often pronounced by Thais very similar to the English word 'cow') เครา beard

khráp ครับ (often pronounced like 'cup' with a high tone) male polite particle

khráw ráai N เคราะห์ร้าย misfortune

khrâwp khrawng V ครอบครอง to occupy, rule over, possess

khrâwp khrua N ครอบครัว family

khrêng khrát ADJ เคร่งครัด strict, observant (of rules, regulations, religious teachings)

khriim N (from English) ครีม cream

khrístian N คริสเตียน Christian; **chaow khrít** N ชาวคริสต์ a Christian

khrohng kaan N โครงการ project, scheme, program (e.g. as in some form of development project etc.)

khrohng sâang N โครงสร้าง structure (of a building, of society)

khrók N (pronounced 'crock') ครก mortar (for pulversing and grinding spices/ingredients for a meal)

khróp ADJ, ADV ครบ to be complete/full (e.g. set of items)

khróp thûan ADJ ครบถ้วน in full

khrù khrà ADJ ขรุขระ rough, uneven, bumpy (surfaces – e.g. a road)

khrua N ครัว kitchen

khruea khàai N เครือข่าย network

khrûeang N เครื่อง machine

khrûeang bin N เครื่องบิน an aeroplane/airplane

khrûeang bin àwk kìi-mohng เครื่องบินออกกี่โมง What is the departure time?

khrûeang bin thǔeng kìi-mohng เครื่องบินถึงกี่โมง What is the arrival time?

khrûeang bin pai... kìi-chûa-mohng เครื่องบินไป...กี่ชั่วโมง How long is the flight to ...?

khrûeang dùehm N เครื่องดื่ม drink(s), refreshment(s)

khrûeang fai fáa N เครื่องไฟฟ้า electrical appliance(s), electrical goods

khrûeang jàk N เครื่องจักร machine(ry)

khrûeang khǐan N เครื่องเขียน stationery

khrûeang khít lêhk N เครื่องคิดเลข calculator

khrûeang mueh N เครื่องมือ tool, utensil, instrument

khrûeang nawn N เครื่องนอน bedding, bedclothes

khrûeang phét phloi N เครื่องเพชร พลอย jewelry

khrûeang prà-dàp kaai N เครื่อง ประดับกาย bodily ornaments, accessories in fashion contexts

khrûeang ráp thoh-rá-sàp N เครื่องรับ โทรศัพท์ an answering machine

khrûeang thêht N เครื่องเทศ spice(s)

khrûeang yon N เครื่องยนต์ an engine, a machine

khrûeng ADJ ครึ่ง half

khruu N ครู teacher

khruu yài N ครูใหญ่ headmaster

khuai N ควย (EXTREMELY RUDE SLANG) penis (or, more accurately – dick/prick/ cock)

khuan AUX V ควร should, ought to

khùan V ข่วน to scratch (as in a cat scratching something with its paws), scrape

khùap N ขวบ year – when used to refer to child's age, used for up to approximately ten years old

khùat N ขวด bottle

khùean N เขื่อน a dam

khuehn V คืน to give back, return N night

khuehn níi N คืนนี้ tonight

khûen V ขึ้น to rise, ascend, go up; to increase; to board/get on (e.g. a bus/ plane)

khûen chàai N ขึ้นฉ่าย Chinese celery

khûen krûeang-bin prà-tou à-rai ขึ้น เครื่องบินประตูอะไร What is the boarding gate?

khûen rót thîi chaan-chaa-laa nǎi ขึ้น

รถที่ชานชาลาไหน At which platform/terminal can I get on the bus/ train?

khûen sǎay nǎi pai... ขึ้นสายไหน ไป… Which number/line does it go to?

khûen yùu kàp ขึ้นอยู่กับ (COLLOQUIAL) it depends on…

khui V คุย to chat

khúk N คุก jail, prison, the slammer

khúkkîi N (from English) คุกกี้ cookie, sweet biscuit

khun pron คุณ you (respectful form of address)

khún khoei คุ้นเคย to be used to, accustomed to (also the more colloquial term chin ชิน)

khún khoei kàp... คุ้นเคยกับ... to be acquainted/familiar with...

khun naai คุณนาย sir/madam (term of address – NOTE: this would only ever be used by a Thai person as it is integral to the very hierarchial nature of Thai society. For a non-Thai to address someone like this would be very odd)

khun-ná-sǒmbàt N คุณสมบัติ (educational) qualification, characteristic

khun pâa PRON คุณป้า aunt (respectful address to an older lady)

khùu V ขู่ to threaten

khûu N คู่ a pair

khûu khàeng N คู่แข่ง rival, competitor

khûu mân N คู่หมั้น fiancé, fiancée

khûu mueh N คู่มือ manual, handbook (e.g. instruction booklet for appliance etc.)

khûu nawn N คู่นอน lover, sexual partner (or, to use that dreadful expression 'fuck buddy')

khûu sǒmrót N (FORMAL) คู่สมรส partner, spouse

khuun V คูณ to multiply

khwǎa ADJ ขวา right (i.e. on the right)

khwǎa mueh ADJ ขวามือ right-hand side

KH

khwaai N ควาย a water buffalo

khwaam N ความ the sense, the substance, the gist (of a matter, an account), also khwaam... ความ ...ness, commonly used by being placed in front of adjectives/verbs to form abstract nouns expressing a state or quality: e.g. '...ness' as in khwaam dii ความดี goodness, virtue (see other examples in the following entries)

khwaam chûai lŭea N ความช่วยเหลือ help, assistance

khwaam chûea N ความเชื่อ belief, faith

khwaam hĕn N ความเห็น opinion

khwaam ìtchǎa N ความอิจฉา jealousy

khwaam jam-pen N ความจำเป็น need, necessity

khwaam jàroehn N ความเจริญ progress

khwaam jèp pùai N ความเจ็บป่วย illness

khwaam jing N ความจริง truth, the truth

khwaam khao-róp N ความเคารพ respect

khwaam khít N ความคิด idea, thoughts

khwaam khlûean wǎi N ความเคลื่อนไหว movement, motion

khwaam khrîat N ความเครียด tension, stress (COLLOQUIAL) khrîat เครียด to be stressed out

khwaam klìat N ความเกลียด hatred

khwaam klua N ความกลัว fear

khwaam kòt dan N ความกดดัน pressure

khwaam kròht N ความโกรธ anger

khwaam kwâang N ความกว้าง width

khwaam lambàak N ความลำบาก hardship

khwaam láp N ความลับ secret, confidentiality

khwaam lóm lĕhw N ความล้มเหลว failure, bankruptcy

khwaam mǎai N ความหมาย meaning (i.e. the 'meaning' of something)

khwaam mâi sà-ngòp N ความไม่สงบ a disturbance, turmoil, absence of peace

khwaam mân-khong N ความมั่นคง security

khwaam mân-jai N ความมั่นใจ confidence

khwaam òp-ùn N ความอบอุ่น warmth

khwaam phá-yaa-yaam N ความพยายาม attempt, effort

khwaam phìt N ความผิด fault, mistake, error

khwaam plàwt phai N ความปลอดภัย safety

khwaam rák N ความรัก love, affection

khwaam ráp phìt châwp N ความรับผิดชอบ responsibility

khwaam ráp rúu N ความรับรู้ awareness

khwaam rew N ความเร็ว speed

khwaam rúu N ความรู้ knowledge

khwaam rúu-sùek N ความรู้สึก feeling, emotion

khwaam sà-àat N ความสะอาด cleanliness

khwaam sǎa-mâat N ความสามารถ ability, capacity (to fulfill a task)

khwaam sǎmkhan N ความสำคัญ importance

khwaam sǎmrèt N ความสำเร็จ success

khwaam song jam N (jam pronounced 'jum' as in 'jumble') ความทรงจำ memory (i.e. one's memory)

khwaam sŏngsǎi N ความสงสัย suspicion, curiosity

khwaam sŏn-jai N ความสนใจ interest (in something)

khwaam sǔung N ความสูง height

khwaam taai N ความตาย death

khwaam tàehk tàang N ความแตกต่าง difference (between this and that)

khwaam tâng-jai N ความตั้งใจ intention

khwaam thâo thiam N ความเท่าเทียม equality

khwaam yâak jon N ความยากจน poverty

khwaam yaow N ความยาว length

khwaan N ควาญ mahout/elephant keeper/driver

khwâang V ขว้าง to throw, hurl

khwǎang V ขวาง to impede, obstruct, thwart

khwǎang thaang V ขวางทาง to bar/block the way

khwâang thíng V ขว้างทิ้ง to throw away, throw out

khwǎehn V แขวน to hang (e.g. a picture on the wall)

khwan N ควัน smoke (e.g. from a fire)

L

lá ละ per, each one: e.g. pii lá khráng ปีละครั้ง once a year

lâ ล่ะ a particle used at the end of an utterance to ask the following sort of question: 'and what about...?'

lâa V ล่า to hunt

láa ADJ ล้า lag, be tired

lá-aai V ละอาย to feel ashamed

laa àwk V ลาออก to resign, quit (a job)

lâa cháa ADJ ล่าช้า late/tardy

laa kàwn ลาก่อน goodbye, farewell

laa-mók ADJ ลามก obscene, lewd, smutty

laa phák V ลาพัก to take leave (from work)

laa pùai V ลาป่วย to take sick leave

lâa sùt ADV ล่าสุด the latest; also – at the latest

lǎai ADJ หลาย many, various, several

laai N, ADJ ลาย design/pattern (e.g. on a T-shirt/piece of material); patterned, striped

laai mue N ลายมือ handwriting, fingerprint

laai sen N ลายเซ็น signature

lǎai sìp หลายสิบ tens of, multiples of ten, many

lâam N ล่าม (an) interpreter

láan NUM ล้าน million

lǎan N หลาน grandchild, niece, nephew

laan N ลาน open space, ground

lǎan chaai N หลานชาย grandson, nephew

laan jàwt rót N ลานจอดรถ a parking lot

lǎan khǒei N หลานเขย the husband of one's niece or granddaughter

lǎan sǎow N หลานสาว granddaughter, niece

lǎan sà-phái N หลานสะใภ้ the wife of one's nephew or grandson

lâat yaang V ลาดยาง paved with asphalt

laang N ลาง omen, portent, sign

lâang ADV ล่าง below, beneath

láang V ล้าง to wash/rinse/cleanse (e.g. dishes, a car, one's face, etc., not clothes)

laang dii N ลางดี good omen, favorable sign

láang jaan V ล้างจาน to wash the dishes

laang ráai N ลางร้าย bad/evil omen

láe CONJ (pronounced something like léh!) และ and

lâehk chék V แลกเช็ค to cash a check/cheque

lâehk ngoehn V (COLLOQUIAL) แลกเงิน to change money

lâehk ngoehn dâi thîi nǎi แลกเงินได้ที่ไหน Where can I exchange money?; khǎw lâek-ngoehn...dawn-lâa ขอแลกเงิน...ดอลลาร์ I'd like to exchange...dollars.

lâehk plìan V แลกเปลี่ยน to trade, exchange

lǎehm ADJ แหลม pointed, jagged; sharp (as in bright/clever)

lâen ruea V แล่นเรือ to sail a boat

láew ADV แล้ว already – a word which indicates completion/past tense: go already = gone pai láew ไปแล้ว; láew แล้ว is also commonly used in conversation to 'connect' statements, meaning, for example, either 'then (so and so happened)', or 'and then (that happened)'

L

láew jà thammai (COLLOQUIAL) แล้วจะ ทำไม So what!

láew tàeh IDIOM (COLLOQUIAL) แล้วแต่ it depends, as you like, (that's) up to (so and so)

lǎi v ไหล to flow

lá-ìat ADJ ละเอียด fine, delicate, to be pulverized (into powder/small pieces), meticulous/careful (craftsmanship)

lâi àwk v ไล่ออก to fire someone

lâi pai v ไล่ไป to chase away, chase out

lâi taam v ไล่ตาม to chase after

lák lâwp v ลักลอบ to smuggle (e.g. drugs, etc.)

lák yím N ลักยิ้ม dimple

làk mueang N หลักเมือง Lak Muang, the city pillar

lá-khawn N (pronounced 'làcorn') ละคร play, theatrical production; lá-khawn thii wii N ละครทีวี television soap opera

láksànà N ลักษณะ characteristic(s), (the) nature or appearance (of something)

làk-thǎn N หลักฐาน evidence

lambàak ADJ (lam pronounced like 'lum' in 'lumber', bàak like 'bark') ลำบาก troublesome, tough (life)

lam iang ADJ ลำเอียง partial

lam-yai N ลำไย longan (fruit)

lǎng N, ADV หลัง back (part of body); back, rear

lǎng jàak CONJ หลังจาก after

lǎng jàak nán ADV หลังจากนั้น afterwards, then

lǎng-khaa N หลังคา roof

lang mái N ลังไม้ wooden box, crate

lâo N เหล้า spirits, liquor, alcohol

lâo v เล่า to tell a story, relate

laow N ลาว Laos (the country), Lao (people/language)

làp v หลับ to sleep, nap; làp taa v หลับตา to close/shut one's eyes

làp nai v หลับใน to daydream

látthí N ลัทธิ sect, doctrine, creed

látthí hǐnná-yaan N ลัทธิหินยาน Lesser vehicle of Buddhism, Hinayana

látthí khaa-thawlìk N ลัทธิคาทอลิก Roman Catholicism

látthí khǒng júeh N ลัทธิขงจื๊อ Confucianism

látthí má-hǎa-yaan N ลัทธิมหายาน Greater vehicle of Buddhism, Mahayana

làw ADJ (pronounced 'lor' with a low tone) หล่อ to be handsome

láw N (pronounced 'lor' with a high tone) ล้อ wheel; sǎam láw สามล้อ a trishaw (and common word for 'tuk-tuk' – a motorized 'trishaw')

láwk v (from English – and pronounced much like the English word) ล็อก to lock

láwk láew ADJ ล็อกแล้ว to be locked

làwk luang v (làwk pronounced like 'lork') หลอกลวง to deceive (in colloquial speech commonly just làwk หลอก)

lawng v ลอง to try, to try out, attempt (to do something), experiment (in the sense of trying something)

lawng sài v ลองใส่ to try on (clothes)

làwt N หลอด tube, (drinking) straw

láwt-toeh-rîi N (from English) ล็อตเตอรี่ lottery

lêhk N เลข number, numeral

lêhk khîi N เลขคี่ (an) odd number; lêhk khûu N เลขคู่ (an) even number

lêhkhǎa N เลขา secretary

lehn N (from English) เลน lane (of a highway)

lehw ADJ เลว bad (of a person)

lěhw ADJ เหลว the opposite of solid, e.g. liquid-like

lék ADJ เล็ก little, small, diminutive

lèk N เหล็ก iron, metal

lèk klâa N เหล็กกล้า steel

lék nói ADJ เล็กน้อย small, not much, a tiny bit

lêm N เล่ม classifier used when counting or referring to numbers of books, candles, knives

len N เลนส์ (from English) lens (of a camera)

lên V เล่น to play

lên don-trii V เล่นดนตรี to play musical instruments

lên pai thûa V เล่นไปทั่ว to play around

lên tôh khlûehn V เล่นโต้คลื่น to surf/ride a surfboard

lép N เล็บ nail(s) – as in fingernail(s), toenail(s), also – for animals – 'claws'

lép mueh N เล็บมือ fingernail

lép tháo N เล็บเท้า toenail

lia V เลีย to lick

lian V เลียน to imitate, copy, mimic; (also, more fully) lian bàehp V เลียนแบบ to copy (e.g. someone else's style of dressing etc.)

lîan ADJ เลี่ยน greasy, oily, fatty (food)

líang V เลี้ยง to bring up, raise (children or animals); to treat (someone/a friend/acquaintance, e.g. by taking them out for drinks or dinner – food or drinks)

líao V เลี้ยว to turn, make a turn

líao klàp V เลี้ยวกลับ to turn around

lín N ลิ้น tongue

lín-chák N ลิ้นชัก drawer

ling N ลิง monkey

lín-jìi N ลิ้นจี่ lychee (fruit)

lip N (from English) ลิฟต์ lift, elevator

lít N (from English) ลิตร liter

lôehk V เลิก to cease/stop/give up (e.g. smoking cigarettes)

lôehk kan V เลิกกัน to break off a relationship

loei เลย a word used in a number of senses such as: 'therefore, so, beyond'; also used to intensify adjective, often in conjunction with 'no/not' – in this sense meaning '... at all'. For example: 'no good at all' mâi dii loei ไม่ดีเลย, or 'not expensive at all' mâi phaehng loei ไม่แพงเลย

lŏh N โหล dozen

lôhk N โลก the earth, world

loi V ลอย to float

loi náam V ลอยน้ำ to float in the water

lom N ลม wind, breeze

lôm ADJ ล่ม capsized/overturned (boat)

lóm V ล้ม to topple, fall over, collapse; to overthrow (a government)

lom bâa mŭu N ลมบ้าหมู epilepsy

lom hăai jai N, V ลมหายใจ breath; to breathe

lom jàp V (COLLOQUIAL) ลมจับ about to faint, about to have a fainting spell; (also, more commonly) pen lom เป็นลม to faint/pass out

lóm lá-laai V ล้มละลาย to go bankrupt, be wiped out financially

lom phát ADJ, V ลมพัด windy; the wind is blowing

lŏng V หลง to be infatuated (with), to be crazy about (someone or something)

long V ลง to go downwards; to land (plane), get off (transport): khăw long thîi… ขอลงที่… I'd like to get off at …

lŏng (thaang) V หลง (ทาง) to get lost, lose one's way (literally and metaphorically)

long kha-naehn sĭang V ลงคะแนนเสียง to vote

long maa V ลงมา to come down

long phung V (COLLOQUIAL) ลงพุง to get paunchy, develop a gut

long tha-bian V ลงทะเบียน to register

long thun V ลงทุน to invest (e.g. in a business)

lóp V ลบ to subtract, deduct, minus (in doing mathematical calculations); to erase (e.g. the writing on a blackboard)

lòp V หลบ to avoid, evade, duck, shy away from

lót V ลด to reduce, decrease, lower

lót long V ลดลง to decrease, lessen, reduce

lót náam-nàk V ลดน้ำหนัก to lose weight, diet (the English word 'diet' has also found its way into Thai and pronounced in a similar way)

lót raa-khaa v ลดราคา to discount or reduce the price

lǔam ADJ หลวม loose (the opposite of 'tight')

lúan ADJ ล้วน all/the whole lot, completely

lǔang ADJ หลวง great, (owned by the) state, royal: thànǒn lǔang N ถนนหลวง public road/thoroughfare; mueang lǔang N เมืองหลวง capital city (COLLOQUIAL) nai lǔang ในหลวง His Majesty the King

lúang v ล่วง to go beyond/exceed (rules, the law); to trespass (against someone), violate, infringe

lúang krà-pǎo v ล้วงกระเป๋า to pickpocket

lûat N ลวด wire

lûat nǎam N ลวดหนาม barbed wire

lǔea v เหลือ to be left over

lûeai N เลื่อย a saw

lúeai v เลื้อย to crawl, slither (as a snake)

lûeak v เลือก to pick, choose, select

lûeak dâi v เลือกได้ to be optional, to have the choice

lûean v เลื่อน to put off, delay

lûean àwk pai v เลื่อนออกไป to postpone, delay

lǔeang เหลือง yellow (for a list of the most common colors see the entry under sǐi สี which means 'color')

lûeat N เลือด blood

luehm v ลืม to forget

luehm taa v ลืมตา to open one's eyes

luehm tua v ลืมตัว to forget oneself, lose one's self-control

lûehn v, ADJ ลื่น to slip, to be slippery

lúek ADJ ลึก deep (e.g. water), profound

lúek láp ADJ ลึกลับ to be mysterious

lúk v ลุก to stand, get up, rise

lúk khûen v ลุกขึ้น to get up (from bed)

lǔm sòp N หลุมศพ grave

lún v (COLLOQUIAL) ลุ้น to back/support/cheer (e.g. a team); to win (a prize in a competition)

lung N, PRON ลุง uncle – either parent's older brother; also used as a pronoun (i.e. 'you' or 'he') to refer to an older unrelated male in a friendly way

lûuk N ลูก child (offspring); classifier for small round objects, e.g. fruit, and 'ball-like' things

lûuk anthá N ลูกอัณฑะ (medical term) testicle(s)

lûuk chaai N ลูกชาย son

lûuk chín N ลูกชิ้น meat/pork/fish ball(s), one of the main ingredients in noodle soup

lûuk fàet N ลูกแฝด twins

lûuk kháa N ลูกค้า customer, client

lûuk khǒei N ลูกเขย son-in-law

lûuk khrûeng N ลูกครึ่ง person of mixed race (e.g. European+Asian = 'Eurasian')

lûuk lǎan N ลูกหลาน descendant(s)

lûuk mǎa N ลูกหมา puppy/puppies

lûuk maew N ลูกแมว kitten(s)

lûuk náwng N ลูกน้อง employee(s)

lûuk phîi lûuk náwng N ลูกพี่ลูกน้อง cousin

lûuk phûu chaai N, ADJ ลูกผู้ชาย man; (to be) manly

lûuk sǎow N ลูกสาว daughter

lûuk-sà-phái N ลูกสะใภ้ daughter-in-law

lûuk taa N (commonly pronounced lûuk-kàtaa ลูกกะตา) ลูกตา eyeball(s)

lûuk thûng N ลูกทุ่ง country/hillbilly; phlehng lûuk thûng N เพลงลูกทุ่ง (Thai) popular country music; also used for 'country music' more generally

M

máa N ม้า horse (NOTE: máa laai ม้าลาย zebra)

mǎa N หมา dog

maa v, n มา to come; also indicates time up to the present; direction

maa jàak v มาจาก to come from, originate

maa jàak nǎi มาจากไหน common question form: 'Where do you come from/where does it come from?' etc.

maa láew v (COLLOQUIAL) มาแล้ว to have arrived, to have come already: e.g. khǎo maa láew เขามาแล้ว 'He's/she's come; he's/she's already here.'

maa nîi v (COLLOQUIAL) มานี่ Come here

maa sǎi v (COLLOQUIAL) มาสาย to be late (e.g. for school, work, etc.)

maa sí v (COLLOQUIAL) มาสิ Come on, come along there

mǎi lêhk thoh-rásàp N หมายเลขโทรศัพท์ telephone number

mâak ADJ มาก many, much, a lot ADV very

màak N หมาก betel nut (which was widely used/chewed in Thailand in the past, leaving a dark reddish stain on the lips, gums, teeth)

màak fàràng N หมากฝรั่ง chewing gum

mâak khûehn ADJ มากขึ้น more, increasing (e.g. the cost of living, the number of tourists)

mâak koehn pai มากเกินไป too much

mâak kwàa ADJ มากกว่า more than (something else), e.g. to like something more than another thing

màak rúk N หมากรุก chess

mâak thîi sùt ADJ มากที่สุด (the) most

maa-lehsia N มาเลเซีย Malaysia, Malaysian

mâan N (pronounced 'marn' with a falling tone) ม่าน curtains, drapes

maandaa N มารดา (FORMAL) mother

maa-rá-yâat N มารยาท conduct, behavior, manners, etiquette

maa-rá-yâat dii ADJ มารยาทดี to have good manners, to be well-mannered

mâat-trà-thǎan N มาตรฐาน standard, specification(s) (e.g. of goods/services, etc.)

mâeh N แม่ mother

mâeh bâan N แม่บ้าน housekeeper, housewife, lady of the house

mâeh khrua N, FEM แม่ครัว cook

mâeh kunjaeh N แม่กุญแจ a padlock

mâeh mâai N แม่ม่าย a widow

mâeh náam N แม่น้ำ river

mâeh sǎa-mii N แม่สามี mother-in-law; also mâeh yaai N แม่ยาย

máeh tàeh แม้แต่ even (though), not even

máeh wâa แม้ว่า though, if, no matter

maew N แมว a cat

maew náam N แมวน้ำ a seal

má-hǎa-chon N มหาชน the public, the masses

má-hǎa sà-mùt N มหาสมุทร ocean

máhǎa sèht-thǐi N มหาเศรษฐี millionare, a very wealthy person

má-hǎa wítthá-yaa-lai N มหาวิทยาลัย university (COLLOQUIAL) máhǎalai มหาลัย

mâi ADV ไม่ no, not (used with verbs and adjectives)

mǎi ไหม common question particle used at the end of an utterance, e.g. 'is it good/is it any good?' (written with a rising tone but commonly pronounced with a high tone) dii mái ดีไหม

mài ADJ ใหม่ new

mái N ไม้ wood

mǎi N ไหม silk

mai N ไมล์ (from English) mile

mâi v ไหม้ to burn

mâi châi ADV ไม่ใช่ is not, are not, am not, No, it's not!, No!

mâi châwp v ไม่ชอบ not to like (something/somebody), to dislike

mâi hâi v ไม่ให้ not to give, not to let, not to, without

mâi hěn dûai v ไม่เห็นด้วย to disagree

mâi jampen ADJ ไม่จำเป็น to be unnecessary, not necessary

mái jîm fan N ไม้จิ้มฟัน toothpick(s)

mái khwǎen sûea N ไม้แขวนเสื้อ coat hanger

M

mái khìit fai N ไม้ขีดไฟ matches

mâi khít ngoehn (COLLOQUIAL) ไม่คิดเงิน free of charge

mâi khoei ADV ไม่เคย never

mâi khôi mii (COLLOQUIAL) ไม่ค่อยมี there's hardly any, hard to find, scarce

mâi kìi... ไม่กี่ few..., e.g. mâi kii khon ไม่กี่คน few people

mái kwàat N ไม้กวาด broom

mâi mâak kâw nói (COLLOQUIAL) ไม่มาก ก็น้อย more or less

mâi mii ไม่มี no (in response to questions such as 'have you a.../have you got any?'), there's none/there isn't any (NOTE: when translated literally mâi mii means 'no have' – an expression you commonly hear in Thailand from those who haven't really studied English)

mâi mii àrai ไม่มีอะไร (COLLOQUIAL) 'no/ nothing' in response to such questions as 'what's the matter?', 'what's on you mind?', 'what are you thinking?'

mâi mii khâw phùuk mát (EXPRESSION) ไม่มีข้อผูกมัด to be free of commitments

mâi mii khrai ไม่มีใคร nobody (e.g. there is nobody at home/I don't have anyone [to help me etc.])

mâi mii khwaam sùk ไม่มีความสุข ADJ to be unhappy

mâi mii prà-yòht ไม่มีประโยชน์ ADJ to be of no use, to be useless

mâi mii thaang (COLLOQUIAL) ไม่มีทาง no way (I'm doing that)

mâi nâa chûeah ไม่น่า (COLLOQUIAL) ADJ เชื่อ unbelievable, incredible

mái pàa diao kan ไม้ป่าเดียวกัน (SLANG EXPRESSION) homosexual (male) – i.e. 'wood from the same jungle/forest'

mâi pen rai (common idiomatic Thai expression) ไม่เป็นไร don't mention it!, never mind!, you're welcome!, it doesn't matter, it's nothing

mâi phaehng ADJ ไม่แพง to be inexpensive

mâi phèt ADJ ไม่เผ็ด mild (not spicy)

mâi prà-sòp phŏn sămrèt ADJ (SOMEWHAT FORMAL) ไม่ประสบผลสำเร็จ to fail, to be unsuccessful

mâi run raehng ADJ ไม่รุนแรง mild (not very strong, e.g. taste), (or, alternatively) not violent (run raehng รุนแรง means 'violent')

mâi rúu-jàk V ไม่รู้จัก (pronounced something like 'roo-juck') (COLLOQUIAL) not to know someone or something

mâi sà-baai ADJ ไม่สบาย sick, ill

mâi sà-baai jai ADJ ไม่สบายใจ (to feel) upset, unhappy

mâi săm-khan ADJ ไม่สำคัญ not important, unimportant

mái sìap N ไม้เสียบ skewer (e.g. a satay stick)

mâi sùk ADJ ไม่สุก (to be) unripe

mâi su-phâap ADJ ไม่สุภาพ impolite, rude

mâi tâwng V ไม่ต้อง not to have to

mái tháo N ไม้เท้า walking stick, cane

mák jà ADV ... มักจะ often, usually, regularly

mák ngâai ADJ มักง่าย careless, sloppy

má-kà-raa-khom N มกราคม January

má-kàwk N มะกอก olive

má-khăam N มะขาม tamarind (fruit)

má-khŭea mûang N มะเขือม่วง eggplant, aubergine

má-khŭea thêht N มะเขือเทศ tomato

mák-khú-thêht N มัคคุเทศก์ guide (i.e. tour guide)

má-laehng N แมลง insect (general term)

má-laehng wan N แมลงวัน fly (insect)

má-laeng-sàap N แมลงสาบ cockroach

má-lá-kaw N (kaw pronounced like 'gore') มะละกอ papaya, pawpaw

málí N มะลิ jasmine

má-mûang N มะม่วง mango

má-naow N มะนาว lemon, lime (citrus fruit)

má-phráow N มะพร้าว coconut

má-reng N มะเร็ง cancer

man มัน (SLANG) excellent, most enjoy-able, to be fun, that's great

man PRON, N, ADJ มัน it; potato-like vegetables; shiny, brilliant

măn ADJ หมัน to be sterile, barren

mân N หมั้น to engage (promise to marry)

man fá-ràng N มันฝรั่ง potato(es)

màn sâi (COLLOQUIAL) หมั่นไส้ to be dis-gusted (with), to be put off (by)

man thêht N มันเทศ yam(s)

mâng khâng ADJ มั่งคั่ง (to be) wealthy

mang sà-wí-rát N, ADJ มังสวิรัติ veg-etarian

mang-khút N มังคุด mangosteen (fruit)

mân jai ADJ มั่นใจ confident, certain

mân-khong ADJ มั่นคง to be firm, definite, secure

mánút N มนุษย์ human (being)

máo N (from English) เมาส์ mouse (computer)

mao ADJ เมา drunk, intoxicated, stoned, wasted

mao kháang V (COLLOQUIAL) เมาค้าง to have a hangover

máruehn níi ADV มะรืนนี้ (the) day af-ter tomorrow

màt N หมัด flea, fist, punch

mâw N (pronounced 'mor' with a fall-ing tone) หม้อ (cooking) pot

măw N (pronounced 'mor' with a ris-ing tone) หมอ doctor

maw-rà-dòk N มรดก inheritance, legacy

maw-rà-kòt N มรกต emerald

maw-rà-sŭm N มรสุม monsoon

màw sŏm ADJ เหมาะสม to be suit-able/appropriate

màwk N หมอก mist, fog

măwn N หมอน pillow, cushion

mawng V มอง to watch, stare at

mawng mâi hěn V มองไม่เห็น to be invisible, unable to see

mâwp hâi V มอบให้ to hand over, bestow (e.g. power to incoming government/a university degree to

a graduate)

mâwp tua V มอบตัว to give oneself up, surrender (to the police); to re-port (for duty, work etc.)

mawtoehsai N (from English) มอเตอร์ไซค์ motorcycle

mêhk mâak ADJ เมฆมาก overcast, cloudy

meh-nuu N (from English) เมนู menu

meh-sǎa-yon N เมษายน April

méht N เมตร meter

měn V, ADJ เหม็น to stink; to be stinky (NOTE: in Thai just this one word can be a whole sentence – the equivalent of 'It stinks/It smells foul' etc.)

mét N เม็ด (also pronounced má-lét เมล็ด) seed; classifier for small seed-like objects, e.g. pills

mí nâa là มิน่าล่ะ (COLLOQUIAL EXPRESSION) no wonder!

mia N เมีย (COLLOQUIAL) wife, defacto partner, sometimes simply 'girl-friend'

mia nói N เมียน้อย mistress

mǐi N หมี a bear

mìi N หมี่ vermicelli, fine noodles

mii V มี to have, own; there is, there are; khun mii...mái? คุณมี...ไหม Do you have...?

mii amnâat ADJ มีอำนาจ to have pow-er, to be powerful

mii chii-wít ADJ มีชีวิต live (be alive), living

mii chûeh ADJ มีชื่อ to be famous, to be well-known

mii chúu V มีชู้ (for a married person) to have a lover

mii ìt-thí-phon V มีอิทธิพล to have in-fluence (to get things done), to have connections

mii jèht-tà-naa V มีเจตนา to intend, have the intention (to)

mii khâa V มีค่า to be valuable, pre-cious, to have worth/be useful

mii khon thoh maa (COLLOQUIAL) มีคนโทรมา someone's on the phone (i.e.

someone's called me/you)

mii khun khâa v มีคุณค่า to have value (e.g. for a medicine to be useful)

mii khwaam mân-jai v มีความมั่นใจ to have confidence, be confident

mii khwaam sùk v มีความสุข to be happy

mii klìn v มีกลิ่น to have an odor, smell bad

mii laai ADJ มีลาย patterned (to have a pattern on it), striped (COLLOQUIAL) tháwng laai ท้องลาย for a woman to have 'stretch marks'

mii-naa-khom N มีนาคม March

mii phìt v มีพิษ to be poisonous

mii phǒn tàw v มีผลต่อ... to affect

mii pràjam duean v มีประจำเดือน (SOMEWHAT FORMAL) to menstruate, have one's period

mii prà-sòbpkaan มีประสบ-การณ์ to have experience, be experienced

mii prà-yòht v มีประโยชน์ to be useful

mii sà-maa-thí v มีสมาธิ to concentrate, be mindful

mii sà-nèh v (COLLOQUIAL) มีเสน่ห์ to be personable, alluring, appealing, to have charm

mii sên v มีเส้น (COLLOQUIAL) to have influence/connections

mii sùan rûam v มีส่วนร่วม to participate/co-operate

mii tháksà v มีทักษะ skilful, to be skilled, to have skills

mii thúrá v มีธุระ to be busy, to have something to do

mîit N (pronounced like 'mead' with a falling tone) มีด knife

mít N มิตร (SOMEWHAT FORMAL) friend

mít-chǎa-chîip N มิจฉาชีพ wrongful/ unlawful occupation; a person who makes their living from some form of criminality

mí-thù-naa-yon N มิถุนายน June

mítì N มิติ dimension (e.g. as in 3D – sǎam mítì สามมิติ)

mòeh ADJ เหม่อ inattentive

móh v โม้ to boast, brag

moh-hǒh ADJ โมโห to be cross/angry

mohng N โมง o'clock, e.g. 6 mohng 6 o'clock, hours

mǒi N หมอย (RUDE) pubic hair

mon-lá-phaa-wá N มลภาวะ pollution, also mon-lá-phít มลพิษ

mòt aàyú หมดอายุ v to expire (e.g. a license, a passport), past its use-by date (e.g. milk, etc.)

mòt láew ADJ (COLLOQUIAL) หมดแล้ว used up, all gone, none left

mót lûuk N มดลูก uterus, womb

mòt raehng (COLLOQUIAL) หมดแรง to have no energy left, tired out

mòt tua N หมดตัว have nothing left, be broke

mûa ADV, ADJ (COLLOQUIAL) มั่ว haphazardly, indiscriminately; chaotic, erratic

muai N มวย boxing (general term)

muai sǎa-kon N มวยสากล Western-style boxing

muai thai N มวยไทย Thai boxing

mùak N หมวก hat, cap

mûang/sǐi mûang N (สี) ม่วง purple

mûea khuehn níi ADV เมื่อคืนนี้, (or simply) mûea khuehn เมื่อคืน last night

mûea kîi níi N (COLLOQUIAL) เมื่อกี้นี้, (or simply) mûea kîi เมื่อกี้ just a moment ago

mûea rài เมื่อไร when?

mûeà rài kâw dâi เมื่อไรก็ได้ (a common response to the question 'when?') whenever, any time

mûea waan níi ADV เมื่อวานนี้, (or simply) mûea waan เมื่อวาน yesterday

mûea waan suehn níi ADV เมื่อวานซืน นี้ the day before yesterday

mǔean ADJ เหมือน to resemble, be similar to, like, as

mueang N เมือง town, city; also 'country' as in the common name for Thailand mueang thai เมืองไทย

mǔeang N (COLLOQUIAL) เหมือง, (more fully) mǔeang râeh เหมืองแร่ a mine

mueang jiin N เมืองจีน China

N

mueang nâwk N (COLLOQUIAL) เมืองนอก foreign country, abroad

mueang thai N เมืองไทย Thailand (NOTE: the most common way Thai people refer to their own country)

mǔean-kan เหมือนกัน to be identical; too, either, (in conversation if you are of the same view as the person you are talking to you can say) likewise

mueh N มือ hand

múeh N มื้อ mealtime, a meal (also commonly used when referring to the number of meals eaten)

mueh thǔeh N มือถือ cell phone, mobile phone

mùehn NUM หมื่น ten thousand

mûeht ADJ มืด dark

mûeht khrúem ADJ มืดครึ้ม to be cloudy, overcast

mùek N หมึก ink

múk N มุก pearl

mum N มุม corner, angle

mǔn V หมุน to turn, rotate (e.g. a knob/dial)

múng N มุ้ง mosquito net

múng lûat N มุ้งลวด fly screen

mûng pai V, PREP มุ่งไป to head for, towards

mút-sàlim N มุสลิม Muslim

mǔu N หมู pig, hog, boar

mùu bâan N หมู่บ้าน a village

mǔu haem N (from English) หมูแฮม ham

mum maam ADJ มูมมาม sloppy, messy, uncouth in manner

N

ná นะ a particle used at the end of a sentence to convey a number of different meanings, e.g. 'right?' mâi dii ná ไม่ดีนะ 'That's no good, right?; 'okay/OK?'; tòk-long pai dûai kan ná ตกลงไปด้วยกันนะ 'Agreed, let's go together, OK?'

nǎa ADJ หนา thick (of things)

naa N นา (irrigated) rice field, paddy field

náa N น้า aunt, uncle (a younger brother or sister of one's mother)

nâa N หน้า face, page, front (ahead); e.g. season – nâa ráwn หน้าร้อน summer (Feb–April); nâa nǎaw หน้าหนาว winter/cool season (Nov–Jan); nâa fǒn หน้าฝน rainy season (May–Oct)

nâa น่า a prefix used with verbs/adjectives to form words with endings such as -ful, -able, -y, -ing; also used to suggest that something's worth doing, trying, sampling etc., e.g. nâa kin น่ากิน – appetizing, tempting, delectable, to look delicious

nâa bùea ADJ น่าเบื่อ boring, dull

nâa duu ADJ น่าดู worth seeing/watching

nâa fang V น่าฟัง worth listening to

nâa ìtchǎa ADJ น่าอิจฉา envious

nâa jà V น่าจะ ought to, might like to, would be

nâa jùup ADJ น่าจูบ kissable

nâa kàak N (pronounced 'gark' with a low tone) หน้ากาก a mask

nâa kàwt ADJ น่ากอด huggable, cuddlesome

nâa khǎai nâa ADJ น่าขายหน้า to be shameful (COLLOQUIAL) khǎai nâa ขาย หน้า to lose face

nâa khít ADJ น่าคิด worth thinking about

nâa klìat ADJ น่าเกลียด ugly – can refer to both a person or thing as well as unseemly behavior

nâa klua ADV น่ากลัว scary, frightening

nâa lá-aai ADJ น่าละอาย (to be) ashamed, embarrassed; to be embarrassing

nâa láeng N หน้าแล้ง dry season

nâa múet V หน้ามืด to black out, have a dizzy spell, lose control of oneself, be blind with passion

nâa òk N หน้าอก chest; also breast(s), chest

nâa phàak N หน้าผาก forehead

nâa plàehk jai ADJ น่าแปลกใจ surprising, weird

nâa prà-làat jai ADJ น่าประหลาดใจ unusual, strange, wonderful

nâa rák ADJ น่ารัก cute, appealing, lovely, pretty (NOTE: this term is used in Thai to refer not only to people or animals, but also behavior)

nâa rák mâak ADJ น่ารักมาก very cute

nâa ram khaan ADJ น่ารำคาญ annoying

nâa rang-kìat ADJ น่ารังเกียจ disgusting

nâa sà-nùk ADJ น่าสนุก to be fun, to look like fun (i.e. it looks like fun)

nâa sàp sŏn ADJ น่าสับสน to be confusing

nâa sŏn-jai น่าสนใจ to be interesting

nâa sŏng săan ADJ น่าสงสาร to feel/express pity/sympathy for someone else: Oh, what a pity!

nâa taa N หน้าตา countenance, look

nâa tàang N หน้าต่าง window (in house) **khăw thîi-nâng rim thaang-doen** ขอที่นั่งริมหน้าต่าง Can I get a window seat?

nâa thîi N หน้าที่ duty (responsibility)

naa thii N นาที a minute

nâa tùehn tên ADJ น่าตื่นเต้น to be exciting

nâa wái jai ADJ น่าไว้ใจ trustworthy, dependable, reliable

naai N นาย Mr, Mister, Sir, owner, employer, chief, boss

naai jâang N นายจ้าง employer

naai phâet N (FORMAL TERM) นายแพทย์ doctor

naai phon N นายพล general (in the armed forces)

naai rueah N นายเรือ captain (of a ship/vessel)

naai tamrùat N นายตำรวจ police officer

naai thá-hăn N นายทหาร army officer

naai thun N นายทุน capitalist

naalí-kaa N นาฬิกา wristwatch, clock; o'clock in 24 hour system (i.e. 1

naalikaa = one o'clock in the morning; 13 naalikaa = one o'clock in the afternoon)

náam N น้ำ water, liquid, fluid (also see entries under náam… below)

náam àt lom N น้ำอัดลม soft drink, fizzy drink (Coke, Pepsi, etc.)

náam chaa N น้ำชา tea

náam hăwm N น้ำหอม perfume

náam jai N น้ำใจ (an important Thai word expressing a very desirable trait – someone with): spirit, heart, goodwill, thoughtfulness, a willingness to help

náam jîm N น้ำจิ้ม sauce (for dipping, e.g. spring rolls, curry puffs, etc.)

náam jùet N น้ำจืด fresh water

náam khăeng N น้ำแข็ง ice

náam khûen N น้ำขึ้น high tide; náam long N น้ำลง low tide

náam man N น้ำมัน gasoline, petrol

náam man khrûeang N น้ำมันเครื่อง engine oil

náam man ngaa N น้ำมันงา sesame oil

náam nàk N น้ำหนัก weight

náam nàk khûen V น้ำหนักขึ้น to gain weight, put on weight

náam nàk lót V น้ำหนักลด to lose weight

náam phŏn-lámái N น้ำผลไม้ fruit juice

náam phrík N น้ำพริก hot chili paste sauce

náam phú N น้ำพุ a spring/fountain

náam phú ráwn N น้ำพุร้อน hot spring

náam phûeng N น้ำผึ้ง honey

náam plaa N น้ำปลา fish sauce

náam prà-paa N น้ำประปา piped water, tap water, water supply (e.g. in a town/city)

naam sà-kun N นามสกุล surname, last name

náam sôm N น้ำส้ม orange juice; also (Thai) vinegar used as a condiment that can used to flavor such things as noodle soup

náam súp N น้ำซุป soup, broth

náam taa N น้ำตา tear(s)

náam taan N น้ำตาล brown (color), sugar

náam thá-leh N น้ำทะเล seawater

náam thûam N, V น้ำท่วม a flood; to flood

náam tòk N น้ำตก a waterfall

náam wăn N น้ำหวาน soft drink, flavored syrup

naan ADJ, ADV นาน long, lasting, for a long time, ages

naan thâo-rài นานเท่าไหร่ (for) how long?

naa-naa châat ADJ นานาชาติ international

naang N นาง woman, lady; Mrs (title)

naang èhk N นางเอก leading actress, female lead, heroine

naang fáa N นางฟ้า angel, fairy

naang ngaam N นางงาม a beauty queen; naang ngaam jàkkrawaan นางงามจักรวาล Miss Universe

naang săow N นางสาว unmarried woman, Miss/Ms (title)

naa-yók N นายก chairman, president (of a company)

naa-yók rát-thà-montrii N นายก รัฐมนตรี prime minister (COLLOQUIALLY) as naa-yók นายก

nâeh jai ADJ แน่ใจ certain, sure

nâeh nawn ADV แน่นอน certainly!, of course, exactly

nâen ADJ แน่น to be crowded; solid, tight

náe-nam V แนะนำ to suggest, advise, recommend

náe-nam tua V แนะนำตัว to introduce someone

náe-nam tua ehng V แนะนำตัวเอง to introduce oneself

naew N แนว line, row (e.g. of chairs etc.)

năi ADV ไหน where? which?

nai PREP ใน in, at (space), inside, within

nai à-dìit ADV ในอดีต in the past

nai à-naàkhót ADV ในอนาคต in the future

nai-lâwn N (from English) ไนลอน nylon

nai lŭang N (COLLOQUIAL) ในหลวง the King (of Thailand)

nai mâi cháa ADV ในไม่ช้า soon, shortly, before long

nai mueang N ในเมือง downtown, urban

nai prá-thêht N ในประเทศ domestic

nai ra-wàng ADV ในระหว่าง during (e.g. the trip to the coast), between

nai rôm ADJ ในร่ม in the shade, indoor

nai thîi sùt ADV ในที่สุด finally, eventually, in the long run

nàk ADJ หนัก to be heavy

nàk jai ADJ หนักใจ depressed, heavy-hearted, anxious

nák นัก used as a prefix to form a word meaning – an expert, one skilled (in), or -er, fancier (see the following entries)

nák bin N นักบิน a pilot, aviator

nák doehn thaang N นักเดินทาง traveler

nák don trii N นักดนตรี musician

nák khàow N นักข่าว journalist

nák khĭan N นักเขียน writer

nák-lehng N นักเลง tough guy, hoodlum, ruffian

nák ráwng N นักร้อง a singer

nák rian N นักเรียน a student

nák thâwng thîao N นักท่องเที่ยว a tourist

nák thúrákìt N นักธุรกิจ businessperson

ná-khawn N นคร city, metropolis, the first part of the name in a number of Thai towns/cities/provinces, e.g. Nakhon Pathom, Nakhon Sawan, Nakhon Phanom, Nakhon Naiyok, Nakhon Sithammarat

nam V นำ to guide, lead; to head, escort

nam khâo V นำเข้า to import

nam pai V นำไป to lead (guide/take someone somewhere)

nam thîao v นำเที่ยว to guide, take (a person) around, lead a tour

nán นั้น that

nân làe! (COLLOQUIAL) นั่นแหละ exactly! just so!

nâng v นั่ง to sit: nâng thîi-nîi dâi-mái นั่งที่นี่ได้ไหม Do you mind if I sit here?

năng N หนัง leather

năng N หนัง film, movie (NOTE: the same word as 'leather', this being related to a perceived likeness between the screening of early films and traditional shadow puppets whose images were illuminated on a thin leather/parchment type of screen)

nâng long v นั่งลง to sit down

nâng rót v นั่งรถ to ride (in a car, van, etc.)

năngsǔeh N หนังสือ book

năngsǔeh doehn thaang N หนังสือเดินทาง passport (the English word 'passport' is commonly used in Thailand, pronounced something like 'pars-port')

năngsǔeh nam thîao N หนังสือนำเที่ยว guidebook (such as Lonely Planet)

năngsǔeh phim N หนังสือพิมพ์ newspaper

nâo ADJ เน่า to be rotten, spoiled, (for food, etc.) to have gone off, decayed, corrupted

năow ADJ หนาว cold weather, to be cold (body temperature)

năow sàn v หนาวสั่น to shiver

náp v นับ to count, reckon

náp thǔeh v นับถือ to respect, hold in high regard, believe in (a particular religion/faith)

nárók N นรก hell, purgatory

nát v (pronounced similar to 'nut' with a high tone) นัด to fix/set a time, make an appointment; also to sniff or snort (a substance) up the nose

nát-mǎai N นัดหมาย an appointment

nàw mái N หน่อไม้ bamboo shoot(s)

ná-wá-níyaai N นวนิยาย novel

nâwk ADJ นอก outside, beyond, outer, external

nâwk jàak PREP นอกจาก apart from, besides, except, unless

nâwk jàak níi นอกจากนี้ besides, in additon, for another thing

nâwk jai v นอกใจ to be unfaithful, adulterous

nâwk khâwk ADJ นอกคอก to be unconventional, offbeat, eccentric, non-conformist

nǎwn N หนอน worm, maggot

nawn v นอน to lie down, recline; to go to bed

nawn khwâm v นอนคว่ำ to lie face down, sleep on one's stomach

nawn làp v นอนหลับ to sleep, be asleep; the opposite – nawn mâi làp นอนไม่หลับ – to be unable to sleep

nawn lên v นอนเล่น to take a rest, lay about, repose

nawn ngǎai v นอนหงาย to lie/sleep on one's back

nâwng N น่อง calf (lower leg)

náwng N น้อง (COLLOQUIAL) younger brother or sister (also commonly used by Thais when speaking to an 'inferior' such as the staff in a restaurant, etc.)

náwng chaai N น้องชาย younger brother

náwng khǒei N น้องเขย younger brother-in-law

náwng mia N น้องเมีย wife's younger sibling

náwng sǎamii N น้องสามี husband's younger sibling

náwng sǎow N น้องสาว younger sister

náwng sà-phái N น้องสะใภ้ younger sister-in-law

náwt N น็อต a bolt, nut (for building etc.)

ná-yoh-baai N นโยบาย policy (e.g. government policy)

nékthai N (from English) เน็คไท necktie

nian rîap ADJ เนียนเรียบ to be smooth (of surfaces)

nǐao ADJ เหนียว sticky, tough (e.g. chewy); (COLLOQUIAL) stingy – more fully khîi nǐao ขี้เหนียว

nîi (PRON) นี่ this; also (COLLOQUIAL; calling attention to something) hey!

nǐi V หนี to flee, run away, escape, get away

níi นี้ ADJ this: e.g. yàang níi อย่างนี้ 'like this'; wan níi วันนี้ 'today (i.e. this day)'

níi sǐn N หนี้สิน debt, obligation

nin thaa V นินทา to gossip about

nîng ADJ นิ่ง still, quiet

ní-sǎi N นิสัย habit, disposition, character

nithǎn N นิทาน fable, tale, story

nít nòi ADV นิดหน่อย slightly, a little bit

níu N นิ้ว finger; also part of the word for 'toe' níu tháo นิ้วเท้า; the names of the different fingers: níu pôhng นิ้วโป้ง thumb; níu chíi นิ้วชี้ index finger; níu klaang นิ้วกลาง middle finger; níu naang นิ้วนาง ring finger; níu kôi นิ้วก้อย little finger/pinky

niu-sii-laehn N นิวซีแลนด์ New Zealand

ní-yom ADJ นิยม to be interested in (e.g. fast cars); rótsàni-yom N รสนิยม taste, preference (e.g. in fashion, music etc.)

noehn khǎo N เนินเขา a hill

noei N เนย butter

noei khǎeng N เนยแข็ง cheese

nôhn ADV โน่น yonder, over there

nóhn ADV โน้น there, way over there (further than nôhn โน่น)

nói ADJ น้อย little, small, not much, few

nói kwàa น้อยกว่า less (smaller amount)

nói nàa N น้อยหน่า custard apple (fruit)

nói thîi sùt น้อยที่สุด least (the smallest amount)

nók N นก bird

nom N นม milk; breasts

nom khôn N นมข้น condensed milk

nonthá-bùrii N นนทบุรี Nonthaburi, provincial capital northwest of central Bangkok on the east bank of the Chaopraya River. Nowadays it is virtually a part of the greater Bangkok metropolitan area

nùat N หนวด mustache

nûat V นวด to massage

nǔea ADV, N เหนือ above, beyond; north

núea N เนื้อ beef, meat

núea kàe N เนื้อแกะ lamb, mutton

núea mǔu N เนื้อหมู pork (NOTE: when ordering food – simply mǔu หมู)

núea sàt N เนื้อสัตว์ meat, flesh

núea wua N เนื้อวัว beef

nùeay ADJ เหนื่อย to be exhausted, weary

núek V นึก to recall, to think of (COLLOQUIAL) nùek àwk láew นึกออกแล้ว 'I've remembered it/I can recall it now'

nùeng หนึ่ง one

nùeng V นึ่ง to steam

nùeng khûu หนึ่งคู่ a pair of

nùeng thii หนึ่งที once

nûm ADJ นุ่ม soft

nùm ADJ, N หนุ่ม young, youthful; young man, adolescent

nùm sǎow N หนุ่มสาว teenagers, young men and women

nûng V นุ่ง to wear, put on, be clad in; nûng phâa thǔng นุ่งผ้าถุง to be wearing a sarong

nǔu N หนู a mouse or rat (NOTE: this word is also used by, generally, younger women as a first person [i.e. 'I'] pronoun)

NG

NG

NOTE: 'ng' ง is a distinct letter in Thai quite separate from 'n' น, although here words beginning with this letter are grouped together under 'N'.

ngaa N งา sesame seeds
ngaa cháang N งาช้าง elephant tusk, ivory
ngâai ADJ ง่าย to be simple, easy
ngǎai tháwng ADJ หงายท้อง overturned, upside down (e.g. a vehicle that has rolled over onto its roof)
ngaam ADJ งาม to be beautiful, attractive; fine, good
ngaan N งาน job, work; also party (as in 'a birthday party'), ceremony; a measure of land the equivalent of 400 sq. m.
ngaan àdìrèhk N งานอดิเรก a hobby
ngaan bâan N งานบ้าน housework
ngaan líang N งานเลี้ยง banquet
ngaan pii mài N งานปีใหม่ new year festival
ngaan sòp N งานศพ funeral
ngaan tàeng-ngaan N งานแต่งงาน wedding
ngaan wát N งานวัด a fair held within the Buddhist temple grounds
ngaan wí jai N งานวิจัย research work
ngâeh N แง่ (an) angle
ngai (COLLOQUIAL) ไง what; how; (COLLOQUIAL EXPRESSIONS) pen ngai เป็นไง 'How are things?', 'How are you?', 'And then what?'; láew ngai แล้วไง 'So?', 'So what'; 'And then?'; wâa ngai ว่าไง 'What did you say?, 'What did he/she say?'
ngán-ngán (COLLOQUIAL) งั้น ๆ average (so-so, just okay)
ngáp V งับ to snap, snap at, nip, clamp, close, shut
ngát V งัด to pry out, force up, raise with a lever
ngǎo ADJ เหงา lonely

ngao N, ADJ เงา shadow, reflection; glossy, shiny, lustrous
ngáw N (áw pronounced very short) เงาะ rambutan (fruit)
ngaw ngae ADJ งอแง fussy, childish, crying like a baby, clumsy
ngâwk V งอก to sprout, shoot, germinate; thùa ngâwk N ถั่วงอก beansprout(s)
ngawn V งอน to pout, show displeasure (esp. women, children), feign displeasure
ngîan N, ADJ เงี่ยน (a) strong urge (for), craving (for); horny, randy, having the hots for (someone)
ngîap ADJ, V เงียบ to be quiet, silent; (also used to say – rather brusquely) 'be quiet!'
ngoehn N เงิน money, silver, cash
ngoehn duean N เงินเดือน salary
ngoehn fàak N เงินฝาก deposit (money deposited in a bank)
ngoehn mát-jam N (pronounced 'mutt-jum') เงินมัดจำ a deposit (e.g. on a car, etc)
ngoehn sòt N เงินสด cash, money
ngoehn traa N (FORMAL) เงินตรา currency
ngôh ADJ โง่ to be stupid
ngôi N ง่อย having a disability
ngók ADJ งก greedy, gluttonous, avaricious, stingy, mean
ngom-ngaai V งมงาย to be credulous, believe in something blindly
ngong ADJ งง to be puzzled, stunned, befuddled
ngòp-prà-maan N งบประมาณ budget
ngùang ADJ ง่วง, ง่วงนอน to be sleepy, tired
ngùea N เหงื่อ sweat; ngùea àwk V เหงื่อออก to perspire, sweat
ngûean khǎi N เงื่อนไข a condition/proviso (e.g. a pre-condition for something to take place)
nguu N งู snake
nguu-nguu plaaplaa (COLLOQUIAL EXPRESSION) งู ๆ ปลา ๆ a little bit, not much,

rudimentary (e.g. to speak a language, be able to do something requiring a degree of skill)
nguu sà-wàt N งูสวัด shingles, *herpes zoster*

O

ôh hoh (exclamation expressing surprise) โอ้โฮ Wow! Gosh! Oh!
oh-kàat N โอกาส chance, opportunity
oh-líang N โอเลี้ยง iced black coffee (Thai-style)
oh-thii (from English) โอที overtime (work)
oh-yúa N โอยั๊วะ hot black coffee (Thai-style)
ohn V โอน to transfer (e.g. money to another bank account/overseas, etc.)
ohn ngoehn V โอนเงิน to transfer money
ohn sǎn châat V โอนสัญชาติ to become naturalized, change one's citizenship
òhng N โอ่ง earthen jar, (large) water jar
ohy/óhy EXCLAM โอย, โอ๊ย Ouch! Oh!
ôi N อ้อย sugarcane
òk/nâa òk N อก, หน้าอก breast, chest
om V อม to keep in the mouth, suck (e.g. a lolly/lozenge)
ong-kaan/ong-kawn N องค์การ/องค์กร (an) organization
ongsǎ N องศา degree(s) (of temperature)
òp V, ADJ อบ to bake, roast; baked
òp choei N อบเชย cinnamon
òp ùn ADJ อบอุ่น warm
òp-phá-yóp V อพยพ to migrate, evacuate
òt V อด to give up, abstain from
òt aa-hǎan V อดอาหาร to fast, go without food, abstain from food
òt taai V อดตาย to starve to death
òt thon V อดทน to be patient, have tenacity, stamina

P

NOTE: this letter should not be confused with the English 'p'. This Thai 'p' ป is not a sound commonly found in English although it is similar to the 'p' sound in the word 'spa'.

pá V ปะ to patch (a tire/inner tube of bicycle/a piece of clothing)
pâa N ป้า aunt, the older sister of either parent
pàa N ป่า forest, jungle ADJ wild (of animals)
pâai N ป้าย sign, signboard; **pâai rót** N ป้ายรถ, ป้ายรถเมล์ bus stop
pàak N ปาก mouth, entrance
pàak sǐa ADJ (COLLOQUIAL) ปากเสีย to say unpleasant things, (to have) a big mouth
pàak soi N ปากซอย the entrance of a Soi (laneway, side road)
pàak-kaa N ปากกา pen
pâehng N แป้ง flour, (talcum) powder
pàeht NUM แปด eight
pàeht sìp NUM แปดสิบ eighty
páep diao (COLLOQUIAL EXPRESSION) แป๊ปเดียว in a jiffy, in a sec (second), (wait) just a second/moment
pai V ไป to go, depart, move; (COLLOQUIAL) to tell someone to 'Go, get out/go away' simply say pai ไป with emphasis. One other sense for which the word is commonly used is to express the idea of 'too/too much', e.g. phaehng pai แพงไป too expensive; dang pai ดังไป too loud
pai ao maa V (COLLOQUIAL) ไปเอามา to fetch, go and get (literally, 'go'-'take'-'come')
pai doehn lên V (COLLOQUIAL) ไปเดินเล่น to go for a walk
pai dûai V (COLLOQUIAL) ไปด้วย to go along, to go as well
pai kan V ไปกัน to go together, let's

go; (COLLOQUIAL) also pai dûai kan ไปด้วย
ยกัน 'let's go together'

pai…khâ/khráp ไป…ค่ะ/ครับ I'd like
to go to…, please.

pai khâang nâa v ไปข้างหน้า to go
forward

pai… kìi chûa-mohng? ไป…กี่ชั่วโมง
How many hours is it to …?

pai klàp N ไปกลับ round trip

pai năi maa (COLLOQUIAL) ไปไหนมา
Where have you been?

pai nawn v ไปนอน to go to bed

pai pen phûean v (COLLOQUIAL) ไปเป็น
เพื่อน to accompany, go along with
someone to keep them company

pai sòng v ไปส่ง to give (someone) a
lift (home), see (someone) off (e.g.
at the airport, etc.)

pai súeh khăwng v ไปซื้อของ to shop,
go shopping

pai…thâo-rài? ไป…เท่าไร How much
is it to go to…?

pai thát-sà-naa-jawn v (thát pronounced 'tat' with a high tone) ไป
ทัศนาจร (somewhat formal) to go
sightseeing

pai thîi năi (QUESTION) ไปที่ไหน where
are you going?; (COLLOQUIAL – also
used as a common greeting) pai năi
ไปไหน

pai thîao v ไปเที่ยว take a trip, travel

pai yîam v ไปเยี่ยม to go visit (e.g. a
friend/relative etc.)

pàk v ปัก to embroider, implant

pàkàtì ADJ ปกติ normal, regular, usual, ordinary

pám náam man N ปั๊มน้ำมัน gas/pet-
rol station

pân v ปั้น to model (clay), mold,
sculpt

panhăa N ปัญหา problem; (COLLOQUIAL)
mâi mii panhăa ไม่มีปัญหา 'No
problems'

pào v เป่า to blow (e.g. the candles
out on a birthday cake)

pào hŭu v (COLLOQUIAL) เป่าหู to insinu-

ate, whisper something in someone's
ear (to get them on your side/believe
you rather than someone else)

pâo măai N เป้าหมาย goal, objective

pàrin-yaa N ปริญญา a degree (i.e. a
university/college degree)

pàtìbàt v ปฏิบัติ (FORMAL) to operate,
perform

pàtìbàt tàw v ปฏิบัติต่อ (FORMAL) to
behave towards

pàtì-kìrí-yaa N ปฏิกิริยา reaction

pàtìsèht v ปฏิเสธ to decline, refuse,
deny

pà-tì-thin N ปฏิทิน calendar

pàt-jù-ban níi ปัจจุบันนี้ (FORMAL) nowadays, these days, currently

pàwk v ปอก to peel (e.g. an orange)

pâwm N ป้อม fortress, citadel

pawn N ปอนด์ pound (money); also
used to refer to a loaf of bread

pâwn v ป้อน to feed someone, spoon-
feed

pâwng kan v ป้องกัน to prevent, protect; defend (in war)

pàwt N ปอด lung(s)

pêh N เป้ a backpack

pen v เป็น (the Thai equivalent to the
verb 'to be') to be someone or something; to know how to do something

pen hèht hâi เป็นเหตุให้ to be the
cause or reason

pen ìtsàrà ADJ เป็นอิสระ to be free,
independent

pen jai v (COLLOQUIAL) เป็นใจ to favor,
sympathize (with), side (with); to be
an accomplice (of)

pen jâo khăwng v, N เป็นเจ้าของ to
own; the owner

pen kan ehng ADJ (COLLOQUIAL) เป็นกัน
เอง to be friendly, outgoing; (COMMON
EXPRESSION) 'make yourself at home/
take it easy, just be yourself'

pen khăwng… เป็นของ to belong
to…, e.g. pen khăwng khăo เป็นของ
เขา 'It's his/hers'

pen man ADJ เป็นมัน oily (skin);

shiny, glossy

pen măn ADJ เป็นหมัน to be sterile, infertile

pen nîi PHR เป็นหนี้ to owe, be in debt to someone

pen pai dâi ADJ (EXPRESSION) เป็นไปได้ to be possible

pen pai mâi dâi ADJ (EXPRESSION) เป็นไปไม่ได้ to be impossible

pen rá-bìap ADJ เป็นระเบียบ to be orderly, organized

pen tham ADJ เป็นธรรม to be fair, just, equitable

pen thammá-châat ADJ เป็นธรรมชาติ natural

pen thammá-daa ADJ เป็นธรรมดา to be typical, normal

pen thîi niyom ADJ เป็นที่นิยม to be popular

pen thîi phaw jai เป็นที่พอใจ to be satisfying

pen wàt เป็นหวัด to have a cold

pèt N เป็ด duck

pìak ADJ เปียก to be wet, soaking

pii N ปี year, years old

pii nâa ปีหน้า next year

pii thîi láew ADV ปีที่แล้ว last year

pìik N ปีก wing (of a bird or aeroplane)

piin V ปีน to climb (e.g. a mountain)

pîng V, ADJ ปิ้ง to grill/toast; to be grilled, toasted

pìt V ปิด to close, cover, shut; off, to turn something off

pìt láew ADJ ปิดแล้ว turned off, closed

pìt prà-tuu V ปิดประตู to close the door

pìt ráan V ปิดร้าน to close the shop/store

pìt thà-nŏn V ปิดถนน to close the road

plaa N ปลา fish

plaa chà-lăam N ปลาฉลาม shark

plaa mùek N ปลาหมึก squid (literally, 'fish'-'ink')

plaai N ปลาย end (e.g. of the road), tip (e.g. of the tongue)

pláatsàtìk N (from English) พลาสติก plastic

plaeh V แปล to translate

plaeh wâa... แปลว่า... it means...; a question to elicit the above response 'it means…': plaeh wâa arai แปลว่าอะไร 'what does it/this mean?'

plàehk ADJ แปลก strange, unusual, odd; khon plàehk nâa N คนแปลกหน้า a stranger

plàehk jai ADJ แปลกใจ surprised, puzzled

plák N (from English) ปลั๊ก plug (bath)

plák fai N ปลั๊กไฟ plug/socket (electric)

plào ADJ เปล่า empty, void; one of the ways of saying 'no' in Thai, for example when someone asks a question assuming a positive reponse but instead gets a reply of 'no' (A: 'Do you want to go and see [name of film]? Everyone says it is great.' B: plào 'No')

plawm V ปลอม to forge, counterfeit, fake

plawm tua V ปลอมตัว to disguise oneself

plàwt phai ADJ ปลอดภัย to be safe (from harm)

plàwt prôhng ADJ ปลอดโปร่ง to be clear (the weather)

plìan V เปลี่ยน to change (e.g. clothes, plans, etc.)

plìan jai V เปลี่ยนใจ to change one's mind

pling N ปลิง a leech

plòi V ปล่อย to free, release, drop/let go

plôn V ปล้น to rob (e.g. a bank), plunder

plòt kàsĭan ADJ ปลดเกษียณ to be retired

plùak N ปลวก termite, white ant

plueai ADJ เปลือย to be naked, nude

plùeak N เปลือก the peel (of an orange), the shell (of a nut)

plùk v ปลุก to awaken/wake up (someone); to arouse, excite

plùuk v ปลูก to plant, grow, build, construct

poehsen N (from English) เปอร์เซ็นต์ percent, percentage

pòeht v เปิด to open; turn or switch something on: pòeht mí-têr mái? เปิดมิเตอร์ไหม Is your meter on?

pòeht banchii v เปิดบัญชี to open an account (e.g. bank account)

pòeht phŏei v เปิดเผย to reveal, make known

póh ADJ โป๊ indecent, revealing (clothing), scantily dressed; nǎng póh หนังโป๊ N an X-rated/pornographic film/ DVD etc.

pòk khrong v ปกครอง to take care of, govern, rule, administer

praa-kòt v ปรากฏ to appear, become visible

pràap v ปราบ to control, suppress (e.g. the drug trade), exterminate

praà-sàat N ปราสาท castle

pràat-sajàak ADV (FORMAL) ปราศจาก without

pràat-thànǎa v ปรารถนา (somewhat more formal than the colloquial wǎng หวัง) to wish (for something), to desire, to be desirous

prà-chaa-chon N ประชาชน the public, the people, populace

prà-chaa-kawn N ประชากร population

pràchaakhom N (FORMAL) ประชาคม community (e.g. used for the EEC, or ASEAN Community)

pràchaa-sǎmphan N ประชาสัมพันธ์ public relations

prà-chót v ประชด to mock, ridicule, deride; to spite (someone)

prà-chum v ประชุม to meet, hold a meeting, have a conference

prà-dàp v ประดับ to decorate, adorn

prà-dìt v ประดิษฐ์ to invent, make up, create

praehng N แปรง a brush

praehng sǐi fan N แปรงสีฟัน toothbrush

prai-sànii N ไปรษณีย์ post office; prai-sànii klaang N ไปรษณีย์กลาง GPO, central post office

prà-jaan v ประจาน (a traditional Thai practice) to humiliate publicly, disgrace, to shame (the modern version of this is for criminals to re-enact their crimes – usually in handcuffs – with the police and general public looking on. Photographs are taken and published in the popular press together with details about the particular crime/offence)

pràjam ADJ, ADV ประจำ regular(ly); prajam thaang N ประจำทาง the regular/scheduled (e.g. bus) route

pràjam duean N (formal medical term) ประจำเดือน (menstrual) period

pràjam pii ADJ, ADV ประจำปี annual

pràjam wan ADJ, ADV ประจำวัน daily

pràjòp v ประจบ to flatter, fawn (on, over); to please or humor someone (i.e. to kiss ass/arse)

prà-kàat v ประกาศ to announce, proclaim, declare, give notice

prà-kàat-sànii-yá-bàt N ประกาศนียบัตร a certificate (for completing a course of study)

prà-kan v ประกัน to guarantee, insure; to put up bail/security

prà-kan chii-wít N ประกันชีวิต life insurance

prà-kàwp v ประกอบ to assemble, put together

prà-kàwp dûai v ประกอบด้วย be made up of, comprising, consist of

prà-kùat v ประกวด to show (in competition), enter a competion, contest

prà-làat ADJ ประหลาด strange, odd, unusual, extraordinary

prà-làat jai ADJ ประหลาดใจ to be surprised

prà-maan v, ADV ประมาณ to estimate; about, approximately, roughly

prà-màat ADJ ประมาท to be negligent, careless (e.g. doing something with a high risk of causing an accident)

prà-muun V ประมูล to bid/tender/auction

prà-muun khǎi V ประมูลขาย (to be) auctioned off

pràp V ปรับ to adjust (e.g. airconditioning)

pràp aa-kaat ADJ ปรับอากาศ air-conditioned

pràp tua V ปรับตัว to adjust, adapt (e.g. oneself to a new situation)

prà-phêht N ประเภท class, category, type

prà-phrúet V (FORMAL) ประพฤติ to behave

prà-sàat N ประสาท nerve; **sên prà-sàat** N เส้นประสาท a nerve; (COLLOQUIAL) **prà-sàat** ประสาท to be nuts/crazy

prà-sòpkaan N ประสบการณ์ experience

prà-thaa-na thíp-bawdii N ประธานาธิบดี president

prà-tháp jai ADJ ประทับใจ to be impressed; impressive

prà-thát N ประทัด fireworks, firecrackers

prà-thêht N ประเทศ country (nation)

prà-thúang V ประท้วง to protest, go on strike

prà-tuu N ประตู door, gate; goal in football/soccer

prà-tuu náam N ประตูน้ำ a water gate; a very busy, lively area in the central part of Bangkok commonly written 'Pratunam'

prà-wàt N ประวัติ history (i.e. a personal history), record, resumé

pràwàttì-sàat N ประวัติศาสตร์ history (the formal discipline of the study of the past)

prà-yàt V, ADJ ประหยัด to economize; economical, to be thrifty, frugal

prà-yòhk N ประโยค a sentence (i.e. a sentence of text)

prà-yòht N ประโยชน์ usefulness, utility, (for the) benefit (of), advantage

prîao ADJ เปรี้ยว sour (to the taste); spirited, vivacious, wild, untamed (of people – generally women still in their prime)

prîao wǎan ADJ เปรี้ยวหวาน sweet and sour (e.g. fish, pork, etc.)

prìap kàp เปรียบกับ compared with

prìap thîap V เปรียบเทียบ to compare

prùek-sǎa V ปรึกษา to consult, talk over with

pùai ADJ ป่วย to be ill, sick

pùat V ปวด to ache (e.g. toothache), be sore (e.g. sore back)

pûean ADJ เปื้อน to be soiled, dirty

puehn N ปืน gun (general term)

pǔi N ปุ๋ย fertilizer

pûm pûi ADJ ปุ้มปุ้ย pudgy, a bit of a fatty (COLLOQUIAL playful)

pùu N ปู่ grandfather (paternal)

puu N, V ปู a crab: to lay, spread, put (sheets/mat) on (bed/floor)

pùu yâa taa yaai ปู่ย่าตายาย grandparents, forebears, ancestors

puun N ปูน cement

PH

NOTE: 'ph' is very similar to the 'p' sound in English

phâa N ผ้า cloth, material, fabric, textile

phàa V ผ่า to split (e.g. a piece of wood with an ax)

phaa V พา to take or lead someone somewhere

phaa pai V พาไป to take someone to

phâa chét tua N ผ้าเช็ดตัว towel

phâa hòm N ผ้าห่ม blanket

phà-jon-phai V ผจญภัย adventure

phâa khîi ríu N ผ้าขี้ริ้ว a rag; tripe/offal

phâa mâan N ผ้าม่าน curtain(s), drapes

phâa puu N ผ้าปู sheet (for bed) (NOTE: the most common way of referring

phâa puu tó

PH

to bedsheets: **phâa puu thîi nawn** ผ้า
ปูที่นอน)

phâa puu tó N ผ้าปูโต๊ะ tablecloth

phâa sîn N ผ้าซิ่น long Thai one-piece
sarong-like skirt

phàa tàt V ผ่าตัด to operate, perform
an operation or surgery

phá-yung V พยุง to carry carefully

phaai N พาย a paddle; **phaai rueah** V
พายเรือ to paddle/row a boat

phaai nai PREP ภายใน in (time, years),
within

phaai nai pràthêht ภายในประเทศ internal, domestic, within the country

phàan V ผ่าน to pass, go past; (to go)
via, through

phâap N ภาพ picture

phâap kwâang N ภาพกว้าง panorama

phâap wâat N ภาพวาด painting

phâap-pháyon N ภาพยนตร์ motion
picture, film

phaa-rá N ภาระ obligation, responsibility, burden

phaa-sǎa N ภาษา language

phaa-sǎa angkrìt N ภาษาอังกฤษ
English (language)

phaa-sǎa jiin N ภาษาจีน Chinese
(language)

phaa-sǎa kha-měhn N ภาษาเขมร
Khmer/Cambodian (language)

phaa-sǎa thai N ภาษาไทย Thai
(language)

phaa-sǎa thìn N (pronounced 'tin',
not 'thin') ภาษาถิ่น local language,
dialect

phaa-sǐi N ภาษี tax(es)

phaa-wá N ภาวะ state, condition,
status

phaa-yú N พายุ storm

phà-choehn V เผชิญ to meet, confront

phà-choehn nâa V เผชิญหน้า to meet,
face up to (someone or something),
confront

phàe N แพะ goat

phaeh N แพ a raft, houseboat

pháeh V แพ้ to lose, be defeated; to be

allergic (e.g. to some types of food,
medication)

phǎen N แผน a plan, scheme

phǎen bohraan ADJ แผนโบราณ traditional, old style, e.g. **nùat phǎehn
bohraan** นวดแผนโบราณ traditional
Thai massage

phǎen thîi N แผนที่ map

phaeng ADJ แพง expensive, dear,
costly

phàen N แผ่น classifier used when
counting flat objects, e.g. CDs/
DVDs, sheets of paper etc.

phàen-din wǎi N แผ่นดินไหว an earthquake

phâet N (FORMAL TERM) แพทย์ doctor,
physician

phâi N ไพ่ card(s) (game); (COLLOQUIAL)
lên phâi เล่นไพ่ to play cards

phai N ภัย danger, peril

phài N ไผ่, (more fully) **mái phài** ไม้ไผ่
bamboo

phai phíbàt N ภัยพิบัติ disaster

phai-lin N ไพลิน sapphire

phàk N ผัก vegetable(s)

phák N พรรค party (political), group

phák V พัก to stay (at, over), to rest,
stop for a while

phàk bûng N ผักบุ้ง Thai morning
glory

phàk chii N ผักชี coriander, cilantro

phàk kàat khǎow N ผักกาดขาว
Chinese cabbage

phák phàwn V พักผ่อน to relax, rest

phàk sòt N ผักสด fresh vegetables

phá-lang N พลัง energy, power (e.g.
physical energy, solar energy, wind
power, etc.)

phá-lang ngaan N พลังงาน energy

phà-lìt V ผลิต to manufacture, produce

phá-mâa N พม่า Burma, Burmese

phan พัน thousand

phan láan พันล้าน billion

phà-nàehk N แผนก division, section
(e.g. of a government department)

phá-naehng/kaehng phanaehng N

54

THAI—ENGLISH

PH

พะแนง/แกงพะแนง name of mild-ish curry (often written in English as 'panang' – apparently originating in Penang, Malaysia)

phánák-ngaan N พนักงาน employee in a department store/large enterprise

phánák-ngaan khăai N พนักงานขาย sales assistant

phá-nan V พนัน to gamble; lên kaan phá-nan เล่นการพนัน to gamble; (COLLOQUIAL) phá-nan kan mái พนันกันไหม do you want to bet?

phà-năng N ผนัง wall, (internal) partition in a building

phá-ùet-phá-om V พะอืดพะอม to feel nauseated

phang ADJ พัง (pronounced like 'hung' with a 'p' in front – 'phung') broken down, destroyed, in ruins, ruined

phanràyaa/phanyaa N (POLITE FORMAL TERM) ภรรยา/ภริยา wife

phansăa N พรรษา rainy season retreat/Buddhist Lent: khâo phansăa เข้าพรรษา to enter/begin the rainy season retreat/Buddhist Lent

phào N เผ่า tribe, ethnic group

phăo V เผา to burn, cremate, set fire (to)

pháp V พับ to fold, double over

pháp phîap V พับเพียบ sit with both legs tucked back to one side

phà-sŏm V ผสม to mix, combine

phàt V, ADJ ผัด to stir fry; stir fried

phát V พัด to fan, blow

phátlom N พัดลม fan (for cooling)

phátsàdù N พัสดุ supplies, things, stores

phát-thá-naa V พัฒนา to develop (e.g. a project); for a child to 'develop/ progress' in their ability/knowledge or understanding

phaw ADV พอ (pronounced 'pour' with a mid tone) enough; as soon as, when

phâw N (pronounced 'pour' with a falling tone) พ่อ father

phaw dii ADV พอดี just right (i.e. just the right amount), just then (i.e. 'just then someone came to the door')

phaw jai ADJ พอใจ to be satisfied, contented, to be pleased

phâw kháa N, MASC พ่อค้า merchant

phaw khuan ADV พอควร enough, moderately, reasonably

phâw mâai N พ่อม่าย widower

phâw mâeh N พ่อแม่ parents

phaw phiang พอเพียง a notion closely associated with King Phumiphon Adunyadet which refers to what is generally called in English 'the sufficiency economy' (i.e. something along the lines of self sufficiency)

phaw săw N (pronounced 'por saw') พ.ศ. Buddhist era, B.E. A year in the Buddhist era (which begins from the year of the Buddha's 'passing') is calculated by adding 543 to a given year in the Christian Era

phaw sŏmkhuan ADJ พอสมควร reasonable (price), appropriate/sufficient

phaw thii (COLLOQUIAL) พอที enough (already), stop (doing what you're doing)

phăwm ADJ ผอม thin, lean, slim

phawn N พร (commonly written in English 'porn' or 'phorn') blessing, benediction, good wishes

phá-yaa-baan N พยาบาล nurse

phá-yaan N พยาน witness

phá-yâat N พยาธิ worm, parasite (in the body)

phá-yaa-yaam V พยายาม to try, attempt, make an effort

pheh-daan N เพดาน ceiling

phêht N เพศ gender, sex

phèt ADJ เผ็ด to be hot (spicy), sharp, peppery

phét N เพชร diamond

phiang ADV เพียง just, only

THAI–ENGLISH

PH

phiang phaw ADV เพียงพอ enough, sufficient, adequate

phiang tàeh ADV เพียงแต่ only

phîi PRON พี่ older brother or sister; commonly used as a polite, somewhat deferential, second person pronoun (you) when talking with a friend, or a stranger, who is older (but often not much older), or in a position of greater power or authority

phǐi N ผี ghost, spirit, ghoul, apparition

phîi chaai N พี่ชาย older brother

phîi khoei N พี่เขย older brother-in-law

phîi náwng N พี่น้อง brothers and sisters/siblings

phîi sǎow N พี่สาว older sister

phîi sà-phái N พี่สะใภ้ older sister-in-law

phǐi sûea N ผีเสื้อ butterfly (literally, 'ghost'-'shirt')

phí-jaàránaa V พิจารณา to consider, have a considered opinion

phí-kaan ADJ พิการ to be disabled, handicapped

phim V พิมพ์ to print, publish; to write on a computer

phim dìit V พิมพ์ดีด to type (with a typewriter)

phí-nai-kam N พินัยกรรม a will, testament

phí-phít thá-phan N พิพิธภัณฑ์ museum

phísèht ADJ พิเศษ special, exceptional, particular

phí-sùut V พิสูจน์ to prove, show, demonstrate

phìt ADJ ผิด to be false (not true); guilty (of a crime); wrong (false)

phí-thii N พิธี ceremony, ritual

phìt kòtmǎai ADJ ผิดกฎหมาย to be illegal

phìt phlâat ADJ ผิดพลาด to be mistaken, to be wrong

phìt wǎng ADJ ผิดหวัง to be disappointed

phǐu N ผิว skin, complexion; surface, covering

phlâat V พลาด to be mistaken, make an error/a mistake; to miss (i.e. the bus, a target)

phlǎeh N แผล scar, cut, wound

phlàk V ผลัก to push

phlehng N เพลง song, tune

phóeh ADJ เพ้อ to ramble on, to be delirious; (COLLOQUIAL) phóeh jôeh เพ้อเจ้อ to refer to utterances that are nonsensical, way over the top, inane

phôehm V, ADJ เพิ่ม to add, increase; extra

phôehm khûen V เพิ่มขึ้น to increase

phôehm toehm ADV เพิ่มเติม further, in addition

phôeng ADV เพิ่ง just now, e.g. kháo phôeng klàp bâan เขาเพิ่งกลับบ้าน he's just gone home

phían ADJ เพี้ยน differing just a little

phǒm N ผม hair (on the head only)

phǒm PRON, MASC ผม I, me

phǒn N ผล effect, result

phǒn prá-yòht N ผลประโยชน์ benefit (which accrues to someone)

phǒn-lá-mái N ผลไม้ fruit

phǒn-sùt-tháai (EXPRESSION) ผลสุดท้าย finally, in the end

phǒng sák fâwk N ผงซักฟอก detergent

phóp V พบ to find, meet

phóp kan mài (COLLOQUIAL EXPRESSION) พบกันใหม่ see you later!

phót-jà naa-ànú-krom N (FORMAL TERM) พจนานุกรม dictionary

phrá พระ (a Buddhist) monk; (also colloquially used to refer to) Buddhist amulets, images

phrá aa-thít N พระอาทิตย์ the sun

phrá aa-thít khûen N พระอาทิตย์ขึ้น sunrise

phrá aa-thít tòk din N พระอาทิตย์ตกดิน sunset

phrá jâo N พระเจ้า, also phrá phûu pen jâo N พระผู้เป็นเจ้า God

phrá má-hǎa kà-sàt N พระมหากษัตริย์ king, monarch

phrá raa-chí-nii N พระราชินี (COLLOQUIAL) raa-chí-nii queen

phrá râat-chá-wang N พระราชวัง royal palace

phráw CONJ เพราะ (or phráw-wâa เพราะว่า) because ADJ mellifluous, to sound pleasing to the ear

phráwm ADJ, ADV พร้อม to be ready

phrík N พริก chilli, chilli pepper

phrík thai N พริกไทย pepper/black pepper

phrom N พรม carpet

phrúet-sà-jì-kaa-yon N พฤศจิกายน November

phrúet-sà-phaa-khom N พฤษภาคม May

phrûng níi N, ADV พรุ่งนี้ tomorrow

phǔa N ผัว husband (colloquial but somewhat rude, better left unsaid in polite company)

phûak N พวก group

phûak khǎo PRON พวกเขา they, them

phûang V พ่วง to trail, trailing; to be attached to (e.g. a trailer)

phuang N พวง bunch, cluster; phuang kunjaeh N พวงกุญแจ key ring/bunch of keys; phuang maa-lai N พวงมาลัย garland; also steering wheel

phûea àrai เพื่ออะไร what for?

phûea thîi เพื่อที่ in order that, so that

phùeak N เผือก taro; also cháang phùeak ช้างเผือก albino – white elephant

phûean N เพื่อน friend

phûean bâan N เพื่อนบ้าน neighbor(s)

phûean rûam ngaan N เพื่อนร่วมงาน co-worker, colleague

phúehn N พื้น floor

phúehn din N พื้นดิน ground, earth

phúehn thîi N พื้นที่ area

phûeng N ผึ้ง bee(s); náam phûeng น้ำผึ้ง honey

phút-thá sàat-sà-nǎa N พุทธศาสนา Buddhism/Buddhist religion

phûu N ผู้ a prefix meaning 'one who (is or does something in particular)'; also male, e.g. to refer to male animals tua phûu ตัวผู้; a male cat is a maeo tua phûu แมวตัวผู้

phûu aa-sǎi N ผู้อาศัย resident, inhabitant

phûu am-nuai-kaan N ผู้อำนวยการ director (of company)

phûu chaai N ผู้ชาย male, man

phûu chá-ná N ผู้ชนะ winner

phûu chûai N ผู้ช่วย assistant, helper

phûu-chûai-sàat-traa-jaan N ผู้ช่วยศาสตราจารย์ assistant professor

phûu dohy-sǎan N ผู้โดยสาร passenger

phûu fang N ผู้ฟัง (pronounced 'fung') listener (e.g. to a radio program)

phûu jàtkaan N (pronounced 'jut garn') ผู้จัดการ manager

phuu-khǎo N ภูเขา mountain

phuu-khǎo fai N ภูเขาไฟ volcano

phûu nam N ผู้นำ leader

phûu phí-phâak-sǎa N ผู้พิพากษา judge (in a court of law)

phûu thaen N ผู้แทน representative (e.g. of a company), delegate

phûu yài N ผู้ใหญ่ adult; (COLLOQUIAL) a person of consequence

phûu yài bâan N ผู้ใหญ่บ้าน village headman

phûu yǐng N ผู้หญิง woman

phùuk V ผูก to tie, fasten, secure

phuu-mí-phâak N ภูมิภาค region

phuum-jai ADJ ภูมิใจ to be proud (of accomplishing something)

phûut V พูด to speak, talk, say

phûut lên V พูดเล่น to be joking/kidding

phûut rûeang... พูดเรื่อง ฯ (to) talk about...

phûut wâa... พูดว่าฯ say/said that, used as follows: kháo phûut wâa kháo mâi sabaai เขาพูดว่าเขาไม่สบาย 'he said he (was) sick'

R

raa-chaa N ราชา king, monarch, rajah

râa-roehng ADJ ร่าเริง cheerful

ráai ADJ ร้าย wicked, evil, malicious, ferocious; **khon ráai** คนร้าย a bad person

raai chûeh N รายชื่อ list (of names)

raai dâi N รายได้ income

raai jàai N รายจ่าย expense(s), expenditure

raai-kaan N รายการ list (of names), item, particulars

raai-kaan aa-hǎan N รายการอาหาร menu

raai-kaan sòt N รายการสด (a live) show, performance

raai ngaan N, V รายงาน a report; to report

ráai raehng ADJ ร้ายแรง serious (severe), violent

râak V ราก root (of plant or a tooth); foundation; also to throw up, retch

raa-khaa N ราคา price, value, worth; (COLLOQUIAL) **raa-khaa khàat tua** ราคา ขาดตัว bottom price, lowest price, best price

ráan N ร้าน shop, store, vendor's stall

ráan aa-hǎan N ร้านอาหาร restaurant

ráan in-ter-nèt N ร้านอินเตอร์เน็ต Internet café: **ráan in-ter-nèt yóu thîi-nǎi?** ร้านอินเตอร์เน็ตอยู่ที่ไหน Where can I find an Internet café?

ráan kaa fae N ร้านกาแฟ coffee shop

ráan khǎi yaa N ร้านขายยา pharmacy, drugstore, chemist

ráan nǎng sǔe N ร้านหนังสือ bookstore

ráan sǒehm sǔai N ร้านเสริมสวย beauty parlor/salon

râang kaai N ร่างกาย body

raangwan N รางวัล a prize, reward (for the arrest of…)

râap ADJ ราบ flat, level, even, smooth

râap rûehn ADJ ราบรื่น harmonious (relations)

râat V ราด to pour (something) on (something else) (e.g. curry over rice **khâaw râat kaehng** ข้าวราดแกง)

râat-chá-kaan N ราชการ government service, the bureaucracy

râat-chá-wong N ราชวงศ์ dynasty, royal house

rábaai sǐi V ระบายสี to paint (in the artistic sense)

rá-biang N ระเบียง verandah, porch

rá-bìap N ระเบียบ order, regulations, rules

rá-bòp N ระบบ a system (e.g. of organizing/processing things)

rá-dàp N ระดับ level (standard), degree

rá-hàt N รหัส code

rá-hàt waai-faai N รหัสวายฟาย a Wi-Fi password

rá-khang N ระฆัง bell

rá-wàang ADV ระหว่าง during, between, among, while

rá-waeng ADJ ระแวง to be wary, suspicious, mistrustful

rá-wang ADJ, V ระวัง to be careful; beware (of), watch out (for)

râeh N แร่ mineral, ore; **náam râeh** น้ำ แร่ mineral water

râehk ADJ แรก beginning, start, original, first, initial

raeng N แรง strength, force, power

raeng-ngaan N แรงงาน labor

râet N แรด rhinoceros

râi N ไร่ a Thai measurement of land (1 râi = 1,600 sq m)

rái khâa ADJ ไร้ค่า worthless

rái sǎa-rá ADJ ไร้สาระ nonsense

rák V รัก to love, be fond of

rák châat V รักชาติ to love one's country, be patriotic

rák ráeh N รักแร้ armpit(s)

ráksǎa V รักษา to care for (someone who is ill); to maintain, preserve (the peace etc.)

ráksǎa khwaam láp V รักษาความลับ to keep a secret

ram V รำ (pronounced 'rum') to dance

(also commonly say **tên ram** เต้นรำ), to perform a Thai traditional dance

ramkhaan v รำคาญ to be annoyed, irritated; to be annoying

rán ADJ รั้น to be stubborn, headstrong

rang N (pronounced like 'rung') รัง nest (e.g. a bird's nest)

rang-kaeh v รังแก to bother, annoy, bully, mistreat

rang khaeh N รังแค dandruff

rangkìat v รังเกียจ to mind (e.g. someone's (bad) behavior); dislike, have an aversion (to/for)

rao PRON เรา we, I, us, me

ráo jai v เร้าใจ to encourage, arouse

raow-raow ADV ราว ๆ around (approximately)

ráp รับ to receive; to take, get; to pick someone up (e.g. from the airport)

ráp chái v รับใช้ to serve

ráp jâang v รับจ้าง to take employment, for hire; to be employed/hired (to do something)

ráp ngoehn duean v รับเงินเดือน to get/receive (one's) salary/wages

ráp phìt châwp v รับผิดชอบ to be responsible

ráp rawng v รับรอง to guarantee

ráp thoh-rá-sàp v (sàp pronounced 'sup' with a low tone) รับโทรศัพท์ to answer the phone

rát N รัฐ (pronounced 'rut' with a high tone) state (of a country), government (in the sense of 'the state')

rát-thà-baan N (the rát sound is pronounced like 'rut' with a high tone) รัฐบาล government

raw v รอ (pronounced 'raw') to wait (for, at, in, on)

ràwk หรอก a particle of speech used at the end of a statement meaning: on the contrary (to what the other party has said or expressed)

ráwn ADJ ร้อน hot (temperature)

rawng-à-thí-kaan-baw-dii N รองอธิการบดี vice president (of a college)

ráwng hâi v ร้องไห้ to cry, weep

rawng-khá-ná-baw-dii N รองคณบดี deputy dean

ráwng phlehng v ร้องเพลง to sing

rawng phôu-am-nuay-kaan N รองผู้อำนวยการ deputy director

rawng sàat-traa-jaan N รองศาสตราจารย์ associate professor

rawng tháo N รองเท้า shoe(s)

rawng tháo tàe N รองเท้าแตะ thongs, flip flops, sandals, slippers

râwp N รอบ (a) round (like a lap of the park), circuit, trip; also used to refer to the 12-year cycle (the Chinese zodiac)

râwp-râwp ADJ รอบ ๆ around (surrounding)

râwt chii-wít v รอดชีวิต to survive (e.g. a car crash)

ráyá N ระยะ interval, distance, bar (in music)

ráyá thaang N ระยะทาง distance (e.g. of a journey)

ráyá wehlaa N ระยะเวลา period (of time)

rêng v เร่ง to hurry, accelerate; (COLLOQUIAL) step on it

rêng dùan ADJ เร่งด่วน to be urgent

rew ADJ เร็ว fast, rapid, quick

rew kwàa pàkatì ADV เร็วกว่าปกติ earlier/faster than usual

rew pai ADV, ADJ เร็วไป too soon, too fast; premature

rew-rew ADV เร็ว ๆ hurry up!

rîak v เรียก to call, demand, summon

rîak chûeh v เรียกชื่อ to call (someone) by name

rîak ráwng v เรียกร้อง to urge, push for, demand

rĭan N เหรียญ a coin, dollar (initial consonant actually written with an 'r' but commonly pronounced with an 'l')

rian v เรียน to learn, study, take lessons

rian năngsŭeh v เรียนหนังสือ to go to school/college etc.

riang khwaam N เรียงความ (university/college/school) essay

rîap ADJ เรียบ even (smooth), flat, level; plain (not fancy)

rîap rói ADJ เรียบร้อย neat, orderly, tidy

rîip V รีบ to hurry, rush

rîit V รีด to squeeze, wring, put through a wringer; to iron, press

rîit sûea V รีดเสื้อ to iron (clothing)

rim N ริม edge, rim

rim fàng mâeh náam N ริมฝั่งแม่น้ำ bank (of river)

rim fii pàak N ริมฝีปาก lip(s)

rin ริน to pour (a drink)

roeh V เรอ to belch, burp

rŏeh (NOTE: this word is actually written rŏeh but commonly pronounced with an 'l' rather than 'r') เหรอ really?, is that so?; a question word at the end of a sentence (often expressed with some doubt or surprise) that seeks confirmation

rôehm V เริ่ม to begin, start, commence, initiate; also rôehm tôn เริ่มต้น to begin, start; rôehm tôn mài เริ่มต้นใหม่ to make a fresh start, begin again

rôhk N โรค disease

rôhk káo N โรคเกาต์ gout

rohng N โรง building, house, hall, shed, factory, godown (general term)

rohng lá-khawn N โรงละคร theater, playhouse (drama)

rohng năng N โรงหนัง cinema, movie house

rohng ngaan N โรงงาน factory

rohng phá-yaa-baan N โรงพยาบาล hospital

rohng raehm N โรงแรม hotel

rohng rian N โรงเรียน school

rohng rót N โรงรถ garage (for parking)

rói NUM ร้อย hundred

roi N รอย trace, mark, track (e.g. fingerprints, footprints)

roi pûean N รอยเปื้อน stain

rók ADJ รก (for a room to be) in a mess, untidy, cluttered; (for a garden to be) overgrown

rôm N ร่ม shade, umbrella

róp kuan V รบกวน to bother, disturb

rót N รถ car, automobile (wheeled vehicles in general)

rót N รส flavor, taste

rót V รด to water (plants); rót náam tôn-mái รดน้ำต้นไม้ to water the plants/garden

rót banthúk N รถบรรทุก truck

rót-dùan N รถด่วน express train: wanníi mii rót-dùan pai...mái? วันนี้มีรถด่วนไป...ไหม Are there express train to … today?

rót-dùan-phí-sèt N รถด่วนพิเศษ special express train

rót fai N รถไฟ train

rót-fai-fáa N รถไฟฟ้า skytrain (BTS)

rót fai tâi din N รถไฟใต้ดิน underground railway, subway (MRT)

rót jàk-kràyaan N รถจักรยาน bicycle, pushbike

rót kĕhng N รถเก๋ง car

rót khĕn N รถเข็น (supermarket) trolley, pram, cart (of the type used by street hawkers)

rót meh N รถเมล์ bus

rót phá-yaa-baan N รถพยาบาล ambulance

rót phûang N รถพ่วง trailer; (COLLOQUIAL) used to refer to a motobike with some sort of attached trailer/sidecar

rót-reow N รถเร็ว rapid train

rót săai níi phàan...mái? รถสายนี้ ผ่าน...ไหม Does this bus/mini bus pass…?

rót-sŏng-thăew N รถสองแถว two-row minibus

rót tûu N รถตู้ van

rót tháeksîi N รถแท็กซี่ taxi (or simply tháeksîi แท็กซี่)

rót-tham-má-daa N รถธรรมดา ordinary train

rót thua N รถทัวร์ an aircONDITIoned tour bus/coach: mii rót-thua/rót-fai

pai…kìi-mong? มีรถทัวร์/รถไฟ ไป…
กี่โมง When is there a bus/train to
…?; rót-thua/rót-fai àwk kìi-mong?
รถทัวร์/รถไฟ ออกกี่โมง What time
does the bus/train leave?; rót-thua/
rót-fai thǔeng kìi-mong? รถทัวร์/รถไฟ
ถึงกี่โมง What time does the bus/
train arrive?

rót tìt N รถติด (a) traffic jam

rót túk-túk N รถตุ๊กตุ๊ก tuk-tuk/mo-
torized trishaw (or simply túk-túk
ตุ๊กตุ๊ก)

rót tûu N (COLLOQUIAL) รถตู้ minibus/
minivan

rót yon N รถยนต์ automobile, car

rúa N รั้ว a fence

rûa V รั่ว to leak

ruai ADJ รวย to be rich, well off,
wealthy

ruam V รวม to total, add together,
join, altogether

rûam V ร่วม to live together, associate
(with), participate (in)

rûam kan V ร่วมกัน (to do/put) together

rûam phêht V (FORMAL/POLITE) ร่วมเพศ to
have sex, or sexual intercourse

ruam tháng V รวมทั้ง to include, including (e.g. service charges, etc.)
CONJ as well as

rûap ruam V รวบรวม to assemble,
gather

ruea N เรือ boat, ship

ruea khâam fâak N เรือข้ามฟาก ferry

ruean N เรือน house, home, dwell-
ing building; the classifier used for
counting (i.e. the number of) watch-
es or clocks

rûeang N เรื่อง story, record, account,
issue (as in 'there are many issues he
has to face')

rûeang lék N เรื่องเล็ก a small matter,
an insignificant thing

rûeang mâak ADJ เรื่องมาก (COLLOQUIAL)
to be fussy; someone who is hard to
please (i.e. a pain in the arse/ass); to
be picky

rúe-duu N (FORMAL TERM) ฤดู season (COL-
LOQUIAL) *see* nâa หน้า

rúe-duu bai mái phlì N ฤดูใบไม้ผลิ
spring (temperate climates)

rúe-duu bai mái rûang N ฤดูใบไม้ร่วง
autumn/fall (temperate climates)

rúe-duu fǒn N (FORMAL) ฤดูฝน rainy
season

rúe-duu nǎaw N (FORMAL) ฤดูหนาว cool
season, winter

rúe-duu ráwn N (FORMAL) ฤดูร้อน hot
season, summer

rǔeh หรือ or **rǒer** (COLLOQUIAL) question
particle that comes at the end of an
utterance asking for confirmation
(perhaps with some doubt or surprise); e.g. jing rǔeh 'is that so?/re-
ally?'. Sometimes it also serves as a
sort of jaded response to a comment/
statement made by someone else
along the lines of 'oh?', or 'oh, yeah?'

rǔeh CONJ หรือ or

rûn N รุ่น model (type), vintage;
'class' of people, e.g. the class of
2001 – those graduating from high
school in 2001

run raeng ADJ รุนแรง severe, violent

rúng N รุ้ง a rainbow

ruu N รู a hole

rúu V รู้ to know, realize, be aware of

rúu-jàk V รู้จัก to know a person/place,
be acquainted with

ruu jà-mùuk N รูจมูก nostril(s)

rǔu rǎa ADJ หรูหรา luxurious

rúu-sùek V รู้สึก to feel/sense, have a
feeling (of, that)

rúu-sùek phìt รู้สึกผิด to feel guilty

rûup N รูป shape, picture

rûup khài N รูปไข่ oval (shape – 'egg-
shaped')

rûup pân N รูปปั้น sculpture, statue

rûup phâap N รูปภาพ picture

rûup râang N รูปร่าง form (shape),
appearance

rûup thàai N รูปถ่าย photograph

rûup wâat N รูปวาด drawing

S

sà-àat ADJ สะอาด to be clean

sà-bùu N สบู่ soap

sà-daeng V แสดง to display, show; to express (an opinion)

sà-dueh N สะดือ navel, belly button

sà phǒm V สระผม to shampoo the hair

sà wâai náam N สระว่ายน้ำ swimming pool

sǎa baan V สาบาน to swear

sǎa-hàt ADJ (hàt pronounced like 'hut' with a low tone) สาหัส severe, serious, grave (condition)

sǎa-hèht N สาเหตุ cause, reason (for)

sǎa-khǎa N สาขา a branch (e.g. the branch of a bank/a particular junk food chain)

sǎa laa N ศาลา rest-house, public rest-house

sǎa laa klaang N ศาลากลาง city hall

sǎa-lii N สาลี wheat

sǎa-man ADJ สามัญ regular, common, ordinary

sǎa-mii N (polite term) สามี husband

sǎa-ràai N สาหร่าย seaweed

sáai ADJ, N (long vowel) ซ้าย left (direction)

saai N (long vowel) ทราย sand

sǎai (long vowel) สาย ADJ (to be) late N classifier for connecting things, e.g. roads, routes and telephone lines

sài V ส่าย to swing, sway, swerve

sǎai mâi wâang (long vowel) สายไม่ว่าง (for the phone) line is engaged/busy

sáai mueh ADV (long vowel) ซ้ายมือ on the left-hand side

sǎai kaan bin N สายการบิน airline

sǎai taa N สายตา eyesight

sǎam NUM สาม three

sǎam lìam N สามเหลี่ยม triangle

sǎam sìp NUM สามสิบ thirty

sǎa-mâat V สามารถ to be able to, be capable of, can

sǎn N ศาล court (of law)

sǎan jâo N ศาลเจ้า a (Chinese) temple, joss house

sâang V สร้าง to build, construct, create

sâang khwaam pràtháp jai สร้างความประทับใจ to create/make an impression

sàang mao V สร่างเมา to become sober

sâap V (pronounced 'sarp' with a falling tone) ทราบ to know (more polite/formal term than rúu รู้)

sâap súeng V, ADJ ซาบซึ้ง to appreciate, to be grateful (for); heartfelt

sàat-sà-nǎa N ศาสนา religion

sàat-sa-nǎa khrít N ศาสนาคริสต์ Christianity

sàat-sà-nǎa phút N ศาสนาพุทธ Buddhism

sàat-traa-jaan N ศาสตราจารย์ professor

sàbaai ADJ สบาย to feel comfortable/relaxed/good; sàbaai-sàbaai สบาย ๆ laid back

sàbaai dii rǔeh/mái (COLLOQUIAL EXPRESSION) สบายดีหรือ/ไหม how are you?

sàbaai jai ADJ สบายใจ to be happy, satisfied

sàdùak ADJ สะดวก to be convenient

sǎen NUM แสน hundred thousand

saeng V แซง to overtake/pass (e.g. another car/vehicle)

sǎeng aa-thít N แสงอาทิตย์ sunlight

sàep V, N แสบ to sting, smart; a stinging sensation

saew V (COLLOQUIAL) แซว to tease (someone)

sàhà-râatchá-aa-naàjàk N สหราชอาณาจักร (formal name of the) United Kingdom (COLLOQUIAL) yuu kheh ยูเค, (or more commonly) ang-grìt – i.e. England

sàhà-rát àmehríkaa N สหรัฐอเมริกา (formal name of the) United States

sài V (shortish vowel) ใส่ to wear, put on; to load; to put in, insert

sǎi ADJ ใส (shortish vowel) clear, bright, unclouded

sài phaw dii (shortish vowel) ใส่พอดี (e.g. for clothing) to fit

săiyá-sàat N ไสยศาสตร์ sorcery, magic (of the non-stage variety), supernatural arts

sàk ADV สัก about, at least, approximately

sàk N, V สัก (a) tattoo; to tattoo (someone); teak (wood) – more fully mái sàk ไม้สัก

sák V ซัก to wash, launder (clothing etc.); to question, interrogate

sàk khráng ADV สักครั้ง just this once

sàk khrûu สักครู่ (in) just a moment

sák phâa V ซักผ้า to do the washing/laundry

sák phák N สักพัก for a while

sák rîit V ซักรีด to wash and iron (clothing)

să-kon ADJ สากล international, universal, western

sà-kòt V สะกด to spell (a word)

sàk-sĭi N ศักดิ์ศรี dignity, honor, prestige

sàksìt ADJ ศักดิ์สิทธิ์ sacred, holy, revered, hallowed

sàlàk V สลัก to carve, chisel out, engrave

sàlàp V สลับ to alternate

sàlàt N สลัด salad; phàk sàlàt ผักสลัด lettuce

sàlòp V สลบ to pass out, lose consciousness

sà-maa-chík N สมาชิก member

sà-maak-hom N สมาคม society/association

sà-măi N สมัย time, period, age, era

sà-măi kàwn N สมัยก่อน in the past

sà-măi mài ADJ สมัยใหม่ modern, contemporary

sà-măi níi ADV สมัยนี้ nowadays, these days

sà-măwng N สมอง brain, mind

sà-mĭan N เสมียน clerk

sămkhan ADJ สำคัญ important, significant

sămlii N สำลี cotton wool

sămnao N สำเนา photocopy, (a) copy

sămnuan N สำนวน an idiom, idiomatic expression; style of writing

sà-mŏeh ADV เสมอ always

sămphâat V, N สัมภาษณ์ (to) interview (someone); (an) interview

sămràp PREP สำหรับ for, to, intended for

sămrawng V สำรอง to reserve (for), to have in reserve, a spare (e.g. tire); put on a waiting list

sămrèt ADJ สำเร็จ to be finished, completed, accomplished, successful V to succeed

sà-mŭn-phrai N สมุนไพร medicinal herbs

sà-mùt N สมุด notebook, exercise book

sà-mùt dai aà-rîi N (from English) สมุดไดอารี่ a diary

sà-năam N สนาม a yard, field, empty space

sà-năam bin N สนามบิน airport

sà-năam yâa N สนามหญ้า lawn

sà-nèh ADJ เสน่ห์ charm, attraction, appeal

sà-ngòp ADJ สงบ peaceful, calm

sà-nŏeh V เสนอ to bring up (topic), propose (a matter) present; to offer, suggest

sà-nùk ADJ สนุก fun, enjoyable, entertaining, to have a good time

sà-òht sà-ong ADJ สะโอดสะอง slender

sà-phaai V สะพาย carry (on the shoulder)

sà-phaan N สะพาน bridge

sà-phaan loi N สะพานลอย a foot bridge (over a road), overpass

sà-phâap N สภาพ condition (of a house, car)

sà-phái N สะใภ้ female in-law

sà-pring N (from English) สปริง (a) spring

sà-rùp V สรุป to summarize, sum up, recapitulate

sà-sŏm V สะสม to accumulate, amass,

save, collect (e.g. stamps), build up

sà-taang N สตางค์ old unit of Thai currency, money; (COLLOQUIAL) tang ตังค์ money

sà-tǎa pàttà-yá-kam N สถาปัตยกรรม architecture

sà-táat V (from English) (pronounced 'sar-tart') สตาร์ท to start (e.g. a car; also used in the broader English sense – 'the sale starts tomorrow')

sà-taehm N (from English) แสตมป์ stamp (postage)

sà-tì N สติ consciousness, mind, thought

sà-thǎa-nii N สถานี station (general term – used in conjunction with other words to form such terms as – radio station, television station, police station, space station, city bus station, etc.)

sà-thǎa-nii-khǒn-sòng N สถานีขนส่ง bus station

sà-thǎa-nii rót fai N สถานีรถไฟ train station

sà-thǎa-nii rót fai hǔa lam-phohng N สถานีรถไฟหัวลำโพง Hualampong, Bangkok's main railway station

sà-thǎa-nii tam-rùat N สถานีตำรวจ police station

sà-thǎan-nákaan N สถานการณ์ situation

sà-thǎan thîi N สถานที่ place

sà-thǎan thûut N สถานทูต embassy

sà-tháwn V สะท้อน to reflect (off the glass, the water, the window, etc.), to rebound, bounce (up, back)

sà-wàang ADJ สว่าง bright, brilliant (light)

sà-wàt-dì-kaan N สวัสดิการ welfare

sà-wìt N (from English) สวิทช์ switch

sân ADJ สั้น brief, short (concise)

sàn V สั่น to shake, vibrate, tremble

sǎnchâat N สัญชาติ nationality

sàng V (pronounced similar to 'sung' with a low tone) สั่ง to order, command; to order something

sǎngkèht V สังเกต to notice

sǎngkhom N สังคม society

sǎntì-phâap N สันติภาพ peace

sǎnyaa V, N สัญญา to promise; a contract

sǎnyálák N สัญลักษณ์ symbol, sign, token

sâo ADJ เศร้า sad, sorrowful

sǎo N เสา post, pole, column

sǎo aa-thít N เสาร์อาทิตย์ the weekend

sǎow N (long vowel) สาว young woman (COLLOQUIAL) sǎow kàeh สาวแก่ an old maid

sàp V สับ to chop, mince, e.g. mǔu sàp หมูสับ minced pork

sáp sáwn ADJ ซับซ้อน complicated, complex

sàp sǒn ADJ สับสน to be confused; disorderly

sàpdaa N (FORMAL) สัปดาห์ week

sàpdaa nâa N (FORMAL) สัปดาห์หน้า next week

sàppàrót N สับปะรด pineapple

sàt N สัตว์ animal (general term)

sàt líang N สัตว์เลี้ยง pet (animal)

sàttà-wát N ศตวรรษ (a) century

sàt-truu N ศัตรู enemy

sàwǎn N สวรรค์ heaven, paradise

sàwàt dii สวัสดี (common polite form of greeting at any time of day) hello (good morning/good afternoon, etc.); also (CASUAL/COLLOQUIAL) wàt dii หวัดดี 'Hi'

sâwm N ส้อม (a) fork (utensil)

sâwm V ซ่อม to repair, mend, fix

sǎwn V สอน to teach, instruct

sâwn V ซ่อน to hide, conceal

sâwn yùu ซ่อนอยู่ (to be) hidden

sawng N ซอง envelope

sǎwng สอง two

sâwng N ซ่อง brothel, hiding place, den (of iniquity)

sâwng kà-rìi N ซ่องกะหรี่ (SLANG – rude, better left unsaid in polite company) whorehouse

sǎwng sǎam ADJ สองสาม (COLLOQUIAL) a few

sǎwng thǎew N (COLLOQUIAL) สองแถว common term for a pick-up truck with bench seats (the name **sǎwng thǎew** means 'two rows [of seats] facing one another') in the back that is used to take paying passengers on shortish journeys – primarily found in provincial towns/cities

sǎwng thâo ADJ สองเท่า double (e.g. double the price), twice as much

sàwp V สอบ to examine, test, take an examination; to verify, inquire

sàwp phàan V สอบผ่าน to pass a test/ an exam

sáwt N (from English) ซอส sauce

sáwt phrík N ซอสพริก chili sauce

sěh-rii ADJ เสรี free, independent

sèht N เศษ remainder, what is left over, scrap(s), fraction

sèht nùeng sùan sìi N เศษหนึ่งส่วนสี่ (¼) one quarter (part of something)

sèht sà-taang N เศษสตางค์ small change

sèht-thà-kìt N (pronounced 'set-àgit') เศรษฐกิจ economy

sèht-thǐi N เศรษฐี a wealthy/rich/af- fluent man

sèht-thǐi-nii N เศรษฐินี a wealthy/rich/ affluent woman

sen N เซ็นต์ centimeter

sen V เซ็น to sign

sên N เส้น thread, line (mark), blood vessel; classifier for counting string- like things, e.g. noodles, hair

seng ADJ (COLLOQUIAL) เซ็ง to be bored, fed up (with)

séng V เซ้ง to sell, for sale; sublet

sèohp V (from English) เสิร์ฟ to serve

sèt V เสร็จ to finish (SLANG) to climax, have an orgasm

sèt láew ADJ เสร็จแล้ว (something) to be done, finished, completed, ready

sèt sîn ADJ เสร็จสิ้น over, done, com- pleted

sí ซิ a particle that is used at the end of an utterance to request/urge (with

some force) or persuade the other party do something, e.g. **pòeht thii wii sí** เปิดทีวีซิ 'come on, turn on that TV will you'; **duu sí** ดูซิ 'Look at that!/do look, will you'

sǐa เสีย ADJ to be spoiled, broken, out of order, spoiled; to have gone off (food) V to spend, pay; to be dead; to die

sǐa chii-wít V เสียชีวิต to die, pass away

sǐa chûeh V เสียชื่อ to get a bad name, spoil one's reputation, be discred- ited, look bad

sǐa daai เสียดาย to regret, be sorry; (EXPRESSION) 'what a shame', 'too bad'

sǐa jai V เสียใจ to feel sorry, regretful, be disappointed

sǐa ngoehn V เสียเงิน to waste money; to pay/spend

sǐa phaa-sǐi V เสียภาษี to pay tax(es)

sǐa sà-là V เสียสละ to sacrifice, give up (something)

sǐa tua V (COLLOQUIAL) เสียตัว (for a wom- an) to lose her virginity, to have sex the first time, to sleep with (a man)

sǐa wehlaa V เสียเวลา to waste time

sǐang N เสียง a sound, noise, tone; voice

sìang V เสี่ยง to risk, take a risk, take a chance

sìang chii-wít V เสี่ยงชีวิต to risk one's life

sǐang dang ADJ เสียงดัง to be loud, noisy

sǐao ADJ เสียว hair-raising, chilling; to feel a thrill of pleasure/pain; (sexu- ally) exciting

sìi NUM สี่ four

sǐi N สี colour, also the word for paint (Here is a list of common colors: white **sǐi khǎaw** สีขาว; black **sǐi dam** สีดำ (pronounced 'dum'); green **sǐi khǐao** สีเขียว; red **sǐi daeng** สีแดง; orange **sǐi sôm** สีส้ม; yellow **sǐi lǔeang** สีเหลือง; brown **sǐi náam-taan**

สีน้ำตาล; (sky) blue sǐi fáa สีฟ้า; (navy/royal) blue sǐi náam ngoehn สีน้ำเงิน; pink sǐi chomphuu สีชมพู; gray/grey sǐi thao สีเทา)

sii dii N (from English) ซีดี CD

sii eíu N ซีอิ๊ว soy sauce (salty)

sii eíu wǎan N ซีอิ๊วหวาน soy sauce (sweet)

sìi lìam N สี่เหลี่ยม square (shape)

sìi sìp NUM สี่สิบ forty

sǐi tòk V สีตก (for the color of clothing, for example) to run

sìi yâehk N สี่แยก (four-way) intersection

sí-kâa N (from English) ซิการ์ cigar

sìng N สิ่ง item, individual thing

sǐng N สิงห์ a lion (NOTE: this is the name of the well-known Thai beer – written in English as Singha but which is actually pronounced sǐng or, more fully bia sǐng เบียร์สิงห์ = Singha beer)

sìng khǎwng N สิ่งของ thing(s), object(s)

sìng kìit khwǎang N สิ่งกีดขวาง (a) hindrance, (an) obstruction

sìng wâeht láwm N สิ่งแวดล้อม the environment, surroundings

sǐng-hǎa-khom N สิงหาคม August

sǐngkhá-poh N สิงคโปร์ Singapore

sǐnlá-pà N ศิลปะ art

sǐnlá-pin N (commonly pronounced sǐnlapin) ศิลปิน artist

sìp NUM สิบ ten; the numbers 11–19 are as follows: sìp èt สิบเอ็ด eleven; sìp sǎwng สิบสอง twelve; sìp sǎam สิบสาม thirteen; sìp sìi สิบสี่ fourteen; sìp hâa สิบห้า fifteen; sìp hòk สิบหก sixteen; sìp jèt สิบเจ็ด seventeen; sìp pàet สิบแปด eighteen; sìp kâo สิบเก้า nineteen

sìrì mongkhon ADJ สิริมงคล (to be) auspicious, lucky, favorable

sìtthí N (commonly pronounced 'sìt' with a low tone) สิทธิ rights (e.g. legal rights)

sôh N โซ่ chain

soh faa N (from English) โซฟา couch, sofa

sǒhm N โสม ginseng

sohm V, ADJ โทรม to deteriorate, decline (of a person); (to look) run down/worn out

sǒh-pheh-nii N (POLITE) โสเภณี prostitute

sòht ADJ โสด single, unmarried

soi N ซอย lane, side street (sometimes virtually a main road)

sôi N สร้อย bracelet

sôi khaw N สร้อยคอ necklace

sòkkàpròk ADJ สกปรก dirty, filthy

sôm N ส้ม orange (citrus fruit)

sǒm hèht phǒn ADJ สมเหตุผล reasonable, sensible, logical

sǒm khuan ADJ สมควร should, worthy (of), proper, appropriate

sôm oh N ส้มโอ pomelo (a type of tropical grapefruit)

sǒmbàt N (pronounced 'som-but') สมบัติ property, wealth

sǒmbuun ADJ สมบูรณ์ to be whole, entire, complete, plentiful; healthy V to have put on weight

sǒmmút V สมมุติ to suppose, assume, hypothetical; e.g. sǒmmút wâa สมมุติว่า 'suppose (that)…'

son ADJ ซน naughty, mischievous, playful

sòng V ส่ง to send, deliver

sòng àwk V ส่งออก to export

sòng fáek V ส่งแฟกซ์ to send a fax

sòng ii-mehl V ส่งอีเมล to (send an) email

sǒng kraan N สงกรานต์ traditional Thai New Year (mid April – 13–15 April)

sǒngkhraam N สงคราม war

sǒngsǎn V สงสาร to pity, feel sorry (for)

sǒngsǎi V สงสัย to doubt, suspect

sǒn-jai ADJ สนใจ (to be) interested in

sòp N ศพ corpse, cadaver

sòt ADJ สด fresh

sòt chûen ADJ สดชื่น fresh, joyful

suai ADJ ซวย to be unlucky, accursed, (to have) bad luck; (mild expletive) Damn it!

sŭai ADJ สวย beautiful, attractive, pretty (of places, things), beautiful

sûam N ส้วม toilet, lavatory

sùan N ส่วน a portion, share, section, piece, part (not the whole)

sŭan N สวน garden, orchard, plantation, park

sùan koehn N ส่วนเกิน (pronounced 'gurn') surplus, excess

sùan nùeng ส่วนหนึ่ง partly, one part

sŭan sǎa-thaa-rá-ná N สวนสาธารณะ public garden/park

sŭan sàt N สวนสัตว์ zoo

sùan tua ADJ ส่วนตัว private, personal (e.g. matters)

sùan yài ADV ส่วนใหญ่ mostly, for the most part

sùat mon V สวดมนต์ to chant/pray (Buddhist style)

sùea N เสื่อ mat

sûea N เสื้อ (general term for items of clothing/upper garments) shirt, blouse, coat

sŭea N เสือ tiger (SLANG) bandit, gangster

sûea bai N (COLLOQUIAL) เสื้อไบ bisexual

sûea chán nai N เสื้อชั้นใน underwear/underclothing (general term)

sûea chóeht N (from English) เสื้อเชิ้ต shirt

sŭea dam N เสือดำ (dam pronounced similar to 'dum') leopard (literally, 'tiger'+'black')

sûea kák N เสื้อกั๊ก a vest, waistcoat

sûea kan nǎow N เสื้อกันหนาว coat, jacket, windcheater

sûea khlum N เสื้อคลุม robe, cloak, cape; bathrobe

sûea klâam N เสื้อกล้าม undershirt, muscle shirt

sûea nâwk N เสื้อนอก jacket, coat

sûea nawn N เสื้อนอน pajamas

sûea phâa N เสื้อผ้า clothes, clothing, garments

sûea yûeht N เสื้อยืด T-shirt, undershirt

súeh V ซื้อ to buy, purchase: khǎw súeh tǔa pai... ขอซื้อตั๋วไป... May I buy a ticket to ...?

sùeh V สื่อ to communicate

sùeh muanchon N สื่อมวลชน mass media

sûeh-sàt ADJ ซื่อสัตย์ to be honest

sùek-sǎa N, V ศึกษา education; to educate, to study

súeng ADJ ซึ่ง deep, profound

sùk ADJ สุก to be ripe, be ready (e.g. to be eaten), be cooked

sùk láew ADJ สุกแล้ว to be done (cooked)

sùksǎn wan kòeht (FORMULAIC EXPRESSION – not commonly used) สุขสันต์วันเกิด happy birthday!

sùksǎn wan pii mài (FORMULAIC EXPRESSION) สุขสันต์วันปีใหม่ happy new year!

su-nák N (FORMAL/POLITE) สุนัข dog/canine

sù-phâap ADJ สุภาพ to be polite, courteous, well-mannered

sù-phâap sàtrii N สุภาพสตรี lady

sù-rào N สุเหร่า mosque

sùt ADJ สุด end, utmost, most, -est, e.g. the tallest person – khon คน (person) sǔung สูง (tall) thîi sùt ที่สุด (-est)

sùt sàpdaa N (FORMAL) สุดสัปดาห์ weekend

sùt tháai ADJ สุดท้าย final, last

sùt yâwt (COLLOQUIAL) สุดยอด That's cool/Great!/Tops! The best!

sùu PREP สู่ to, towards

sûu V สู้ to fight (physically), fight back, oppose, resist

sùu khǎw V สู่ขอ to ask for the hand (of someone) in marriage

sûu khwaam V สู้ความ to contest a legal action

S

suu-poehmaa-ket N (from English) ซูเปอร์มาร์เก็ต supermarket

sûu róp V สู้รบ to do battle, engage in combat

sûu taai V (COLLOQUIAL) สู้ตาย to fight to the bitter end

sǔun N ศูนย์ zero, naught

sǔun klaang ADJ ศูนย์กลาง center

sǔung ADJ สูง high, tall

sùup V สูบ to smoke (e.g. smoke cigarettes sùup bù rì สูบบุหรี่); to pump (in, out, up, away)

sùut N (from English) สูท suit (clothes)

sùut N สูตร formula, method, recipe

sùut aa-hǎan N สูตรอาหาร recipe (for food)

T

NOTE: This letter should not be confused with the normal English 't' sound. It is pronounced somewhere between a 'd' and a 't', similar to the sound of the 't' in the word 'star'

taa N ตา eye; (maternal) grandfather

taa bàwt ADJ ตาบอด to be blind, sightless

taa châng N ตาชั่ง scales

taa daeng N, ADJ ตาแดง conjunctivitis; bleary eyed, red-eyed

taa tùm N ตาตุ่ม anklebone

taai V ตาย to die, pass away EXCLAM 'Oh!', 'Damn!'

taai jai V ตายใจ have implicit faith in, trust implicitly

taai tua ADJ ตายตัว to be fixed (e.g. a fixed or set price of something)

tàak V ตาก to dry, expose to the air

tàak hâehng V ตากแห้ง (to) dry out (in the sun)

tàak phâa V ตากผ้า to dry the clothing out (in the sun)

taa khàai N ตาข่าย net

taa khǎow N, ADJ ตาขาว the white of the eye; cowardly

tàak dàet V ตากแดด to expose to the sun, spread out in the sun

taa khěh ADJ ตาเข slightly cross-eyed, squint-eyed

taam V ตาม to follow, accompany; in accordance with; along

taam doehm ADV ตามเดิม as before

taam jai V ตามใจ to go along with (whatever you think/want to do); to give in to; to please, indulge (someone)

taam khoei ADV ตามเคย as usual (as expected/as he/she does habitually)

taam kòtmǎai ADV ตามกฎหมาย legally, according to the law

taam lamdàp ADV ตามลำดับ in order, respectively

taam lam phang ADV ตามลำพัง alone

taam lǎng V ตามหลัง to follow behind

taam pàkàti ADV ตามปกติ ordinarily, usually, normally

taam thîi ADJ ตามที่.... according to... (e.g. what he said)

tàang ADJ, V ต่าง each; other, different; to differ

tàang châat ADJ ต่างชาติ alien, foreign (e.g. people)

tàang dâow N ต่างด้าว alien

tàang hàak ADV ต่างหาก extra, separately (i.e. additional/extra fees apply, etc.)

tàang hǔu N ต่างหู earring(s)

tàang jang-wàt N, ADJ ต่างจังหวัด out of town; provincial

tàang prà-thêht N ต่างประเทศ overseas, abroad, international

tàang-tàang ADJ ต่าง ๆ different, diverse, various

taàraang wehlaa N ตารางเวลา timetable, schedule

taa-raang N ตาราง square (also used to refer to square meters taa-raang méht ตารางเมตร)

tà-bai N, V ตะไบ file (e.g. nail)

tà-bai lép N ตะไบเล็บ nail file

tà-bawng-phét N ตะบองเพชร cactus

tàe v (pronounced with a very short vowel sound) แตะ to touch

tàeh CONJ แต่ but, however, only; (COLLOQUIAL) tàeh wâa แต่ว่า 'but (she said…)'

tàeh kàwn ADV แต่ก่อน formerly, previously

tàeh lá ADJ แต่ละ each, every: e.g. tàeh lá pii แต่ละปี each/every year; tàeh lá khon แต่ละคน each/every person

tàehk v, ADJ แตก to be broken, shattered, cracked

tàehk là-iat v แตกละเอียด to break, shatter into tiny pieces

tàehk ngâai ADJ แตกง่าย breakable

tàehk ngoehn v (COLLOQUIAL) แตกเงิน to get change, to break (a bill)

tàehk yâek ADJ แตกแยก divided, disunited, broken apart

taen N แตน hornet

taeng N แตง melon (general term)

tàeng v แต่ง to write, arrange, compose (letters, books, music)

taeng kwaa N แตงกวา cucumber

taeng moh N แตงโม watermelon

tàeng nâa v แต่งหน้า to make up

tàeng ngaan v แต่งงาน to marry, get married

tàeng ngaan láeo ADJ แต่งงานแล้ว to be married

tàeng phlehng v แต่งเพลง to write or compose a song

tàeng tua v แต่งตัว to get dressed

tâi PREP ใต้ under, below; south

tai N ไต kidney(s)

tài v ไต่ to go up, climb (hills, mountains)

tâi din ADJ ใต้ดิน underground

tài săn v ไต่สวน to interrogate (a witness or accused person)

tâifùn N ไต้ฝุ่น typhoon

tàk N ตัก lap (i.e. 'the baby is sitting on her lap')

tàk v ตัก (pronounced similar to 'tuck' with the 'star' sound and a low tone) to draw, scoop up – tàk khâow v ตัก

ข้าว to help oneself/others to rice; to dish out the rice

tà-kawn N ตะกอน sediment, silt

ták-kà-taen N ตั๊กแตน grasshopper, locust

tà-khàap N ตะขาบ centipede

tà-khăw N ตะขอ hook

tà-khrâi N ตะไคร่ moss

tà-khrái N ตะไคร้ lemon grass

tà-khriu N ตะคริว cramp

tà-kìap N ตะเกียบ chopstick(s)

tà-kiang N ตะเกียง lamp, lantern

tà-kohn v ตะโกน to cry out, shout, yell

tà-krâa N ตะกร้า basket

tà-kraeng N ตะแกรง shallow basket used as a sieve or strainer, sieve

tà-krâw N ตะกร้อ rattan ball, kind of a Thai ball game

tà-kùa N ตะกั่ว lead

tà-làat N ตลาด market, bazaar

tà-làat hûn N ตลาดหุ้น stock market

tà-làat náam N ตลาดน้ำ floating market (the most notable being in Ratburi/Ratchaburi province)

tà-làat nát N ตลาดนัด occasional market (common in Thailand) – perhaps once or twice a week/month, etc. in different spots in a given locality

tà-làat sòt N ตลาดสด food market, market in which raw or perishable food stuffs are sold

tà-làp N ตลับ (very) small box, compact (for make-up), case

tà-làwt PREP, ADV ตลอด through, throughout, all the time, from beginning to end

tà-làwt chii-wít ADV ตลอดชีวิต for life, throughout one's life

tà-làwt pai ADV ตลอดไป forever, always, all the time

tà-làwt thaang ADV ตลอดทาง all the way

tà-lìng N ตลิ่ง bank (of a river)

tà-lòk ADJ ตลก funny, comical, ridiculous

tàm ADJ ต่ำ low, inferior, base

tam v ตำ to pound, beat (part of the word for the Northeastern Thai dish 'green papaya salad' sôm tam ส้มตำ)

tambon N ตำบล sub-district: an administrative unit in Thailand, often spelled in English as 'tambol'. In the Thai spelling the final letter is the letter 'l' but it is pronounced as an 'n'

tam-lueng N ตำลึง old Thai monetary unit, a kind of Thai plant

tam-naan N ตำนาน legend, chronicle

tam-nàeng N ตำแหน่ง position (in an organization)

tam-rùat N ตำรวจ police

tan N ตัน ton ADJ clogged up, solid (not hollow), stopped up

tâng v ตั้ง to set, place, erect, establish, settle, locate, appoint, form

tang chûe v ตั้งชื่อ to give a name to

tâng jai v ตั้งใจ to intend, pay attention

tâng sà-tì v ตั้งสติ to concentrate

tâng-tàeh CONJ ตั้งแต่ since

tâng tôn N ตั้งต้น start, beginning

tâng yùu v ตั้งอยู่ to be situated, located

tao N เตา a stove (gas/electric), a traditional-style charcoal cooker/brazier

tao pîng N เตาปิ้ง toaster

tao káet N เตาแก๊ส gas stove

tào N เต่า turtle

tâo hûu N เต้าหู้ beancurd, tofu

tao òp N เตาอบ oven

tao rîit N เตารีด iron

tào tà-nù N เต่าตนุ (sea) turtle

tàp N (pronounced similar to 'tup' with a low tone) ตับ liver (vital organ)

tàp àwn N ตับอ่อน pancreas

tà-puu N ตะปู a nail (spike)

tàt v ตัด to cut, cut off, sever

tàt phŏm v ตัดผม to have a haircut

tàt sĭn jai v ตัดสินใจ to decide, make a decision

tàw v ต่อ to extend (e.g. a visa); to lengthen; to join, reconnect (e.g. a severed limb)

taw-lǎe v ตอแหล to lie, talk a lot (COLLOQUIAL) babble, chatter

tàw pai ต่อไป next (in line, sequence)

tàw ráwng v ต่อรอง to bargain, negotiate

tàw tâan v ต่อต้าน to oppose

tàw waay-faay v ต่อวายฟาย connect to Wi-Fi

tà-wan àwk N ตะวันออก east

tà-wan àwk chĭang nŭea N ตะวันออกเฉียงเหนือ north-east

tà-wan àwk chĭang tâi N ตะวันออกเฉียงใต้ south-east

tà-wan tòk N ตะวันตก west

tà-wan tòk chĭang nŭea N ตะวันตกเฉียงเหนือ north-west

tà-wan tòk chĭang tâi N ตะวันตกเฉียงใต้ south-west

tàwm náam laai N ต่อมน้ำลาย saliva gland

tàwm náam lŭeang N ต่อมน้ำเหลือง lymph gland

tawn N ตอน part, period; episode

tâwn v ต้อน to castrate, geld, neuter, spay

tawn bàai N ตอนบ่าย in the afternoon

tawn klaang khuehn N ตอนกลางคืน at night, during the night

tawn năi ตอนไหน when?, what time?

tawn níi ADV ตอนนี้ now

tawn lăng ADV ตอนหลัง later on, subsequently

tâwn ráp v ต้อนรับ to welcome, greet, receive (someone)

tawn rôehm tôn N ตอนเริ่มต้น (at the) beginning

tawn săai N ตอนสาย late morning

tawn tîi PREP ตอนที่ as

tawn thîang N ตอนเที่ยง at noon, noontime

tawn yen N ตอนเย็น evening

tâwng AUX v ต้อง have to, must

tâwng hâam ADJ, N ต้องห้าม to be forbidden, prohibited; taboo

T

tâwng kaan AUX V ต้องการ to want, desire, must have

tàwp V ตอบ to answer, respond; reply

tàwp sà-nǎwng ตอบสนอง to respond, react

tèh V เตะ to kick, boot (e.g. a football)

tem ADJ เต็ม to be full, complete, filled up

tem jai ADJ เต็มใจ willing

tên/tên ram V เต้น, เต้นรำ to dance

tîa ADJ เตี้ย to be short, low

tiang N เตียง bed, bedstead

tiang dìao N เตียงเดี่ยว single bed

tiang khûu N เตียงคู่ double bed

tì-chom V ติชม to find fault with, find both good and bad points

tii V ตี to hit, strike, beat

tii klawng V ตีกลอง to drum

tiin N ตีน foot, paw (sometimes considered vulgar)

tiin kòp N ตีนกบ diving fins

tii phim V ตีพิมพ์ to print, publish

tii raa-khaa V ตีราคา to estimate the value/price, give an estimate; set the price (of something)

tii sà-nìt V (COLLOQUIAL) ตีสนิท to get on familiar terms, get close (to), become 'mates/buddies'; to befriend (for ulterior motives)

tìng N ติ่ง outgrowth, appendage ไส้ติ่ง appendix (body part)

tìt V (not pronounced like the English word 'tit') ติด to stick, get stuck; be addicted to; to be close to; to owe, be owed

tìt àang V ติดอ่าง to stutter, stammer

tìt kan ADJ ติดกัน next, adjoining; stuck together

tìt kàp V ติดกับ to be trapped; next to

tìt khúk V ติดคุก to be gaoled/jailed, go to gaol/jail; to be imprisoned

tìt lâo ADJ ติดเหล้า alcohol addicted

tìt lòm V ติดหล่ม to get stuck in the mud

tìt rôôhk V ติดโรค catch a disease

tìt taam V ติดตาม follow

tìt tâng V ติดตั้ง to install, put in (e.g. air conditioning)

tìt tàw V ติดต่อ to communicate with, contact, get in touch with; contagious/infectious (e.g. disease)

tìt jai V ติดใจ to like, be fond of, be attracted or impressed

tìt thúrá V ติดธุระ to be busy, tied up (with some other matter)

toehm V เติม to add, put in (e.g. petrol)

toehm náam man V เติมน้ำมัน to refuel (gasoline)

tì V ติ to criticize, blame

toh ADJ (pronounced with a long vowel sound) โต to be big, large, mature

tó! N (pronounced very short!) โต๊ะ desk, table

toh khûen V โตขึ้น to grow larger (e.g. a tree); growing up (e.g. children)

tôh tàwp V โต้ตอบ to reply to, retort, argue

tòi V ต่อย to punch, box, strike; (for a bee) to sting

tòk V ตก to fall, drop, diminish, decrease

tòk jai ADJ ตกใจ alarmed, startled

tòk ngaan V ตกงาน to be out of work, to lose one's job

tòk plaa V ตกปลา to fish

tòk rót V (COLLOQUIAL) ตกรถ to miss (a bus, train)

tòk yâak V ตกยาก to fall on hard times; to be impoverished; to suffer misfortune

tòk-long V ตกลง to agree; OK, agreed!

tòk-long tham V ตกลงทำ to agree to do something

tom N ตม bog, mud

tôm V ต้ม to boil (water); (COLLOQUIAL/SLANG) take (someone) for a ride, swindle; to be taken in, cheated (out of something)

tôm khàa N ต้มข่า mildish coconut/cream soup flavored with galangal, kaffir lime, etc.

T

tôm yam N (pronounced similar to 'tom yum') ต้มยำ a Thai (generally clear) soup with a spicy, lemony taste

tôn N ต้น classifier for trees or plants

tôn mai N ต้นไม้ plant, tree

tôn chà-bàp N ต้นฉบับ script, manuscript

tôn khǎa N ต้นขา thigh

tôn khaw N ต้นคอ neck

tôn náam N ต้นน้ำ spring (river)

tòp V ตบ to clap, slap

tòp mueh V ตบมือ to clap hands

tòp tàeng V ตบแต่ง to beautify, improve the appearance; to marry off one's daughter

tòt N, V ตด a fart; to fart, pass wind

traa N ตรา seal, stamp, chop, brand

traa châng N ตราชั่ง scale

trài trawng V ไตร่ตรอง to consider, think (something over), ponder

traeh N แตร horn, trumpet, bugle

trà-kuun N ตระกูล lineage, family

tràwk N ตรอก alley, narrow passage

triam V เตรียม to prepare, make ready

triam phráwm V เตรียมพร้อม to be prepared, ready for action

triam tua V เตรียมตัว to get ready

trong ADJ ตรง straight; accurate; direct, non-stop (e.g. flight)

trong khâam ADJ, PREP ตรงข้าม opposite (facing): trong kan khâam ตรงกันข้าม on the contrary; conversely

trong kan V ตรงกัน to correspond, coincide

trong klaang ADJ ตรงกลาง in the middle/center

trong pai khâng nâa ADJ, ADV ตรงไปข้างหน้า (go/it's) straight ahead

trong wehlaa ADJ ตรงเวลา (to be) on time, punctual

trùat V ตรวจ to inspect, examine, check

trùat sàwp V ตรวจสอบ to check, verify, test

tua N ตัว body; thing classifier for counting animals, tables, chairs and clothes

tǔa N ตั๋ว ticket (for transport, entertainment)

tua àksǎwn N ตัวอักษร letter, character (written), alphabet

tua ehng PRON ตัวเอง oneself

tua jing N ตัวจริง original, (the) genuine (article), (the) real (thing)

tua lêhk N ตัวเลข number, numeral, figure

túk-kà-taa N ตุ๊กตา doll

tua mia N ตัวเมีย female (used for animals/plants)

tua nǎng sǔe N ตัวหนังสือ letter, character (of the alphabet)

tua nóht N ตัวโน๊ต musical note

tǔa pai klàp N ตั๋วไปกลับ return ticket: khâa-tǔa pai-klàp thâo-rài? ค่าตั๋วไปกลับเท่าไร How much is a round-trip ticket?

tua phûu N ตัวผู้ male (used for animals/plants)

tua ráwn V ตัวร้อน to have a high temperature

tua sàn V ตัวสั่น to shake, tremble

tǔa thîao diao N ตั๋วเที่ยวเดียว one-way ticket

tua yàang N ตัวอย่าง example, sample

tua yàang chên ADV ตัวอย่างเช่น such as, for example

tua yâw N ตัวย่อ abbreviation

tuean V เตือน to remind, warn

tùek N ตึก building

tueng ADJ ตึง tight

tûehn ADJ ตื้น to be shallow, not deep, superficial

tùehn/tùehn nawn V ตื่น, ตื่นนอน to wake up, be awake, get up (from sleeping)

tùehn tên V, ADJ ตื่นเต้น to be excited; exciting

tù-laa-khom N ตุลาคม October

tûm hǔu N ตุ้มหู earring(s)

tûu N ตู้ cupboard, cabinet, closet, bogie (of train)

tûu e-thii-em N ตู้เอทีเอ็ม ATM machine: mii tûu-e-thii-em mái? มีตู้เอทีเอ็มไหม Is there an ATM machine around here?

tûu nâng N ตู้นั่ง passenger car (of train)

tûu-nawn N ตู้นอน sleeping car (of train)

tûu prai-sà-nii N ตู้ไปรษณีย์ letter box

tûu-sà-biang N ตู้เสบียง dining car (of train)

tûu thoh-rá-sàp N ตู้โทรศัพท์ telephone box

tûu năngsŭeh N ตู้หนังสือ bookshelf

tûu yen N ตู้เย็น refrigerator

tùut N ตูด ass, bottom, anus (vulgar)

TH

NOTE: This 'th' sound is the same as the English 't'. For example, in the words 'tie–Thai' – spelled differently, but pronounced exactly the same way

thaa V ทา to coat, paint, apply (e.g. sunscreen)

thâa CONJ ถ้า if, although; suppose

thâa ruea N ท่าเรือ harbor, port; wharf, pier

thaa sĭi V ทาสี to paint (e.g. a house, a wall)

tháa thaai V ท้าทาย to challenge, defy; to provoke

thâa thaang N ท่าทาง appearance, manner, bearing

thàai V ถ่าย to decant, pour out, discharge, throw away (FORMAL/POLITE) to defecate

thàai rûup V ถ่ายรูป to take a picture, photograph

thàai sămnao V ถ่ายสำเนา to make a photocopy

thăam V ถาม to ask, enquire

thăam kìao kàp V ถามเกี่ยวกับ to ask about

thăn N ฐาน base (e.g. military), foundation, basis

thâan PRON ท่าน (polite form of address directly to, or when talking about, a higher status individual) he, she; him, her, you; sir

thaan V (COLLOQUIAL/POLITE) ทาน to eat (also 'drink'; the colloquial equivalent is kin); donation, charity

thaan aa-hăan yen V (COLLOQUIAL/POLITE) ทานอาหารเย็น to eat dinner

thaan khâaw thîang (COLLOQUIAL/POLITE) ทานข้าวเที่ยง to eat lunch

thă-ná N ฐานะ position, status, standing

thaang N ทาง way, path, direction

thaang àwk N ทางออก exit, way out

thaang doenh N ทางเดิน aisle: khăw thîi-nâng rim thaang doenh ขอที่นั่งริมทางเดิน Can I get an aisle seat please?

thaang kaan ADJ ทางการ official, formal; phaa-săa thaang kaan N ภาษาทางการ official/formal language

thaang khâo N ทางเข้า entrance, way in

thaang lûeak V, ADJ ทางเลือก choice; alternative

thaang rótfai N ทางรถไฟ railroad, railway

thaa-rók N (FORMAL) ทารก baby, infant

thàat N ถาด a tray

thă-wawn ADJ ถาวร permanent, fixed, enduring

thaa-yâat N ทายาท heir, descendant

thá-bian bâan N ทะเบียนบ้าน census registration

thaen V, ADJ แทน to represent; to substitute (for), in place of, instead (of); tua thaen ตัวแทน an agent, a representative (e.g. of a company)

thaen thîi แทนที่ instead of

thaen thîi jà... แทนที่จะ rather than...

tháeksîi N (from English) แท็กซี่ taxi: khăw táek-sîi khâ/khráp ขอแท็กซี่ค่ะ/ครับ I need a taxi, please.

thăem V แถม to give something extra, give in addition (e.g department store giveaways that often go with purchases above a certain amount; when a vendor gives you something 'extra' when buying fruit/fish etc. in a market)

thaeng v แทง to stab, pierce, prick

tháeng v แท้ง to abort; tham tháeng ทำแท้ง to have an abortion; tháeng lûuk แท้งลูก to have a miscarriage

thǎew N แถว a row, line; area

thǎew níi ADJ แถวนี้ around here (e.g. 'where's the bike shop?' 'around here/in this area')

thá-hǎan N ทหาร soldier (COLLOQUIAL) general term for someone in the armed services

thá-hǎan aa-kàat N ทหารอากาศ airman, airwoman; (the) air force (in general)

thá-hǎan bòk N ทหารบก soldier in the army; (the) army (in general)

thá-hǎan ruea N ทหารเรือ sailor; (the) navy (in general)

thai ไทย Thai, Thailand; khon thai คนไทย a Thai person/Thai people; châat thai ชาติไทย the Thai nation; prà-thêht thai ประเทศไทย (the country) Thailand; phaa-sǎa thai ภาษาไทย (the) Thai language

thák thaai v ทักทาย to greet, say hello

thá láw v, N ทะเลาะ to argue; an argument

thá-leh N ทะเล sea

thá-leh saai N ทะเลทราย a desert

thá-leh sàap N ทะเลสาบ a lake

thâm N ถ้ำ a cave

tham N ธรรม Dharma, the Buddha's teaching, the Doctrine

tham v ทำ to do, perform an action, make, act, undergo; see tham hâi ทำให้ below – a very important aspect of the Thai language – commonly these two words go together to express the idea of 'to do (something) to/for (someone else)'

tham aa-hǎan v ทำอาหาร to cook

tham bun v ทำบุญ to make merit, perform good deeds, give to charity

tham dii thîi sùt v ทำดีที่สุด do one's best

tham dûai ADJ ทำด้วย made of/made from; tham dûai mueh ทำด้วยมือ made by hand, handmade

tham dûai mái/tham jàak mái ทำด้วยไม้/ทำจากไม้ to be made from wood/timber; wooden

tham fan v ทำฟัน go to the dentist

tham hǎai v ทำหาย to lose, mislay

tham hâi v ทำให้ to make/do something to/for someone; to cause: e.g. tham hâi khǎo jep ทำให้เขาเจ็บ to hurt him (to cause him pain/grief)

tham hâi chamrút v ทำให้ชำรุด to cause damage

tham hâi hâeng v ทำให้แห้ง to (make something) dry

tham hâi jom náam v ทำให้จมน้ำ (to cause someone – the cause, for example, being the rough sea) to drown

tham hâi lâa cháa v ทำให้ล่าช้า to delay

tham hâi mâi phaw jai v ทำให้ไม่พอใจ to offend; to offend (someone else)

tham hâi pen rûup v ทำให้เป็นรูป to form/make into (the) shape (of)

tham hâi pháeh v ทำให้แพ้ to defeat, (or, more precisely) to make (someone) lose

tham hâi phráwm v ทำให้พร้อม to make ready

tham hâi pùat v ทำให้ปวด to (make) ache/to cause (some bodily part) to ache

tham hâi ráwn v ทำให้ร้อน to heat, make hot

tham hâi sèt v ทำให้เสร็จ to complete, finish off

tham hâi yen v ทำให้เย็น to (make) cool

tham jai v ทำใจ to accept (e.g. unpleasant news), manage one's emotions/feelings; come to terms with (it); make the best of (it, a situation, etc.)

TH

tham jing-jing v ทำจริง ๆ to seriously, do (something) in earnest

tham khwaam sà-àat v ทำความสะอาด to clean

tham ngaan v ทำงาน to work, function

tham phìt ADJ ทำผิด (to do something morally) wrong

tham ráai v ทำร้าย to harm, injure, hurt; do violence to

tham sŭan N ทำสวน gardening

tham sám v (sám pronounced similar to 'sum' with a high tone) ทำซ้ำ to repeat

tham sĭa v ทำเสีย to spoil something, ruin; to break

tham sŏngkhraam v ทำสงคราม to wage war, make war

tham tàw pai ทำต่อไป v to continue on (doing something), to keep doing something

tham tua v ทำตัว to act, behave

tham tua dii ADJ ทำตัวดี to be well-behaved

tham tua hâi sà-nùk v ทำตัวให้สนุก to enjoy oneself

tham wí-jai v ทำวิจัย to research, to do research

thamlaai v ทำลาย to destroy, demolish, ruin

thamleh N ทำเล location (e.g. a good location for a business), district

thammá-châat N, ADJ ธรรมชาติ nature; natural

thammá-daa ADJ ธรรมดา ordinary, common, simple, normal, undistinguished

tham-mai (question word) ทำไม why?, what for?, what?

tham naa v ทำนา to grow rice

tham naai v ทำนาย to predict, foretell, prophesy

tham thôht v ทำโทษ to punish

tham-niam N ธรรมเนียม custom, tradition, practice; **khâa tham-niam** N ค่าธรรมเนียม a fee (e.g. for a government/offical service)

than ทัน in time (e.g. to get the bus), to have time (to do something); to catch, catch up with

than sà-mǎi ADJ ทันสมัย to be modern, contemporary

than thii ADV ทันที at once, immediately

thá-naai khwaam N ทนายความ, (COLLOQUIAL) thanai ทนาย lawyer

thá-naa-khaan N ธนาคาร bank (financial institution): **thá-naa-khaan pòeht kìi-mohng?** ธนาคารเปิดกี่โมง What time does the bank open?

thá-ná-bàt N ธนบัตร (bank) note

thà-nǎwm v ถนอม to take care of, treat with care, cherish, nurture, conserve (e.g. one's complexion, a vintage car, etc.)

thà-nǎwm aa-hǎan v, ADJ ถนอมอาหาร to preserve food; food preservation

thà-nǒn N ถนน road, street, avenue

thá nuu N ธนู bow, arrow

tháng ADJ ทั้ง all, entire, the whole of

tháng khuehn N ทั้งคืน all night (long)

tháng khûu PRON ทั้งคู่ both, both of them

tháng mòt ADV ทั้งหมด altogether, all, the whole lot

tháng prà-thêht N ทั้งประเทศ the whole country

tháng wan ADV ทั้งวัน the whole day

than jai ADV ทันใจ as quickly as desired

thanwaa-khom N ธันวาคม December

thâo ADJ เท่า as much as, the same as, equal (to), equivalent (to)

tháo N เท้า foot/feet (used for humans only)

thâo kan ADJ เท่ากัน equal (e.g. amounts of something)

thâo nán ADV, ADJ เท่านั้น just, only (used at the end of a sentence)

thâo rài (question word) เท่าไร how much? (used at the end of a sentence)

thâo thiam ADJ เท่าเทียม to be equal

tháp-phii N ทัพพี a ladle, dipper

THAI–ENGLISH

thàt pai ADJ ถัดไป (the) next, succeeding (e.g. client, government)

thátsà-ná-khá-tì N ทัศนคติ opinion, view, outlook (on particular matters), attitude

thaw V ทอ to weave

thá-waan nàk N (medical term) ทวารหนัก anus

thá-wîip N ทวีป continent

thá-yer-thá-yaan ADJ ทะเยอทะยาน ambitious

thǎwn V ถอน to withdraw (e.g. money from the bank), retract; to uproot, extract, pull out, e.g. thǎwn fan ถอนฟัน to pull out a tooth

thǎwn-ngoehn V ถอนเงิน to withdraw money

thawng N ทอง gold

tháwng N, ADJ ท้อง stomach, belly; to be pregnant

thawng daeng N ทองแดง copper

thawng samrít N ทองสัมฤทธิ์ bronze

thawrá-maan V ทรมาน to torture, punish, torment; to suffer agonizing pain

thàwt V ถอด to take off, remove (clothes, shoes)

thâwt V ทอด to (deep) fry; fried

theh V เท to pour (e.g. water out of a container)

thehp N (from English) เทป adhesive tape

thêht-sà-kaan N เทศกาล festival

thennít N (from English) เทนนิส tennis

thiam ADJ เทียม artificial (e.g. leg), synthetic

thian N เทียน candle

thǐang V เถียง to argue, dispute, bicker

thîang khuehn N เที่ยงคืน midnight

thîang wan N เที่ยงวัน midday

thîao N เที่ยว trip, journey

thîao V เที่ยว to go out for fun/pleasure; to go around; to visit

thîao bin N เที่ยวบิน a flight (a trip on an airplane)

thîaw-bin-trong N เที่ยวบินตรง direct flight

thîao diao N เที่ยวเดียว a single trip; one-way ticket: khâa-tǔa thîao diao thâo-rài? ค่าตั๋วเที่ยวเดียวเท่าไร How much is a one-way ticket?

thîao phûu-yǐng V (COLLOQUIAL) เที่ยวผู้หญิง to go whoring, for a man to go out and have sex with a prostitute/prostitutes

thii N ที time, occasion; chance, opportunity; classifier for counting the number of times

thîi ที่ PREP in, at (space) N site, place, space; that, which, the one who; portion, serve (food)

thîi bâan ADV ที่บ้าน at home

thîi din N ที่ดิน land (a piece of land)

thîi jàwt rót N ที่จอดรถ (a) carpark, parking lot

thîi jing ADV ที่จริง in fact, actually

thîi kìao khâwng ที่เกี่ยวข้อง (that which is) involved; concerning

thîi kwâang ADJ ที่กว้าง spacious

thîi lá khon (COLLOQUIAL) ที่ละคน one by one (e.g. were given a vaccination shot one by one)

thîi lá lék thîi lá nói (COLLOQUIAL) ที่ละเล็กทีละน้อย little by little, bit by bit; also (COLLOQUIAL) thii la nit ทีละนิด gradually, bit by bit

thîi láew ADV ที่แล้ว ago: e.g. sǎwng pii thîi láew สองปีที่แล้ว two years ago

thîi lǎng ADV ที่หลัง later (on), afterwards

thîi lǔea ADJ ที่เหลือ left, leftover, remaining, the rest

thîi maa N ที่มา origin, source

thîi nǎi (question tag) ที่ไหน where?

thîi nǎi kâw dâi (COLLOQUIAL) ที่ไหนก็ได้ anywhere (at all)

thîi nân ADV ที่นั่น there

thîi nâng N ที่นั่ง a seat, a place to sit

thîi nawn N ที่นอน a mattress

thîi nîi ADV ที่นี่ here

thîi nôhn ADV ที่โน่น over there

thîi phák N ที่พัก accommodation

thîi râap N ที่ราบ (a) plain, flatland, flat area

thîi rák N ที่รัก darling, dear

thîi rawng jaan N ที่รองจาน tablemat

thîi săam ADJ ที่สาม third (e.g. the third person to go, third place in a race, etc.); in Thai ordinal numbers (1st, 2nd, 3rd, etc.) are created by placing thîi ที่ in front of a given number: 1st thîi nèung ที่หนึ่ง; 2nd thîi săwng ที่สอง, etc.

thîi să-thaa-rá-ná N ที่สาธารณะ public place

thîi sìap plúk N ที่เสียบปลั๊ก socket (electric)

thîi sùt ADV ที่สุด the end, finally; -est (superlative), most, extremely; e.g. dii thîi sùt ดีที่สุด the best; rew thîi sùt เร็วที่สุด the fastest; sŭai thîi sùt สวยที่สุด the most beautiful

thîi tham ngaan N ที่ทำงาน place of work, office, etc.

thîi thŭeh N ที่ถือ (a) handle

thîi wâang ที่ว่าง (to have) room, space

thii wii N (from English) ทีวี TV, television

thîi yùu N ที่อยู่ address

thîi yùu ii-mehl ที่อยู่อีเมล email address

thiim N (from English) (pronounced similar to the English word) ทีม team

thíng V (pronounced like 'ting' with a high tone) ทิ้ง to throw away; desert, abandon

thíng wái V ทิ้งไว้ (to) leave something somewhere (with intent) (The form of use is as follows – thíng (object) wái, e.g. khǎo thíng rót wái thîi bâan phûean เขาทิ้งรถไว้ที่บ้านเพื่อน) she left her car at her friend's place

thíp N, V (from English) ทิป (to) tip (gratuity)

thoeh PRON (pronounced similar to 'ter') เธอ you (intimate)

thoehm N (from English) เทอม

school term; pìt thoehm ปิด เทอม the end of (the school) term

thohrá-sàp N โทรศัพท์ telephone

thohrá-sàp mueh thŭeh N โทรศัพท์มือถือ, (COLLOQUIAL) mueh thŭeh มือถือ mobile phone

thohrá-thát N โทรทัศน์ (somewhat formal) television

thôht V, N โทษ to blame; punishment, penalty, sentence

thŏi V ถอย to retreat, draw back; to back up

thŏi lăng V ถอยหลัง to go in reverse, back up, backwards

thòk panhăa V ถกปัญหา to discuss

thon V ทน to put up with, tolerate, bear, stand, endure

thon fai ADJ ทนไฟ fireproof

thon náam ADJ ทนน้ำ waterproof

thon thaan ADJ ทนทาน lasting, durable, sturdy

thon thúk V ทนทุกข์ to suffer

thonbùrii N ธนบุรี Thonburi, area opposite Bangkok on the west bank of the Chaophraya River. The capital of the Thai kingdom before Bangkok (**Krungthep**) assumed this role in 1782

thong N ธง flag

thong châat N ธงชาติ national flag

thót lawng V ทดลอง to try, experiment, test, give (something) a trial

thûa ADJ ทั่ว all over, throughout

thùa N ถั่ว bean(s), pea(s) (general term)

thùa daehng N ถั่วแดง kidney bean(s)

thùa dam N ถั่วดำ black bean(s)

thùa fàk yaow N ถั่วฝักยาว (long) green bean(s), stringbean(s)

thùa lantao N ถั่วลันเตา snowpea(s)

thùa lí-sŏng N ถั่วลิสง peanut(s)

thùa ngâwk N ถั่วงอก (mung) bean sprout(s)

thûa pai ADV ทั่วไป in general, generally

thûa prà-thêht ADV ทั่วประเทศ all over the country; throughout the country

TH

thûai N (pronounced 'two-ay' with a falling tone) ถ้วย cup

thŭeh V ถือ to hold something (in the hands); to believe in (e.g. a religion, faith, set of ideas); to mind (i.e. to be offended by some form of behavior, way of dress, etc.)

thŭeh sĭin V ถือศีล to keep/observe the rules/precepts (of religion)

thŭeh tua ADJ ถือตัว to be aloof, reserved; to have a high opinion of oneself

thŭeng V ถึง to reach, arrive (at), get to

thŭeng láew ถึงแล้ว to have arrived; (COLLOQUIAL) we're here (at the destination)

thŭeng máeh wâa... ถึงแม้ว่า although, even though

thúk ADJ ทุก each, every, all

thúk chá-nít N ทุกชนิด every type, every kind of

thúk khon PRON ทุกคน everybody, everyone

thúk khuehn ADV, ADJ ทุกคืน every night, nightly

thúk sìng PRON ทุกสิ่ง everything

thúk sìng thúk yàng PRON (COLLOQUIAL) ทุกสิ่งทุกอย่าง everything

thúk thîi ADV ทุกที่ everywhere

thúk thii ADV ทุกที every time, also (more commonly) thúk khráng ทุกครั้ง

thun N ทุน funds, funding, capital

thŭng N ถุง bag (i.e. plastic or paper bag)

thŭng mueh N ถุงมือ glove(s)

thŭng tháo N ถุงเท้า sock(s)

thŭng yaang (à-naa-mai) N ถุงยาง (อนามัย), (commonly) thŭng yaang ถุงยาง condom

thú-rá N ธุระ business, affairs, work, something to do; tìt thúrá ติดธุระ to be busy, tied up, engaged, occupied

thú-rákìt N ธุรกิจ business; nák thurakit นักธุรกิจ business man/woman

thú-rian N ทุเรียน durian (tropical fruit)

thút-jàrìt ADJ ทุจริต dishonest, corrupt, crooked (e.g. officials, etc.)

thŭu V ถู to rub, scrub, polish, wipe, clean (e.g. the floor)

thùuk ADJ, V ถูก to be cheap, inexpensive; to be right, correct; to touch; also used to create the passive form: e.g. he was hit by a car kháo thùuk rót chon เขาถูกรถชน

thùuk jai ADJ (COLLOQUIAL) ถูกใจ to be pleased, satisfied, content (with the outcome of something)

thùuk jàp V ถูกจับ (jàp pronounced similar to 'jup' with a low tone) (COLLOQUIAL) to be arrested, apprehended, caught

thùuk láew ADJ (COLLOQUIAL) ถูกแล้ว yes, that's right

thùuk làwk V (COLLOQUIAL) ถูกหลอก to be duped, conned

thùuk luehm V ถูกลืม (to be) forgotten

thùuk tâwng ADJ ถูกต้อง to be correct

thùuk tham laai V ถูกทำลาย (for something to be) destroyed, ruined

thûup N ธูป incense, joss stick

thûut N ทูต diplomat

U

ûak V อ้วก (COLLOQUIAL) to be sick; vomit, spew, puke

ûan ADJ อ้วน to be fat, stout

ùap ADJ อวบ to be chubby

ùat V อวด to show off, strut, flaunt

ùat dii V อวดดี to be vainglorious, put on airs

ùat kèng V อวดเก่ง to show off

ùat rúu V อวดรู้ to be a know-it-all; pretentious

ù-bàat ADJ อุบาทว์ evil, sinister

ù-battihèht N อุบัติเหตุ accident

ù-bohsòt N อุโบสถ temple, consecrated assembly hall

ùdom ADJ อุดม rich in (i.e. fertile); great, excellent

ù-mohng N อุโมงค์ tunnel

ù-thaan v อุทาน to exclaim, cry out

ùt-thá-yaan n อุทยาน garden, park, national park

ùe (pronounced very short) อี้ (COLLOQUIAL) v to defecate n poop

ueam ADJ เอือม fed up

ùehn ADJ อื่น other; khon ùehn คนอื่น other people/another person

ùehn-ùehn PRON, n อื่น ๆ others

ù-jàat ADJ อุจาด obscene, filthy, shameful

ûm v อุ้ม to carry (e.g. a baby), hold in one's arms; (COLLOQUIAL/SLANG) dohn ûm โดนอุ้ม to be illegally taken and (usually) secretly killed

ùn v, ADJ อุ่น to heat, warm

un-hà-phuum n อุณหภูมิ temperature

ùn kaehng v อุ่นแกง to warm up the curry

ù-pà-kaa-rá v อุปการะ to support, look after, take care (of)

ù-pà-kawn n อุปกรณ์ equipment, instrument, implement

ù-pà-sàk n อุปสรรค obstacle, difficulty, impediment

ù-pà-thǎm v อุปถัมภ์ patronage; support; to give patronage

ùt-jaà-rá n (FORMAL MEDICAL TERM) อุจจาระ feces, stool, excrement

ùt nǔn v อุดหนุน to support, aid, back (someone or something)

ùtsàa v อุตส่าห์ to take the trouble (to do something), make an effort (to)

ùt-sǎa-hà-kam n, ADJ อุตสาหกรรม industry; industrial

ùu n อู่ cradle; drydock, boathouse

ûu ngaan v อู้งาน to work with unnessary delay

ùu rót n อู่รถ garage (for mechanical repairs)

ùut n อูฐ a camel

W

waa n วา a linear Thai measure equal to 2 meters; taa-rang waa ตารางวา 1 square waa (or 4 sq.m.)

wâa... ว่า to speak, say, state, tell; that (introducing a spoken comment, remark, or quotation) – kháo phûut wâa kháo mâi sàbaai เขาพูดว่าเขาไม่สบาย he said that he was sick; to scold, rebuke, criticize (someone)

wáai n (from English) ไวน์ wine

wáai EXCLAM (COLLOQUIAL) ว้าย Eek!, Oh! Oh my God, etc.

waai-faai n วายฟาย Wi-Fi connection

wâai náam v ว่ายน้ำ to swim

wǎn ADJ หวาน sweet (taste); (COLLOQUIAL) pàak wǎn ปากหวาน a smooth talker who uses sweet words and flattery with another person

wàan v หว่าน to sow, cast

waang v วาง to lay (something) down, place (something somewhere)

waang jai ADJ วางใจ confident

wâang ADJ ว่าง to be unoccupied, vacant, free, available; (COLLOQUIAL) weh-laa wâang เวลาว่าง to have spare/free time

wâang ngaan ADJ ว่างงาน to be unemployed, jobless

waang phǎehn v วางแผน to lay plans; to plot, scheme

wâang plào ADJ ว่างเปล่า to be vacant, unoccupied (e.g. piece of land), empty

waa-rá-sǎan n วารสาร magazine, periodical, journal

wâat v วาด to draw, paint, sketch

wâat phâap v วาดภาพ to draw/paint a picture; to portray, depict

wâatsà-nǎa n วาสนา fortune, good luck

wáe v (pronounced very short) แวะ to stop by, pay a (quick) visit: (COLLOQUIAL) wáe pai hǎa แวะไปหา to pop in/drop by and visit (someone)

wàeng ADJ แหว่ง chipped, partly broken

wǎehn n แหวน a ring (jewellery)

wǎehn phét n แหวนเพชร (a) diamond ring

wâen taa

W

wâen taa N แว่นตา (COLLOQUIAL) wâen แว่น (eye) glasses, spectacles; wâen kan (pronounced like 'gun') dàet N แว่นกันแดด sunglasses

wái V ไว้ an important 'function' word in Thai – meaning 'to place, put; to keep, preserve, reserve'. Some examples of usage: to keep (name of object) [for the foreseeable future] kèp (name of object) wái เก็บไว้; to do something (for some ongoing/continuing purpose) tham wái ทำไว้; to leave (something somewhere for a period of time – either for a short period or for an unspecified length of time) thíng (pronounced 'ting' with a high tone) wái ทิ้งไว้: e.g. leave the bag at home (and come back and get it later) thíng kràpǎo wái thîi bâan ทิ้งกระเป๋าไว้ที่บ้าน

wǎi V ไหว to be able (to do something), capable (of doing), up to it (a job, task, doing something, etc.); (COLLOQUIAL) wǎi mǎi ไหวไหม Can you do it? Are you up to it? Can you manage it?: (to respond in the negative) mâi wǎi ไม่ไหว It's too much, I give up, I don't think I can manage (it)

wǎi-phríp N ไหวพริบ adroitness

wai N วัย age (general term used with other words to refer to a particular age demographic or grouping); e.g. wai rûn วัยรุ่น youth, adolescent(s), teenager(s); wai dèk วัยเด็ก childhood; wai chá-raa วัยชรา old age, geriatic

wâi V ไหว้ the traditional Thai form of greeting and fundamental aspect of Thai social relations – to raise the hands pressed together up to the head as a sign of respect (an indicator of the relative status/position of those interacting – a 'junior/inferior' will always 'wâi' a 'superior' – the height of the 'wâi' is a clear indicator of the social standing of the parties involved); pay homage to. The wâi is a practice that is best avoided until one has developed a good deal of familiarity with Thai society.

wái jai V ไว้ใจ to trust

wâi jâo V ไหว้เจ้า to make a spirit offering; wâi phrá ไหว้พระ to salute/pay homage to a monk; to do one's chanting (in homage of Buddhism's Triple Gems)

wan N (pronounced similar to 'one') วัน day of the week

wan aa-thít N วันอาทิตย์ Sunday

wan angkhaan N วันอังคาร Tuesday

wan duean pii kòeht N วันเดือน ปีเกิด date of birth (literally, 'day'-'month'-'year'-'birth')

wan jan N วันจันทร์ Monday

wan kàwn ADV (COLLOQUIAL) วันก่อน the day before; some days before

wan kòeht N วันเกิด birthday

wan níi ADV วันนี้ today

wan phà-rúe-hàt N วันพฤหัส Thursday (the full word for Thursday is wan phà-rúe-hàt sà-baw-dii วันพฤหัสบดี)

wan phút N วันพุธ Wednesday

wan sǎo N วันเสาร์ Saturday

wan sùk N วันศุกร์ Friday

wan thîi… วันที่ (the) date (of the month), on the (date)

wan wén wan ADV (COLLOQUIAL) วันเว้นวัน every other day

wan yùt N วันหยุด day off

wan yùt phák phàwn N วันหยุดพัก ผ่อน holiday, vacation

wan yùt râat-chá-kaan N วันหยุด ราชการ public holiday

wan yùt thêht-sà-kaan N วันหยุด เทศกาล festival holiday

wang N วัง palace

wǎng V หวัง to hope

wanná-khádii N วรรณคดี literature

wâow N ว่าว (a) kite; chák wâow V ชัก ว่าว to fly a kite (COLLOQUIAL/SLANG) to masturbate (males only)

THAI–ENGLISH

80

wát N วัด temple, monastery (e.g.Thai, Hindu-Balinese); v to measure (e.g. the length of something); **wát tua** วัด ตัว to take someone's measurements

wàt N หวัด (a) cold (i.e. to catch a cold)

wát bohraan N วัดโบราณ (an ancient) temple

wát phrá kâew N วัดพระแก้ว Temple of the Emerald Buddha in the precincts of the old Grand Palace in Bangkok

wát-sàdù N วัสดุ material (e.g. building material), ingredient

wát-táná-tham N วัฒนธรรม culture

wátthù N วัตถุ (general term similar to wát-sàdù วัสดุ above) thing, object, material (e.g. building material), substance; **wát-thù dìp** N วัตถุดิบ raw material(s); **wát-thù níyom** N วัตถุนิยม materialism

wehlaa N เวลา time, at the time; when; **tà-làwt wehlaa** ตลอดเวลา all of the time, continuously, always; than (pronounced similar to 'ton') **wehlaa** ทันเวลา (to be) in time (e.g. to catch a flight)

wehlaa wâang N เวลาว่าง spare time, free time, leisure time

wehn N เวร turn, shift, fate

wehn-kam N เวรกรรม misfortune, ill fated; (COLLOQUIAL) exclam How awful! God almighty! etc.

weh-thii N เวที a stage, ring (e.g. boxing ring)

wéhn PREP เว้น to skip; excepting; **yók wén** ยกเว้น except, excluding, with the exception of

wép sái N (from English) เว็บไซต์ website

wìang v เหวี่ยง to hurl

wian hŭa ADJ เวียนหัว dizzy

wîat-naam N เวียดนาม Vietnam

wí-chaa N วิชา knowledge; subject/ branch of study

wí-chaa chîip N วิชาชีพ profession, occupation

wí-hăan N วิหาร Buddhist assembly hall (often written in English as 'Vihear' or 'Viharn' – despite the fact that there is no 'v' sound in Thai)

wĭi N หวี comb

wii-sâa N (from English) วีซ่า visa

wí-jaan v วิจารณ์ to criticize, comment (on), review (e.g. a book, film, etc.); **nák wi-jaan** นักวิจารณ์ a (professional) critic, commentator

wí-naa-thii N วินาที a second (of time)

wínai N วินัย discipline, orderly conduct; Buddhist disciplinary rules; **mii winai** ADJ มีวินัย (to be) orderly, disciplined

win maw-ter-sai N วินมอเตอร์ไซค์ motorbike taxis

wîng v วิ่ง to run

wing wian ADJ วิงเวียน dizzy

wîng nĭi v วิ่งหนี to run away, to flee

win-yaan N วิญญาณ (pronounced 'win yarn') spirit, soul (of the dead)

wít-tha-yaa N วิทยา knowledge, science; **wít-tha-yaàkawn** วิทยากร speaker, lecturer; expert

wít-thá-yaa-lai N วิทยาลัย college; **wít-thá-yaa-lai khruu** วิทยาลัยครู teachers' college

wít-thá-yaa-sàat N วิทยาศาสตร์ science; **nák wít-thá-yaa-sàat** N นัก วิทยาศาสตร์ (a) scientist

wí-thii N วิธี way, method, means; **wí-thii chái** วิธีใช้ directions (for use, e.g. medication)

wí-thíi N วิถี path, way; **wí-thii chii-wít** วิถีชีวิต way of life, lifestyle (NOTE: the English term 'lifestyle' has made its way into Thai, pronounced something like **lai sàtai**)

wít-thá-yú N วิทยุ radio

wiu N (from English 'view') วิว scenery, view, panorama

wòht N (from English and pronounced something like 'whoat') โหวต to vote; there are also a number of Thai words for 'to vote' such as **àwk sĭang**

81

W

ออกเสียง and long khà-naehn ลง
คะแนน

wohy waai v โวยวาย to make a fuss/
make a big to do (about/over something), complain (in an animated
fashion)

wói mehl N (from English) วอยซ์เมล
voicemail

won v วน to whirl

wong N วง a ring, circle

wong dontrii N วงดนตรี (a musical)
band/group, orchestra

wong jawn N วงจร (a) circuit (e.g. an
electrical circuit)

wong klom N วงกลม (a round) circle

wong phâi N (COLLOQUIAL) วงไพ่ a circle
of card players

wong wian N วงเวียน circle (e.g. a
traffic circle), roundabout

wua N วัว cow

wún N วุ้น jelly, gelatin, agar; **wún sên**
N วุ้นเส้น glass noodles

wûn waai ADJ วุ่นวาย to be busy
(crowded); chaotic, turbulent

wùt wìt ADV หวูดหวิด almost, nearly,
narrowly

Y

yaa N ยา drug, medicine, pills; **yaa
bâa** N (literally, 'drug'-'crazy/mad')
ยาบ้า methamphetamine (type
of smokeable speed); **yaa thàai** N
ยาถ่าย (a) laxative

yàa INTERJ อย่า don't (do that)!

yâa N หญ้า grass (of the lawn variety)

yâa N ย่า (paternal) grandmother

yàa v หย่า to divorce

yàa láew ADJ หย่าแล้ว to be divorced

yaa mét N ยาเม็ด tablet(s)

yaa phít N ยาพิษ poison

yaa raksǎa rôhk N ยารักษาโรค
pharmaceutical(s)

yaa sà phǒm N ยาสระผม (hair)
shampoo

yaa sàmǔn phrai N ยาสมุนไพร herbal

medicine(s)

yaa sèp tìt N ยาเสพติด narcotic(s),
addictive drug (in Thailand this term
is used to refer to all illicit drugs
from heroin and ice to marijuana)

yaa sǐi fan N ยาสีฟัน toothpaste

yaa sùup N ยาสูบ tobacco

yaai N ยาย (maternal) grandmother

yáai v ย้าย to move (from one place
to another), transfer, shift; **yáai bâan**
v ย้ายบ้าน to move house

yâak ADJ ยาก (to be) difficult, hard (to
do, say, make, etc.), not so easy

yàak v อยาก to want, desire, need,
require; to be thirsty/hungry (adventure, sex, etc.)

yàak dâi v อยากได้ would like to get
(something), e.g. on seeing a flashy
new car a young man/woman says
'I want one/to get one of those' **yàak
dâi** อยากได้

yâak jon ADJ ยากจน poor, needy, impoverished, hard up

yàak yâi N หยากไย่ cobweb

yaam N ยาม watch (i.e. as in the military 'be on watch/guard duty'); time,
era (in a general sense); watchman,
sentry

yâam N ย่าม (a) shoulder bag (e.g. the
type of cloth shoulder bag used by
monks and, once upon a time – hip-
pies, aka freaks)

yaam dùek N ยามดึก at night; late
at night

yaam kháp khǎn N ยามคับขัน time of
emergency

yâan N ย่าน district; area, quarter (of
a city/town)

yaan yon N (formal term, rarely spoken) ยานยนต์ motor vehicle

yaang N ยาง rubber (substance); res-
in, sap, latex, tar

yàang N อย่าง kind, type, sort, variety; classifier for things

yâang v ย่าง to roast, grill, barbecue

yaang baen N ยางแบน a flat tire; also

yaang tàehk ยางแตก to have a flat tire, have a blowout

yàang dii ADJ อย่างดี good quality (e.g. material); well (e.g. makes furniture)

yàang nán ADV อย่างนั้น (COLLOQUIAL; nán pronounced like 'nun' with a high tone) (do it) like that; that's right, correct

yàang níi ADV อย่างนี้ (COLLOQUIAL) (do it) like this

yàang nói ADV อย่างน้อย at least (e.g. they should try it)

yàang prà-yàt ADJ อย่างประหยัด economical

yàang rai (question marker) อย่างไร how? (used at the end of an utterance); (COLLOQUIAL) yang-ngai (pronounced something like 'yang-ngai') ยังไง how?; (COLLOQUIAL - GREETING) pen yang-ngai เป็นยังไง how are you/ how are you doing?

yàang rai kâw taam CONJ อย่างไร ก็ตาม however

yaang rót N ยางรถ (a rubber) tire (on a vehicle)

yàang rûat rew ADV อย่างรวดเร็ว quickly, speedily

yàap ADJ หยาบ rough, rude

yàap khaai ADJ หยาบคาย to be rude, crude

yâat N (pronounced like 'yart' with a falling tone) ญาติ relatives (family)

yâeh ADJ (pronounced like 'yair' or 'yeah' with a falling tone) แย่ terrible

yàeh V แหย่ to insert, poke, tease, provoke, disturb

yâeh long ADJ แย่ลง (to get) worse

yâeh thîi sùt ADJ แย่ที่สุด (the) worst

yâehk V แยก to separate, divide, split; spread apart

yâehk kan V แยกกัน to separate, split up, divide

yaehm N (from English) แยม jam

yâeng V แย่ง to grab, snatch; scramble for; to vie/compete (for)

yài ADJ ใหญ่ large, big, great; major

(important); in charge, in command; **yài toh** ADJ ใหญ่โต very big, huge; formidable; powerful

yai N ใย filament, fiber; thread

yai maeng mum N ใยแมงมุม spider web, cobweb

yai sǎngkhráw N ใยสังเคราะห์ synthetic (thread)

yák N ยักษ์ a giant, ogre (frequently appearing in traditional Thai poetic literature and folk tales)

yák lài V ยักไหล่ to shrug

yam N (pronounced like 'yum') ยำ Thai-style spicy salad

yang ADV ยัง still, even now; not yet (as a reply)

yang dèk ADJ (COLLOQUIAL) ยังเด็ก (he/ she is) still a child/still young

yang dii ADJ ยังดี (it's) still good

yang mii... (COLLOQUIAL) ยังมี there is still some left, remaining

yang mii chii-wít yùu ADJ ยังมีชีวิตอยู่, (or, more colloquially) yang yùu ยัง อยู่ (to still be) alive

yaow ADJ ยาว long (in length); khwaam yaaw N ความยาว length

yao-wáchon N เยาวชน youth (general term – plural)

yáp ADJ ยับ (pronounced similar to 'yup') wrinkled (clothing), crushed

yát V ยัด to stuff (in, with), cram (in, with), stuffed (with)

yâw V ย่อ to abbreviate, make shorter; summarize

yaw V ยอ to flatter (somebody)

yâw tua V ย่อตัว to bow down

yáwm V ย้อม to dye, tint (cloth, hair, etc.)

yawm V ยอม to yield, give in, submit; to allow, consent

yawm hâi V ยอมให้ to permit, allow (someone to do something)

yawm pháeh V ยอมแพ้ to surrender, give up, give in (to)

yawm ráp V ยอมรับ to acknowledge, accept, agree; to admit, confess

Y

yawm taai v (COLLOQUIAL) ยอมตาย I'll never give in

yâwng v ย่อง to walk quietly, creep up, walk on tiptoes

yàwt v หยอด to drop

yâwt N ยอด summit, peak, top

yâwt yîam ADJ ยอดเยี่ยม to be excellent

yeh suu N เยซู (although this may seem somewhat odd, the name is pronounced 'yeah sue') Jesus; also phrá yeh-suu พระเยซู

yen ADJ เย็น to be cool, cold

yép v เย็บ to sew, stitch, pin; to staple

yét v เย็ด (COLLOQUIAL – EXTREMELY RUDE) to fuck

yîam ADJ เยี่ยม first rate, great, tops; yâwt yîam ADJ ยอดเยี่ยม top, superb

yîam v เยี่ยม to visit, call on, go to see (someone)

yîao N, v (COLLOQUIAL) เยี่ยว urine; to urinate, piss, pee

yìap v เหยียบ to step on, put one's foot on; yìap brèhk v (brèhk from English) เหยียบเบรค to brake, put one's foot on the brakes (of a car)

yìat v เหยียด to look down on, hold in contempt, despise, be contemptuous (of); yìat phǐu N เหยียดผิว (to be a) racist (literally, 'despise'+'skin')

yîi-pùn N ญี่ปุ่น Japan

yîi sìp NUM ยี่สิบ twenty; yîi sìp èt ยี่สิบ เอ็ด twenty one (COLLOQUIAL) yíp èt ยีบ เอ็ด

yìk v หยิก to pinch phǒm yìk ADJ ผม หยิก wrinkled/kinky/curly/fuzzy hair

yím v ยิ้ม to smile

yím yaehm ADJ ยิ้มแย้ม (to be) cheerful

yin dii ADJ ยินดี to be glad, pleased, be happy (for, to); yin dii thîi dâi rúu-jàk (EXPRESSION) ยินดีที่ได้รู้จัก 'glad to meet you'; 'it's a pleasure to meet you'

yin dii tâwn ráp (formal public type of greeting) ยินดีต้อนรับ welcome!

yìng ADJ หยิ่ง (to be) haughty, stuck-up, conceited, vain, proud, aloof

yìng ADV ยิ่ง exceedingly

yǐng N หญิง female (humans only)

ying v ยิง to shoot, fire (a gun/cannon)

yìng khûen ADV ยิ่งขึ้น more and more, increasingly

yìng yài ADJ ยิ่งใหญ่ grand, great, momentous

yóeh yáe (COLLOQUIAL) (both words pronounced with very short vowels) เยอะแยะ lots of, many (SLANG) heaps of/tons of (e.g. great music)

yôhk v โยก to rock, shake from side to side

yoh khá N โยคะ yoga

yohn v โยน to throw, toss

yôi v ย่อย to digest, crush, dissolve

yòk N หยก jade (semi precious stone)

yók v ยก to raise, lift; also a round in boxing

yók lôehk v ยกเลิก to cancel (e.g. a contract)

yók rá-dàp v ยกระดับ to elevate, upgrade, raise the level/standard (e.g. of teaching)

yók song N ยกทรง a bra, brassiere (literally, 'lift'+'shape')

yók thôht v ยกโทษ to forgive, pardon (someone/a prisoner)

yók tua yàang ยกตัวอย่าง for example, for instance; to give an example

yók wén v ยกเว้น to except, excluding, not including; exempt from

yók yaw v ยกยอ to flatter, praise

yók yâwng v ยกย่อง to praise

yót N ยศ rank (military, police); insignia of rank

yòt v หยด to drop

yú v ยุ to incite, provoke

yûa ADJ, v ยั่ว provocative; to provoke, arouse, entice; yûa yuan ADJ ยั่วยวน provocative, sexy, seductive

yùea N เหยื่อ prey, bait, victim

yùeak N เหยือก a jug, pitcher

yuehm v ยืม to borrow

yuehn v ยืน to stand, get on one's feet
yûehn ADJ ยื่น to project, stick out; to hand, offer, present
yûehn àwk maa v ยื่นออกมา to protrude
yuehn khûen v ยืนขึ้น to stand (up)
yuen yan v ยืนยัน to confirm
yûet ADJ ยืด to expand, stretch; **yûet wehlaa** ADV ยืดเวลา to prolong; to extend the time (for doing something)
yúet thǔeh v ยึดถือ to grasp hold of; to seize
yúk N ยุค time; period, age: e.g. **yúk hǐn** ยุคหิน the Stone Age
yung N ยุง mosquito
yung kàt N ยุงกัด mosquito bites
yûng v, ADJ ยุ่ง to be busy/hectic (work, etc.); to interfere/meddle (in someone else's affairs); to fool around (with); troublesome, bothersome; (COLLOQUIAL) **yàa yûng** อย่ายุ่ง 'leave it/me/alone', 'don't interfere', 'don't mess/fool around with (someone or something)'

yûng yǒehng ADJ ยุ่งเหยิง tangled up; to be in a muddle, in a state of
yú-rôhp N ยุโรป Europe
yùt v หยุด to stop, halt
yùt ná (COLLOQUIAL) หยุดนะ stop it!
yút-tì-tham ADJ ยุติธรรม to be just, fair, equitable
yùu v อยู่ to stay, remain; to live, dwell; to be alive
yùu bâan v (COLLOQUIAL) อยู่บ้าน to be at home, stay home
yùu kàp thîi v อยู่กับที่ to stay, remain
yùu kin ADJ (COLLOQUIAL) อยู่กิน, (or, more fully) yùu kin dûai/dûai kan อยู่กินด้วย/ด้วยกัน to live (together, with)
yùu pen phûean v (COLLOQUIAL) อยู่เป็นเพื่อน to keep another company
yùu trong khâam ADV อยู่ตรงข้าม to be opposite (facing) (e.g. the cinema)

Y

THAI–ENGLISH

A

abandon v (leave – a car, a girlfriend, etc.) láthîng ละทิ้ง, or simply thîng ทิ้ง

abbreviation N kham-yâw คำย่อ

abbot N jâo-aa-wâat เจ้าอาวาส

abdomen N châwng-tháwng ช่องท้อง

abduct v lák-phaa ลักพา

able to ADJ săa-mâat สามารถ

ability N khwaam săa-mâat ความสามารถ

abnormal ADJ phìt-pòk-kà-tì ผิดปกติ

aboard See 'on board'

abolish v lêrk-lóm เลิกล้ม

abort, an abortion v, N tháeng แท้ง, tham tháeng ทำแท้ง

about (approximately) ADV prà-maan ประมาณ, or raaw raaw ราว ๆ

about (regarding, concerning) PREP kìao-kàp เกี่ยวกับ, or rûeang เรื่อง (used in a meaning of 'subject/topic' for informal expression)

above, on top (of) ADV khâang bon ข้างบน

abroad, overseas ADV, ADJ tàang prà-thêht ต่างประเทศ, or mueang nâwk เมืองนอก; to be abroad/overseas—to be living abroad/overseas—either of these equally common expressions: yùu tàang prà-thêht อยู่ต่างประเทศ, or yùu mueang nâwk อยู่เมืองนอก

absence N, **absent** ADJ (not be here/there) mâi yùu ไม่อยู่, e.g. he/she is not here khăo mâi yùu เขาไม่อยู่

absent-minded ADJ jai-loi ใจลอย

absolute ADJ, **absolutely** ADV nâe-nawn แน่นอน

absorb v dòut-suem ดูดซึม

abstain (to give up something) v lóek เลิก

abstract N naam-má-tham นามธรรม

absurd ADJ rái-săa-rá ไร้สาระ

abundance N, **abundant** ADJ ù-dom-sŏm-buun อุดมสมบูรณ์

abuse v (mistreat/hurt) tham rái ทำร้าย; to abuse (verbally, to scold/berate) dàa (somebody) ด่า, or, equally common — wâa (somebody) ว่า

abyss N thá-leh-lúek ทะเลลึก

academic (an academic – a university lecturer) aajaan (pronounced like 'ah-jarn') อาจารย์; (the general term for) things 'academic' wíchaa-kaan วิชาการ

academy N rohng-rian โรงเรียน

accelerate v rêng เร่ง

accent N (when speaking) săm-niang สำเนียง

accept v yawm ráp ยอมรับ

acceptable ADJ yawm ráp dâi ยอมรับได้

access v (get access to) khâo เข้า e.g. I can't get access to the Internet khâo in-toe-nèt mâi-dâi เข้าอินเตอร์เน็ตไม่ได้

accessories N (accompanying item of dress) khrûeang-prà-dàp เครื่องประดับ

accidentally, by chance ADV dohy bang-oehn โดยบังเอิญ (COLLOQUIALLY) bang-oehn บังเอิญ

accommodation N thîi phák ที่พัก

accompany v pai pen phûean ไปเป็นเพื่อน (literally, 'go'-'be'-'friend')

accomplish, achieve v tham săm-rèt ทำสำเร็จ

accomplishment, achievement N. khwaam-săm-rèt ความสำเร็จ

according to (what he/she said) PREP taam thîi... ตามที่...

account (e.g. bank account) N ban-chii

บัญชี; an accountant N nák ban-chii นักบัญชี

accumulate v sà-sŏm สะสม

accuracy N, **accurate** ADJ mâen yam แม่นยำ

accuse v klàow hǎa กล่าวหา

accustom v khún khoei คุ้นเคย

ache (as in 'headache/toothache, etc.) N pùat ปวด

acid N kròt กรด

acne (pimple/s) N rán สิว

acquaintance (not a friend as such) N khon rúu jàk คนรู้จัก

acquainted/familiar (e.g. to be acquainted with something) ADJ khún khoei kàp คุ้นเคยกับ

acquire v dâi rian-rúu ได้เรียนรู้ (to gain knowledge)

across from... PREP trong khâam kàp... ตรงข้ามกับ

act (do) v (COLLOQUIAL) tham ทำ, or (in more formal, bureaucratic language) pàtìbàt ปฏิบัติ

action N kaan kràtham การกระทำ

active ADJ khlâwng-khlâew คล่อง แคล่ว

activity N kìt-jà-kam กิจกรรม

activist N (i.e. a social activist) nák kìt-jà-kam นักกิจกรรม

actor/actress (general term for 'performer') N nák sà-daehng นักแสดง

actual (real) ADJ pen jing เป็นจริง

actually (as in 'actually he doesn't have a car') ADV thîi jing ที่จริง

acupuncture N fǎng-khěm ฝังเข็ม

adapt/adjust v pràp ปรับ; pràp-tua ปรับตัว (as to a new environment)

add v phôehm เพิ่ม, bùak บวก (plus, i.e. +)

addict (drug) N khon tìt yaa คนติดยา

addicted v (to drugs, sex, types of food, soap operas, etc.) (COLLOQUIAL) tìt ติด

additional ADJ thîi phôehm-toehm ที่ เพิ่มเติม

address thîi yùu ที่อยู่

administer v jàt kaan จัดการ, baw-rí-haan บริหาร (manage as an administrator)

admire/praise v chom ชม

admit/confess v yawm ráp ยอมรับ

adolescent N wai rún วัยรุ่น

adopt v ráp líang รับเลี้ยง; N an adopted child bùt bun tham บุตรบุญธรรม

adorable (lovable) ADJ nâa rák น่ารัก

adore v rák mâak รักมาก

adult N phûu yài ผู้ใหญ่

adultery N (for someone to engage in adultery – an affair with a 'married' man/woman) pen chúu เป็นชู้ (NOTE: for an adulterer often just the single word chúu ชู้ is used. *Also see* entry under 'womanizer')

advance, go/move forward v kâow nâa ก้าวหน้า

advance money, a deposit N ngoehn mát jam เงินมัดจำ

advantage (benefit) N phǒn prà-yòht ผลประโยชน์; to take advantage (of someone) ao prìap เอาเปรียบ

adventure N phà-jon-phai ผจญภัย, adventurous ADJ châwp phà-jon-phai ชอบผจญภัย

advertise v **advertisement** N khôht-sà-naa โฆษณา (NOTE: this word also means 'propaganda')

advice N kham náe nam คำแนะนำ, advise/suggest v náe nam แนะนำ

aerobics (from English) N ae-rohbìk แอ โรบิกส์; to do aerobics lên ae-rohbìk (literally, 'dance'-'aerobics') เต้นแอโร บิกส์

aeroplane/airplane N khrûeang bin เครื่องบิน

affair N (as in that's 'my affair/my business'—the word for 'story' is used) rûeang เรื่อง, (for a married person to have a lover, i.e. an affair) (COLLOQUIAL) mii chúu มีชู้

affect v mii phǒn tàw มีผลต่อ

affection N khwaam rák khrâi ความรัก ใคร่

affirm/confirm v yuehn yan ยืนยัน
afford v săa-mâat mii dâi (literally, 'able'-'have'-'can') สามารถมีได้
afraid/scared, to be ADJ klua กลัว
Africa N (from English) áep-frí-kaa แอฟริกา
after CONJ lăng jàak หลังจาก; (later) ADV thii lăng ที่หลัง
afternoon N (after midday till 4 p.m.) tawn bàai ตอนบ่าย, late afternoon (4 p.m. to dusk) tawn yen ตอนเย็น
afterwards, then ADV lăng jàak nán หลังจากนั้น
again ADV (another – person, bottle of beer, etc.) ...ìik ...อีก: e.g. 'play (name of game) again' lên ìik เล่นอีก; 'can I have another bottle of beer?' khăw bia ìik khùat (literally, 'request/ask for'-'beer'-'another'-'bottle') ขอเบียร์อีกขวด
against PREP tàw tâan ต่อต้าน
age N aa-yú อายุ; to ask someone's age, i.e. 'How old are you? khun aa-yú thâo-rài (literally, 'you'-'age'-'how much?') คุณอายุเท่าไหร่
agency N (company) bawrísàt tua thaen บริษัทตัวแทน
agent/representative N tua thaen ตัวแทน (NOTE: often the English word 'agent' is used with Thai pronunciation 'a yên' เอเย่นต์)
aggression N rúk raan รุกราน
aggressive ADJ kâaw ráaw ก้าวร้าว; (COLLOQUIAL) someone looking for trouble khon hăa rûeang (literally, 'person'-'looking for'-'a story/an issue') คนหาเรื่อง; to look for trouble hăa rûeang หาเรื่อง
agile ADJ wâwng-wai ว่องไว
ago ADV thî láew ที่แล้ว; two years ago săwng pii thî láew (literally, 'two'-'year'-'ago') สองปีที่แล้ว
agony N jèp เจ็บ, pùat ปวด
agree v (with someone) hĕn dûai เห็นด้วย
agree to do something v tòk-long

tham ตกลงทำ
agreed! ADJ tòklong ตกลง
agreement N khâw tòklong ข้อตกลง
agriculture N kà-sèht-trà-kam เกษตรกรรม
ahead ADV lûang nâa ล่วงหน้า
aid v See 'help'
AIDS rôhk èhds โรคเอดส์
aim N pâo-măai เป้าหมาย
aimless ADJ mâi-mii jùt-măai ไม่มีจุดหมาย
air N aa-kàat อากาศ
air conditioned ADJ ...pràp aa-kàat (literally, 'adjust'- 'air') ...ปรับอากาศ, or (MORE COLLOQUIALLY) ae แอร์
aircraft, airplane N khrûeang-bin เครื่องบิน
air force N kawng tháp aa-kàat กองทัพอากาศ
air hostess N (COLLOQUIAL, from English) ae แอร์; the term naang fáa (literally, 'woman'-'sky') นางฟ้า is also used colloquially
airline N săi kaan bin สายการบิน
airmail N mehl aa-kàat เมลอากาศ
airport N (COLLOQUIAL) sà-năam bin สนามบิน
airsick ADJ mao khrûeang-bin เมาเครื่องบิน
aisle N thaang-doehn ทางเดิน
alarm tuean phai (literally, 'warn'-'danger') เตือนภัย; alarm clock naàlí-kaa plùk (literally, 'clock'-'wake') นาฬิกาปลุก
alcohol, liquor N (spirits) lâo เหล้า
alcoholic ADJ tìt lâo ติดเหล้า
alert v tuean เตือน, ADJ tùehn tua ตื่นตัว
alien N (as in strange, different, unusual) plàehk แปลก; alien (from outer space) má-nút tàang daow (literally, 'human'-'different'-'planet') มนุษย์ต่างดาว
alienate v hŏehn hàang เหินห่าง
alike, the same ADV mŭean เหมือน
alive ADJ yang mii chii-wít yùu ยังมีชีวิตอยู่

all ADJ (the whole lot), altogether ADV
tháng mòt ทั้งหมด

all-around ADJ râwp rúu รอบรู้

allergic ADJ (to something)/an allergy N
pháeh แพ้

alley, lane, side street N (in Bangkok,
in particular, can also refer to a sub-
stantial road) soi ซอย

alligator N *See* 'crocodile'

all-out ADJ tem thîi เต็มที่

allow/give permission V à-nú-yâat hâi
อนุญาตให้

allow V (let someone) yawm ยอม

allowed/permitted to ADJ dâi ráp à-nú-
yâat ได้รับอนุญาต

all right ADJ *See* 'okay'

almost ADV kùeap เกือบ

alone ADV (be by oneself) khon diao
คนเดียว

along ADV taam ตาม (i.e. walk along
the path), dûai ด้วย (i.e. as company)

alongside ADV yùu khâang อยู่ข้าง

a lot ADV yér เยอะ

aloud ADV dang ดัง

alphabet N àk-săwn อักษร

already ADV láew แล้ว (a term that
indicates completion); 'gone' pai láew
(literally, 'go'-'already') ไปแล้ว

although, even though CONJ thŭeng
máeh wâa ถึงแม้ว่า

also (as well) ADV dûai ด้วย: e.g. he/
she will go also/as well khăo pai dûai
(literally, 'he/she'-'go'-'also/as well')
เขาไปด้วย

alternative/choice N mii thîi lûeak มีที่
เลือก, or mii thaang lûeak มีทาง
เลือก

altogether ADV *See* 'all'

alumni N sìt kào ศิษย์เก่า

always ADV sà-mŏeh เสมอ

amateur N sà-màk-lên สมัครเล่น

amaze V plàek jai แปลกใจ

amazing ADJ (as in 'that's un-believ-
able!' 'incredible') mâi nâa chûea
ไม่น่าเชื่อ, also má-hàt sà-jan
มหัศจรรย์

ambassador, diplomat (general term) N
thûut ทูต

amber ADJ sĭi lŭeang-thawng สีเหลือง
ทอง

ambulance N rót phá-yaa-baan รถ
พยาบาล

ambush N lâwp tham-ráai ลอบทำร้าย

America N à-meh-rí-kaa อเมริกา

American N khon à-meh-rí-kan คน
อเมริกัน

among, between PREP rá-wàang
ระหว่าง

amount N jam-nuan จำนวน

amphetamine N (COLLOQUIAL) yaa bâa
(literally, 'drug/medicine'-'crazy/mad')
ยาบ้า; ice yaa ái ยาไอซ์

amputate V tàt àwk ตัดออก

amulet N (i.e. the ubiquitous Buddha
image amulets worn by many Thai
people, both male and female) phrá
khrûeang พระเครื่อง

amusement park N sŭan sà-nùk
สวนสนุก

amusing/funny ADJ tà-lòk ตลก, or
tà-lòk khòpkhăn ตลกขบขัน

analyze V wí-khráw วิเคราะห์

ancestor N banphá-bu-rùt บรรพบุรุษ

ancient ADJ bohraan โบราณ; very old
kào kàe เก่าแก่

and CONJ láe และ (pronounced with a very
short sound of 'air'), or kàp กับ
(most common and informal word)

anemia N loh-hìt-jaang โลหิตจาง

angel N naang fáa นางฟ้า (female),
the-wá-daa เทวดา (male)

anger N khwaam kròht ความโกรธ

Angkor/Angkor Wat ná-khawn wát
(literally, 'city'-[of] 'temple(s)') นครวัด

angry ADJ kròht โกรธ, also moh-hŏh
โมโห

animal N sàt สัตว์

ankle N khâw tháo ข้อเท้า

anklet N kamlai khâw tháo กำไลข้อเท้า

anniversary N khróp râwp ครบรอบ

announce V prà-kàat ประกาศ

annoy/bother V róp kuan รบกวน

annoyed ADJ ramkhaan รำคาญ

annual ADJ prà-jam pii ประจำปี

another (more) ADJ ìik… อีก…: e.g. 'another one' (as in 'another plate of food' etc. ìik jaan nùeng อีกจานหนึ่ง); a second word for 'another' is ùehn อื่น (which is used in this sense: 'another person' khon ùehn คนอื่น)

answer (response) N kham tàwp คำตอบ

answer (respond) V tàwp ตอบ

answer the phone V ràp thoh rá sàp รับโทรศัพท์

answering machine N khrûeang ràp thoh-rá-sàp เครื่องรับโทรศัพท์

ant(s) N mót มด

antenna (TV, radio) N săo aa-kàat เสาอากาศ

anthem N phleng cháat เพลงชาติ

anti- PREFIX tàw-tâan ต่อต้าน

antibiotic N yaa khâa-chúea ยาฆ่าเชื้อ

anticipate V khâat wàng คาดหวัง

antique(s) N khăwng kào ของเก่า

anus (polite/medical term) N thawaan nàk ทวารหนัก; (vulgar, common term) ruu tùut (literally, 'hole'-'arse') รูตูด

anxiety N khwaam kang-won ความกังวล

anxious ADJ kang-won กังวล

any ADJ (the equivalent of the English word 'any' is generally implied in Thai questions and responses without any specific word as such. For example, to say 'do you have any money?' is khun mii ngoehn mái [literally, 'you'-'have'-'money'-'question marker'] คุณมีเงินไหม; here there is no word that specifically means 'any', it is understood. To respond 'yes, I do' is simply mii มี which means 'have'. To answer 'no, I don't have any' you can say either mâi mii [literally, 'no'-'have'] ไม่มี or, mâi mii loei [literally, 'no'-'have'-'at all'] ไม่มีเลย. The idea of 'any' is understood, but not expressed as a word. In certain limited cases,

however, there is a Thai word that means 'any/some'. This is used in the following example, the same English question asked above but in another form in Thai: 'do you have any/some money?' khun mii ngoehn bâang mái [literally, 'you'-'have'-'money'-'any/some'-'question marker'] คุณมีเงินบ้างไหม. Here the word bâang บ้าง may be translated as 'any/some')

anybody, anyone PRON (at all) (the word kâw ก็ is pronounced very similar to the English word 'gore', but short and with a falling tone) khrai kâw dâi ใครก็ได้

anyhow, anyway ADV yang-ngai kâw taam ยังไงก็ตาม

anything ADV (at all) àrai kâw dâi อะไรก็ได้

anywhere ADV (at all) thîi năi kâw dâi ที่ไหนก็ได้

apart (from….), in addition to… PREP náwk jàak…. นอกจาก

apartment N (from English) à-páatméhn อะพาร์ตเมนต์

ape/monkey N ling ลิง

apologize to V (e.g. for stepping on someone's foot) khăw thôht ขอโทษ

apology N (e.g. 'my apologies' – on hearing of someone's serious illness/death) sà-daeng khwaam sĭajai แสดงความเสียใจ

apparently ADV yàang hĕn dâi chát อย่างเห็นได้ชัด; apparently (it seems as if…) praa-kòt wâa ปรากฏว่า

appear/become visible V praa-kòt ปรากฏ

appearance/attitude, looks N thâa thaang ท่าทาง

appendicitis N sâi-tìng àk-sèp ไส้ติ่งอักเสบ

appetizer/entrée/starter N khăwng wâang ของว่าง

applaud V pròp-mueh ปรบมือ

apple N (from English) áep-pôen แอปเปิล

appliance N (electrical) khrûeang fai fáa เครื่องไฟฟ้า

apply V (for permission) khăw à-nú-yâat ขออนุญาต

apply V (for work/a job) sà-màk สมัคร

appointment N nát-măai นัดหมาย, or simply nát นัด; to have an appointment mii nát มีนัด

apprehend V jàp จับ (to arrest), khâo jai เข้าใจ (to understand)

approach V (in space) khâo hăa เข้าหา

approach V (in time) klâi wehlaa ใกล้เวลา

appropriate/suitable ADJ màw-sŏm เหมาะสม

approve (of something) V hĕn sŏmkhuan เห็นสมควร; to approve (something) à-nú-mát อนุมัติ

approximately ADV prà-maan ประมาณ

April N meh-săa-yon เมษายน

apron N phâa-kan-pûean ผ้ากันเปื้อน

aquarium N phí-phít-thá-phan sàt-nám พิพิธภัณฑ์สัตว์น้ำ

aquatic ADJ nai nám ในน้ำ

architect N sà-tăa-pà-ník สถาปนิก

architecture N sà-tăa pàt-tà-yá-kam สถาปัตยกรรม

area N phúechn thîi พื้นที่, or bawrí-wehn บริเวณ

area code, post code N rá-hàt รหัส

Are you busy? PHR khun wâang mái? คุณว่างไหม

argue V thá lá-w ทะเลาะ (NOTE: a very common Thai term meaning 'to argue/dispute an issue/contradict/talk back' is thĭang เถียง)

argument N kaan thòk thĭang การถกเถียง

arm N khăen แขน

armpit N rák-ráe รักแร้

army N kawng thá-hăan กองทหาร, or commonly kawng tháp กองทัพ

aroma N (pleasant smell) klìn hăwm กลิ่นหอม

around ADV (approximately) raow raow ราว ๆ

around PREP (here, nearby) thăew níi แถวนี้

around ADV (surrounding) râwp râwp รอบ ๆ

arouse V krà-tûn กระตุ้น

arrange V jàt kaan จัดการ

arrangements N kaan jàt kaan, การจัดการ; to make plans waang phăehn วางแผน

arrest V jàp จับ, or jàp kum จับกุม; to be arrested dohn jàp โดนจับ

arrive/reach V maa thŭeng มาถึง, or simply thŭeng ถึง

arrogant ADJ yìng หยิ่ง, or jawng hăwng จองหอง

art N sĭnlápà ศิลปะ, or simply sĭn ศิลป์; artist sĭnlápin ศิลปิน

arthritis N rôhk káo โรคเกาต์

article N (in newspaper) bòt khwaam บทความ

artificial ADV (as in an artificial limb, or copy of a brand name product) thiam เทียม

artist N sĭn-lá-pin ศิลปิน

artistic ADJ mii sĭn-lá-pà มีศิลปะ

as ADV taam-thîi ตามที่, CONJ tawn-thîi ตอนที่

ashamed, embarrassed ADJ nâa lá-aai น่าละอาย

ashtray N thîi khìa bùrìi ที่เขี่ยบุหรี่

Asia N eh-chia เอเชีย

Asian N khon eh-chia คนเอเชีย

ask V (a question) thăam ถาม, ask about V thăam kìao kàp ถามเกี่ยวกับ, or simply thăam rûeang ถามเรื่อง

ask for, request V khăw ขอ

asleep ADJ slept V nawn làp นอนหลับ, or nawn นอน

ass/arse N (bottom) (COLLOQUIAL) tùut ตูด

assault V tham-rái ทำร้าย

assemble/gather together V rûap ruam รวบรวม

assemble, put together V (e.g. a bicycle) prà-kàwp ประกอบ

assess V prà-moehn ประเมิน

asset N sáp-sĭn ทรัพย์สิน

assist v chûai ช่วย

assistance N khwaam chûai lǔea ความช่วยเหลือ

association N sà-maa-khom สมาคม

as soon as CONJ (COLLOQUIAL) phaw พอ

assume v (suppose, imagine) sǒmmút สมมุติ/สมมติ

asthma N (medical condition) rôhk hàwp hùeht โรคหอบหืด (COLLOQUIALLY) hàwp หอบ

astonished ADJ prà-làat jai ประหลาดใจ

as well ADV dûai ด้วย

at PREP thîi ที่; at home thîi bâan ที่บ้าน

athlete N (sports person, male/female) nák kii-laa นักกีฬา

athletic ADJ khǎeng-raeng แข็งแรง

ATM (from English) eh-thii-em เอทีเอ็ม

atmosphere/ambience N ban-yaa-kàat บรรยากาศ

at night, nighttime N tawn klaang khuehn ตอนกลางคืน, or simply klaang khuehn กลางคืน

atom N (from English) à-tawm อะตอม

at once, immediately ADV than thii ทันที

at the latest, the latest ADJ lâa sùt ล่าสุด

attached file, attachment N fai thîi nâep maa ไฟล์ที่แนบมา (NOTE: the most commonly used English terms related to computers, the Internet, etc. are generally also used in Thai – the word 'file', for example, is fai ไฟล์)

attack v (in war) johm tii โจมตี

attack v (with words) dàa wâa ด่าว่า

attain, reach, arrive v thǔeng ถึง

attempt N khwaam phá-yaa-yaam ความพยายาม

attempt/try v phá-yaa-yaam พยายาม

attend v (a party/meeting, etc.) khâo rûam เข้าร่วม

attire N chút ชุด

attitude N (opinion – formal) thàt sà ná khá tì ทัศนคติ

attorney N thá-naai-khwaam ทนายความ

attractive ADJ (appealing to the eye) nâ dueng dùut น่าดึงดูด

aubergine/eggplant N má-khǔea มะเขือ

auction v (to tender) prà-muun ประมูล

auction off v prà-muun khǎai ประมูลขาย

audience N (looking at a performance) phûu chom ผู้ชม, or phûu fang (listening to a radio broadcast, etc.) ผู้ฟัง

August N sǐng-hǎa-khom สิงหาคม

aunt N (elder sister of mother or father) pâa ป้า

aunt N (mother's younger sister) náa น้า (also 'uncle' – mother's younger brother)

aunt N (father's younger sister) aa อา (also 'uncle' – father's younger brother)

aunt N (respectful address to a mature lady) khun pâa คุณป้า

Australia N áwt sà treh lia ออสเตรเลีย

Australian N khon áwt sà treh lia คนออสเตรเลีย

authentic ADJ tháe แท้, jing จริง

author N See 'writer'

authority N (official) jâo nâa thîi เจ้าหน้าที่

authority N (power) amnâat อำนาจ

autograph N laai sen ลายเซ็น

automatic ADJ àt-tà-noh-mát อัตโนมัติ

automobile/car N rót yon รถยนต์; sedan rót kěng รถเก๋ง

autumn N rúeduu bai mái rûang ฤดูใบไม้ร่วง

available ADJ, to have v (e.g. to sell/rent) mii มี

available, to make v jàt hâi mii... จัดให้มี...

avenue N thà-nǒn ถนน

average N (numbers) chàlìa เฉลี่ย

average, to feel v (so-so, just OK) yang-ngán ยังงั้น

avoid v lìik-lîang หลีกเลี่ยง

awake ADJ (to have woken up) tùehn láew ตื่นแล้ว

awaken v tùehn ตื่น

aware ADJ rúu tua รู้ตัว

awareness N khwaam rúp rúu ความ รับรู้

away ADV: either the same word as 'go' pai ไป or 'leave' jàak pai จากไป

awesome ADJ sùt-yâwt สุดยอด

awful N nâa-klua น่ากลัว, yâe-mâak แย่มาก (badly)

awkward ADJ ùeht-àt-jai อึดอัดใจ

ax, axe N khwǎan ขวาน

B

babble v phûut phlâam พูดพล่าม

baby N thaa-rók ทารก (generally used in formal or written language; colloquially the term lûuk ลูก is used. This word is also used to refer to one's own or somebody else's children no matter their age)

babysitter N phîi lîang dèk พี่เลี้ยงเด็ก

back N (part of body) lǎng หลัง

back, rear ADJ lǎng หลัง

back, to go ADV klàp pai กลับไป

backache N pùat lǎng ปวดหลัง

backbone N krà-dùuk-sǎn-lǎng กระดูก สันหลัง

background N khwam-pen-maa ความ เป็นมา

back up/reverse v thǒi pai ถอยไป

backpack N (bag) pêh เป้

backward ADV thǒi lǎng ถอยหลัง

bad ADJ lehw เลว, bad (e.g. food that has gone off) sǐa เสีย; no good mâi dii ไม่ดี; awful/terrible/atrocious (e.g. person, film, situation) yâeh แย่

bad luck N (unlucky, accursed) suai ซวย, (alternatively) chôhk ráai โชคร้าย

bag N (paper or plastic) thǔng ถุง

bag N (general term for bags; also used for 'pocket' in a garment) krà-pǎo กระ เป๋า; bag (suitcase) krà-pǎo doehn thaang กระเป๋าเดินทาง

bake v (to be baked) òp อบ

balance N sǒm-dun สมดุล (NOTE: the English word 'balance' is often used with Thai pronunciation, something like baa láan บาลานซ์)

balcony, verandah N rá biang ระเบียง

bald ADJ hǔa láan (literally, 'head'-'million') หัวล้าน

ball N bawn บอล (also the common colloquial word used to refer to foot-ball/soccer)

balloon N lûuk pòhng ลูกโป่ง

bamboo N mái phài ไม้ไผ่

ban v hâam ห้าม

banana N klûai กล้วย

band N (of musicians) wong don-trii วง ดนตรี

bandage N phâa phan phlǎeh ผ้าพัน แผล

Bangkok N krung-thêp กรุงเทพฯ

bank N (financial institution) thá-naa-khaan ธนาคาร

bank N (of river) rim fàng mâeh náam ริมฝั่งแม่น้ำ

bank account N banchii thá-naa-khaan บัญชีธนาคาร

banknote N See 'note'

bankrupt, to go N (a business) lóm lá-laai ล้มละลาย (COLLOQUIAL) jéng เจ๊ง (NOTE: this is also used as a slang term meaning to be 'broken/worn out' as in 'my mobile/cell phone is broken')

banquet N ngaan líang งานเลี้ยง

bar N (serving drinks) baa บาร์

barber N châang tat phǒm ช่างตัดผม

barefoot ADJ tháo plào เท้าเปล่า

barely ADV nói mâak น้อยมาก

bargain v tàw rawng ต่อรอง

bark (dog bark) v hào เห่า; to howl hǎwn หอน

barren ADJ (arid, dry environment) hâeng-láeng แห้งแล้ง

barrier N sìng-kìit-khwǎang สิ่ง กีดขวาง, ùp-pà-sàk อุปสรรค

base, foundation N thǎan ฐาน; military base thǎan tháp ฐานทัพ

basic ADJ (the beginning level, elementary) bûeang tôn เบื้องต้น, or phúen-thǎan พื้นฐาน

basis N thǎan ฐาน

basket N tà-krâa ตะกร้า

basketball N (from English) báat-sàkèht-bawn บาสเก็ตบอล, (COLLOQUIAL) báat บาส

bastard (as in 'you bastard!' – the term given here is, in fact, considerably stronger and far more vulgar in meaning so you can use your imagination) âi-hîa ไอ้เหี้ย

bat N (animal) kháang-khaow ค้างคาว

bathe/take a bath/have a wash V àap náam อาบน้ำ

bathrobe N sûea khlum àap náam เสื้อคลุมอาบน้ำ

bathroom N hâwng náam ห้องน้ำ

bathtub N àang àap náam อ่างอาบน้ำ

battery N thàan ถ่าน, or (from English) bàet-toeh-rîi แบตเตอรี่ (COLLOQUIALLY) bàet แบต

battle N kaan sûu róp การสู้รบ

bay (or gulf) N àow อ่าว (NOTE: the 'Gulf of Thailand' is àow thai อ่าวไทย)

be (at) V yùu thîi อยู่ที่

beach N chaai hàat ชายหาด

bean(s) N thùa ถั่ว

beancurd N tâo hûu เต้าหู้

bear N mǐi หมี

beard N khrao เครา

beat N (to defeat) ao cháná เอาชนะ

beat V (to strike) tii ตี

beat N (as in music, rhythm) jang-wà จังหวะ

beautiful ADJ (in appearance) sǔai สวย

beauty parlor/beauty salon N ráan sǒehm sǔai (literally, 'shop/store'-'enhance'-'beauty') ร้านเสริมสวย

because CONJ phráw wâa เพราะว่า, or simply phráw เพราะ

become V klaai pen กลายเป็น

bed N tiang เตียง

bedbug N rûet เรือด

bedding, bedclothes N khrûeang nawn เครื่องนอน

bedroom N hâwng nawn ห้องนอน

bedsheet N phâa puu thîi nawn ผ้าปูที่นอน

bee N phûeng ผึ้ง

beef, meat/flesh N (in general) núea เนื้อ (NOTE: also common slang word for marijuana)

beehive N rang phûeng รังผึ้ง

beer N bia เบียร์

before PREP (in front of) khâang nâa ข้างหน้า

before ADV (in time) kàwn ก่อน

beg V khǎw ráwng ขอร้อง

beggar N khǎw-thaan (literally, 're-quest'-'things given') ขอทาน

begin V rôehm เริ่ม

beginning N tawn rôehm tôn ตอนเริ่มต้น; (COLLOQUIAL) in the beginning/at first tawn râehk ตอนแรก

behave V (FORMAL) prà-phrúet ประพฤติ; behavior N khwaam prà-phrúet ความประพฤติ

behind PREP (location) khâang lǎng ข้างหลัง

belated ADJ lâa cháa ล่าช้า

belief, faith N khwaam chûea ความเชื่อ

believe V chûea เชื่อ

bell N rá khang ระฆัง, krà ding กระดิ่ง (i.e. bicycle bell)

bellboy N phá-nák-ngaan yók-krà-pǎo พนักงานยกกระเป๋า

belly N (stomach) tháwng ท้อง (NOTE: also the general way of referring to a woman falling pregnant/being pregnant

belongings N (personal) khǎwng sùan tua ของส่วนตัว, (COLLOQUIAL) khǎow khǎwng (literally, 'rice/food'-'things') ข้าวของ

belong to V pen khǎwng เป็นของ: e.g. 'it belongs to him/it's his' pen khǎwng khǎo (literally, 'belong'-'him') เป็นของเขา

below, downstairs, beneath PREP khâang lâang ข้างล่าง

belt N khěm khàt เข็มขัด; safety belt/

seatbelt (in a car) N khěm khàt níráphai เข็มขัดนิรภัย

beneficial ADJ mii prà-yòht มีประโยชน์

benefit N phǒn-prà-yòht ผลประโยชน์

beside PREP khâang ข้าง, or khâang khâang ข้าง ๆ

besides ADV (in addition, apart from) nâwk jàak… นอกจาก

best ADJ (i.e the best) dii thîi sùt ดีที่สุด

best wishes dûai khwaam pràat-thǎ-nǎa dii ด้วยความปรารถนาดี

bet/gamble V lên kaan phá-nan เล่นการพนัน, or simply lên phá-nan เล่นพนัน

betel nut N màak หมาก

betray V hàk lǎng หักหลัง

better ADJ (than something else) dii kwàa ดีกว่า

better, to get ADJ (improve) dii khûen ดีขึ้น, (from an illness) khôi yang chûa ค่อยยังชั่ว

between PREP rá-wàang ระหว่าง

beverage (refreshment) N khrûeng-dùehm เครื่องดื่ม

bias N à-khá-tì อคติ

Bible N (Christian) phrá kham-phii พระคัมภีร์

bicycle N (rót) jàk-krà-yaan (รถ) จักรยาน

big ADJ yài ใหญ่

bikini N (from English) chút bì-kì-nîi ชุดบิกินี

bill N (as in a restaurant – from English) bin บิล Also see under the entry 'pay'

billion ADJ phan láan (literally, 'thousand'-'million') พันล้าน

billionaire N sèht-thǐi phan láan เศรษฐีพันล้าน (the word sèht-thǐi เศรษฐี means a 'wealthy man')

bind V phùuk ผูก, mát มัด

binoculars N klâwng sǎwng taa กล้องสองตา

biology N chii-wá-wít-thá-yaa ชีววิทยา

bird N nók นก

birth, to give V khlâwt lûuk คลอดลูก

birth certificate N sǔu-ti-bàt สูติบัตร

birth control pill N See 'contraceptive pill'

birthday N wan kòeht (pronounced like 'one gurt') วันเกิด

birthplace N thîi kòeht ที่เกิด

biscuit N (sweet, cookie) (from English) khúk-kîi คุกกี้

bit N (just a bit, a little bit) nít nòi นิดหน่อย

bite V kàt กัด

bitter (taste) ADJ khǒm ขม

black ADJ sǐi dam สีดำ

black beans N thùa dam ถั่วดำ (also part of a Thai slang expression meaning gay 'anal sex' àt thùa dam อัดถั่วดำ, àt อัด = 'stuff/compress')

black eye N taa chám ตาช้ำ

black magic N See 'voodoo'

blackout, faint N pen lom เป็นลม

bladder N krà-páw phàt-sǎa-wá กระเพาะปัสสาวะ

blame V thôht โทษ

bland/tasteless ADJ jùeht จืด

blanket N phâa hòm ผ้าห่ม

bleed V sǐa lûeat (literally, 'lose'-'blood') เสียเลือด

blemish N (flaw e.g. in a jewel, a person's complexion) tam nì ตำหนิ

blend/mix V (a drink) phàsǒm ผสม

bless V ouai phawn อวยพร

blind N (person) taa bàwt ตาบอด

blink V krà phríp taa กะพริบตา

blog N/V (from English) bláwk บล็อก

blood N lûeat เลือด

blood group N mùu lûeat หมู่เลือด

blood pressure N khwaam dan lûeat ความดันเลือด, (COLLOQUIALLY, SIMPLY) khwaam dan ความดัน (NOTE: 'high blood pressure' is khwaam dan sǔung ความดันสูง; 'low blood pressure' khwaam dan tàm ความดันต่ำ)

blood test N kaan trùat lûeat การตรวจเลือด

blossom N dàwk-mái baan ดอกไม้บาน

blouse N sûea sà trii เสื้อสตรี

ENGLISH–THAI

blow v (the wind) phát พัด

blue ADJ (sky blue) sĭi fáa สีฟ้า *Also see* 'navy blue'

blunt ADJ (not sharp) thûeh ทื่อ

blur v mua มัว

blush N nâa daeng หน้าแดง

board N kràdaan กระดาน; blackboard kràdaan dam (literally, 'board'-'black') กระดานดำ *Also see* 'surfboard'

board v (bus, train) khûen ขึ้น

boarding pass N bàt khûehn khrûeang บัตรขึ้นเครื่อง

boast v (brag) ùat อวด, or ('talk big') khui móh คุยโม้

boat/ship N ruea เรือ

body N râang kaai ร่างกาย; dead body, corpse sòp ศพ

bodybuilding N (COLLOQUIAL) lên klâam (literally, 'play'-'muscle') เล่นกล้าม

boil v tôm ต้ม (NOTE: also used as slang meaning 'cheat' or 'swindle')

boiling/boiled ADJ (e.g. water) dùeat เดือด

bomb/hand grenade N lûuk rá-bòet ลูกระเบิด

bon voyage! (Have a safe trip) doehn thaang plàwt phai ná เดินทาง ปลอดภัยนะ

bone N krà-dùuk กระดูก

bong N (bamboo water pipe for smoking tobacco or marijuana) bâwng บ้อง, or bâwng kan-chaa บ้องกัญชา

book N nǎngsǔeh หนังสือ

bookstore N ráan nǎng-sǔeh ร้าน หนังสือ

boost v phôehm เพิ่ม (FORMAL) sǒehm เสริม

boot N rawng-tháo búut รองเท้าบู๊ท

border, edge N khàwp ขอบ

border N (between countries) chaai daehn ชายแดน

bored ADJ bùea เบื่อ

boring ADJ (a film, a person) nâa bùea น่าเบื่อ

born v kòeht (pronounced like 'gurt') เกิด

borrow v khǎw yuehm ขอยืม, or simply yuehm ยืม

boss, master N jâo-naai เจ้านาย (in short) naai นาย

bossy ADJ (COLLOQUIAL) jâo-kîi jâo-kaan เจ้ากี้เจ้าการ

both PRON (of them) tháng khûu ทั้งคู่

bother/disturb v róp-kuan รบกวน

bother, disturbance N kaan róp-kuan การรบกวน

bottle N khùat ขวด

bottom ADJ (at the bottom) khâang tâi ข้างใต้

bottom N (buttocks; also used in the broader sense to mean 'the deepest or lowest part') kôn ก้น

bouquet N châw dàwk-mái ช่อดอกไม้

bow v khóhng โค้ง (i.e. to bend the head or body to express greeting, kôm ก้ม (i.e. to lower the head quickly, as in greeting or acknowledgment)

bowl N chaam ชาม

bowling N lêhn boh-lîng เล่นโบว์ลิ่ง

box N (general term) klàwng กล่อง, (cardboard) klàwng krà-dàat กล่อง กระดาษ

box v, **boxing** N (fighting) muai มวย; Thai boxing muai thai มวยไทย

boy N dèk chaai เด็กชาย

boyfriend/girlfriend N faehn แฟน

bra, brassiere N yók song ยกทรง

bracelet N kamlai mueh กำไลมือ

brag v *See* 'boast'

braid v thàk ถัก, N phǒm pia ผมเปีย (i.e. a length of hair that has been braided)

brain N sà-mǎwng สมอง

brainwash v láang sà-mǎwng ล้างสมอง

brake N (in a vehicle) (from English) brèhk เบรก, v yìap brèhk เหยียบ เบรก (to reduce the speed)

branch N (of a bank, business franchise) sǎa-khǎa สาขา, (of a tree) kìng-mái กิ่งไม้

brand N yîi-hâw ยี่ห้อ: also 'brand

name' (from English) bran nehm แบรนด์เนม

brandy N (from English) bà-ràn-dii บรั่นดี

brass N thawng lŭeang (literally, 'gold'-'yellow') ทองเหลือง

brave/daring ADJ klâa hǎan กล้าหาญ

bread, bun N khànŏm pang ขนมปัง

break V (glasses, plates) tàehk แตก; break (a leg, bones) hàk หัก

break apart V tàehk yâehk แตกแยก

break down V (car, machine) sǐa เสีย

breakfast, morning meal N aa-hǎan cháo อาหารเช้า

breakfast, to eat V kin aa-hǎan cháo กินอาหารเช้า

breakup N lôehk kan เลิกกัน (the discontinuance of a relationship)

breast(s) N (also chest, male or female) nâa òk หน้าอก; breasts/tits (COLLOQUIAL; also the word for 'milk') nom นม

breathe V hǎai-jai หายใจ; breathe in hǎai-jai khâo หายใจเข้า; breathe out hǎai-jai àwk หายใจออก

breed V (of cat or dog) phan พันธุ์; 'what sort of breed is it (dog/cat etc.)?' phan àrai พันธุ์อะไร

breeze N lom àwn àwn (literally, 'wind'-'gentle') ลมอ่อน ๆ

bribe N sǐn bon สินบน

bride N jâo sǎow เจ้าสาว

bridegroom N jâo bàow เจ้าบ่าว

bridge N sà-phaan สะพาน (NOTE: the same word is used for 'bridge' in dental work); footbridge (over a busy road) sà-phaan loi (literally, 'bridge'-'float') สะพานลอย

brief ADJ sân-sân สั้น ๆ

briefcase N krà-pǎo tham ngaan กระเป๋าทำงาน

bright ADJ (of light) sà-wàang สว่าง

brighten V tham hâi sà-wàang ทำให้สว่าง

bring V ao maa (literally, 'take'-'come') เอามา (Often used like this: when the object, say an umbrella (rôm ร่ม), is

understood. Otherwise if you wished to say the full sentence 'bring an umbrella' it would be ao rôm maa เอา ร่มมา, i.e. ao–'umbrella'–maa)

bring up V (e.g. a topic/submit plans) sà-nǒeh เสนอ, (raise children) líang เลี้ยง

British ADJ angkrìt อังกฤษ; a British person khon angkrìt คนอังกฤษ

broad/wide/spacious ADJ kwâang กว้าง

broadcast, program N raai-kaan krà-jaai sǐang รายการกระจายเสียง

broadcast V krà-jaai sǐang กระจายเสียง

broadminded ADJ jai kwâang ใจกว้าง

broccoli N (from English) bráwk-koh-lîi บรอกโคลี

broke ADJ (SLANG; meaning 'to have no money') See 'money'

broken, does not work, spoiled ADJ sǐa เสีย, (COLLOQUIAL) jéng เจ๊ง

broken, shattered ADJ tàehk แตก

broken, snapped ADJ (of bones, etc.) hàk หัก

broken hearted ADJ (COLLOQUIAL) òk-hàk อกหัก

bronze N thawng sǎmrít ทองสัมฤทธิ์

broom N mái kwàat ไม้กวาด

broth, soup N náam súp น้ำซุป

brothel N sâwng ซ่อง, or sâwng sǒh-pheh-nii ซ่องโสเภณี

brother N (older) phîi chaai พี่ชาย, (younger) náwng chaai น้องชาย

brother-in-law N (older) phîi khǒei พี่ เขย, (younger) náwng khǒei น้องเขย

brow N khíw คิ้ว

brown ADJ sǐi náamtaan สีน้ำตาล

bruise N, **to be bruised** ADJ chám ช้ำ

brush V (for scrubbing) praehng แปรง

brush N (paint brush) phû-kan พู่กัน

bubble N fawng ฟอง

bucket/bin N thǎng ถัง

Buddha N (The Lord) phrá phút-thá-jâo พระพุทธเจ้า

Buddhism N sàat-sà-nǎaphút ศาสนา พุทธ

Buddhist(s) N chaow phút ชาวพุทธ

buddy N (friend) phûean เพื่อน
budget N ngóp prà-maan งบประมาณ
buffalo N (water buffalo) khwaai ควาย
buffet N (from English) búp-fêh บุฟเฟต์
bug N má-laeng แมลง
build V sâang สร้าง
building N (made of brick/stone) tùek ตึก
bull N wua tua phûu วัวตัวผู้
bully V klâeng แกล้ง (treat somebody badly), N nák leng นักเลง (a thug)
bump V chon ชน
burden N phaa-rá ภาระ
bureaucrat/public servant N khâa râat-chákaan ข้าราชการ
burglar N khà-mohi ขโมย
Burma N phá-mâa พม่า; also Myanmar mian-mâa เมียนมาร์
Burmese N (person) chaow phá-mâa ชาวพม่า, or khon phá-mâa คนพม่า; Burmese (language) phaa-săa phá-mâa ภาษาพม่า
burn N (injury) phlăeh mâi แผลไหม้, V phăo เผา
burp V roeh เรอ
bury V făng ฝัง
bus N (the general term for bus, non-airconditioned, is either) rót meh รถเมล์ or rót bút (from the English 'bus') รถบัส. An airconditioned bus or coach is commonly referred to as a rót thua รถทัวร์, or 'tour bus'.
bush N phûm-mái พุ่มไม้
bus station N (COLLOQUIAL) sá-thăa-nii-khŏn-sòng สถานีขนส่ง (literally, 'transport'-'send')
business N thú-rá-kìt ธุรกิจ
businessperson N nák thú-rá-kìt นักธุรกิจ
busy ADJ (bothersome – e.g. in a busy work environment where there is no let up) yûng ยุ่ง, (crowded and noisy) wûn waai วุ่นวาย, (telephone) săai mâi wâang สายไม่ว่าง
but CONJ tàeh แต่
butter N noei เนย

butterfly N phĭi sûea ผีเสื้อ
button N krà-dum กระดุม
buy V súeh ซื้อ
by PREP (created by name of author/artist) dohy โดย
bye, goodbye INTERJ (from English) báai-baai บ๊ายบาย, sà-wàt-dii สวัสดี
by means of PREP dûai wíthii… ด้วยวิธี
by the way, in addition ADV nâwk jàak níi นอกจากนี้; furthermore ìik yàang nùeng อีกอย่างหนึ่ง

C

cab N (taxi cab) rót tháek-sîi รถแท็กซี่
cabbage N kàlàm plii กะหล่ำปลี, (Chinese cabbage) phàk kàat khăow ผักกาดขาว
café N ráan kaa-faeh (literally, 'shop'-'coffee') ร้านกาแฟ
cafeteria N rohng aa-hăan โรงอาหาร
cake N khànŏm khéhk (khéhk from English 'cake') ขนมเค้ก
calculate V khamnuan คำนวณ
calculator N khrûeang khít lêhk เครื่องคิดเลข
calendar N pà-tì-thin ปฏิทิน
calf N (lower leg) nâwng น่อง
call, summon V rîak เรียก
called, named V chûeh ชื่อ
calm, peaceful ADJ sà-ngòp สงบ
Cambodia N khà-mĕhn เขมร
Cambodian/Khmer N chaow khà-mĕhn ชาวเขมร, or khon khà-mĕhn คนเขมร, (language) phaa-săa khà-mĕhn ภาษาเขมร
camel N ùut อูฐ
camera N klâwng thàai rûup กล้องถ่ายรูป
camp N khâai ค่าย, (from English) kháem แคมป์; V khâo khâai เข้าค่าย, tâng kháem ตั้งแคมป์
campus N wít-thá-yaa-khèht วิทยาเขต (other institution), má-hăa-wít-thá-yaa-lai มหาวิทยาลัย (a college or university)

can, be able to, capable săa-mâat สามารถ, (COLLOQUIAL) ...dâi ...ได้ (put at the end of a sentence)

can/tin N krà-păwng กระป๋อง

canal N khlong คลอง

cancel V yók lôehk ยกเลิก

cancer N má-reng มะเร็ง

candid ADJ jing-jai จริงใจ

candidate N phûu sà-màk ผู้สมัคร

candle N thian thian thiian เทียน

candy, toffee, sweets N (from English) táwp-fîi ทอฟฟี่; a sweet/lolly you suck on lûuk om ลูกอม

cane N mái tháo ไม้เท้า

canvas N phâa bai ผ้าใบ

canyon N hùp khăo หุบเขา

cap N mùak หมวก

capability N khwaam săa mâat ความสามารถ

capital N (money, funds for investment) thun ทุน; capitalist/entrepreneur naai thun นายทุน

capitol N (city of a country, state) mueang lŭang เมืองหลวง

captain N kàp tan กัปตัน

caption N kham ban yaai phâap คำบรรยายภาพ

capture V (arrest) jàp จับ

car, automobile N rót รถ

card N (as in a credit card, name card, etc.) bàt บัตร (pronounced in a very similar way to the English word 'but'). *Also see* 'ID (identity card)'

cardboard N krà-dàat khăeng กระดาษแข็ง

cards N (game) phâi ไพ่; to play cards lên phâi เล่นไพ่

career N aa-chîip อาชีพ

care for, to love and V rák láe ao-jai sài รักและเอาใจใส่, also: take care ték khae (from English; COLLOQUIAL) เทคแคร์ (Also note: 'I don't care' phŏm/chăn mâi khae ผม/ฉันไม่แคร์)

care of (a child), to take V duu-laeh ดูแล

careful, cautious ADJ ra-wang ระวัง

careless ADJ mâi rá-mát rá-wang ไม่ระมัดระวัง, or sà-phrâo สะเพร่า

carpenter N châang máai ช่างไม้

carpet N phrom พรม

carrot N (from English) khaeràwt แครอต

carry V (largish or heavy objects e.g. suitcase) hîu หิ้ว

cart N (street vendor pushcart, supermarket trolley, pram) rót khěn รถเข็น

cartoon N (from English) kaa tuun การ์ตูน

carve V (a piece of meat) cham-lâe ชำแหละ, or simply lâeh แล่, (a statue) kàe sàlàk แกะสลัก

case N (box) klàwng กล่อง

cash N (money) ngoehn sòt เงินสด

cash a check V lâehk chék แลกเช็ค

cashew N (nut) mét má-mûang hĭm-má-phaan เม็ดมะม่วงหิมพานต์; (COLLOQUIALLY) mét má-mûang เม็ดมะม่วง

cast N fùeak เฝือก

casual ADJ (for informal wear) lam-lawng ลำลอง, (without formality) mâi pen thaang kaan ไม่เป็นทางการ

cat N maew แมว

catch N (a ball; to arrest) jàp จับ

category N prà phêht ประเภท

catfish N plaa-dùk ปลาดุก

cauliflower N dàwk kà-làm ดอกกะหล่ำ

cause N (the cause of something) săa-hèht สาเหตุ

cave N thâm ถ้ำ

cavity N (hole) lŭm หลุม, (a pit in a tooth) fan-phù ฟันผุ

CD N (from English) sii dii ซีดี

ceiling N pheh-daan เพดาน

celebrate V chà-lăwng ฉลอง

celebrity N khon dang คนดัง

celery N ceh-loeh-rîi เซเลอรี่

cell phone N thoh-rá-sàp-mueh thŭeh โทรศัพท์มือถือ, commonly referred to in speech as mueh thŭeh มือถือ

censor V (from English) sen-sôeh เซ็นเซอร์

center/centre, middle

center/centre, middle N trong klaang ตรงกลาง, or simply klaang กลาง

center N (of city) klaang mueang กลางเมือง

central N sǔun klaang ศูนย์กลาง (NOTE the use of central in 'central Thailand' – i.e. the middle and most populous region of Thailand spreading out in all directions from Bangkok. The 'central region' as it is known is referred to as phâak klaang ภาคกลาง.) *Also see* 'region'. It should be pointed out that Central Thai, also referred to as Bangkok Thai, is the official national language used in all forms of media and the education system. 'Central Thai' is known as phasǎa klaang (literally, 'language'-'centre/middle') ภาษากลาง

century N sàtà-wát ศตวรรษ

cereal N (from English) sii-rîaw ซีเรียล, than-yá-phûeht ธัญพืช

ceremony N phí-thii พิธี

certain, sure ADJ nâeh jai แน่ใจ, or nâeh nawn แน่นอน

certainly ADV nâeh nawn แน่นอน

certificate N prà-kàat-sànii-yábàt ประกาศนียบัตร

chain N sôh โซ่

chair N kâo-îi เก้าอี้

challenge V tháa thaai ท้าทาย

champion N (from English) cháehm-pîan แชมเปี้ยน

chance, opportunity N oh-kàat โอกาส

chance, by ADV dohy bang-oen โดยบังเอิญ

change, small N sèht sà-taang เศษสตางค์, (MORE COLLOQUIAL) sèht tang เศษตังค์

change V (conditions, situations, clothes, plans) plìan เปลี่ยน

change, exchange V (money) lâehk plìan แลกเปลี่ยน (NOTE: for 'change or exchange money' you would say lâehk ngoehn แลกเงิน, and for 'change clothes' plìan sûeàphâa เปลี่ยนเสื้อผ้า)

change one's mind V plìan jai เปลี่ยนใจ

channel N châwng thaang ช่องทาง

chaos N khwaam wûn waai ความวุ่นวาย

chapter N bòt บท, tawn ตอน

character N (personality) (FORMAL) bùk-khá-lík láksànà บุคลิกลักษณะ, (MORE COLLOQUIALLY) ní-sǎi นิสัย

character, letter N (from an alphabet) tua àksǎwn ตัวอักษร, also (COLLOQUIALLY) tua nǎngsǔeh ตัวหนังสือ

characteristic, qualities N láksana ลักษณะ

charge V (to energize a storage battery) cháat bàet ชาร์จแบต, (demand a price) khít-ngoehn คิดเงิน

charity N kaan kùsǒn การกุศล

charming ADJ mii sà-nèh มีเสน่ห์

chase V lâi taam ไล่ตาม

chase away/chase out V lâi pai ไล่ไป

chat V khui คุย

cheap ADJ (in price) thùuk ถูก

cheat V kohng โกง

cheat, cheater N khon kohng คนโกง; someone who habitually cheats khon khîi kohng คนขี้โกง

check/verify V trùat sàwp ตรวจสอบ

checked N (pattern) laai màak rúk ลายหมากรุก

checkup N trùat râang-kaai ตรวจร่างกาย

cheek N kâem แก้ม

cheers! INTERJ (Hooray!) chai yoh ไชโย

cheese N noei khǎeng เนยแข็ง

chef N phâw krua (literally, 'father'-'kitchen') พ่อครัว FEM mâeh khrua (literally, 'mother'-'kitchen') แม่ครัว

chemist N (pharmacy) ráan khǎai yaa ร้านขายยา; chemist (proprietor of pharmacy) phehsàt-chá-kawn เภสัชกร; chemist (scientist) nák khehmii นักเคมี

chess N màak rúk หมากรุก

chest N (box) hìip หีบ, (breast) nâa òk หน้าอก

chew v khíao เคี้ยว; chewing gum màak fàràng หมากฝรั่ง (NOTE: the choice of words: literally, 'betel nut'- 'foreign/western' – i.e. 'foreign betel nut')

chicken N kài ไก่

child N dèk เด็ก (NOTE: also generally used to refer to very junior staff in a work environment i.e. subordinates), offspring lûuk ลูก

chili N (pepper) phrík พริก

chili sauce N sáwt phrík ซอสพริก

chilled ADJ châeh yen แช่เย็น

chilly ADJ (weather) năow หนาว

chin N khaang คาง

China N mueang jiin (pronounced like 'jean') เมืองจีน

Chinese N khon jiin คนจีน, (language) phaa-săa jiin ภาษาจีน

Chinese New Year (celebrated on differing dates from later January until around the middle of February) trùt jiin ตรุษจีน

chip N (as in computer chip) (from English) chip ชิป

chip(s) N See 'French fries'

chocolate N (from English) cháwk-koh-láet ช็อกโกแลต

choke v (on something) săm-lák สำลัก, (someone) bìip khaw (literally, 'squeeze' –'neck/throat') บีบคอ

cholera N rôhk à-hì-waa โรคอหิวาต์

cholesterol N khăi man nai lûeat (literally, 'fat'-'in'-'blood') ไขมันในเลือด

choose v lûeak เลือก; choice thaang lûeak ทางเลือก

chop/mince v sàp สับ

chopsticks N tà-kìap ตะเกียบ

chore N ngaan bâan งานบ้าน

Christ, Jesus N phrá yeh-suu พระเยซู

Christian N khrís-tian คริสเตียน; Christian(s) chaow khrít ชาวคริสต์

Christianity N sàatsà-năa khrít ศาสนาคริสต์

Christmas N khrít-sà-mâat คริสต์มาส

church N bòht โบสถ์

cigar N síkâa ซิการ์

cigarette N bùrìi บุหรี่

cigarette lighter N fai cháek ไฟแช็ก

cinema N rohng năng โรงหนัง

cinnamon N (spice) òb-choei อบเชย

circle N (shape) wong klom วงกลม

circle N (traffic) wong-wian วงเวียน

circumstance N sà-thăan-ná-kaan สถานการณ์

citizen N prà-chaàchon ประชาชน, or phon-lá-mueang พลเมือง

citrus: orange N sôm ส้ม; lemon má-naow มะนาว

city, large town N mueang เมือง

civilization N (from English) sìwílai ศิวิไลซ์, or aa-ráyá-tham อารยธรรม

claim v rîak ráwng เรียกร้อง (to demand), âang อ้าง (to state to be true)

clap v tòp mueh ตบมือ

class, category N chán ชั้น, or prà-phêht ประเภท

classroom N hâwng rian ห้องเรียน

clean ADJ sà-àat สะอาด

clean v (e.g. the bathroom) tham khwaam sà-àat ทำความสะอาด

cleanliness N khwaam sà-àat ความสะอาด

clear ADJ (water, soup, liquid) săi ใส, (of weather) plàwt pròhng ปลอดโปร่ง

clearly ADV (to see something clearly, to speak clearly) chát ชัด (NOTE: it is a genuine compliment in Thai when someone says you speak the language 'clearly' phûut thai chát (literally, 'speak'-'Thai'–'clear[ly]') พูดไทยชัด)

clever ADJ chà-làat ฉลาด, or kèng เก่ง

client/customer N lûuk-kháa ลูกค้า

climate N ban-yaa-kàat บรรยากาศ

climb v (a tree, a hill, a mountain) tài ไต่, or piin ปีน

clinic N (from English) khlii-ník คลินิก

clitoris N mét lá-mút เม็ดละมุด, (SLANG) mét tháp-tim เม็ดทับทิม, (EXTREMELY VULGAR) tàet แตด

clock N (or a watch) naalí-kaa นาฬิกา (NOTE: also term meaning 'hour' in the

C

24 hour system of time keeping i.e. 15 hours = 3 p.m.)

close/near ADJ klâi ใกล้

close V (to close a door), **cover** V (to cover something, to put a lid on a jar) pìt ปิด

closet N tûu sûea phâa ตู้เสื้อผ้า

close together, stuck together ADV tìt kan ติดกัน

cloth N phâa ผ้า

clothes, clothing N sûea phâa เสื้อผ้า

cloud N mêhk เมฆ

cloudy, overcast ADJ mûeht khrúem มืดครึ้ม, or simply mii mêhk (literally, 'have'-'cloud[s]') มีเมฆ

cloves N kaan phluu กานพลู

club, association N sà-moh-sǎwn สโมสร

clumsy ADJ sûm sâam ซุ่มซ่าม

coach N (a bus used for long-distance service) rót thua รถทัวร์, (a trainer) khruu fùek ครูฝึก

coarse ADJ (to the touch) yàap หยาบ, (vulgar, crude manner) yàap khaai หยาบคาย

coast N (of the sea) chaai tháleh ชายทะเล

coat N (jacket) sûea jáek-kêt เสื้อแจ็คเก็ต, (overcoat) sûea nâwk เสื้อนอก

cockroach N (COLLOQUIAL) má-laehng-sàap แมลงสาบ

cocky ADJ yìng หยิ่ง

cocoa N koh-kôh โกโก้

coconut N má-phráo มะพร้าว; young coconut má-phráo àwn มะพร้าวอ่อน; coconut milk/cream (used in curries) kà-thí กะทิ

coffee N kaa-faeh กาแฟ: black coffee kaa-faeh dam (literally, 'coffee'-'black') กาแฟดำ; white coffee kaa-faeh sài nom (literally, 'coffee'-'put'-'milk') กาแฟใส่นม

coin N rĭan เหรียญ

cold ADJ (drink) yen เย็น

cold N (common cold) wàt หวัด; to have a cold pen wàt เป็นหวัด

cold ADJ (weather) nǎow หนาว

collapse V phang พัง (break down), lôm ล้ม (fall down)

colleague, coworker N phûean rûam ngaan เพื่อนร่วมงาน

collect N (a parcel, a present, etc.) ráp รับ

college N wít-thá-yaà-lai วิทยาลัย

collide V chon ชน

collision N kaan chon การชน

color N sǐi สี (also the word for the noun 'paint')

colorblind ADJ taa bàwt sǐi ตาบอดสี

colorful ADJ mii sǐi sǎn มีสีสัน

comb N wǐi หวี

combine V ruam รวม; combine with ruam kàp รวมกับ; join together rûam kan ร่วมกัน

come V maa มา

come back V klàp maa กลับมา

come in V (enter) khâo maa เข้ามา

comedian N tua tà-lòk ตัวตลก

comedy N rûeang tà-lòk เรื่องตลก, or simply tà-lòk ตลก (which also means 'funny')

comfortable ADJ sàbaai สบาย (a key Thai term which means something like 'relaxed and comfortable', a highly desirable state [often also used with the implicit sense of without worry or concern]). Two very common expressions meaning 'Are you feeling comfortable/ Are you feeling well/How do you feel? [generally asked with the expectation that the answer will be yes] are khun sàbaai dii rǔeh คุณสบายดีหรือ, khun sàbaai dii mái คุณสบายดีไหม

command, order N kham sàng คำสั่ง

command V (or, to order food in a restaurant) sàng สั่ง

commercial N khôht-sà-naa โฆษณา

common, ordinary ADJ tham-màdaa ธรรมดา

communicate V (with someone) sùeh-sǎan สื่อสาร

community N chum chon ชุมชน

ENGLISH—THAI

conscious

C

company, firm N bawrí-sàt บริษัท
compare V prìap thîap เปรียบเทียบ
compared with V prìap kàp เปรียบกับ
compel V (to force) bangkháp บังคับ
compensate V (to make up for) chót choei ชดเชย
compete V khàeng แข่ง
competition N (contest) kaan khàeng khǎn การแข่งขัน
complain V bòn บ่น; a grouchy/cranky person given to complaining khon khîi bòn คนขี้บ่น
complaint N kham ráwng thúk คำร้องทุกข์
complete ADJ (accomplished) sǎmrèt สำเร็จ, or simply sèt เสร็จ, (thorough) dohy sîn choehng โดยสิ้นเชิง, (to make whole) sǒmbuun สมบูรณ์, or khróp thûan ครบถ้วน
complete V tham hâi sèt ทำให้เสร็จ
completely ADV yàang sǒmbuun อย่างสมบูรณ์
complicated/complex ADJ (a piece of machinery, a relationship) sáp sáwn ซับซ้อน
compose, write V (letters, books, music) tàeng แต่ง, or khǐan เขียน
composition, writings N kaan tàeng การแต่ง, kaan khǐan การเขียน
compromise V prà-nii prà-nawm ประนีประนอม
compulsory/mandatory ADJ bangkháp บังคับ
computer N (from English) khawm-phiu-tôeh คอมพิวเตอร์, or (COLLOQUIALLY) khawm คอม (NOTE: a laptop computer is [from the English 'notebook'] notèbúk โน้ตบุ๊ค.) *Also see* 'tablet PC'
concentrate V (think) mii sà-maa-thí มีสมาธิ, or ao jai sài เอาใจใส่
concentrated ADJ (liquid, substance) khêm khôn เข้มข้น
concept N khwaam khít ความคิด
concern N khwaam kang won ความกังวล

concerned ADJ pen hùang เป็นห่วง,
concerning PREP kìao kàp เกี่ยวกับ
conclude V sà-rùp สรุป
concrete N rûup-pà-tham รูปธรรม, khawn krìit คอนกรีต (construction material)
condition/proviso N ngûean-khǎi เงื่อนไข
condition N (of a secondhand car) sà-phâap สภาพ, (symptom, indication, state, e.g. when discussing sickness, illness) aa-kaan อาการ
condom N thǔng yang ถุงยาง, (from English) khawn-dâwm คอนดอม
condominium N (condo) (from English) khawndoh-mi-nîam (khondo) คอนโดมิเนียม (คอนโด)
confectionery/sweets N khànǒm wǎan ขนมหวาน
confess V (admit something) yawm ráp ยอมรับ
conference N *See* 'meeting'
confidence N khwaam mân-jai ความมั่นใจ (i.e. having confidence mii khwaam mân-jai มีความมั่นใจ)
confident ADJ mân-jai มั่นใจ
confirm V yuehn yan ยืนยัน
Confucianism N lát-thí khǒng júeh ลัทธิขงจื๊อ
confuse V sàp sǒn สับสน
confused ADJ (in a mess) yûng yǒehng ยุ่งเหยิง, (filled with confusion) sàp sǒn สับสน, (perplexed) ngong งง
confusing ADJ nâa sàpsǒn น่าสับสน
congratulations! INTERJ (I congratulate you) khǎw sà-daehng khwaam yin-dii dûai ขอแสดงความยินดีด้วย, or (in short) yin-dii-dûai ยินดีด้วย
connect V tàw ต่อ, (together) tìt tàw kan ติดต่อกัน
connection(s) N (SLANG) sên เส้น, (COLLOQUIAL) to have connections with people of influence mii sên มีเส้น, (FORMAL) khwaam sǎm phan ความสัมพันธ์
conscious ADJ mii sà-tì มีสติ; be aware rúu tua รู้ตัว

ENGLISH–THAI

103

conscious of, to be rúu sămnúek
รู้สำนึก

consent v yin yawm ยินยอม

consider v (consider an issue) phí-jaa-
rá-naa พิจารณา, (to think over) phí-
jaa-rá-naa พิจารณา, or trài trawng
ไตร่ตรอง

considerate ADJ khreng-jai เกรงใจ

constipation N **to be constipated** ADJ
tháwng phùuk (literally, 'stomach'-'tie'/
'tied') ท้องผูก

constitution N rát-thá-tham-má-nuun
รัฐธรรมนูญ

construct v sâang สร้าง

consult, talk over with v prùek săa
ปรึกษา

contact, get in touch with v tìt tàw ติด
ต่อ

content N nûea hăa เนื้อหา

contest v prà-kùat ประกวด

context N bawrí-bòt บริบท

continent N thá-wîip ทวีป

continue v tham tàw pai ทำต่อไป

contraceptive N (pill) (COLLOQUIAL) yaa
khum ยาคุม

contract N (legal) săn-yaa สัญญา (NOTE:
the same word also means 'to promise')

contrast N khwaam tàek tàang ความ
แตกต่าง

control v (something) khûap-khum
ควบคุม

convenient ADJ sà-dùak สะดวก

conversation N (COLLOQUIAL) phûut khui
พูดคุย

converse v (FORMAL) sŏn-thá-naa
สนทนา, (COLLOQUIAL) to chat khui คุย

convince v tham hâi chûea ทำให้เชื่อ

cook N (person) khon tham aa-hăan
คนทำอาหาร; also (from English) khúk
กุ๊ก, or simply (COLLOQUIAL) M phâw krua
พ่อครัว F mâeh krua แม่ครัว

cook v tham aa-hăan ทำอาหาร

cooked ADJ (also, of fruit, 'to be ripe')
sùk สุก

cooker N (charcoal)/**stove** N (oven) tao
เตา

cookie, sweet biscuit N (from English)
khúk-kîi คุกกี้

cool ADJ yen เย็น

cool v (e.g. in a fridge) châeh yen แช่เย็น

cool ADJ (COLLOQUIAL – as in 'hip',
'trendy') têh เท่, or kĕh เก๋

cop N (police) tam-rùat ตำรวจ

copper N (metal) thawng daehng
ทองแดง

copy v (imitate) lian bàep เลียนแบบ

copy N (e.g. a photocopy) sămnao
สำเนา; v make a photocopy thàai
èkkà-săan ถ่ายเอกสาร, or simply
(from English) 'copy' kóp-pîi ก๊อปปี้

copyright N lík-khá-sìt ลิขสิทธิ์

coral N hĭn pà-kaa-rang หินปะการัง, or
simply pà-kaa-rang ปะการัง

coriander, cilantro N phàk chii ผักชี

corn N khâaw phôht ข้าวโพด

corner N mum มุม

cornstarch N pâeng khâaw phôht
แป้งข้าวโพด

corpse N (dead body) sòp ศพ

correct/to be right ADJ (answer to a
question) thùuk tâwng ถูกต้อง

correct v (a mistake/error) kâeh แก้

correspond v (write letters, email)
khĭan jòtmăi เขียนจดหมาย, khĭan
ii-mehl เขียนอีเมล

correspondent/reporter/journalist N
phûu sùeh khàaw ผู้สื่อข่าว, or nák
khàaw นักข่าว

corridor N thaang doehn nai tùek ทาง
เดินในตึก

corrupt v thút-jà-rìt ทุจริต

cosmetics N See 'makeup'

cosmetic surgery N See 'plastic surgery'

cost(s) N (i.e. expenses) khâa chái jàai
ค่าใช้จ่าย, (price) raa-khaa ราคา: How
much does it/this cost?/What's the
price? raa-khaa thâo-rài ราคาเท่าไร

costume N sûea phâa เสื้อผ้า

cotton N fâai ฝ้าย

cotton wool N săm-lii สำลี

couch, sofa N (from English) soh-faa
โซฟา

cough v ai ไอ

could, might AUX v àat jà อาจจะ: (e.g. he could/might go khǎo àat jà pai เขา อาจจะไป)

count, to v náp นับ

country (nation) prà-thêht ประเทศ; Thailand prà-thêht thai ประเทศไทย

country/countryside N (FORMAL) chon-ná-bòt ชนบท, (COLLOQUIAL) bâan nâwk บ้านนอก

coup d'etat N rát-prà-hǎan (literally, 'state'–'execute') รัฐประหาร

courgette, zucchini N suu-kì-nîi ซูกินี

court N (of law) sǎan ศาล

cousin N lûuk phîi lûuk náwng ลูกพี่ ลูกน้อง

cover v pít ปิด, or khlum คลุม

cow N wua วัว

coworker, colleague N phûean rûam ngaan เพื่อนร่วมงาน

cozy ADJ sà-baai สบาย

crab N puu ปู

cracked ADJ roi tàehk รอยแตก

cracker/salty biscuit N khà-nǒmpang kràwp ขนมปังกรอบ

crafts N ngaan fǐi-mueh งานฝีมือ

craftsperson/craftsman N châang fǐi-mueh ช่างฝีมือ

cramp N (muscle pain in arm/leg) tà-kriu ตะคริว; to have a cramp tà-kriu kin ตะคริวกิน; a stomach cramp tháwng jùk ท้องจุก

cranky ADJ aa-rom-sǐa อารมณ์เสีย

crash/bump v (into) chon ชน; car crash rót chon รถชน; crash helmet/motorcycle helmet (COLLOQUIAL) mùak kan nók หมวกกันน็อก

crate N lang mái ลังไม้

crazy, mad ADJ bâa-bâa baw-baw บ้า ๆ บอ ๆ, or simply bâa บ้า, also (COLLOQUIAL TERM) ting-táwng ติงต๊อง (NOTE: a crazy/mad person is khon bâa คนบ้า)

cream N (from English) khriim ครีม

create/build v sâang สร้าง

creature N (an animal) sàt สัตว์, (a human) khon คน

credit N (from English) khreh-dìt เครดิต, nâa chûae thǔeh น่าเชื่อถือ

criminal N (FORMAL) àat-yaa-kawn อาชญากร, (COLLOQUIAL) phûu-ráai ผู้ร้าย

crisis N wí-khrìt วิกฤต

critical ADJ sǎm khan สำคัญ

criticism N kaan wí jaan การวิจารณ์

crocodile/alligator N jawrá-khêh จระเข้

crook N (a cheat) khon khîi kohng คน ขี้โกง

cross/angry ADJ kròht โกรธ, or moh hǒh โมโห

cross, go over v (the road) khâam ข้าม

crosswalk N (COLLOQUIAL) thaang máa laai ทางม้าลาย

crow N (bird) kaa กา

crowded/congested; tight ADJ (to grip someone's hand tightly, to feel stuffed after eating a lot of food, etc.) nâen แน่น

crown N (as in dental work) khrâwp fan ครอบฟัน (NOTE: fan ฟัน or 'tooth' is pronounced like the English word 'fun')

cruel ADJ hòht ráai โหดร้าย

crush v bòt บด, bìip-àt บีบอัด

crush on v (SLANG) àep-châwp แอบชอบ

cry v (with tears) ráwng hâi ร้องไห้, (cry out) ráwng ร้อง, (shout) tà-kohn ตะโกน

cucumber N taeng kwaa แตงกวา

cuisine, food N aa-hǎan อาหาร; style of cooking/cuisine, e.g. Chinese food/cuisine aa-hǎan jiin อาหารจีน

culture N wát-tháná-tham วัฒนธรรม

cup N thûai ถ้วย

cupboard, wardrobe, chest of drawers N tûu ตู้

cure/treat v (an illness) ráksǎa รักษา

cured, preserved, pickled ADJ (fruit) dawng ดอง

curious ADJ yàak rúu yàak hěn (literally, 'want know'–'want see') อยาก รู้อยากเห็น, or simply sǒng-sǎi สงสัย

curly ADJ (as in 'curly hair') See 'frizzy'

currency (FORMAL) ngoehn traa เงินตรา,

C

(SIMPLY COLLOQUIAL) ngoehn 'money' เงิน

curry N kaeng แกง

curtains, drapes N mâan ม่าน

curve N (a line) sên khôhng เส้นโค้ง, (a road) thaang khôhng ทางโค้ง

cushion N (pillow) măwn หมอน

custom/tradition N prà-pheh-nii ประเพณี, or tham-niam ธรรมเนียม

customer/client N lûuk kháa ลูกค้า

cut/slice V hàn หั่น

cut V tàt ตัด, N phlăe (a wound)/cut by a knife See 'knife'

cute/appealing ADJ nâa rák น่ารัก

cycling N khìi jàk-kà-yaan ขี่จักรยาน

D

dad/father N (COLLOQUIAL) phâw พ่อ, (MORE FORMAL) bì-daa บิดา

daily ADV (in the sense of a regular activity) prà-jam-wan ประจำวัน, (every day) thúk wan ทุกวัน

dam N khùean เขื่อน

damage V (i.e. to be damaged) chamrút ชำรุด, or sĭa hăi เสียหาย, (SIMPLY COLLO-QUIAL) phang พัง, (to cause damage to) tham hâi chamrút ทำให้ชำรุด

damp/humid ADJ chúehn ชื้น

dance V tên ram เต้นรำ, or simply tên เต้น

dandruff V rang-khaeh รังแค

danger/dangerous ADJ an-tà-raai อันตราย

dark ADJ mûehd มืด

dark blue ADJ See 'navy blue'

dark skin N (in colloquial Thai it is com-mon to use the abbreviated word for 'black' dam ดำ even for someone many westerners would consider to have a moderate tan) 'Dark skin' phĭw dam ผิวดำ or phĭw klám ผิวคล้ำ

darling/my love N (expression of affec-tion) thîi rák ที่รัก

date N (of the month) wan thîi วันที่

date of birth N wan duean pii kòeht (literally, 'day'-'month'-'year'-'birth')

วันเดือนปีเกิด

daughter N lûuk săow ลูกสาว

daughter-in-law N lûuk sà-phái ลูกสะใภ้

dawn N cháo trùu เช้าตรู่

day N wan วัน; today wan níi วันนี้; yes-terday mûea waan (níi) เมื่อวาน(นี้)

day after tomorrow ADV mà-ruehn (níi) มะรืน(นี้)

day before yesterday ADV mûeawaan suehn níi เมื่อวานซืน (นี้)

day-care center N sà-thăan-líang-dèk สถานเลี้ยงเด็ก

daydream V făn klaang wan ฝันกลาง วัน

daylight N săeng dàet แสงแดด

day off N (also used for 'holiday', i.e. day off work) wan yùt วันหยุด

daytime N klaang wan กลางวัน

dead ADJ (COLLOQUIAL) taai láew ตาย แล้ว, (MORE FORMAL) sĭa láew เสียแล้ว; death khwaam taai ความตาย

deaf ADJ hŭu nùak หูหนวก

dear N thîi rák ที่รัก

debate V tôh waa thii โต้วาที, tôh yáeng โต้แย้ง'

debt(s) N nîi sĭn หนี้สิน

decade N thót-sà-wát ทศวรรษ

decay V nâo pùeay เน่าเปื่อย (rot), phù ผุ (i.e. tooth decay)

deceive V làwk-luang หลอกลวง (in colloquial speech the single word làwk หลอก is used)

December N than-waa-khom ธันวาคม

decide V tàt-sĭn jai ตัดสินใจ

decision N kaan tàt-sĭn jai การตัดสินใจ

decisive ADJ (to act decisively) dèt-khàat เด็ดขาด

decline/decrease/get less V lót long ลดลง

decline/refuse/deny V pàtì-sèht ปฏิเสธ

decorate V tòk tàeng ตกแต่ง

deejay N (DJ or 'disk jockey' playing music on the radio or in a club etc.) dii jeh (pronounced very similar to the English) ดีเจ

deep ADJ lúek ลึก

defeat v (someone else, i.e. to win) ao
cháná เอาชนะ, or simply cháná ชนะ

defeated ADJ (beaten, lose a contest)
pháeh แพ้

defecate v (POLITE) thàai ถ่าย, (COLLOQUIAL;
the first of the following two terms is
more appropriate in general) ùeh อึ,
khîi ขี้ (NOTE: the word khîi ขี้ which is the
common way of referring to feces
should not be thought of as equivalent
to the English term 'shit'; khîi is not a
vulgar word and such bodily functions
are often talked of by Thai people in an
unself-conscious, matter-of-fact way)

defect N (or fault in something) khâw
bòk phrâwng ข้อบกพร่อง

defend v (in war), **protect** v (oneself or
somebody else), also to **prevent** v (the
outbreak of disease) pâwng kan ป้อง
กัน

define v hâi khwaam mǎai ให้ความ
หมาย

definite ADJ nêh nawn แน่นอน

deformed/crippled/disabled ADJ phí-
kaan พิการ

degree, level, standard N (e.g. 'high
standard') rá-dàp ระดับ

degree N (awarded by college or university) pà-rin-yaa ปริญญา

degree(s) N (temperature) ongsǎa องศา

dehydrate v khàat náam ขาดน้ำ

delay v tham hâi lâa cháa ทำให้ล่าช้า

delayed ADJ lâa cháa ล่าช้า

delete/rub out v lóp àwk ลบออก

delicate ADJ (fine, detailed work/crafts-
manship) lá-ìat ละเอียด, prà-nîit
ประณีต, (constitution/not strong)
àwn-aeh อ่อนแอ

delicious/tasty ADJ àròi อร่อย

delinquent N (SLANG) dèk wáen เด็ก
แว้น, or dèk sakói เด็กสก๊อย (young
members of motorcycle gangs); jìk-
kǒh จิ๊กโก๋ (more general types of
delinquents), and kúi กุ๊ย (a distinct
low-life variety)

deliver v sòng ส่ง

demand v rîak ráwng เรียกร้อง

democracy N prà-chaa-thí-pà-tai
ประชาธิปไตย

demonstrate v (show how to) sǎa-thít
สาธิต

dense ADJ nǎa nâen หนาแน่น, thùe
ทึบ

dental floss N mǎi khàt fan ไหมขัด
ฟัน

dentist N (MORE FORMAL) thantà-phâet
ทันตแพทย์, (COMMON) mǎw fan (literally, 'doctor'-'tooth') หมอฟัน

depart v àwk jàak ออกจาก; **departure**
àawk doehn thaang ออกเดินทาง;
department (in bureaucracy) phà-nàek
แผนก

department store v hâang sàpphá-sǐn-
kháa ห้างสรรพสินค้า, (SIMPLY COLLOQUIAL)
hâang ห้าง

departure N (boarding at the airport)
khǎa àwk ขาออก, (leaving) àwk
doehn thaang ออกเดินทาง

depend v (on somebody for help)
phôeng พึ่ง, (it depends on…)
khûen yùu kàp… ขึ้นอยู่กับ, or
alternatively láew tàeh แล้วแต่

deposit v (money in a bank, to leave
something somewhere) fàak ฝาก
(NOTE: it is also very common to use
this word in the following sense – e.g.
to ask somebody going out to the
shops to buy something in particular
for you 'Can you get (buy) me some
bread as well?' – fàak súeh [= buy]
khanǒm pang [= bread] dûai ฝากซื้อ
ขนมปังด้วย)

deposit N (of payment on a car, a
house) ngoehn mát jam เงินมัดจำ,
(money deposited in the bank) ngoen
fàak เงินฝาก

depression N (mental condition) rôhk
suem sâo โรคซึมเศร้า

depressed ADJ klûm jai กลุ้มใจ

descendant, heir/heiress N thaà-yâat
ทายาท

describe v banyaai บรรยาย; description kham banyaai คำบรรยาย, or kaan banyaai การบรรยาย

desert N (arid land) thá-leh saai (literally, 'sea'-'sand') ทะเลทราย

desert V (abandon) thíng ทิ้ง

deserve V sŏm khuan dâi ráp สมควรได้รับ

design V (a house) àwk bàehp ออกแบบ

designer N (from English) dii saai nôeh, (MORE FORMAL) nák àwk bàep นักออกแบบ

desire V (to do something) khwaam pràat-thà-nă ความปรารถนา; to desire (to do something) yàak อยาก

desire N (sexual) khwaam khrâi ความใคร่, tan-hăa ตัณหา (NOTE: the word yàak อยาก (previous entry) can also convey this particular meaning)

desk, table N tó โต๊ะ

desperate ADJ mòt wăng หมดหวัง

dessert N khăwng wăn (literally, 'thing'-'sweet') ของหวาน

destination N plaai thaang ปลายทาง

destiny N chôhk chá-taa โชคชะตา

destroy, devastate V tham-laai ทำลาย

destroyed/ruined ADJ thùuk tham-laai ถูกทำลาย

destruction N kaan tham-laai การทำลาย

destructive ADJ châwp tham-laai ชอบทำลาย

detail(s) N (e.g. in a contract – 'the fine print') raai-lá-ìat รายละเอียด

detect V (to spy) sùehp สืบ, (to find out) khôn-hăa ค้นหา

detective N nák-sùehp นักสืบ

detention N kaan khum tua การคุมตัว

detergent N (washing powder) phŏng sák fâwk ผงซักฟอก; detergent (liquid – for washing plates etc.) náam-yaa láang jaan น้ำยาล้างจาน, (for washing clothing) náam-yaa sák phâa น้ำยาซักผ้า

determined, intent on getting something done/accomplished ADJ tâng-jai ตั้งใจ

detour N thaang âwm ทางอ้อม

develop V phát-thá-naa พัฒนา; development kaan phát-thá-naa การพัฒนา, (grow) tòep toh เติบโต

device N ùp-pà-kawn อุปกรณ์

devilish ADJ hòht ráai โหดร้าย

dial V (telephone) kòt กด

diabetes N rôhk bao-wăan โรคเบาหวาน

diagnose V wí-nít-chăi-rôhk วินิจฉัยโรค

diagram N phăn phâap แผนภาพ

dialect N phaa-săa thìn ภาษาถิ่น

diamond N phét เพชร

diaper N (baby's diaper) phâa-âwm ผ้าอ้อม

diarrhea, diarrhoea N tháwng sĭa ท้องเสีย, tháwng doehn (literally, 'stomach'-'walk') ท้องเดิน, tháwng rûang ท้องร่วง

diary N sà-mùt dai aa-rîi สมุดไดอารี่

dictate, command V sàng สั่ง

dictionary N phót-jà-naanúkrom พจนานุกรม, (COLLOQUIAL) dìk (from English 'dictionary') ดิก

die V (COLLOQUIAL) taai ตาย, or (POLITE) sĭa เสีย

diesel N (petrol, gasoline) (petrol = náam-man) náam-man dii-sel น้ำมันดีเซล

diet V lót náamnàk ลดน้ำหนัก, (also from English) dai-èt ไดเอท

difference N (e.g. in quality) khwaam tàehk tàang ความแตกต่าง

different ADJ tàehk tàang แตกต่าง; other ùehn อื่น

difficult ADJ (i.e. a difficult task) yâak ยาก, difficult in the sense of not being easy to do things (e.g. going somewhere, etc. or 'having a hard/difficult life') lambàak ลำบาก

dig V (a hole in the ground) khùt ขุด

digest V (food) yôi (aa-hăan) ย่อย (อาหาร)

digit N tua-lêhk ตัวเลข **digital** ADJ (from English) dí-jì-tâwn ดิจิตอล

diligent ADJ khà-yăn ขยัน

dilute V juea jaang เจือจาง

dimple N lák yím ลักยิ้ม

dinner N aa-hǎan yen; **to eat dinner** (POLITE) thaan aa-hǎan yen ทานอาหารเย็น, (COLLOQUIAL) kin khâaw yen กินข้าวเย็น

dinosaur N (from English) dai-noh-sǎo ไดโนเสาร์

dip V jùm จุ่ม

diploma N (from college or school – also see 'degree') à-nú-pàrin-yaa อนุปริญญา

dipper, ladle N (implement used when cooking stir-fry dishes) tháp-phii ทัพพี

direct ADJ (directly, non-stop) trong ตรง

direct V (somebody to do something) sàng สั่ง

direction N (according to the compass) thít thaang ทิศทาง

director N (of company) phûu jàt-kaan ผู้จัดการ

dirt N din ดิน, (dust) fùn ฝุ่น

dirty, filthy ADJ sòk-kà-pròk สกปรก

disability N phí-kaan พิการ

disadvantage N khâw sǐa ข้อเสีย, khwaam sǐa prìap ความเสียเปรียบ

disagree V (with someone) mâi hěn dûai ไม่เห็นด้วย

disappear V See 'vanish'

disappointed ADJ phìt wǎng ผิดหวัง

disapprove V mâi à-nú-mát ไม่อนุมัติ

disaster N phai phíbàt ภัยพิบัติ

discard V thing ทิ้ง

discipline N wí-nai วินัย

disco N (from English) dis-kôh ดิสโก้, (COLLOQUIAL) ték เทค; nightclub (from English) nái-khláp ไนท์คลับ

discomfort N khwaam ùet-àt ความอึดอัด

disconnect V (to shut off an appliance) dueng-àwk ดึงออก, (to sever) yâek แยก

discount V, N (in the price of something) lót raa-khaa ลดราคา

discover V khón phóp ค้นพบ

discredit V tham-hâi sǐa chûeh-sǐang

ทำให้เสียชื่อเสียง

discuss V (ways to solve a problem) thòk panhǎa ถกปัญหา; discuss (exchange ideas) lâek-plìan khwaam khít hěn แลกเปลี่ยนความคิดเห็น

disease N (general term) rôhk โรค

disguise V plawm plaeng ปลอมแปลง

disgusting ADJ nâa rangkìat น่ารังเกียจ; to be disgusted (COLLOQUIAL) màn sâi หมั่นไส้

dish/plate N jaan จาน

dishonest ADJ mâi sûeh-sàt ไม่ซื่อสัตย์

dishwasher N khrûeang láang-jaan เครื่องล้างจาน

disk N (CD, DVD) phàen dís แผ่นดิสก์

dislike V mâi châwp (literally, 'no'-'like') ไม่ชอบ

dissolve/melt V lá-laai ละลาย

display N (a show, a performance) kaan sà-daehng การแสดง

display V sà-daehng แสดง

distance N (from one place to another) rá-yá thang ระยะทาง

distribute V jàek แจก

district N (in Bangkok) khèht เขต, (in other provinces) amphoe อำเภอ

disturb V róp-kuan รบกวน

disturbance N khwaam mâi sà-ngòp ความไม่สงบ

dive V (into the sea, go diving) dam náam ดำน้ำ

divide V (up – e.g. between different people) bàeng แบ่ง; separate/split up yâehk แยก

divided by V hǎan dûai (e.g. twenty divided by five, 20 hǎan dûai 5) หารด้วย

divorce V yàa หย่า

divorced ADJ yàa láew หย่าแล้ว

do V (to perform an action) tham ทำ

don't! V (do something) yàa อย่า

don't mention it PHR (or 'it doesn't matter', 'that's OK, don't worry about it') mâi pen rai ไม่เป็นไร

do one's best tham dii thîi sùt ทำดีที่สุด

109

doctor N (COLLOQUIAL) măw หมอ, (MORE FORMAL) phâeht แพทย์

document N èhkkà-săan เอกสาร

dog N (COMMON, COLLOQUIAL) măa หมา, (MORE GENTEEL, FORMAL) sù-nák สุนัข

doll N (toy) tùkkà-taa ตุ๊กตา

dollar N (from English) dawn-lâa ดอลลาร์, (COLLOQUIAL) dawn ดอล

dolphin N plaa-loh-maa ปลาโลมา

domestic ADJ (involving one's own country) nai prà-thêht ในประเทศ, (involving the family) nai khrâwp-khrua ในครอบครัว

donate V baw-rí-jàak บริจาค

done ADJ (cooked) sùk láew สุกแล้ว

done ADJ (finished) sèt láew เสร็จแล้ว

donut N (from English) doh-nát โดนัท

door/gate N prà-tuu ประตู

doorbell N àwt ออด

dormitory N hăw-phák หอพัก

double N (a pair, or as in 'double' bed) pen khûu เป็นคู่, (twice in amount) săwng thâo สองเท่า

doubt/suspect/curious V sŏng-săi สงสัย

down, downward ADV long maa ลงมา

downstairs ADV khâang lâang ข้างล่าง

down-to-earth ADJ (to be natural, un-pretentious) pen tham-má-châat เป็น ธรรมชาติ

downtown N nai mueang ในเมือง

dozen N lŏh โหล

drag V lâak ลาก

dragon N mang-kawn มังกร

drama N (as in TV soap opera) lá-khawn ละคร; TV soap opera lá-khawn thii-wii ละครทีวี

drapes, curtains N mâan ม่าน

draw V (a picture) wâat วาด; draw a picture wâat rûup วาดรูป; a drawing rûup wâat รูปวาด

drawer N (in a desk) línchák ลิ้นชัก

dream N khwaam făn ความฝัน

dream V făn ฝัน; Dream on! (as in 'In your dreams' or 'You must be kid-ding!') făn pai thóeh ฝันไปเถอะ

dress, frock N chút krà-prohng ชุด กระโปรง

dressed, to get V tàeng tua แต่งตัว

dressing N náam sà-làt น้ำสลัด

dressing gown N sûea khlum เสื้อคลุม

drill N (tools) sà-wàan สว่าน, (repeti-tious exercise) kaan fùek การฝึก

drink V (in formal situations) dùehm ดื่ม, (COLLOQUIAL) gin-náam กินน้ำ (literally: 'eat water' is used in casual conversa-tions)

drink/beverage N khrûeang dùehm เครื่องดื่ม

drive V (a car) khàp ขับ

driver V khon khàp คนขับ

driving license N (for either car or mo-torcycle) (COLLOQUIAL) bai khàp khìi ใบ ขับขี่

drop V yòt หยด

drought ADJ (very dry weather condi-tions, land, etc.) hâehng láehng แห้งแล้ง

drown V jom náam taai จมน้ำตาย

drug N (medicine) yaa ยา, drug (narcot-ic) yaa sèhp tìt (literally, 'drug/medi-cine'-'consume'-'stuck') ยาเสพติด

drugstore, pharmacy, chemist N ráan khăai yaa ร้านขายยา

drunk/intoxicated ADJ mao เมา; a drunk (drunkard) khîi mao ขี้เมา. (NOTE: the word mao เมา is not only used to refer to someone being drunk on alcohol, it is also used to refer to someone being 'high' or 'stoned' on any type of drug. Stoned on marijua-na, for example, is mao kan-chaa เมา กัญชา. A habitual user of illegal drugs is referred to as khîi yaa ขี้ยา. The word khîi ขี้ in this instance means 'habitual', 'being prone to' some type of behavior')

dry ADJ hâehng แห้ง, (weather) hâehng láehng แห้งแล้ง

dry V tham hâi hâehng ทำให้แห้ง, tàak ตาก; to dry clothing tàak phâa ตากผ้า

dry clean(ing) V sák hâehng ซักแห้ง

dryer N (clothes dryer) khrûeang òp-phâa เครื่องอบผ้า, (hair dryer) dai-pào-phŏm ไดร์เป่าผม

dry out v (in the sun) tàak dàet ตากแดด

duck N pèt เป็ด

dull ADJ (boring) nâa bùea น่าเบื่อ, (weather) khà-mùk-khà-mŭa ขมุกขมัว

dumb ADJ (COLLOQUIAL) ngôh โง่

dump v thíng ทิ้ง

dumpling N (meat) saa lá pao ซาละเปา

duplicate, make a copy v tham săm-nao ทำสำเนา

durable ADJ châi-thon ใช้ทน

durian N (fruit) thú-rian ทุเรียน

during, in between PREP nai rá-wàang ในระหว่าง

dusk ADJ klâi mûeht (literally, 'close'-'dark') ใกล้มืด

dust N fùn ฝุ่น; dustbin/rubbish bin/garbage bin thăng khà-yà ถังขยะ

duty N (tax) phaa-sĭi ภาษี, (responsibility) nâa thîi หน้าที่

DVD N (from English) dii wii dii ดีวีดี

dye v yáwm ย้อม

dysentery N rôhk bìt โรคบิด

E

each ADJ (as in 'each particular person', 'each particular book') tàeh lá แต่ละ; every... thúk... ทุกๆ

eager, enthusiastic ADJ krà-tueh-rueh-rón กระตือรือร้น

eagle N nók in-sii นกอินทรี

ear N hŭu หู; earphone(s), headphones hŭufang หูฟัง; ear wax khîi hŭu (literally, 'excrement'-'ear') ขี้หู

earlier, beforehand ADJ & ADV lûang nâa ล่วงหน้า

early ADV (come before usual time) kàwn weh-laa ก่อนเวลา

early in the morning ADV cháo trùu เช้าตรู่

earn v (a wage) dâi khâa jâang ได้ค่าจ้าง

earrings N tûm hŭu ตุ้มหู

earth, soil N din ดิน

Earth, the world N lôhk โลก

earthenware N khrûeng din-phăo เครื่องดินเผา

earthquake N phàen din wăi แผ่นดินไหว

east ADJ (direction) tà-wan àwk ตะวันออก

ease v tham-hâi ngâai ทำให้ง่าย **easy** ADJ ngâai ง่าย

easygoing ADJ sà-baai sà-baai สบาย ๆ, rûeay rûeay เรื่อย ๆ

eat v—there are a number of words in Thai that mean 'to eat'. These range from the colloquial to more formal. They include: kin กิน or more fully kin khâaw (literally, 'eat'-'rice') กินข้าว (NOTE: the colloquial term kin กิน is also used as slang to refer to corrupt practices such as taking bribes); thaan (more polite, colloquial) ทาน; ráp prà-thaan (formal) รับ-ประทาน; chăn (for monks) ฉัน. When animals 'eat' another word is often used: dàek แดก. If dàek is used to refer to people eating, it is extremely rude and should be avoided. It is generally used in informal settings among intimate male friends, and rougher, rowdier elements of Thai society.

ecology N níwêt-wít-thá-yaa นิเวศวิทยา; ecologist nák ní-wêht-wít-tháyaa นักนิเวศวิทยา

economical/frugal ADJ prà-yàt ประหยัด

economy, the N sèht-thà-kìt เศรษฐกิจ

ecstasy N khwaam sùk mâak ความสุขมาก; ecstasy (the drug) yaa ii ยาอี

edge N khàwp ขอบ

edible ADJ kin dâi กินได้

edit v kâe-kăi แก้ไข

educate v sùek-săa ศึกษา

education N kaan sùek-săa การศึกษา

effect, result N phŏn ผล

effective ADJ dâi phŏn ได้ผล

effort N khwaam phá-yaa-yaam ความพยายาม

effort, to make an; try v phá-yaa-yaam พยายาม

egg N khài ไข่

eggplant, aubergine N (general term) má-khùea มะเขือ

eight NUM (the number) pàeht แปด

eighteen NUM sìp pàeht (literally, 'ten'-'eight') สิบแปด

eighty NUM pàeht sìp (literally, 'eight'-'ten') แปดสิบ

either…or CONJ mâi… kâw… ไม…ก็

ejaculate/to come v (COLLOQUIAL; used for both men and women) sèt เสร็จ, or sèt láew เสร็จแล้ว. (The word sèt เสร็จ also means 'finished')

elbow N khâw sàwk ข้อศอก

elder ADJ (i.e. 'older than') kàeh kwàa แก่กว่า

elder N (older person) khon kàe คนแก่

election N kaan lûeak tâng การเลือกตั้ง

electric, electricity ADJ, N fai-fáa ไฟฟ้า

electrician N châang fai-fáa ช่างไฟฟ้า

electronic ADJ (from English) i-lék thraw-ník อิเล็กทรอนิก

elegant ADJ sŭai-ngaam สวยงาม

elementary ADJ (basic) phúehn-thǎan พื้นฐาน, prà-thǒm ประถม (i.e. an elementary school)

elephant N cháang ช้าง; a white elephant (regarded as auspicious in Thailand) cháang phùeak (literally, 'elephant'-'albino') ช้างเผือก

elevator N (from English 'lift') líp ลิฟต์

eleven NUM sìp èt สิบเอ็ด

eligible ADJ màw-sŏm เหมาะสม

eliminate v tàt-àwk ตัดออก

elite N khon chán sǔung (literally, 'person/people'-'class/level'-'high') คนชั้นสูง

else ADJ (as in 'anything else?') àrai ìik อะไรอีก

elsewhere ADV thîi-ùehn ที่อื่น

email N (message) (from English) ii-mehl อีเมล

email v (send an email) sòng ii-mehl ส่งอีเมล

email address N thîi yùu ii-mehl ที่อยู่อีเมล

embarrassed/shy ADJ aai (pronounced like 'eye') อาย

embarrassing ADJ nâa lá-aai น่าละอาย

embassy N sà-thǎan thûut สถานทูต

embrace/hug v kàwt กอด

embroider v pàk ปัก

embroidery N yép pàk thàk rói เย็บปักถักร้อย

emerald N mawra-kòt มรกต

emergency N chùk chǒehn ฉุกเฉิน

emotion, feeling N khwaam rúu-sèuk ความรู้สึก

emotional ADJ àwn-wǎi อ่อนไหว

empathy N khwaam-hěn-jai ความเห็นใจ

emphasize/stress something v nén เน้น

employ v (to hire someone) jâang จ้าง

employee N (generally used with un-skilled or lowly skilled workers) lûuk jâang ลูกจ้าง

employer N (boss) naai jâang นายจ้าง

empty, to be v wâang plào ว่างเปล่า

enchanted ADJ mii-sà-nèh มีสเน่ห์

encounter v phà-choehn-nâa เผชิญหน้า, pà-thá ปะทะ

end N (ending) jòp จบ, (the tip, e.g. of the tongue, nose, etc.) plaai ปลาย

end v sèt sîn เสร็จสิ้น, also jòp จบ

endless ADJ mâi-sîn-sùt ไม่สิ้นสุด

endure v òt-thon อดทน

enemy N sàt-truu ศัตรู

energy N phá-lang ngaan พลังงาน

engaged, busy ADJ (telephone) sǎai mâi wâang สายไม่ว่าง, (to be married) mân หมั้น

engine/motor N khrûeang yon เครื่องยนต์, or (simply and more colloquially) khrûeang เครื่อง

engineer N wítsà-wá-kawn วิศวกร

England N angkrìt อังกฤษ

English N (people) khon angkrìt คนอังกฤษ; (language) phaa-sǎa angkrìt ภาษาอังกฤษ

engrave v (to carve a piece of stone, wood, etc.) kàe-sà-làk แกะสลัก

enjoy v (to be fun/pleasurable) sà-nùk สนุก (This is a quintessential Thai word and the full sense of the term is not really adequately conveyed by the English word 'enjoy'. In Thai being sà-nùk is highly desirable)

enjoyable ADJ nâa sà-nùk น่าสนุก

enjoy oneself v tham tua hâi sà-nùk ทำตัวให้สนุก (sometimes the English word 'enjoy' is also used in Thai: en-joy เอนจอย)

enlarge v khà-yǎai ขยาย

enormous ADJ má-hùe-maa มหึมา

enough, sufficient ADJ phaw พอ

enquire/ask v thǎam ถาม

enroll v long thá-bian ลงทะเบียน

enter v khâo เข้า (NOTE: this word is frequently used in conjunction with either the word 'come' maa มา, or 'go' pai ไป; e.g. 'come in [here]' khâo maa เข้ามา, or 'go in [there]' khâo pai เข้าไป)

entertain v tham-hâi sà-nùk ทำให้สนุก

entire, whole N tháng mòt ทั้งหมด

entrance, way in N thaang khâo ทางเข้า

entrée N aa-hǎan jaan-râek อาหารจานแรก

entrepreneur/business person N nák thúrá-kìt นักธุรกิจ

envelope N sawng ซอง

environment N sìng wâeht láwm สิ่งแวดล้อม

envy v ìtchǎa อิจฉา; envious ADJ nâa ìtchǎa น่าอิจฉา

episode N tawn ตอน

equal ADJ thâo kan เท่ากัน

equality N khwaam thâo thiam ความเท่าเทียม

equipment/implement N ù-pà-kawn อุปกรณ์

era N sà-mǎi สมัย, yúk ยุค

errand N thú-rá ธุระ

error, mistake N khwaam phìt ความผิด

escalator N bandai lûean บันไดเลื่อน

escape/flee v nǐi หนี

especially ADV dohy chà-phá-w โดยเฉพาะ

essay N (e.g. term essay at university) riang khwaam เรียงความ, or (essay/article in a newspaper) bòt khwaam บทความ

establish, set up v kàw tâng ก่อตั้ง

estate N thîi din ที่ดิน

estimate v prà-maan ประมาณ; estimate the price/give a quote tii raa-khaa ตีราคา

ethnic group, minority group N chon klùm nói ชนกลุ่มน้อย

Eurasian N (the offspring of an Asian and European/Caucasian parent) lûuk khrûeng (literally, 'child'-'half') ลูกครึ่ง

Euro N (currency) ngoen yuù-roh เงินยูโร

Europe N yú-ròhp ยุโรป

evacuate v òp-phá-yóp อพยพ

evaluate v prà-moehn ประเมิน

even ADV (e.g. even young people like it) máeh tàeh แม้แต่

even ADJ (smooth) rîap เรียบ, (evenly matched, equal in a race/competition, e.g. a tie in a football game) sà-mǒeh kan เสมอกัน

evening N tawn yen ตอนเย็น

event N hèht kaan เหตุการณ์

ever ADV (e.g. 'have you ever been to…?') khoei เคย (NOTE: for fuller description of how this word is used see 'have'.)

every ADJ thúk ทุก

everybody, everyone PRON thúk khon ทุกคน (NOTE: common idiom – 'everybody for themselves/every man for himself' tua khrai tua man ตัวใครตัวมัน)

every day ADJ thúk wan ทุกวัน

every kind of… N thúk chá-nít ทุกชนิด

everything PRON thúk sìng ทุกสิ่ง, also thúk-yàang ทุกอย่าง

every time ADV thúk khráng ทุกครั้ง

everywhere ADV thúk thîi ทุกที่

evidence, proof N làk thăan หลักฐาน

evil ADJ chûa ráai ชั่วร้าย N khwaam chûa ความชั่ว

exact ADJ (COLLOQUIAL) trong péh ตรง เป๊ะ, (or in short) péh เป๊ะ

exactly! just so! ADV (COLLOQUIAL) nân lâe นั่นแหละ

exaggerate V phûut koehn jing พูด เกินจริง

exam, test N (knowledge or skill) sàwp สอบ

examine, inspect V trùat-sàwp ตรวจ สอบ

example N tua yàang ตัวอย่าง

example, for CONJ chên... เช่น

exceed V koehn kwàa เกินกว่า

excellent ADJ yâwt yîam ยอดเยี่ยม; great, (COLLOQUIAL) 'that's great!' sùt yâwt สุดยอด

except CONJ, **to be exempt** ADJ (e.g. 'everyone can go except him') yók wéhn ยกเว้น; an exception khâw yók wéhn ข้อยกเว้น

except PREP (i.e. in the sense of being 'apart from' or 'in addition to') nâwk jàak นอกจาก

exchange V (money, opinions) lâehk plìan แลกเปลี่ยน

exchange rate N àttraa lâek plìan อัตราแลกเปลี่ยน

excited ADJ tùehn tên ตื่นเต้น

exciting ADJ nâa tùehn tên น่าตื่นเต้น

excrement/feces N (FORMAL MEDICAL TERM) ùt-jaará อุจจาระ, (COLLOQUIAL) khîi ขี้ (in English the common colloquial for this is 'shit' of course, but the Thai word does not have the same type of crude/vulgar sense to it and, while not exactly polite, is not particularly rude. Thus khîi ขี้ is not used in situations, common in English, when someone is angry or has made a mistake, etc.)

excuse me! PHR (attracting attention) used as an apology, e.g. 'I'm sorry' (for bumping into you) khăw thôht ขอโทษ (literally, 'request/ask for'-

'punishment')

excuse me! PHR (said trying to get past someone in a crowded place) khăw thaang nòi ขอทางหน่อย

excuse N khâw kâe tua ข้อแก้ตัว

exercise V àwk kamlang kaai ออก กำลังกาย

exhausted ADJ nùeay เหนื่อย

exhibition N ní-thát-sà-kaan นิทรรศการ

exist V (to be alive) mii chiiwít yùn มีชี วิตอยู่

exit, way out N thaang àwk ทางออก

expand, grow larger V khà-yăai ขยาย

expect V khâat wâa... คาดว่า

expel V lâi àwk ไล่ออก

expense(s), expenditure N raai jàai รายจ่าย, khâa chái jàai ค่าใช้จ่าย

expensive ADJ phaehng แพง

experience N prà-sòp-kaan ประสบการณ์

experience V (to have experienced something) mii pràsòp-kaan มีประสบการณ์

expert ADJ & N (have expertise) chamnaan ชำนาญ; an expert (in a particular field) phûu chîao-chaan ผู้เชี่ยวชาญ

expire V (e.g. a driving license) mòt aa-yú หมดอายุ

explain V à-thí-baai อธิบาย (NOTE: the first two syllables of this word à and thí are very short); '(I) can't explain' à-thí-baai mâi dâi อธิบายไม่ได้; explanation kham à-thí-baai คำอธิบาย

explode V (e.g. a bomb) rá-bòet ระเบิด

explore V săm-rùat สำรวจ

export V sòng àwk ส่งออก

express, urgent ADJ dùan ด่วน

express V (emotion, one's feelings) sà-daehng แสดง

expressway, freeway N thaang dùan ทางด่วน

extend V (make larger/longer, add to) tàw ต่อ; extension (telephone) tàw ต่อ (NOTE: to 'extend a visa' is tàw wii-sâa ต่อวีซ่า)

extinguisher N khrûeang dàp phloehng เครื่องดับเพลิง

extra, additional ADJ phôehm เพิ่ม

extraordinary ADJ (special) phí-sèht พิเศษ

extravagant ADJ (spendthrift) fûm fueai ฟุ่มเฟือย

extremely ADV (COLLOQUIAL) sùt khìit สุดขีด, or (in short) sùt sùt สุด ๆ (e.g. 'extremely hot' ráwn sùt sùt ร้อน สุด ๆ, 'hot' = ráwn ร้อน)

extrovert N châwp khâo sang khom ชอบเข้าสังคม

eye N taa ตา

eyebrow N khíu คิ้ว (it is pronounced like 'cute' in English)

eyeglasses, glasses, spectacles N wâen taa แว่นตา

eyelash N khŏn taa ขนตา

eyelid N plùeak taa เปลือกตา

eyesight N săi taa สายตา

eyewitness N phá-yaan พยาน

F

fable/legend N ní-thaan นิทาน

fabric/textile/cloth N phâa ผ้า

face N nâa หน้า; lose face (dignity, to be embarrassed) khăi nâa (literally, 'sell'-'face') ขายหน้า, or sĭa nâa (literally, 'ruined/spoiled'-'face') เสียหน้า

face/confront V phà-choehn nâa เผชิญ หน้า

fact, facts N khâw thét jing ข้อเท็จจริง

factory N rohng ngaan โรงงาน

fail V (to be unsuccessful) mâi sămrèt ไม่สำเร็จ; to fail a test/exam sàwp tòk (literally, 'test'-'fall') สอบตก

failure N khwaam lóm lĕow ความล้ม เหลว

faint/swoon V pen lom เป็นลม

fair ADJ (to be just)/fair-minded yút-tì-tham ยุติธรรม (NOTE: the English word 'fair' is commonly used in Thai but generally in the negative sense, i.e. something that is 'not fair' mâi fae ไม่แฟร์)

faith N khwaam chûea ความเชื่อ, (MORE FORMAL) sàt-thaa ศรัทธา

fake N (an imitation) plawm ปลอม, e.g. referring to a fake Rolex – 'it's a fake!' khăwng plawm ของปลอม

fall, autumn N (season) rúe-duu bai mái rûang ฤดูใบไม้ร่วง

fall V (drop, decrease) tòk ตก

fall/fell over V hòk-lóm หกล้ม, or simply lóm ล้ม

false ADJ (not genuine) plawm ปลอม, (not true) mâi jing ไม่จริง; wrong phìt ผิด

familiar ADJ khún-kheoi คุ้นเคย

family N khrâwp krua ครอบครัว

famine N khwaam òt yàak ความอดอยาก

famous ADJ mii chûeh sĭang (literally, 'have'-'name'-'sound/voice') มีชื่อเสี ยง, (COLLOQUIAL) 'to be famous' dang ดัง; a famous/well-known person khon dang คนดัง (NOTE: dang ดัง is also the word for a 'loud' sound/noise)

fan N (of a singer/movie star) faehn แฟน (from English: also colloquial term for either girl or boyfriend), (a machine for cooling) phát-lom พัดลม

fancy/luxurious/opulent ADJ rŭurăa หรูหรา

fantasy N (from English) faen-taa-sii, jin-tà-naa-kaan จินตนาการ

far/distant ADJ klai ไกล See 'note' under the entry for 'near' to help differentiate these two terms

fare N khâa dohy-săan ค่าโดยสาร (for buses and minivans), or simply, and more colloquially khâa rót ค่ารถ

farewell N am-laa อำลา (i.e. a farewell party is 'ngaan-líang am-laa' งาน เลี้ยงอำลา)

farm N (from English) faam (is commonly used with a unit of land for rearing animal or fish or livestock, for example; chicken farm is 'faam kài' ฟาร์มไก่, (a paddy field) râi naa ไร่นา

farmer N chaow naa (literally, 'people'- 'rice field') ชาวนา

fart

fart N & V (COLLOQUIAL) tòt ตด

fascinate V chûehn châwp ชื่นชอบ

fashion N (clothing) In Thai the English word is commonly used but with slightly different pronunciation fae-chân (NOTE: unfashionable/old-fashioned/out-of date choei เชย)

fast, rapid ADJ rew เร็ว; the expression to tell someone to 'go faster' or 'hurry up' is rew-rew เร็ว ๆ

fast V (go without food) òt aa-hǎan อดอาหาร

fat, grease N khǎi man ไขมัน (NOTE: the word for cholesterol is khǎi man nai lûeat (literally, 'fat'-'in'-'blood') ไขมันในเลือด)

fat, plump, obese ADJ ûan อ้วน (NOTE: the word 'fat' does not quite have the same negative connotations in Thai conversation as it does in the west, although this could be changing. A more polite word to refer to someone who is carrying a few extra kilograms is sǒmbuun สมบูรณ์ which means 'healthy', 'complete', 'perfect')

fate N chôhk chá-taa โชคชะตา

father N (COLLOQUIAL) phâw พ่อ, (FORMAL) bì-daa บิดา

father-in-law N phâw taa พ่อตา

fatigued, tired ADJ nùeay เหนื่อย

fault N khwaam phìt ความผิด

favorite N (to like the most) châwp mâak thîi sùt ชอบมากที่สุด

fax N (machine/message) fáek(s) แฟกซ์; to send a fax sòng fáek(s) ส่งแฟกซ์

fear N khwaam klua ความกลัว

fearful ADJ nâa klua น่ากลัว

fearless ADJ mâi klua ไม่กลัว, (brave) jai klâa ใจกล้า

feasible, possible ADJ pen pai dâi เป็นไปได้

feast N ngaan-líang งานเลี้ยง

feather N khǒn nòk ขนนก

feature N jùt dèhn จุดเด่น

February N kum-phaa-phan กุมภาพันธ์

federal N sà-hà-phan สหพันธ์

federation N sà-hà-phâap สหภาพ

fee N (generally for a public sector service) khâa tham-niam ค่าธรรมเนียม; service fee khâa bawrí-kaan ค่าบริการ

feeble ADJ mâi mii raeng ไม่มีแรง

feeble-minded, stupid ADJ (COLLOQUIAL) ngôh โง่

feed V hâi aa-hǎan ให้อาหาร

feel V rúu-sùek รู้สึก

feeling N khwaam rúù-sùek ความรู้สึก

feet/foot N (for humans) tháo เท้า, foot/feet (for animals) tiin ตีน (NOTE: in central Thai the word tiin, when applied to people, is extremely rude)

felicity N khwaam sùk ความสุข

fellow N phûean เพื่อน

female N (human being) yǐng หญิง, female (animal) tua mia ตัวเมีย

fence N rúa รั้ว

fend V pâwng kan ป้องกัน

feng shui N huang jûi ฮวงจุ้ย

ferry N ruea khâam fâak เรือข้ามฟาก

fertile ADJ (of land) ù-dom sǒmbuun อุดมสมบูรณ์

festival N (very common in Thailand) thêht-sàkaan เทศกาล; also 'temple fair' (similarly very common) ngaan wát งานวัด

fetch V (to go and get) pai ao maa (literally, 'go'-'take'-'come') ไปเอามา

fever N khâi ไข้; to have a fever pen khâi เป็นไข้

few ADJ mâi kìi… ไม่กี่

few N sǎwng sǎam (literally, 'two'-'three') สองสาม

fiancé, fiancée N khûu mân คู่หมั้น

fiction N ní yaai นิยาย

fidelity N khwaam sûeh sàt ความซื่อสัตย์

field N (a sporting field, a parade ground) sà-nǎam สนาม; a rice field thûng naa ทุ่งนา, or simply naa นา

fierce, vicious ADJ (to describe either an animal or person) dù ดุ

fifteen NUM sìp hâa (literally, 'ten'-'five') สิบห้า

fifth ADJ thî hâa ที่ห้า

fifty NUM hâa sìp (literally, 'five'-'ten') ห้าสิบ

fight V (physically) sûu สู้

fight over V (e.g. the control of a piece of land, a child, etc.) yâehng แย่ง

figure N (number) tua lêhk ตัวเลข, (body shape) hùn ห่น: e.g. 'a good figure' hùn dii หุ่นดี

fill V (e.g. up a car with petrol) toehm เติม

fill out V (a form) kràwk กรอก (*also see* 'form')

film, movie N (COLLOQUIAL) nǎng หนัง, (more formal) phâap-phá-yon ภาพยนตร์

filthy ADJ See 'dirty'

final N & ADJ sùt tháai สุดท้าย

finally ADV ...nai thîi sùt ในที่สุด (in Thai, usually used at the end of a sentence)

finance N kaan-ngoehn การเงิน

find V phóp พบ; trying to find/ to look for something hǎa หา

fine ADJ (okay) dii ดี, OK (from English) oh-kheh โอเค

fine N (for some type of infringement) khâa pràp ค่าปรับ. (In the 'entertainment scene' in Thailand there is also something known as a 'bar fine' – the English words pronounced in the Thai manner. This is the 'fee' a patron has to pay to take a woman (dancer, hostess) out of the premises. A separate 'fee' for 'services rendered' is negotiated between these two individuals)

finger N níu นิ้ว; fingernail lép mueh เล็บมือ

finish, finish off V (stop doing an activity or task) sèt เสร็จ

finished ADJ (complete) sèt láew เสร็จแล้ว, (used up) mòt láew หมดแล้ว

fire N fai ไฟ; 'there's a fire (burning)!' fai mâi ไฟไหม้

fire alarm N sǎn-yaan fai-mâi สัญญาณไฟไหม้

fire someone V lâi àwk ไล่ออก

fireworks N prà-thát ประทัด

firm, company N bawrí-sàt บริษัท

firm ADJ (skin, muscles) nâen แน่น; firm (mattress) khǎeng แข็ง; firm (secure) mânkhong มั่นคง

first ADJ râehk แรก; at first thii râehk ที่แรก, or tawn râehk ตอนแรก

first, earlier, beforehand ADV kàwn ก่อน

first ADJ thîi nùeng ที่หนึ่ง

fish N plaa ปลา

fish V (to go fishing) tòk plaa ตกปลา

fish ball N lûuk chin plaa ลูกชิ้นปลา

fisherman N (formal) chaow prà-mong ชาวประมง, (informal) khon hǎa plaa คนหาปลา

fish sauce N náam plaa (literally, 'water'-'fish') น้ำปลา

fist N kam pân กำปั้น

fistfight N chók tòi ชกต่อย

fit V (clothing; 'it fits perfectly') sài phaw dii ใส่พอดี

fitting, suitable, appropriate ADJ màwsǒm เหมาะสม

five NUM hâa ห้า

fix V (a time, appointment) nát นัด, (repair) kâeh แก้, sâwm ซ่อม

flag N thong ธง; national flag thong châat ธงชาติ

flake N klèt เกล็ด

flame N pleow fai เปลวไฟ

flashlight/torch N fai chǎai ไฟฉาย

flat, apartment N (from English) flàet แฟลต

flat, smooth ADJ (e.g. the sea) rîap เรียบ; flat (e.g. a flat tire/tyre) baen แบน

flavor N rót รส

flaw N roi รอย, tam-nì ตำหนิ

flea N màt หมัด

flea market N tà-làat khǎwng-kào ตลาดของเก่า

flee V nǐi หนี

fleece N khǒn kàe ขนแกะ

flesh, meat N núea เนื้อ

flexible/adaptable ADJ yûet yùn ยืดหยุ่น

flight N (on an airline) thîao bin เที่ยวบิน

flip V plík พลิก

flip flops/thongs N See 'slipper'

flippers N (fins – used for snorkeling, diving, etc.) tiin kòp (literally, 'feet'-'frog') ตีนกบ, also (from English) fin ฟิน

flirt V jìip (pronounced like the word 'jeep' with a low tone) จีบ

float V loi ลอย

flock N fǔung ฝูง

flood N & V náam thûam น้ำท่วม

floor N phúehn พื้น

flour N pâehng แป้ง (Note: the same word pâehng แป้ง also means 'face powder', 'baby powder' etc.)

flow V lǎi ไหล

flower N dàwk mái ดอกไม้

flu/influenza N khâi wàt yài ไข้หวัดใหญ่

fluent ADJ (to do something – e.g. speak a language – fluently) khlâwng คล่อง

fluid/liquid N khǎwng lěhw ของเหลว

flute N khlùi ขลุ่ย

fly N (insect) má-laehng-wan แมลงวัน

fly V bin บิน

foam N fawng ฟอง, (from English) fohm โฟม (is mostly used to refer to a facial foam)

fog N màwk หมอก

fold V (e.g. a piece of paper) pháp พับ

folk ADJ phúehn mueang พื้นเมือง

folk music N don-trii phúehn mueang ดนตรีพื้นเมือง

folktale N ní-thaan phúehn mueang นิทานพื้นเมือง

follow along V taam ตาม

follow behind V taam lǎng ตามหลัง

fond of ADJ (to like someone) châwp ชอบ

food N aa-hǎan อาหาร (Note: the word 'rice' khâaw ข้าว is often colloquially used to refer to 'food')

fool N (COLLOQUIAL) khon ngôh คนโง่

foolish, stupid ADJ (COLLOQUIAL) ngôh โง่

foot/feet N tháo เท้า (Note: the word used for animals' foot/feet is tiin ตีน. It is extremely rude and inappropriate to use this term when referring to humans in polite, or even informal, conversation)

footprint N (FORMAL) roi-tháo รอยเท้า, (very informal) roi-tiin รอยตีน (see note on 'foot/feet' above)

for PREP sǎmràp สำหรับ, also pûea เพื่อ

forbear V lìil lîang หลีกเลี่ยง

forbid V hâam ห้าม

forbidden ADJ tâwng hâam ต้องห้าม, or simply hâam ห้าม

force, energy N kamlang กำลัง

force/compel V bangkháp บังคับ

forecast/predict V (as in weather forecast) phá-yaa-kawn พยากรณ์

forefinger N níu chíi นิ้วชี้

forehead N nâa phàak หน้าผาก

foreign/overseas ADJ tàang prà-thêht ต่างประเทศ

foreigner N chaow tàangchâat ชาวต่างชาติ. Also the common word fàràng ฝรั่ง. This can be an ambiguous term (meaning 'foreigner – westerner-caucasian') that, for some, has negative connotations. The term chaow tàangchâat ชาวต่างชาติ – noted above – does not have such connotations.

forest, jungle N pàa ป่า

forever N & ADV tà-làwt pai ตลอดไป

forget V luehm ลืม

forgetful ADJ khîi-luehm ขี้ลืม

forgive V hâi à-phai ให้อภัย

forgiveness, mercy N kaan hâi à-phai การให้อภัย

forgotten ADJ thùuk luehm ถูกลืม

fork N (utensil) sâwm ส้อม

form N (shape) rûup râang รูปร่าง

form V (to organize or arrange) jàt จัด

formal, official; officially ADJ, ADV thaang kaan ทางการ

format N rûup bàep รูปแบบ

former ADJ khon kàwn คนก่อน

formula N sùut สูตร

fortress, fort N pâwm ป้อม

fortunately/luckily... ADV chôhk dii thîi... โชคดีที่...

fortune teller N mǎw duu หมอดู; to have one's fortune told (COLLOQUIAL) duu mǎw ดูหมอ

forty N sìi sìp สี่สิบ

forward, to go V pai khâang nâa ไปข้างหน้า

foster V líang duu เลี้ยงดู

foul ADJ (bad odor) měn เหม็น, (rotten) nâo เน่า; foul-mouth(ed) ADJ (to speak rudely/coarsely) pàak rái ปากร้าย, (slang; very rude, best left unsaid) pàak mǎa (literally, 'mouth'–'dog') ปากหมา

foundation N muun ní-thí มูลนิธิ

fountain N náam phú น้ำพุ

four NUM sìi สี่

fourteen NUM sìp sìi สิบสี่

fraction N (a fraction of something) sèht-sùan เศษส่วน (NOTE: to make fractions in Thai the 'formula' is sèht เศษ (top number), sùan ส่วน (bottom number), e.g. ¾ – three quarters sèht sǎam sùan sìi เศษสามส่วนสี่. Also see the entry under a 'quarter')

fragile ADJ (delicate) bàwp-baang บอบบาง, (easily broken) tàek ngâai แตกง่าย

fragrance N náam hǎwm น้ำหอม

fragrant ADJ hǎwm หอม

frame N (e.g. picture frame) kràwp กรอบ

France N (country) prà-thêht fà-ràng-sèht ประเทศฝรั่งเศส; French (person) khon fà-ràngsèht คนฝรั่งเศส; (language) phaa-sǎa fà-ràngsèht ภาษาฝรั่งเศส

fraud N kaan kohng การโกง; a fraud/fraudster khon khîi kohng คนขี้โกง

free ADJ (of charge) mâi khít ngoen ไม่คิดเงิน, (also commonly used – from English) frii ฟรี

free of commitments ADJ mâi mii khâw phùuk mát ไม่มีข้อผูกมัด

free/independent ADJ ìtsàrà อิสระ

freedom N ìtsàrà-phâap อิสรภาพ

freewill N sà-màk jai สมัครใจ

freeze V (as with frozen food) châeh khǎeng แช่แข็ง

French fries/chips N (from English) frén fraai เฟรนช์-ฟราย, or man fàràng thâwt มันฝรั่งทอด

frequent ADJ bòi บ่อย; frequently bòi-bòi บ่อย ๆ

fresh ADJ sòt สด

freshwater N náam jùeht น้ำจืด

Friday N wan sùk วันศุกร์

fried V (deep fried), fry V thâwt ทอด; stir-fry/stir fried phàt ผัด

friend N phûean เพื่อน. NOTE: friends phûean-phûean เพื่อน ๆ; a close friend phûean sànìt เพื่อนสนิท, (COLLOQUIAL/SLANG) phûean síi เพื่อนซี้. Also note the following idiomatic expressions: phûean kin เพื่อนกิน (casual, fair-weather friends) (literally, 'friend'-'eat'); phûean taai เพื่อนตาย (friends who will do anything for you) (literally, 'friend'-'die')

friendly, outgoing ADJ pen kan ehng เป็นกันเอง (This expression also means 'take it easy, make yourself at home')

friendship N mít-tà-phâap มิตรภาพ

frightened ADJ tòk jai ตกใจ (NOTE: often said as tòk-kà-jai)

frizzy/curly/kinked ADJ yìk หยิก (i.e. frizzy hair is phǒm yìk ผมหยิก)

frog N kòp กบ

from PREP jàak จาก: e.g. 'what country do you come from?' khun maa jàak prathêht arai (literally, 'you'-'come'-'from'-'country'-'what'?) คุณมาจากประเทศอะไร

front ADJ (in front of) khâang nâa ข้างหน้า

frontier N phrom daen พรมแดน

frost N náam kháang khǎeng น้ำค้างแข็ง, or mâeh khá-níng แม่คะนิ้ง

frown V khà-mùat khíu ขมวดคิ้ว

frozen V & ADJ châeh khǎeng แช่แข็ง

frugal ADJ *See* 'economical'

fruit N phŏnlá-mái ผลไม้

fry V *See* 'fried'

fuel oil N náam man น้ำมัน

fugitive ADJ lòp nĭi หลบหนี

fulfill V (to complete something successfully) sămrèt สำเร็จ

full ADJ tem เต็ม, (having consumed enough food or drink) ìm อิ่ม; to be full already ìm láeo อิ่มแล้ว

fume N kwan ควัน

fun, to have ADJ sà-nùk สนุก

function/work V tham ngaan ทำงาน

funds, funding, capital N thun ทุน

funeral N ngaan sòp งานศพ

fungus/mould N chúea raa เชื้อรา; to be mouldy (COLLOQUIAL) raa khûen ราขึ้น

funny ADJ tà-lòk ตลก, or khăm khăm ขำ ขำ

fur N khŏn-sàt ขนสัตว์

furious ADJ kròht โกรธ

furniture N (from English) foeh-ní-jôeh เฟอร์นิเจอร์

further, additional ADJ phôehm toehm เพิ่มเติม

fussy ADJ (COLLOQUIAL) rûeang mâak (literally, 'issues'-'many') เรื่องมาก, or (alternatively) jûu jíi จู้จี้

future N à-naà-khót อนาคต; in (the) future nai à-naakhót ในอนาคต

G

gain V dâi ráp ได้รับ

gallery N (from English) kael-loeh-lîi แกลเลอรี่

gallon N (from English) kael-lawn แกลลอน

gallstone N kâwn nìu ก้อนนิ่ว; gallstones nìu นิ่ว

gamble V lên kaan phá-nan เล่นการพนัน

game N (from English) kehm เกม

gang N (from English) káeng แก๊ง, klùm กลุ่ม

gangster N nák lehng นักเลง

gap N châwng wâang ช่องว่าง

garage N (for car repairs) ùu sâwm rót อู่ซ่อมรถ, (for parking) rohng rót โรงรถ

garbage/rubbish/trash N khà-yà ขยะ

garden, yard N (also 'plantation') sŭan สวน

gardens (public), park N sŭan săa-thaa rá-ná สวนสาธารณะ

garland N (garlands of flowers are very common in Thailand) phuang maa-lai พวงมาลัย (NOTE: the same word is also used for 'steering wheel'), garland – also simply maalai มาลัย

garlic N kra-thiam กระเทียม

garment, clothing N sûea phâa เสื้อผ้า

gas N (from English, for cooking etc.) káet แก๊ส

gasoline, petrol N náam-man น้ำมัน

gasoline/gas/petrol station N pám náam-man ปั๊มน้ำมัน

gasp V hàwp หอบ

gate, door N prà-tuu ประตู

gateway N thaang khâo ทางเข้า

gather V rûap ruam รวบรวม

gauze N (from English) phâa káwt ผ้าก๊อซ

gay N (homosexual) (from English) keh เกย์, (SLANG) effeminate homosexual tút ตุ๊ด

gaze V jáwng mawng จ้องมอง

gazette N năng-sŭeh-pim หนังสือพิมพ์

gecko N túk-kae ตุ๊กแก

gem N pét phloi เพชรพลอย

gender N (sex – i.e. male/female) phêht เพศ

general, all-purpose N & ADJ thûa pai ทั่วไป

generally, in general ADV dohy thûa pai โดยทั่วไป

generation N (used for people, the particular year/vintage of a car etc.) rûn รุ่น

generous ADJ jai kwâang (literally, 'heart'-'broad/wide') ใจกว้าง

gentle, graceful ADJ (behavior, movement) àwn yohn อ่อนโยน; to do

something (e.g. like a massage) gently
bao-bao เบา ๆ

gentleman N sù-phâap bùrùt สุภาพบุรุษ

genuine/authentic/real ADJ (the opposite of an imitation/fake) tháeh แท้; the
genuine article/the real thing khǎwng
tháeh ของแท้

germ N chúea rôhk เชื้อโรค

German N (person) khon yoeh-rá-man
คนเยอรมัน; German (language)
phaa-sǎa yoeh-rá-man ภาษาเยอรมัน;
Germany (the country) prà-thêht
yoeh-rá-má-nii ประเทศเยอรมนี

**gesture, manner, expression, bearing,
attitude** N (i.e. the way one appears to
another – friendly, unfriendly, disinter-
ested) thâa thaang ท่าทาง

get V (receive) dâi ได้, or dâi ráp ได้รับ

get off V (e.g. a bus) long ลง

get on V (e.g. a bus) khûen ขึ้น

get up/stand up V lúk khûen ลุกขึ้น

get well soon! hǎi wai-wai หายไว ๆ

ghost N phǐi ผี

giant N yák yài ยักษ์ ใหญ่

gift/present N khǎwng khwǎn ของขวัญ

giggle V hǔa ráw khík khák หัวเราะคิก
คัก

ginger N khǐng ขิง

girl (child) N dèk phûu yǐng เด็ก
ผู้หญิง, or simply dèk yǐng เด็กหญิง

girlfriend/boyfriend N (steady) faehn
แฟน; (SLANG) a casual girlfriend, mainly
for sex and a bit of fun without much,
if any, commitment kík กิ๊ก

give V hâi ให้ (NOTE: this important word
is also used in a variety of ways with
various meanings – see the Thai-English section)

give in/give up V (as in 'I give in, you
can go out if you want to' or, 'I give
up, I can't fix it') yawm pháeh (literally,
'allow/permit'-'defeat') ยอมแพ้

glad ADJ dii jai ดีใจ

glamorous ADJ mii sà-nèh มีเสน่ห์

glance V lùeap mawng เหลือบมอง

glass N (for drinking) kâew แก้ว, (mate-

rial – as in a window or the windscreen of a car. It is also the Thai word
for 'mirror') krà-jòk กระจก

glasses, spectacles N wâen taa
แว่นตา

glide V lûehn lǎi ลื่นไหล

globe N lôhk โลก

glorious ADJ sà-ngàa-ngaam สง่างาม

glory N kìat-tì-yót เกียรติยศ

glossy ADJ man waow มันวาว

glove N thûng mueh ถุงมือ

glow V plèhng plàng เปล่งปลั่ง

glue/paste N kaaw กาว

glutinous ADJ (or sticky) rice khâaw
nǐao ข้าวเหนียว

go V pai ไป – a common greeting in
Thai is 'Where are you going?' pai nǎi
(literally, 'go'-'where') ไปไหน. To ask
'where have you been?' is pai nǎi maa
(literally, 'go'-'where'-'come') ไปไหน
มา

go along, join in V pai dûai ไปด้วย

go around, visit V pai yîam ไปเยี่ยม

go back/return V klàp pai กลับไป, or
simply klàp กลับ

go for a walk V pai doehn lên ไปเดิน
เล่น

go home V klàp bâan กลับบ้าน

go out, exit V àwk pai ออกไป

go out V (for fun) (pai) thîao (ไป)เที่ยว
(NOTE: the word thîao is another quintessential Thai term and used in various
ways – e.g. to go to a friend's house
(for fun) is thîao bâan phûean เที่ยว
บ้านเพื่อน; to go to the beach (for
fun) is thîao chaai hàat เที่ยวชายหาด;
to go to a bar (for fun) is thîao baa
เที่ยวบาร์; (for men) to go out and fool
around with loose women is thîao
phûu-yǐng เที่ยวผู้หญิง; and someone
(invariably male) who is habitually
interested in going out on the town at
night is a nák thîao นักเที่ยว)

go out (fire, candle, electricity – as in a
blackout) dàp ดับ (also slang meaning
'to die')

go to bed

G

go to bed v pai nawn ไปนอน

goal N (objective) pâo mǎai เป้าหมาย, (in football/soccer) prà-tuu ประตู (NOTE: the same word for 'door' or 'gate')

goat N pháe แพะ

God N phrá phûu pen jâo พระผู้เป็นเจ้า, or simply phrá jâo พระเจ้า

goddess N jâo mâeh เจ้าแม่

gold N (precious metal) thawng kham ทองคำ, or simply thawng ทอง; the Golden Triangle (the area in northern Thailand where the borders of Burma, Laos, and Thailand meet) sǎam lìam thawng kham สามเหลี่ยมทองคำ

gold ADJ (color) sǐi thawng สีทอง

golf N (from English) káwp กอล์ฟ; to play golf lên káwp เล่นกอล์ฟ

gone ADJ (no longer available; used up) mòt láew หมดแล้ว

gonorrhea N (VD) rôhk nǎwng nai (literally, 'disease'-'pus'-'in') โรคหนองใน

good ADJ dii ดี; very good dii mâak ดีมาก

goodbye INTERJ (from English) báai baai บ๊ายบาย, (FORMAL) laa kàwn ลาก่อน, (MORE COLLOQUIALLY) pai kàwn ná ไปก่อนนะ

good-looking ADJ duu dii ดูดี

good luck! N chôhk dii โชคดี

goodness (me)! INTERJ ôh hoh โอ้โฮ

goods N sǐn kháa สินค้า

goose N hàan ห่าน

gossip N súp síp ninthaa ซุบซิบนินทา, or simply (to talk behind one's back) ninthaa นินทา

govern v pòk khrawng ปกครอง

government N rát-thà-baan รัฐบาล

gown N sûea khlum เสื้อคลุม

GPO (General Post Office, i.e. the main post office or, following the Thai, central post office) prai-sànii klaang ไปรษณีย์กลาง (klaang กลาง means 'central/middle')

GPS (navigation system – from English; pronounced very similar to the English 'GPS') จีพีเอส

grab/snatch v yâeng แย่ง

grace N khwaam sà-ngàa-ngaam ความสง่างาม

graceful ADJ sà-ngàa-ngaam สง่างาม

gradually, bit by bit ADV thii lá nít ทีละนิด

graduate v rian jòp เรียนจบ

grain N than-yá-púeht ธัญพืช

gram N (weight) (from English) kram กรัม

grand, great ADJ yîng yài ยิ่งใหญ่, yài toh ใหญ่โต

grandchild N lǎan หลาน

granddaughter N lǎan sǎow หลานสาว

grandfather N (maternal) taa ตา, (paternal) pùu ปู่

grandmother N (maternal) yaai ยาย, (paternal) yâa ย่า

grandparents N pùu yâa taa yaai ปู่ย่าตายาย

grandson N lǎan chaai หลานชาย

grant v yin yawm ยินยอม

grant N (public fund to finance educational study) thun kaan-sùek-sǎa ทุนการศึกษา

grapes N à-ngùn องุ่น

graph N (from English) kráap กราฟ

grasp v khwáa คว้า

grass N yâa หญ้า

grasshopper N ták-kà-taen ตั๊กแตน

grateful ADJ khàwp-khun ขอบคุณ

grave N lǔm sòp หลุมศพ

gray, grey ADJ sǐi thao สีเทา

grease N (as used in cars/trucks etc.) jaa-rá-bii จารบี

greasy ADJ See 'oily'

great (COLLOQUIAL – as in 'that's great/fantastic'/'tops!') sùt yâwt สุดยอด

Greater vehicle of Buddhism – the Mahayana doctrine lát-thí máhǎa-yaan ลัทธิมหายาน

greed N lôhp โลภ, lá-môhp ละโมบ

green ADJ (color) sǐi khǐao สีเขียว

green beans N thùa fàk yaow ถั่วฝักยาว

green light N fai-khǐao ไฟเขียว, phàan ผ่าน

greens N (green vegetables) phàk sǐi khǐao ผักสีเขียว, or simply phàk khǐao ผักเขียว

greet/welcome V thák thaai ทักทาย, or tâwn ráp ต้อนรับ

greetings N kaan thák thaai การทักทาย

grenade N lûuk rá-bùeat ลูกระเบิด

grief N khwaam sâo ความเศร้า

grill/toast N pîng ปิ้ง, or yâang ย่าง

grind V bòt บด

grocery N khǎwng cham ของชำ

grocery store N ráan khǎai khǎwng cham ร้านขายของชำ

ground, earth, soil, dirt N din ดิน; ground, earth phúehn din พื้นดิน

group N klùm กลุ่ม, phùak พวก, (COLLOQUIAL) group of friends/mates/buddies/entourage phák phùak พรรคพวก

grow, plant V plùuk ปลูก

grow up V toh โต

grow larger V toh khûehn โตขึ้น

grown ADJ pen phûu yài เป็นผู้ใหญ่

grumpy ADJ ngùt-ngìt หงุดหงิด

guarantee V (insure) prà-kan ประกัน, also làk prà-kan หลักประกัน

guard V fâo yaam เฝ้ายาม; a guard (nightwatchman) yaam ยาม

guess V dao เดา

guest N (visitor in one's home, hotel guest) khàehk แขก (NOTE: this word is also used to refer to swarthy people with darker complexions such as Indians, Pakistanis, and Arabs in general)

guesthouse N ruean ráp-rawng khàek เรือนรับรองแขก (NOTE: the English word 'guesthouse' is commonly used in Thai, pronounced something like 'guest-how')

guest of honor N khàek phûu mii kìat แขกผู้มีเกียรติ

guide/lead V nam นำ

guidebook N nǎngsǔeh nam thîao หนังสือนำเที่ยว

guilty (of a crime), **to be wrong** ADJ phìt ผิด

guilty, to feel V rúu-sùek phìt รู้สึกผิด

guitar N kii-tâa กีตาร์

gulf N àow อ่าว

gum N (chewing gum) mǎak-fá-ràng หมากฝรั่ง, (the tissue that surrounds the bases of the teeth) ngùeak เหงือก

gun N (general term) peuhn ปืน; pistol/handgun peuhn phók ปืนพก; rifle peuhn yaow (literally, 'gun'-'long') ปืนยาว; shotgun peuhn lûuk sǎwng ปืนลูกซอง; machine gun peuhn kon ปืนกล; gunman/hitman/hired killer mueh-peuhn (literally, 'hand'-'gun') มือปืน

gut N (intestine) lam-sâi ลำไส้, guts (courage) ความกล้า

guy N (fellow) phûean เพื่อน, guys túk khon ทุกคน

gym N (from English) yim ยิม; (COLLOQUIAL) to work out in the gym/go to the gym lên yim (literally, 'play'-'gym') เล่นยิม

gypsy N (from English) yíp-sii ยิปซี

H

habit N (habitual behavior, often used to refer to a person's character – what sort of person they happen to be) ní-sǎi นิสัย

hacker N (i.e. computer hacker – from English) háek-kôeh แฮกเกอร์

hail N (hailstones) lûuk hép ลูกเห็บ

hair N (on the head – humans) phǒm ผม, (hair on rest of the human body apart from the head; also for animals, i.e. fur) khǒn ขน

half N khrûeng ครึ่ง *Also see* 'Eurasian'

hall N (or large room) hâwng thǒhng ห้องโถง

ham N muu haem หมูแฮม

hammer N kháwn ค้อน

hammock N pleh yuan เปลยวน, (COLLOQUIAL) pleh เปล

hand N mueh มือ

handcuffs N kun-jaeh mueh (literally, 'key'-'hand') กุญแจมือ

handicap/handicapped/disabled N phí-kaan พิการ

handicraft N ngaan fǐi-mueh งานฝีมือ, or (FORMAL) hàt-thà-kam หัตถกรรม

handle N (of an object, e.g. a knife) dâam ด้าม

handle V (to deal with) jàt kaan จัดการ

hand out, distribute V jàehk แจก

hand over V mâwp hâi มอบให้

handsome ADJ làw หล่อ; (COLLOQUIAL) a good-looking, handsome man rûup làw รูปหล่อ

handwriting N laai mueh ลายมือ

handy ADJ sà-dùak สะดวก

hang V (a painting) khwǎehn แขวน; to hang down/dangle (e.g. fruit hanging down from a tree) hôi ห้อย

hang out V (meet up and chill out) joeh kan เจอกัน, (spend time in a certain place) pai thîaw ไปเที่ยว

hangover N mao kháang เมาค้าง

happen/occur V kòeht khûen เกิดขึ้น

happened V (as in 'what happened?') kòeht àrai khûen เกิดอะไรขึ้น

happiness N khwaam sùk ความสุข

happy ADJ mii khwaam sùk มีความสุข

happy birthday! EXP sùksǎn wan kòeht สุขสันต์วันเกิด (or simply the expression 'happy birthday' pronounced in the Thai way – something like 'háeppîi bértday')

happy new year! EXP sà-wàt-dii pii-mài สวัสดีปีใหม่

harbor, pier, port N thâa ruea ท่าเรือ

hard ADJ (to be difficult) yâak ยาก, (solid, stiff) khǎeng แข็ง

hard disk N (from English) háad-dís ฮาร์ดดิสก์; (from English) hard drive háad-drái ฮาร์ดไดร์ว

hardly ADV (e.g. able to do something, any left, etc.) thâehp jà mâi… แทบ จะไม่

hardship N (difficult circumstances) khwaam lambàak ความลำบาก, or simply lambàak ลำบาก

hardworking, industrious, diligent ADJ

khà-yǎn ขยัน

harm N an-tà-raai อันตราย

harmonious ADJ (e.g. relations with others) khâo kan dâi เข้ากันได้

harsh ADJ run raeng รุนแรง

harvest V (gathering crops) kèp kìaw เก็บเกี่ยว

harvest N (yield, output) phǒn phá-lìt ผลผลิต

haste V rêhng rîip เร่ง รีบ

hat, cap N mùak หมวก; *also see* entry under 'helmet'

hate V klìat เกลียด

hatred N khwaam klìat ความเกลียด

haunted ADJ lǎwn หลอน

have… V mii… มี (the Thai word is used in various ways, e.g. to have available, to own, there is…)

have been somewhere khoei pai เคย ไป: e.g. If someone asks you 'have you ever been to Chiang Mai?' – in Thai the question is khun khoei pai chiang mài mǎi คุณเคยไป เชียงใหม่ไหม. If you have, the answer 'yes' is khoei pai เคยไป, or simply just khoei เคย. To answer in the negative 'I've never been' is mâi khoei pai, or simply mâi khoei ไม่เคย

have done something khoei tham เคย ทำ: e.g. If some asks you 'have you ever ridden a horse?' – in Thai the question is khun khoei khìi máa mǎi คุณเคยขี่ม้าไหม. If you have, the answer 'yes' is khoei khìi เคยขี่, or simply just khoei เคย. To answer in the negative see the previous entry.

have to, must V tâwng ต้อง

haven N thâa ruea ท่าเรือ

hawk N yìaw เหยี่ยว

hay N faang ฟาง

hazard, danger N an-tà-raai อันตราย

haze N màwk หมอก

he, him PRON (also she, her and the third person plural pronoun 'they') khǎo เขา

head N (COLLOQUIAL) hǔa หัว, (the more formal medical term is) sǐi-sà ศีรษะ,

(the boss, person in charge) hŭa nâa หัวหน้า

head for, toward PREP mûng pai มุ่งไป

headdress N khrûeang prà-dàp sĭi-sà เครื่องประดับศีรษะ

heal V rák-sǎa รักษา

health N sùk-khà-phâap สุขภาพ

healthy ADJ sŏmbuun สมบูรณ์; to be healthy sùk-khà-phâap dii สุขภาพดี, or khǎeng raehng แข็งแรง (which normally would be translated as 'strong', but also means 'healthy and well')

hear V dâi-yin ได้ยิน; listen to (the radio) fang ฟัง

heart N hŭa jai หัวใจ (NOTE: in a more metaphorical sense i.e. 'my heart is not in it' just the word jai ใจ is used. In Thai there are numerous compound words that incorporate jai ใจ: e.g. to 'feel sorry' as in 'feeling sorry on hearing bad news' is sĭa jai (literally, 'spoiled'-'heart') เสียใจ

heart attack N hŭa jai waai หัวใจวาย

heartbreak N òk-hàk อกหัก

heartwarming ADJ òp-ùn-jai อบอุ่นใจ

heat V tham hâi ráwn ทำให้ร้อน

heat N khwaam ráwn ความร้อน

heaven/paradise N sà wǎn สวรรค์

heavy ADJ nàk หนัก; *also see* 'weight'

heel N (of the foot) sôn tháo ส้นเท้า

height N khwaam sǔung ความสูง

hell N ná-rók นรก

hello, hi INTERJ (greeting used at any time of the day) sàwàt dii สวัสดี

hello! INTERJ (answering the phone, from English) han-lŏh ฮัลโหล

helmet N (i.e. crash helmet/motorcycle helmet) mùak kan nók หมวกกันน็อก

help V chûai ช่วย or chûai lŭea ช่วยเหลือ

help! INTERJ ('Please help!') chûai dûai ช่วยด้วย

helper, assistance N phûu chûai ผู้ช่วย

hen N mâe kài แม่ไก่

hence, therefore ADV dang nán ดังนั้น

hepatitis N rôhk tàp àk-sèhp (literally, 'disease/illness'-'liver'-'inflamed') โรคตับอักเสบ

her, his, their PRON khǎwng kháo ของเขา; hers, his, theirs khǎwng khǎo ของเขา

herb N sà-mǔn-phrai สมุนไพร

herd N fǔung ฝูง

herd V tâwn ต้อน

herdman, herder N khon lîang sàt คนเลี้ยงสัตว์

here ADV thîi nii ที่นี่

hereditary N kammá-phan (pronounced 'gum-àpun') กรรมพันธุ์

heritage N maw-rá-dòk มรดก

hero N phrá-èk (e.g. in a film – 'leading man') พระเอก; wii-rá bù-rùt (e.g. in a war, in a disaster saving lives) วีรบุรุษ, hii-rôh (from English) ฮีโร่; heroine naang-èk (e.g. in a film – 'leading woman') นางเอก, wii-rá sà-trii (e.g. in a conflict etc.) วีรสตรี

heroin N (narcotic) (from English) heroh-iin เฮโรอีน, (COLLOQUIAL) phŏng khǎow (literally, 'powder'-'white') ผงขาว

herpes (STD) N rôhk roem โรคเริม

hiccup N sà-ùek สะอึก

hidden ADJ sâwn yùu ซ่อนอยู่

hide V (from someone) (do something furtively) àehp แอบ; to hide something/to be hidden sâwn wái ซ่อนไว้

hide-and-seek N lên sawn hǎa เล่นซ่อนหา

hierarchy N lam-dàp-chán ลำดับชั้น

higgle V tàw rawng ต่อรอง

higgledy-piggledy ADJ yûng yǒehng ยุ่งเหยิง

high ADJ (in or at a lofty position, level, or degree, i.e. mountain, prices etc.) sǔung สูง

high-five V tii-moeh ตีมือ

highland N thîi râap sǔung ที่ราบสูง

highlight V tham hâi dèhn ทำให้เด่น

high-voltage ADJ fai-fáa raeng sǔung ไฟฟ้าแรงสูง

highway N thaang lǔang ทางหลวง

hijack v jîi khrûeang bin จี้เครื่องบิน

hike v, **hiking** n doehn pàa เดินป่า

hilarious ADJ tà-lòk ตลก

hill n noehn khǎo เนินเขา, or simply noehn เนิน

hill tribe n chaow khǎo (literally, 'people'-'mountain') ชาวเขา

hinder/obstruct v kìit khwǎang กีดขวาง

hindrance n sìng kìit khwǎang สิ่งกีดขวาง

hint n bàwk bâi บอกใบ้

hip n sà-phôhk สะโพก

hippy n (from English) híp-pîi ฮิปปี้

hire/rent v châo เช่า (NOTE: to hire/rent a car is châo rót เช่ารถ, while a rental car is rót châo รถเช่า)

his PRON (or 'hers' or 'their(s)') khǎwng khǎo ของเขา

history prà-wàt-ti-sàat ประวัติศาสตร์; one's own personal history prà-wàt sùan tua ประวัติส่วนตัว

hit, strike, beat v (for a person to hit, strike, or beat another person or object) tii ตี; to hit or collide with.... chon ชน

hit-and-run ADJ chon láew nǐi ชนแล้วหนี

HIV n (also see 'AIDS' – from English) etch-ai-wii เอชไอวี

hive n rang phûeang รังผึ้ง

hoarse ADJ sǐang hàep เสียงแหบ

hobby/pastime n ngaan à-dì-rèhk งานอดิเรก

hockey n (from English) hawk-kîi ฮ็อกกี้

hoe n jàwp จอบ

hoist v yók khûen ยกขึ้น

hold, grasp v thǔeh ถือ or jàp จับ

hold back v yùt wái หยุดไว้

hole n (but not of the 'hole in the ground' variety) ruu รู; hole in the ground lǔm หลุม

holiday n (festival) wan yùt thèht-sà-kaan วันหยุดเทศกาล, (vacation) wan yùt phák phàwn วันหยุดพักผ่อน, (public) wan yùt râatchá-kaan วันหยุดราชการ, or simply wan yùt วันหยุด

holy, sacred ADJ sàksìt ศักดิ์สิทธิ์

home, house n bâan บ้าน

homework n (from school, college) kaan bâan การบ้าน; housework ngaan bâan งานบ้าน

homicide n kaan khâa khon การฆ่าคน

homosexual See 'gay'

honest ADJ sûeh-sàt ซื่อสัตย์

honey n náam phûeang (literally, 'water'-'bee') น้ำผึ้ง

honeymoon n (from English) han-nii-muun ฮันนีมูน

Hong Kong n hâwng kong ฮ่องกง

honk v bìip trae บีบแตร

honor n kìat-tì-yót เกียรติยศ

honor v hâi kìat ให้เกียรติ

hoodlum/tough guy/thug n anthá-phaan อันธพาล, or (MORE COLLOQUIALLY) nák-leng นักเลง

hooker, whore n (prostitute) (POLITE) sǒhphehnii โสเภณี, (COLLOQUIAL) phûu-yǐng hǎa kin (literally, 'woman'-'look for'-'eat') ผู้หญิงหากิน, phûu-yǐng hǎa ngoen (literally, 'woman'-'look for'-'money') ผู้หญิงหาเงิน

hop v krà-dòht กระโดด

hope v wǎng หวัง, or 'to hope that...' wǎng wâa...หวังว่า

hope n khwaam wǎng ความหวัง

hopeful ADJ mii khwaam wǎng มีความหวัง

hopefully ADV dûai khwaam wǎng ด้วยความหวัง

horizon n khàwp-fáa ขอบฟ้า

hormone n (from English) haw-mohn ฮอร์โมน

horny ADJ (desirous of sex) (SLANG, RUDE) ngîan เงี่ยน; also yàak อยาก (which, in general usage, means 'want')

horrible, horrific ADJ (frightening) nâa klua น่ากลัว

horrify v tham hâi klua ทำให้กลัว

hors d'oeuvre(s), entrée, starter N khǎwng wâang ของว่าง

horse N máa ม้า

horseman N thá-hǎan-máa ทหารม้า

hospital N rohng phá-yaa-baan โรงพยาบาล

host N jâo phâap เจ้าภาพ

hostage N tua prá-kan ตัวประกัน

hostel N thîi-phák ที่พัก, (from English) hóhs-tehl โฮสเทล

hostess N (in an entertainment establishment) phûu-yǐng bawrí-kaan (literally, 'woman'-'service') ผู้หญิงบริการ

hostile N sàt-truu ศัตรู

hot ADJ (spicy) phèt เผ็ด, (temperature) ráwn ร้อน, (as in 'sexy' – from English) háwt ฮอท (NOTE: the word 'sexy' is also commonly used in Thai sék-sîi เซ็กซี่)

hotheaded ADJ jai ráwn ใจร้อน

hotel N rohng-raehm โรงแรม (NOTE: in Thailand there are many 'short-time' hotels with 'canvas curtains' so a car can be parked discreetly. These are known as rohng-raehm mâan rûut (literally, 'hotel'-'curtain'-'zip') โรงแรมม่านรูด)

hot spring N náam phú ráwn น้ำพุร้อน

hour N chûa-mohng ชั่วโมง

house N See 'home'

houseboat N See 'raft'

housekeeper N (servant), maid (in hotel) mâeh bâan (literally, 'mother'-'house/home') แม่บ้าน

how? ADV yàang-rai อย่างไร, or yang-ngai ยังไง: e.g. 'how do you do it?' tham yàang-rai ทำอย่างไร, or (in colloquial speech like this) tham yang ngai ทำยังไง (NOTE: in contrast to the English form this question tag comes at the end of the sentence)

how are you? sa-baai dii rǒeh? (Note: the word rǒeh here, although spelled with an 'r', is commonly pronounced lǒeh) สบายดีหรือ, also sa-baai dii mǎi สบายดีไหม

however ADV yàang-rai kâw taam อย่างไรก็ตาม

how long (does it take)?/**for how long?** naan thâo-rài นานเท่าไหร่ (the word naan means 'a long time' so the question – naan thâorài – has the following pattern 'long time' – 'how much?')

how long? (length) yaaw thâorài ยาวเท่าไร (the word yaaw means 'long' with the question yaaw thâorài having the following pattern 'long' – 'how much?')

how many...? kìi... กี่

how much? thâo rài เท่าไหร่ – to say 'how much is it?', 'what's the price?', or 'what does it cost?' (the word for price/cost is raa-khaa ราคา) the pattern is raa-khaa thâorài i.e. 'price/cost' – 'how much?' ราคาเท่าไหร่

how old? aa-yú thâorài อายุเท่าไหร่ (the word for 'age' is aa-yú อายุ – again the pattern is the same as above i.e. 'age' – 'how much?')

hug V kàwt กอด

huge ADJ yài ใหญ่

human/human being N má-nút มนุษย์

humane ADJ mii náam jai มีน้ำใจ

humble ADJ thàwm tua ถ่อมตัว

humid ADJ chúehn ชื้น

humiliate V khǎai nâa ขายหน้า, sǐa nâa เสียหน้า

humorous, funny, amusing ADJ khòp khǎn ขบขัน, or tà-lòk ตลก

hundred NUM rói ร้อย

hundred thousand NUM sǎehn แสน

hungry ADJ hǐu หิว: the common expression for 'I'm hungry' is hǐu khâaw (literally, 'hungry'-'rice/food') หิวข้าว; for 'I'm thirsty' the expression is hǐu náam (literally, 'hungry'-'water') หิวน้ำ

hunt V lâa ล่า

hurricane N phaa-yú hoeh-rí-khehn พายุเฮอริเคน

hurry up! V rew-rew เร็ว ๆ

hurt (injured), sore ADJ jèp เจ็บ

hurt

H

hurt v (cause pain) tham hâi jèp ทำให้เจ็บ

husband N (POLITE) sǎa-mii สามี, (SLANG) phǔa ผัว (in more educated circles considered rude, generally seen as low class language – referring to the sexual partner of a woman, the couple not being formally married)

husk N plùehk เปลือก

hut, shack, shed N krà-thâwm กระท่อม, or krà-táwp กระต๊อบ

hybrid car N ('hybrid' from English) rót-yon hai-brìd รถยนต์ไฮบริด

hydrate v toehm náam เติมน้ำ

hydration N chum chûehn ชุ่มชื่น

hygiene/cleanliness N khwaam sà-àat ความสะอาด

I

I, me PRON (NOTE: there are numerous first person pronouns, i.e. the words for 'I' and 'me', and other ways to refer to oneself in Thai. This issue is too complex to be discussed here. For our purposes the following common polite terms will suffice: for males phǒm (the same word as 'hair on the head') ผม; for females dìchǎn ดิฉัน, or simply chǎn ฉัน)

ice N náam khǎeng น้ำแข็ง (literally, 'water'-'hard')

ice cream N (from English) ai-sà-khriim ไอศกรีม

ice pack N thǔng náam khǎeng ถุงน้ำแข็ง

icon N (from English) ai-khâwn ไอคอน

ICU (from the English abbreviation of the term 'Intensive Care Unit' – in common usage in Thai hospitals and used by the general public) ai-sii-yuu ไอซียู

ID (in this entry referring to 'Identity card' which all Thai citizens possess) bàt prà-chaàchon (literally, 'card'-'people/populace') บัตรประชาชน

idea N khwaam khít ความคิด

ideal N ù-dom-khá-tì อุดมคติ

identical, alike, the same as ADJ mǔean-kan เหมือนกัน, or simply mǔean เหมือน

identification card N bàt-prá-chaa-chon บัตรประชาชน

identity N (as in 'national identity/characteristics') èkkàlák เอกลักษณ์; Thai identity èkkàlák thai เอกลักษณ์ไทย

ideologist N nák khít นักคิด

ideology N naew khít แนวคิด

idiom N (figure of speech) sǎm-nuan สำนวน

idiot N (a fool) khon ngô (literally, 'person'-'stupid') คนโง่

idol N (from English) ai-dâwl ไอดอล

if CONJ (used in much the same way as English) thâa ถ้า

ignite v jùt fai จุดไฟ

ignorant ADJ (to be unaware of something, not to know what's going on) (COLLOQUIAL) mâi rúu rûeang ไม่รู้เรื่อง; ignorant ('unschooled' or 'uneducated') khàat kaan sùek-sǎa (literally, 'missing/without'-'education') ขาดการศึกษา or mâi mii kaan sùek-sǎa (literally, 'no'-'have'-'education') ไม่มีการศึกษา

ignore v lá loei ละเลย, or mâi sǒn-jai (literally, 'no'-'interest') ไม่สนใจ

ill/sick ADJ pùai ป่วย, or simply mâi-sàbaai ไม่สบาย

ill will N mâi jing jai ไม่จริงใจ

illegal/illicit ADJ phìt kòt-mǎai ผิดกฎหมาย

illiterate ADJ (very informal) mâi rúu nǎng-sǔeh ไม่รู้หนังสือ, (more formal) mâi mii kan sùek-sǎa ไม่มีการศึกษา

illness N khwaam jèp pùai ความเจ็บป่วย

illude, deceive v làwk luang หลอกลวง

illuminate v tham-hâi sà-wàang ทำให้สว่าง

illusion N phâap luang taa ภาพลวงตา

illustration N phâap prà-kàwp ภาพประกอบ

incredible

image N phâap ภาพ, or rûup phâap รูปภาพ

imagination N jin-tà-naa-kaan (NOTE: the first syllable jin is pronounced like the English word 'gin') จินตนาการ

imagine V (visualize an image) néuk phâap นึกภาพ, (in the sense 'imagine/suppose that....?') sŏm-mút wâa สมมุติว่า

imbalance N mâi sŏm-dun ไม่สมดุล

imitate V lian bàep เลียนแบบ

imitation N kaan lian bàep การเลียนแบบ

immature ADJ yang dèk ยังเด็ก

immediately ADV than thii ทันที

immense ADJ jam nuan maâak จำนวนมาก

immigrant N phûu òp-phá-yóp ผู้อพยพ

immigration N (as in the Immigration Bureau where visas are extended, etc.) sam nák ngaan trùat khon khâo mueang สำนักงานตรวจคนเข้าเมือง, (colloquially referred to by the abbreviation taw maw [pronounced like 'tore more', from the words trùat ตรวจ – 'check/inspect' and mueang เมือง – 'country] ตอมอ)

immoral ADJ phìt sĭin ผิดศีล

immortal ADJ (FORMAL) am-má-tà อมตะ, mâi taai ไม่ตาย

immune ADJ mii phuum tâan thaan มีภูมิต้านทาน

impart V hâi khwaam rúu ให้ความรู้

impartial, fair ADJ yú-tì-tham ยุติธรรม

impatient ADJ jai ráwn (literally, 'heart'-'hot') ใจร้อน

impeach V fáwng ráwng ฟ้องร้อง

implicate V kìaw khâwng เกี่ยวข้อง

implicit ADJ chat jehn ชัดเจน

implore, beg for V khăw ráwng ขอร้อง

imply V bàwk thŭeng บอกถึง

impolite, rude ADJ mâi sù-phâap ไม่สุภาพ

import N (imported goods) sĭn-kháa nam khâo สินค้านำเข้า

import V nam khâo นำเข้า

importance N khwaam sămkhan ความสำคัญ

important ADJ sămkhan สำคัญ

impossible ADJ pen pai mâi dâi เป็นไปไม่ได้

impotent ADJ mâi mii raeng ไม่มีแรง

impress V tham-hâi prà-tháp jai ทำให้ประทับใจ

impression N khwaam prà-tháp jai ความประทับใจ

impressive ADJ nâa-prà-tháp jai น่าประทับใจ

improve V pràp-prung ปรับปรุง

improvement N kaan pràp-prung การปรับปรุง

impudence N mâi mii maa-rá-yâat ไม่มีมารยาท

impure ADJ mâi baw-rí-sùt ไม่บริสุทธิ์

in PREP (inside) nai ใน, (a period of time) phaai nai ภายใน

inaccurate ADJ mâi thùuk tâwng ไม่ถูกต้อง

inadequate ADJ mâi phaw ไม่พอ

incense N (joss sticks) thûup ธูป

inch ADJ níw นิ้ว

incident N hèht kaan เหตุการณ์

incite, provoke V yûa-yú ยั่วยุ

incline V (to have a certain tendency) mii naew nôhm มีแนวโน้ม, (to slope) iang เอียง

include V ruam รวม; including... ruam tháng... รวมทั้ง

income, wages, salary N raai dâi รายได้, (MORE COLLOQUIAL) ngoen duean เงินเดือน

incomparable ADJ thîap kan mâi dâi เทียบกันไม่ได้

incompatible ADJ (e.g. two people who do not get on) khâo kan mâi dâi เข้ากันไม่ได้

inconvenient ADJ mâi sà-dùak ไม่สะดวก

increase V phôehm เพิ่ม, or phôehm khûen เพิ่มขึ้น

incredible ADJ (as in 'amazing!', 'unbelivable!') mâi nâa chûea ไม่น่าเชื่อ

ENGLISH–THAI

indeed! INTERJ (to emphasize something as in 'really, it's true!') jing-jing จริง ๆ

independent ADJ (to be free, not to be controlled by others) ìtsàrà อิสระ

index N (in a printed work) dàt-chá-nii ดัชนี, (finger) níw chíi นิ้วชี้

India N prà-thêht in-dia ประเทศ อินเดีย, Indian N khon in-dia คน อินเดีย

indifferent/blasé ADJ chŏei-chŏei เฉย ๆ (NOTE: a very commonly used expression in Thai)

indigenous ADJ (person) chaow phúehn mueang ชาวพื้นเมือง; for something that is indigenous to a particular place simply – phúehn mueang พื้นเมือง

indigo N sĭi khraam สีคราม

indirect ADJ thaang âwm ทางอ้อม

Indonesia N (the country) indohnii-sia อินโดนีเซีย (in colloquial speech Indonesia is often referred to simply as indo อินโด)

Indonesian N chaow indohnii-sia ชาว อินโดนีเซีย, or khon indohnii-sia คน อินโดนีเซีย; Indonesian (language) phaa-sǎa indohnii-sia ภาษา อินโดนีเซีย

induct V náe nam แนะนำ

industry N (factories etc.) ùt-sǎahà-kam อุตสาหกรรม

inequality N mâi thâo kan ไม่เท่ากัน

inexpensive ADJ mâi phaehng ไม่แพง

inexperience N ไม่มีประสบการณ์

infamous ADJ sĭa chûeh เสียชื่อ

infant N thaa rók ทารก

infect N tìt chúea ติดเชื้อ, or tìt rôhk ติดโรค

infection N kaan tìt chúea การติดเชื้อ, kaan tìt rôhk การติดโรค

influence N ìt-thí-phon อิทธิพล

influence V (to have influence – in Thai this generally means to have 'connections' enabling one to engage in 'extra legal' activities) mii ìt-thí-phon มี อิทธิพล (There is also the expression

ìt-thí-phon mûehd อิทธิพลมืด which means 'dark influence(s)' or, more correctly in English, 'dark force(s)' which is used to refer to well-placed individuals involved behind the scenes in political intrigue, extortion, bribery, murder)

influenza N (the flu) khâi wàt yài ไข้หวัดใหญ่

inform V (e.g. the police about a problem) jâehng แจ้ง; inform (tell) bàwk บอก

informal ADJ mâi pen thaang kaan ไม่เป็นทางการ

information, data N khâw-muun ข้อมูล; knowledge khwaam rúu ความรู้

information booth/hotel reception N (where information about various things is available)/public relations prà-chaa sǎmphan ประชาสัมพันธ์

ingredient(s) N (in a recipe) sùan prà-kàwp ส่วนประกอบ

inhabit/live V yùu aa-sǎi อยู่อาศัย, or simply yùu อยู่

inhabitant N phûu yùu aa-sǎi ผู้อยู่อาศัย

inhale V sùut สูด

inhibit V hâam ห้าม

inhumane ADJ hòht ráai โหดร้าย

initial ADJ rôehm tôn เริ่มต้น

initiate V rí-rôehm ริเริ่ม

inject V chìit ฉีด; an injection of medicine/vaccine/drug chìit yaa ฉีดยา

injured ADJ dâi ráp bàat jèp (literally, 'receive/get'-'injury') ได้รับบาดเจ็บ

injury N bàat jèp บาดเจ็บ

injustice N mâi yú-tì-tham ไม่ยุติธรรม

ink N mùek หมึก

innocent ADJ bawrí-sùt บริสุทธิ์ (NOTE: the English word 'innocent' – in-noh-sén อินโนเซนท์ – is also used in Thai. Additionally, the Thai term bawrí-sùt is also used to refer to a virgin)

innovation N ná-wàt tà-kam นวัตกรรม

in order that, so that CONJ phûea thîi เพื่อที่

inquire V sàwp thǎam สอบถาม

insane ADJ rôhk jìt โรคจิต; (or simply the word for) mad/crazy bâa บ้า – a simple slang expression to express the same thing is to refer to such a person as mâi tem (literally, 'not'-'full') ไม่เต็ม

insect N (general term for insects) má-laehng แมลง

insecure ADJ mâi mân khong ไม่มั่นคง

insert V saek แทรก

inside PREP khâang nai ข้างใน

insignificant ADJ mâi săm khan ไม่สำคัญ

insist V yuehn kraan ยืนกราน

inspect V trùat ตรวจ

inspector N phûu trùat sàwp ผู้ตรวจสอบ

inspire V ban-daan jai บันดาลใจ; inspiration N raeng ban-daan jai แรงบันดาลใจ

install V tìt tang ติดตั้ง

installment N phàwn jàai ผ่อนจ่าย

instance N tua yàang ตัวอย่าง

instant ADJ than thii ทันที

instead of PREP thaen thîi แทนที่, or simply thaen แทน

institute N sà-thăa-ban สถาบัน

instruct (to give advice) V hâi kham náe-nam ให้คำแนะนำ

instrument/tool N khrûeang mueh เครื่องมือ

insufficient ADJ mâi phaw ไม่พอ

insult/look down (someone) V duu thùuk ดูถูก

insure V prà-kan ประกัน; insurance prà-kan phai ประกันภัย

integrate V phà-sŏm phá-săan ผสมผสาน

intellect N pan yaa ปัญญา, or sàtì-pan yaa สติปัญญา

intelligent ADJ mii sàtì-pan yaa มีสติปัญญา, (MORE COLLOQUIAL) chà-làat ฉลาด

intend V tâng-jai ตั้งใจ

intended for ADJ săm-ràp สำหรับ

intense ADJ khêhm khôn เข้มข้น

intention N khwaam tâng-jai ความตั้งใจ

interest N (a charge for a loan) dàwk bîa ดอกเบี้ย, (or colloquially, simply) **dàwk** ดอก

interest N (personal) khwaam sŏn-jai ความสนใจ

interested ADJ sŏn-jai สนใจ

interesting ADJ nâa sŏn-jai น่าสนใจ

interior ADJ phaai nai ภายใน

international ADJ naa-naa châat นานาชาติ

Internet N (from English) inthoehnèt อินเทอร์เน็ต, (COLLOQUIAL) nèt เน็ต

interpret/translate V plaeh แปล (NOTE: one common way to ask 'what does this/that mean?' is plaeh wâa àrai แปลว่าอะไร)

interpreter N lâam ล่าม

interrogate V sàwp sŭan สอบสวน

interrupt V khàt-jang-wà ขัดจังหวะ

intersection N (i.e. four-way intersection) sìi yâehk สี่แยก (the word yâehk แยก means 'to separate'); a five-way intersection hâa yâehk ห้าแยก

intervene V saek saeng แทรกแซง

interview V săm-phâat สัมภาษณ์

intimate ADJ (to be close to, a close friend) sà-nìt สนิท; also see 'friend'

intimidate V khùu ขู่

into PREP (to the inside) khâo pai khâang nai (literally, 'enter'-'go'-'inside') เข้าไปข้างใน

intolerant ADJ òt-thon อดทน

introduce V náe-nam tua แนะนำตัว

intrude, invade V bùk rúk บุกรุก

invent V prà-dìt ประดิษฐ์

invest V (in a business etc.) long thun ลงทุน

investigate V sùep สืบ

invisible ADJ mawng mâi hĕn มองไม่เห็น

invitation N kham choehn คำเชิญ

invite V (COLLOQUIAL) chuan ชวน, (FORMAL) choehn เชิญ

invoice, receipt N bai kèp ngoehn ใบเก็บเงิน, (COLLOQUIAL) bai sèht ใบเสร็จ

involve V kìao khâwng เกี่ยวข้อง

I

iron N (steel) lèk เหล็ก, (an appliance) tao rîit เตารีด

iron V (clothes) rîit phâa รีดผ้า

ironic ADJ prà-chót ประชด

irregular ADJ mâi pòk-kà-tì ไม่ปกติ

irrelevant ADJ mâi kìaw khâwng ไม่เกี่ยวข้อง

irritate V kuan jai กวนใจ

Islam N (the religion of Islam) sàat-sà-nǎa ìt-sàlaam ศาสนาอิสลาม

island N kàw (pronounced very short like 'oh!' in 'Oh! Ooh' with a 'g' sound in front) เกาะ

isolate V yâek tua แยกตัว

issue N pan hǎa ปัญหา

it PRON man (the an pronounced like 'un' in 'unlucky') มัน (used for things, animals, an event, an issue, etc. – NOTE: when used to refer to a person it is extremely rude; at times some Thai people may use this to refer to for-eigners which reflects a contemptu-ous attitude)

itch N khan คัน

itchy ADJ mii aa-kaan khan มีอาการคัน

item, individual thing N sìng สิ่ง

itinerary N phǎen kaan doehn thaang แผนการเดินทาง

itself PRON tua-ehng ตัวเอง

ivory N ngaa cháang งาช้าง

J

jabber V phûut rua พูดรัว

jacket N (from English) jáekkêt แจ็คเก็ต

jade N yòk หยก

jail/gaol N khúk คุก; to be in jail/gaol/incarcerated tìt khúk ติดคุก

jam N (from English, e.g. 'strawberry jam') yaehm แยม

January N má-ká raa-khom มกราคม

Japan N yîipùn ญี่ปุ่น

Japanese N chaow yîipùn ชาวญี่ปุ่น, or khon yîipùn คนญี่ปุ่น

jar N (i.e. a large water jar) òhng โอ่ง; a (very) small jar (e.g. containing face powder/ointment etc.) krà-pùk กระปุก

jaw N kraam กราม

jealous/envious ADJ ìt-chǎa อิจฉา; jealous (a jealous boyfriend, wife etc.) hǔeng หึง; someone who is extremely jealous khîi hǔeng ขี้หึง

jealousy N khwaam ìt-chǎa ความอิจฉา

jeans N (from English) kaang keng yiin กางเกงยีน

jelly N wún วุ้น, (from English) yen lîi เยลลี่

jellyfish N maehng-kà-phrun แมงกะพรุน

jet ski N (from English) jét sà-kii เจ็ตสกี

jewel N phét phloi เพชรพลอย

jewelry N khrûeang phét phloi เครื่องเพชรพลอย

jinx N tua chôhk ráai ตัวโชคร้าย, (COLLO-QUIAL) tua suai ตัวซวย

job, work N ngaan งาน (NOTE: the same word also means 'a party' or 'a festive occasion')

jockey N nák khìi máa นักขี่ม้า

jogging N wing cháa cháa วิ่งช้า ๆ

join, go along V pai dûai ไปด้วย

join together/participate V khâo ruâm เข้าร่วม

joint N (in the body) khâw ข้อ

joke V (with someone) phûut lên พูดเล่น

jot down V jòt yâw yâw จดย่อ ๆ

journal N (periodical) waa-rá-sǎan วารสาร, (personal record) ban-thúek บันทึก

journalist N nák khàaw นักข่าว

journey N kaan doehn thaang การเดินทาง

joy N khwaam sà-nùk ความสนุก

joyful ADJ sà-nùk สนุก

judge N See 'magistrate'

judge/decide V tàt-sǐn ตัดสิน

jug (of beer), **pitcher** N yùeak เหยือก

juice N (i.e. fruit juice) náam phǒnlá-mái น้ำผลไม้

July N kà-rákàdaakhom กรกฎาคม

jump V krà-dòht กระโดด

junction N thaang yâek ทางแยก

June mí-thù-naayon มิถุนายน

jungle N pàa ป่า

junior N rûn náwng รุ่นน้อง

junk food N aa-hǎan khà-yà อาหารขยะ

junta N rát-thá-baan thá-hǎan รัฐบาล ทหาร

juristic ADJ kòt-mǎai กฎหมาย

jury N khá-ná lûuk khǔn คณะลูกขุน

just, only ADV thâonán เท่านั้น; 'only/ just ten baht' sìp bàat thâonán สิบบาท เท่านั้น (NOTE: a very useful and com- mon expression meaning 'just this/ that amount' is khâe níi (this) แค่นี้, or khâe nán (that) แค่นั้น. And for the sentence 'I just want this much' you say ('I' is understood) – ao khâe níi (literally, 'want'-'just'-'this') เอาแค่นี้)

just/fair ADJ yút-tì-tham ยุติธรรม

justice N khwaam yút-tì-tham ความ ยุติธรรม

justify V phí-sùut พิสูจน์

just now ADV dǐao níi ehng เดี๋ยวนี้เอง, or phaw dii พอดี

juvenile ADJ (FORMAL) yao-wá-chon เยาวชน, (COLLOQUIAL) wai-rûn วัยรุ่น

K

kale N khá-náa คะน้า

kangaroo N jing-jôh จิงโจ้

karaoke N khaa-raa oh-kè คาราโอเกะ

Karen N (ethnic group living in different areas along the Thai-Burmese/Myan- mar border) kà-rìang กะเหรี่ยง

karma N kam (pronounced like 'gum' as in 'chewing gum') กรรม

keen ADJ mii wǎi phríp มีไหวพริบ

keep V kèp เก็บ, also kèp wái เก็บไว้ (NOTE: wái ไว้ is an important word in Thai. In conjunction with other words it serves a number of functions. In a broader sense it means to 'preserve/ conserve/uphold' and to 'place/leave/ replace, restore/wear') See Thai-Eng- lish section.

keeper N phûu duu-lae ผู้ดูแล

kettle N (hot water jug) kaa náam กาน้ำ

key N (to a room) kunjaeh กุญแจ

key ADJ sǎm-khan สำคัญ

keyboard N (of computer – from Eng- lish) khii-bàwt คีย์บอร์ด

Khmer N See 'Cambodia'

kick V tèh เตะ

kickboxing N (i.e. Thai boxing) muai thai มวยไทย

kickoff N rôehm tôn เริ่มต้น

kid N (child) dèk เด็ก

kidnap/abduct V lák phaa ลักพา

kidney(s) N tai ไต

kidney beans N thùa daehng (literally, 'beans'-'red') ถั่วแดง

kill/murder V khâa ฆ่า

killer N khâat-tà-kawn ฆาตกร

kilogram N kì-loh kram กิโลกรัม, or simply kì-loh กิโล

kilometer N kì-loh mêht กิโลเมตร, or simply ki-loh กิโล

kind, good ADJ jai dii ใจดี

kind N (type) prà-phêht ประเภท

kindergarten N rohng rian à-nú-baan โรงเรียนอนุบาล

king N phrá-má-hǎa kà-sàt พระมหา กษัตริย์ (NOTE: in everyday speech the Thai monarch is referred to as nai lǔang ในหลวง)

kingdom N aà-naa-jàk อาณาจักร

kinship N khrâwp khrua ครอบครัว

kiss V jùup (pronounced 'joop') จูบ

kitchen N hâwng khrua ห้องครัว, or simply khrua ครัว

kite N wâow ว่าว

kitten N lûuk maew ลูกแมว

knee N hǔa khào หัวเข่า or simply khào เข่า

kneel V khúk khào คุกเข่า

knife N mîit มีด; to be cut by a knife (i.e. wound inflicted by knife) mîit bàat มีดบาด; similarly 'cut by a piece of glass' kâew bàat แก้วบาด

knight N àt-sà-win อัศวิน

knit V thàk ถัก

knock v (on a door) kháw (pronounced with a very short vowel – similar to the first part of the exclamation 'oh! ooh' preceded by a 'k' sound) เคาะ; knock on the door kháw prà-tuu เคาะประตู

know v rúu รู้ (somewhat more formal, and in certain contexts more polite, is the word sâap ทราบ)

know, be acquainted with v rúu-jàk รู้จัก

knowledge N khwaam rúu ความรู้

koala N (bear) khoh-aa-lâa โคอาล่า

Korea (North) kao-lǐi nǔea เกาหลีเหนือ

Korea (South) kao-lǐi tâi เกาหลีใต้

Korean N (person) khon kao-lǐi คน เกาหลี

kungfu N muai jiin (literally, 'boxing'-'Chinese') มวยจีน

L

label N pâai ป้าย, or khrûeang mǎai เครื่องหมาย

labor, labour chái raeng ngaan ใช้แรงงาน

labor, labour N (construction worker) kam-má-kawn กรรมกร

lack v khàat khlaehn ขาดแคลน; lacking ADJ khàat ขาด

ladder N bandai บันได

ladle, dipper N krà-buai กระบวย

lady N sù-phâap sà-trii สุภาพสตรี

lake N thá-leh sàap ทะเลสาบ

lamb N (mutton) núea kàe เนื้อแกะ

lamp N (lantern) tà-kiang ตะเกียง, (an electric lamp) kohm-fai โคมไฟ

land, plot, lot, property N thîi din ที่ดิน

land/go down v (plane) long ลง

landlord N jâo khǎwng bâan châo (literally, 'owner'-'house'-'rent') เจ้าของ บ้านเช่า

lane N (of a highway – from English) lehn เลน, (anywhere in size from a small lane to what many would consider a significant road) soi ซอย

language N phaa-sǎa ภาษา; sign language phaa-sǎa bâi ภาษาใบ้

Laos N (country) prà-thêht lao ประเทศ ลาว, (COLLOQUIAL) lao ลาว

Laotian N khon lao คนลาว

laptop/notebook computer N See 'computer'

large, big ADJ yài ใหญ่

laser N sǎeng leh-sôeh แสงเลเซอร์

last ADJ (e.g. last piece of cake; to be last in a race) sùt tháai สุดท้าย

last name, surname N naam sà-kun นามสกุล

last night N mûea khuehn níi เมื่อคืนนี้

last week N aa thít thîi láew อาทิตย์ที่ แล้ว

last year N pii thîi láew ปีที่แล้ว

late ADV (after the expected time) sǎai สาย, ADJ (delayed) cháa ช้า

late at night ADV dùek ดึก

lately/recently ADV mûea rew-rew níi เมื่อเร็ว ๆ นี้

later ADV thii lǎng ทีหลัง

laugh v hǔa ráw หัวเราะ

laugh at v hǔa ráw yáw หัวเราะเยาะ

launch N plòi ปล่อย

laundry N sák phâa ซักผ้า

lavatory/toilet N hâwng náam (literally, 'room'-'water') ห้องน้ำ

lavish ADJ fûm-fueay ฟุ่มเฟือย

lawn, oval, playing fields N sà-nǎam yâa สนามหญ้า

law, legislation N kòtmǎai กฎหมาย

lawyer N thá-naai-khwaam ทนายความ, (COLLOQUIAL) thá-naai ทนาย

lay v (to put something down i.e. 'to put a book on the table') waang วาง, (as in 'lay down on the bed') nawn long นอนลง; to lay/sleep on one's stomach nawn khwâm นอนคว่ำ; to lay/sleep on one's back nawn ngǎai นอนหงาย; to lay/sleep on one's side nawn tà-khaehng นอนตะแคง

lay or set the table v (i.e. before dinner) jàt tó จัดโต๊ะ

layer, floor in a building N (e.g. on the

tenth floor) chán ชั้น

layoff N lôehk kìat เลิกจ้าง

layout N phǎen-ngaan แผนงาน

lazy ADJ khîi kìat ขี้เกียจ

lead N (metal) tà kùa ตะกั่ว

lead V (or take someone somewhere) nam นำ, or phaa พา, (to guide someone somewhere) nam pai นำไป

leader N phûu nam ผู้นำ

leaf N bai mái ใบไม้

leak V rûa รั่ว, N (a crack or hole) roi-rûa รอยรั่ว

lean V ehn เอน

leap, jump V krá-dòht กระโดด

learn/study V rian เรียน

lease V (a property) hâi châo ให้เช่า

least ADJ (smallest amount) nói thîi sùt น้อยที่สุด

least ADV (at least) yàang nói อย่างน้อย

leather N nǎng หนัง

leave, depart (for) V àwk pai ออกไป

leave behind by accident V (i.e. forget) luehm ลืม

leave behind on purpose V thíng wái ทิ้งไว้

leave behind for safe-keeping V (deposit, store, leave something somewhere to be picked up later) fàak ฝาก

lecture V kaan banyaai การบรรยาย

leech N pling ปลิง

left N (opposite of 'right') sáai ซ้าย; on the left khâang sáai ข้างซ้าย; left-hand side sáai mueh ซ้ายมือ; to be left-handed thà-nàt mueh sáai ถนัดมือซ้าย

left, remaining ADJ thîi lǔea ที่เหลือ

leg(s) N khǎa ขา

legal ADJ taam kòtmǎai ตามกฎหมาย

legend N tam naan ตำนาน

leisure N (free time) wehlaa wâang เวลาว่าง

lemon N (citrus) má-naaw มะนาว

lemongrass N tà-khrái ตะไคร้

lend V hâi yuehm ให้ยืม

length N khwaam yaow ความยาว

lens N (i.e. a camera lens – from English) len เลนส์

lesbian N (SLANG/COLLOQUIAL) feminine lesbian – from the English word 'lady') dîi ดี้, (butch lesbian – from the English word 'tom') tawm ทอม

less ADJ (a lesser amount) nói kwàa น้อยกว่า

lessen, reduce V lót long ลดลง, or simply lót ลด (as in 'reduce the price' lót raa-khaa ลดราคา)

Lesser vehicle of Buddhism, Hinayana N latthí hǐnnáyaan ลัทธิหินยาน

lesson N (at school; also used in the sense as a 'lesson' learned through experience) bòt rian บทเรียน

let, allow, permit V à-nú-yâat อนุญาต, let (someone do something etc.) hâi ให้ (NOTE: this is an important word in Thai used in a variety of ways – see the Thai-English section)

let someone know V (i.e to tell someone) bàwk บอก

letter N (as in a 'letter in the mail') jòt mǎai จดหมาย, (in the alphabet) àk-sǎwn อักษร, tua àk-sǎwn ตัวอักษร, or tua nǎng-sǔeh ตัวหนังสือ

lettuce N phàk salàt (literally, 'vegetable'-'salad') ผักสลัด

level N (even, flat) rîap เรียบ, or râap ราบ, (storey in a tall building) chán ชั้น, (position or rank on a scale) rá-dàp ระดับ

lewd ADJ (crude, obscene) laa-mók ลามก

liable ADJ ráp phìt châwp รับผิดชอบ

liberty N ìt-sà-rà-phâap อิสรภาพ

library N hâwng sà-mùt ห้องสมุด

license N (i.e. driver's license) bai khàp khìi ใบขับขี่, permit N bai à-nú-yâat ใบอนุญาต

lick V lia เลีย

lid N (of a jar etc.) fǎa ฝา

lie, tell a falsehood V koh-hòk โกหก, (COLLOQUIAL/SLANG) taw-lǎeh ตอแหล; a liar khon koh-hòk คนโกหก

lie down V nawn นอน

life N chii-wít ชีวิต, (as in 'this life', 'this incarnation') châat níi ชาตินี้

lifejacket N (on a boat) sûea chuuchîip เสื้อชูชีพ

lifetime N & ADJ (throughout one's life) tà-làwt chii-wít ตลอดชีวิต

lift, elevator N (from English) líp ลิฟท์

lift V (to give someone a lift in a car) pai sòng ไปส่ง, (to raise) yók ยก

light V (light a match) jùt จุด; (light a fire) jùt fai จุดไฟ

light ADJ (not heavy) bao เบา, (bright) sà-wàang สว่าง

light N (lamp) fai ไฟ

light bulb N làwt fai หลอดไฟ

lighter N (cigarette lighter) fai cháek ไฟแช็ค

lightning N fáa phàa ฟ้าผ่า

like ADJ (to be the same) mǔean เหมือน

like V (to be pleased by) châwp ชอบ

like this ADV (COLLOQUIAL) (i.e. in this way/ in this manner) bàehp níi แบบนี้; 'do it like this' (e.g. holding chopsticks) tham bàehp níi ทำแบบนี้

likely N pen pai dâi เป็นไปได้

like-minded ADJ (having the same ideas/tastes) mii jai trong kan (literally, 'have'-'heart/mind'-'straight/ direct'-'together') มีใจตรงกัน

likewise ADV mǔean kan เหมือนกัน

lime/lemon N má naaw มะนาว

limited/restricted ADJ (in time, space) jam-kàt จำกัด

line N (mark) sên เส้น, (queue – from English) khiu คิว

line up V (queue up) khâo khiu เข้าคิว

lineage N (ancestry) trà-kuun ตระกูล

link V chûeam เชื่อม

lion N sǐng-toh สิงโต, or simply sǐng สิงห์

lip(s) N rim fǐi pàak ริมฝีปาก

liquor, alcohol N lâo เหล้า

list N raai kaan รายการ

listen to V fang ฟัง

listening V (to someone talking, the

radio) fang yùu ฟังอยู่

literate ADJ mii kaan sùek-sǎa มีการศึกษา

literature N wanná-khá-dii วรรณคดี

little ADJ (not much) nói น้อย; a little bit nít nòi นิดหน่อย, (small) lék เล็ก

livable ADJ nâa yùu น่าอยู่

live ADJ (alive) mii chii-wít yùu มีชีวิตอยู่

live, to be located V (stay in a place) yùu อยู่

lively/full of life ADJ chii-wít chii-waa ชีวิตชีวา

liver N tàp ตับ

load, burden N (i.e. responsibility) phaa-rá ภาระ

load V (up/pack a suitcase) banjù บรรจุ

loan V hâi yuehm ให้ยืม

loan N (of money) ngoehn kûu เงินกู้; go and get a loan (from a bank/money lender) kûu ngoehn กู้เงิน

loathe/dislike/despise V rang kìat รังเกียจ

lobster N kûng mangkawn (literally, 'prawn/shrimp'-'dragon') กุ้งมังกร

local ADJ thâwng thìn ท้องถิ่น

located ADJ tâng yùu ตั้งอยู่, or simply yùu อยู่

location/site N (e.g. a good/bad location for a home, business, etc.) tham-leh ทำเล

lock N mâeh kunjaeh (literally, 'mother'-'key') แม่กุญแจ (NOTE: colloquially the word for 'key' kunjaeh กุญแจ is also used to refer to a lock)

lock V (from English) láwk ล็อก

locked ADJ láwk láew ล็อกแล้ว

lodge, bungalow N (from English) bang-kà-loh บังกะโล

logic N hèht phǒn เหตุผล

logical ADJ mii hèht-phǒn (literally, 'have'-'reason') มีเหตุผล

loincloth N phâa khǎaw máa ผ้าขาวม้า

lonely ADJ ngǎo เหงา

long ADJ (length) yaaw ยาว, (distance) klai ไกล, (time) naan นาน

look! EXCLAM (look at that!) duu sí ดูซิ

look after v (e.g. children) duulaeh ดูแล

look at v duu ดู

look for/search/look up v (find in book) hăa หา

look(s) like v duu mŭean ดูเหมือน

look out! EXP (be careful) rá wang ระวัง

loose ADJ (not tight) lŭam หลวม

lose v (fail to win) pháeh แพ้, (mislay) tham hăai ทำหาย, (unable to keep alive) sĭa chii-wít เสียชีวิต

lose money v (on a business venture) (COLLOQUIAL) khàat thun; lose money (on something and get nothing in return) sĭa ngoehn frii (literally, 'waste'-'money'-'free') เสียเงินฟรี

lost ADJ (vanished) hăai หาย (i.e. lost property is 'khăwng hăai' ของหาย), (can't find way) lŏng (thaang) หลง (ทาง)

lot, lots N (COLLOQUIAL) yóe yáe (both words pronounced very short) เยอะ แยะ, or yóe mâak เยอะมาก

lottery N (from English) láwt toeh rîi ล็อตเตอรี่, (COLLOQUIAL) hŭai หวย; (COLLOQUIAL) to win the lottery thùuk hŭai ถูกหวย

loud ADJ dang ดัง (also colloquial term for 'famous')

lounge room/living room N hâwng ráp khàek (literally, 'room'-'receive'-'guest[s]') ห้องรับแขก, or hâwng nâng lên (literally, 'room'-'sit'-'play') ห้องนั่งเล่น

love N khwaam rák ความรัก

love v rák รัก

lovely/adorable ADJ (of a person/cute behavior) nâa rák น่ารัก, (beautiful) sŭai-ngaam สวยงาม

low ADJ (opposite of 'high') tàm ต่ำ

loyal ADJ sûe-sàt ซื่อสัตย์

lubricate v tham-hâi lûen ทำให้ลื่น

luck N chôhk โชค

lucky ADJ chôhk dii โชคดี

luggage/bag/suitcase N krà păo กระเป๋า

luminous ADJ sà-wàang สว่าง

lump N (e.g. of rock; also a lump/growth on the body) kâwn ก้อน

lunch N aa-hăan klaang wan อาหารกลางวัน (i.e. eating lunch is 'thaan khâow thîang' ทานข้าวเที่ยง, or MORE COLLOQUIAL is 'kin khâaw thîang' กินข้าวเที่ยง)

lung(s) N pàwt ปอด

lure v lâw jai ล่อใจ

lust/desire N tanhăa ตัณหา

luxury N khwaam rŭn răa ความหรูหรา; luxurious rŭn răa หรูหรา

lychee N (fruit) lín-jìi ลิ้นจี่

lyric N núea phleng เนื้อเพลง

M

machine N khrûeang jàk เครื่องจักร

mad ADJ See 'crazy/insane'

madam, ma'am N (term of address) maà-daam มาดาม, mâem แหม่ม

made-to-order ADJ taam sàng ตามสั่ง

Mafia N maafia มาเฟีย (NOTE: this term is commonly used in Thailand to refer to local criminal organizations or foreign gangs operating in Thailand)

magazine nít-tà-yá-săan นิตยสาร

magic N (with spells, incantations – not stage magic) khaa-thăa aa-khom คาถาอาคม

magistrate/judge N phûu-phí phâak-săa ผู้พิพากษา

magnet N mâeh lèk (literally, 'mother'-'iron/steel') แม่เหล็ก

mahout N (elephant keeper/handler) khwaan cháang ควาญช้าง

maid N (female servant in a private residence) săow chái (literally, 'woman'-'use') สาวใช้; room maid (in a hotel/private residence) mâeh bâan แม่บ้าน

mail, post N (from English) mehl เมล

mail v sòng ส่ง

mailman/postman N bùrùt praisànii บุรุษไปรษณีย์

main ADJ (most important) sămkhan สำคัญ

mainly ADV, **majority** N sùan yài ส่วน
ใหญ่, or sùan mâak ส่วนมาก

maintain v khong wái คงไว้

major/big ADJ (something important/
significant) yài ใหญ่

make/do v tham ทำ

make up v (to apply cosmetics) tàeng
nâa แต่งหน้า

makeup N (cosmetics) khrûeang
sămaang เครื่องสำอาง

Malaysia N maalehsia มาเลเซีย

Malaysian N (people) chaow maàlehsia
ชาวมาเลเซีย

male N (human being) chaai ชาย; male
(animal) tua phûin ตัวผู้

mama-san N (brothel keeper, female bar
keeper) mâe láo แม่เล้า (NOTE: the word
'mama-san' is also commonly used)

man/men N phûin chaai ผู้ชาย

manage/organize v jàt-kaan จัดการ

manager N phûin jàt-kaan ผู้จัดการ

Mandarin N (official language of China)
phaa-săa jiin klaang ภาษาจีนกลาง

mandate N kham sang คำสั่ง

mango N má-mûang มะม่วง

mangosteen N (fruit) mang-khút มังคุด

manhood N khwaam klâa hăan ความ
กล้าหาญ

maniac ADJ See 'crazy/insane'

manicure N tham lép ทำเล็บ

manifest ADJ chát jehn ชัดเจน

manikin N khon khráe คนแคระ

manipulate v ját kaan จัดการ

mankind/humans/humanity N má-nút
มนุษย์

manners N (etiquette/behavior) maa-rá-
yâat มารยาท

manual ADJ (to work with one's hands)
tham dûai mueh (literally, 'do'-'by/
with'-'hand') ทำด้วยมือ

manual N (instructional book, e.g. in-
structions on how to operate a DVD
player) khûu mueh คู่มือ

manufacture v phà-lìt ผลิต

many, massive, much ADJ mâak มาก
(COMMON COLLOQUIAL) yóe (pronounced

something like 'yer!' very short with a
high tone) เยอะ

map N phăehn thîi แผนที่

March N mii-naakhom มีนาคม

margin N khàwp ขอบ

marijuana/marihuana N kan-chaa (pronounced 'gun-jar') กัญชา (NOTE: common slang for marijuana is núea [the
normal word for 'meat/beef/flesh']
เนื้อ)

mark N (symbol, sign) khrûeang-măai
เครื่องหมาย, marks (score in a test or
examination) khá-naen คะแนน

market N tà-làat ตลาด (NOTE: in Thailand there are markets that move from
one location to another in the same
town. For example on a Monday the
market may be in one place, the next
day somewhere else, and so on. Markets of this variety are referred to as
tà-làat nát ตลาดนัด. The word nát
นัด means 'appointment', 'to arrange
to meet', 'to set a date')

married ADJ tàeng-ngaan láew
แต่งงานแล้ว

marry/get married v tàeng-ngaan
แต่งงาน

mask v nâa kàak หน้ากาก

massage v nûat นวด, such as Thai
traditional massage nûat thai นวด
ไทย, or nûat phăehn bohraan นวด
แผนโบราณ

massage parlor N (these establish-
ments, while generally offering normal
straight massages, are primarily
geared towards providing customers
with sexual services) àap òb nûat อาบ
อบนวด

master N hŭa-nâa หัวหน้า

masturbate v (COLLOQUIAL/SLANG) for men
chák wâow (literally, 'to pull/draw'-
'kite') ชักว่าว; the equivalent for wom-
en tòk bèt ตกเบ็ด (which normally
means 'to go fishing')

mat N (e.g. a woven floor mat) sùea เสื่อ

match/game N (from English) kehm เกม

matches N (COLLOQUIAL) mái-khìit ไม้ขีด, (or more fully) mái-khìit-fai ไม้ขีดไฟ

matchmaker N mâe-sùeh แม่สื่อ

mate N phûean เพื่อน

material N (e.g. building material) wát-thù วัตถุ (NOTE: the syllable thù here is pronounced very short), or wàtsà-dù วัสดุ

mathematics N khá-nít-sàat คณิตศาสตร์

matter (of) N (a subject of concern) rûeang เรื่อง, (as in 'It doesn't matter') i.e. when someone apologizes to you, you can say 'mâi pen rai' ไม่เป็นไร

mattress N thîi nawn ที่นอน

maximum/the most N mâak thîi sùt มากที่สุด

May N (month) phrúet-sà-phaa-khom พฤษภาคม

may AUX V àat jà อาจจะ: e.g. I may go chǎn/phǒm àat jà pai ฉัน/ผมอาจจะไป

maybe, perhaps ADV àat jà อาจจะ, also baang thii บางที (which may also be translated as 'sometimes')

me See the entry under 'I'

meal N múeh มื้อ

mean ADJ (stingy) (COLLOQUIAL) khîi nǐao (literally, 'feces/shit'-'sticky'), i.e. someone who is so tight they want to keep their own excrement) ขี้เหนียว, (unkind, cruel) jai-ráai ใจร้าย

mean V (intend) mii jehttà-naa มีเจตนา, (denote) mǎai khwaam หมายความ (NOTE: the expression 'What does it/this/do you mean is?' is mǎai khwaam wâa àrai หมายความว่าอะไร) Also see 'interpret/translate'

meaning N (the 'meaning' of something) khwaam mǎi ความหมาย

meanwhile ADV (in the meantime/at the same time) nai wehlaa diao kan ใน เวลาเดียวกัน

measure V wát วัด

meat/flesh N núea เนื้อ

meatball N (which, in fact, may either

be beef, pork, or fish) lûuk chín ลูกชิ้น

mechanic N (the general term for a skilled tradesman is châang ช่าง followed by the particular area of expertise: note motor vehicle = rót รถ; engine = khrûeang เครื่อง). The full word for a motor mechanic is either châang rót ช่างรถ, or châang khrûeang ช่างเครื่อง

meddle V (interfere in someone else's affairs) yûng ยุ่ง

media N (mass media, radio, television, Internet etc.) sùeh muanchon สื่อมวลชน, (COLLOQUIAL) sùeh สื่อ

medical ADJ thaang kaan phâeht ทางการแพทย์

medicine/drug N yaa ยา

meditate V tham sà-maa-thí ทำสมาธิ

meditation N kaan tham sà-maa-thí การทำสมาธิ

medium N (size – neither big nor small) khà-nàat klaang ขนาดกลาง

meet V phóp พบ

meeting N (e.g. a conference) pràchum ประชุม

melodious ADJ (pleasing to the ear, a beautiful sound) phai-ráw ไพเราะ, (or simply and more commonly) phrá-w เพราะ

melon N (i.e. fruit/vegetables in the melon family) taeng แตง: e.g. watermelon taeng moh แตงโม; cucumber taeng kwaa แตงกวา

melt V lá-laai ละลาย (the same word also means 'dissolve')

member N (e.g. of a club) sà-maa-chík สมาชิก

memory N (one's memory) khwaam song jam ความทรงจำ

mend/fix/repair V sâwm ซ่อม

menstruate V (a woman's period) mii prà-jam duean มีประจำเดือน, (COLLOQUIAL) pen men เป็นเมนส์

mentally retarded ADJ panyaa àwn (literally, 'intellect'-'weak/tender/soft') ปัญญาอ่อน

mention

mention v klàaw thǔeng กล่าวถึง

menu N (from English) mehnuu เมนู, or raai-kaan aa-hǎan รายการอาหาร

merchandise N (commercial products, goods) sǐn-kháa สินค้า

merchant N khon khǎai คนขาย

merely/only ADV phiang เพียง

merge v ruam รวม

mess N, **messy** ADJ rók รก (i.e. a messy house bâan rók บ้านรก)

message N khâw khwaam ข้อความ; SMS message (from English) es-em-es เอสเอ็มเอส

metal N (COLLOQUIAL) lèk เหล็ก (NOTE: this term actually means 'iron' or 'steel'; the proper word for 'metal' is loh-hà โลหะ)

meter/metre N (length – from English) méht เมตร

method N (of doing something) wí-thii วิธี

microwave N (oven) (COLLOQUIAL – from English) wéhf (pronounced similar to 'wave') เวฟ

midday N thîang wan เที่ยงวัน

middle/center N sǔun klaang ศูนย์กลาง

middle ADJ klaang กลาง (i.e. the middle of a road is 'klaang thà-nǒn กลาง ถนน)

midnight N thîang khuehn เที่ยงคืน

migrate v òp-phá-yóp อพยพ; a migrant N phûu òp-phá-yóp ผู้อพยพ

mild ADJ (not spicy) mâi phèt ไม่เผ็ด, (not severe – as in a storm, a protest, etc.) mâi run raehng ไม่รุนแรง, (gentle) àwn yohn อ่อนโยน

mile N (distance – from English) mai ไมล์

militant ADJ bùk-rúk บุกรุก

military N thá-hǎan ทหาร

milk N nom นม (also the common word for a woman's breasts)

milkshake N nom-pàn นมปั่น

million NUM láan ล้าน

millionaire N (or a wealthy person) sèht-thǐi เศรษฐี

mince v (meat/pork etc.) sàp สับ

mind N (remembrance; memory) khwaam jam ความจำ, (manner of feeling or thought) jìt-jai จิตใจ, or simply jai ใจ

mind, care, to be concerned (about) rang kìat รังเกียจ, (COLLOQUIAL) tǔeh ถือ

mine N (i.e. diamond mine) mǔeang เหมือง, or mǔeang râeh เหมืองแร่

mineral N râeh แร่

minibus/van N rót tûn รถตู้

ministry N (as in a government ministry) krà-suang กระทรวง

minor ADJ (not important) mâi sǎmkhan ไม่สำคัญ

minority N (group) chon klùm nói ชน กลุ่มน้อย

minus N (–) lóp ลบ

minute N naa thii นาที

miracle N sing àt-sà-jan สิ่งอัศจรรย์

mirror krà-jòk กระจก

miscellaneous ADJ (misc) bèt tà-lèt เบ็ดเตล็ด

miser/skinflint/tightwad N khon khîi nîao คนขี้เหนียว

misery N khwaam thúk ความทุกข์

misfortune, bad luck N chôhk ráai โชค ร้าย

miss v (too late for, i.e. a bus, a flight) phlâat พลาด, (think of somebody) khít thǔeng คิดถึง

Miss N (title for an unmarried woman) naang sǎow นางสาว

missing ADJ (absent) hǎai หาย, or hǎai pai หายไป

mist, fog N màwk หมอก

mistake N khwaam phìt ความผิด

mistaken ADJ (incorrect in understanding) phìt phlâat ผิดพลาด

mistress/minor wife N (a complex and significant area of Thai social life) mia nói เมียน้อย (NOTE: a man's 'major wife' is known colloquially as a mia lǔang เมียหลวง) *Also see* entry under 'wife'

misunderstand v, **misunderstanding** N khâojai phìt เข้าใจผิด

mix/blend v phà-sŏm ผสม

moan N sĭang khraang เสียงคราง

mobile/cell phone N (*also see* 'telephone') thoh-rá-sàp mueh tŭeh โทรศัพท์มือถือ, (COLLOQUIAL) mueh tŭeh มือถือ, smartphone (from English) sà-márt fohn สมาร์ทโฟน

mock/make fun of v yáw yóei เยาะเย้ย

model N (a design of an item) bàep แบบ, (one who models clothes or cosmetics) naang bàep นางแบบ

moderate ADJ paan klaang ปานกลาง

modern ADJ than sà-măi ทันสมัย

modest, simple, ordinary ADJ thammá-daa ธรรมดา

modify v kâe khăi แก้ไข

molar N fan-kraam ฟันกราม

mold/mould N raa รา

moment N (the present time, i.e. at the moment) tawn níi ตอนนี้, (a short period of time, i.e. in a moment) dĭao (COLLOQUIAL) เดี๋ยว (in a more formal environment – e.g. office/surgery etc. a receptionist would say 'please wait a moment' raw sák khrûu รอสักครู่)

moment ago ADV (i.e. just a moment/second/minute ago) mûea kîi níi เมื่อกี้นี้

Monday N wan jan วันจันทร์

monarch N kà-sàt กษัตริย์

money N ngoehn เงิน (this word also means 'silver'), (MORE COLLOQUIAL) tang ตังค์ (shortened from another old Thai term for 'money' sà-taang สตางค์: 100 sàtaang = one baht); to have no money/to be broke (SLANG) mâi mii tang ไม่มีตังค์, or thăng tàehk (literally, 'bucket'-'broken') ถังแตก

monitor N (of computer), **screen** N jaw (pronounced like the English word 'jaw') จอ

monk N (a Buddhist monk) phrá พระ

monkey N ling ลิง

monotonous ADJ nâa bùea น่าเบื่อ

month N duean เดือน

monument N ànú-săa-wárii อนุสาวรีย์

mood N *See* 'passion' (NOTE: 'to be in a bad mood' aa rom sĭa อารมณ์เสีย)

moody/irritable ADJ ngùt-ngìt หงุดหงิด

moon N duang jan ดวงจันทร์

moonlight N săeng jan แสงจันทร์

mop v thŭu phúen ถูพื้น

morality N sĭin-lá-tham ศีลธรรม

more ADJ (comparative) kwàa กว่า: e.g. better dii kwàa (literally, 'good'-'more') ดีกว่า

more of N (things) **/more than** ADV mâak kwàa มากกว่า

more or less IDIOM mâi mâak kâw nói ไม่มากก็น้อย

moreover ADV nâwk jàak nán นอกจากนั้น

morning N (time), cháo เช้า, or tawn cháo ตอนเช้า

moron/stupid person N khon ngôh คนโง่

mortgage N jam nawng จำนอง

mosque N sù-rào สุเหร่า

mosquito N yung ยุง

most ADJ (superlative) thîi sùt ที่สุด: e.g. the most expensive phaeng thîi sùt แพงที่สุด, (the most) mâak thîi sùt มากที่สุด

mostly, for the most part ADV sùan yài ส่วนใหญ่

mother N (COMMON/COLLOQUIAL) mâeh แม่, (MORE FORMAL) maan daa มารดา; stepmother mâeh líang แม่เลี้ยง

mother-in-law N (wife's mother) mâeh yaai แม่ยาย; (husband's mother) mâeh săa-mii แม่สามี

motor/engine N khrûeang yon เครื่องยนต์, or simply khrûeang เครื่อง

motorcycle N maw-toeh-sai มอเตอร์ไซค์, (MORE COLLOQUIAL) rót khrûeang รถเครื่อง (*also see* 'taxi' for 'motorcycle taxi')

motor vehicle N (specifically 'a car') rót yon รถยนต์

mountain N phuu khăo ภูเขา

mouse N (rat) nŭu หนู, (computer) máo เมาส์ (from English)

mouth N pàak ปาก

mouthwash N (i.e. Listerine) náam yaa bûan pàak น้ำยาบ้วนปาก

move V khlûean thîi เคลื่อนที่, (from one place to another e.g. to move house) yáai ย้าย

movement, motion N khwaam khlûean wǎi ความเคลื่อนไหว

movie N nǎng หนัง

movie house/cinema N rohng nǎng โรงหนัง

mow, cut V (the lawn/grass) tàt ตัด

Mr N (title) naai นาย

Mrs N (title) naang นาง

MSG/msg N (flavor enhancer) phǒng chuu rót (literally, 'powder'-'boost/lift/elevate'-'taste') ผงชูรส

mug N yùeak เหยือก

multiple ADJ lǎai หลาย

municipality N têht-sà-baan เทศบาล

muscle N klâam núea กล้ามเนื้อ

museum N phíphít-tháphan พิพิธภัณฑ์

mushroom(s) N hèt เห็ด

music N dontrii ดนตรี

musician N nák don trii นักดนตรี

Muslim N mút-sà-lim มุสลิม

must AUX V tâwng ต้อง: e.g. (I) must go (chǎn) tâwng pai ต้องไป

mustache/moustache N nùat หนวด

mute ADJ (unable to speak) bâi ใบ้; to be mute pen bâi เป็นใบ้ See 'language' (for 'sign language')

my, mine PRON (male speaking) khǎwng phǒm ของผม; (female) khǎwng dìchǎn/chǎn ของดิฉัน/ฉัน

Myanmar N See 'Burma'

N

nail N (finger, toe, claws of an animal) lép เล็บ, (used in carpentry/building) tà-puu ตะปู

naive ADJ sûeh ซื่อ

naked ADJ plueai เปลือย; a naked body/to be in the nude (FORMAL) plueai kaai เปลือยกาย, or (SIMPLE COLLOQUIAL) póh โป๊

name N chûeh ชื่อ; 'what's your name?' khun chûeh àrai (literally, 'you'-'name'-'what'?) คุณชื่ออะไร

nap N ngîip งีบ

narcotic(s) N yaa sèp tìt (literally, 'drug'-'consume'-'stuck/addicted') ยาเสพติด

narrow ADJ khâehp แคบ; to be narrow-minded/petty jai khâehp (literally, 'narrow'-'heart') ใจแคบ

nation, country N châat ชาติ

national ADJ hàeng châat แห่งชาติ

national anthem N phlehng châat เพลงชาติ

national park N ùt-thá-yaan hàeng châat อุทยานแห่งชาติ

nationality N sǎnchâat สัญชาติ: e.g. Thai nationality sǎnchâat thai สัญชาติไทย

native ADJ (indigenous) phúen mueang พื้นเมือง

natural ADJ pen thammá-châat เป็นธรรมชาติ

nature N thammá-châat ธรรมชาติ

naughty ADJ son (pronounced like the English word 'on' with 's' in front) ซน

nauseous ADJ khlûehn sâi คลื่นไส้

navel N (belly button) sà dueh สะดือ

navy N kawng tháp ruea กองทัพเรือ

navy blue/dark blue/royal blue N sǐi náam-ngoehn สีน้ำเงิน

navigate V nam-thaang นำทาง

near, nearby ADJ klâi ใกล้ (Note: the Thai words 'near' klâi ใกล้ and 'far' klai ไกล are perhaps the most significant examples of the importance of getting the tones correct as they convey the completely opposite meaning. Hint: the word for 'near' has a falling tone and when said, is shorter than the mid-tone word for 'far' klai ไกล. To say 'very near' simply repeat the word twice klâi-klâi ใกล้ ๆ)

nearly ADV kùeap เกือบ

neat, orderly, well-behaved ADJ rîap rói เรียบร้อย – This term is widely used and conveys the notion of ideal behavior and deportment. (NOTE: this term is also commonly used to express the idea that a job/task has been successfully completed, something like 'done!')

necessary ADJ jam-pen (jam จำ is pronounced like 'jum' in the English word 'jump') จำเป็น

neck N khaw คอ

necklace N sôi khaw สร้อยคอ

necktie N (from English) nékthai เน็คไท

need N khwaam jam-pen ความจำเป็น

need V jam-pen-tâwng จำเป็นต้อง

needle khêm เข็ม

neglect V mâi sŏn jai ไม่สนใจ

negotiate V tàw rawng ต่อรอง

neighbor N phûean bâan เพื่อนบ้าน

nephew N lăn chaai หลานชาย

nerve N sên prà-sàat เส้นประสาท

nervous/anxious ADJ kang-won jai กังวลใจ

nest N (e.g. bird's nest) rang รัง; bird's nest rang nók รังนก

net N taa-khàai ตาข่าย, (mosquito net) múng มุ้ง

network N khruea khàai เครือข่าย; social network khruea khàai săngkhom เครือข่ายสังคม

neutral ADJ (impartial) pen klaang เป็นกลาง

never ADV mâi khoei ไม่เคย (NOTE: for a fuller description of how the word khoei เคย is used see 'have')

never mind! IDIOM mâi pen rai ไม่เป็นไร

nevertheless ADV (FORMAL) yàang-rai kâw taam อย่างไรก็ตาม, or (COLLOQUIAL) yang-ngai kâw taam ยังไงก็ตาม

new ADJ mài ใหม่

news N khàow ข่าว

newspaper N năng sŭeh phim หนังสือพิมพ์

new year pii mài ปีใหม่, (the expression) 'Happy New Year' sàwàt dii pii mài สวัสดีปีใหม่ (NOTE: the traditional Thai new year (13—15 April) is called sŏng-kraan สงกรานต์)

New Zealand N niu sii-laehn นิวซีแลนด์

next ADJ (in line, sequence) tàw pai ต่อไป

next to PREP thàt pai ถัดไป

next week N aa-thít nâa อาทิตย์หน้า

next year N pii nâa ปีหน้า

nice/good ADJ dii ดี

nickname N (NOTE: most Thai people have both a first name and a nickname – frequently a shortened version of their first name — or something else, invariably short, altogether) chûeh lên (literally, 'name'-'play') ชื่อเล่น

niece N lăn săow หลานสาว

night N klaang khuehn กลางคืน

nightclothes/nightdress/pajamas N chút nawn ชุดนอน

nightclub N (from English) nái-khláp ไนท์คลับ

nightly ADJ thúk khuehn ทุกคืน

nine NUM kâo เก้า

nineteen NUM sìp kâo สิบเก้า

nipple N hŭa nom หัวนม

ninety NUM kâo sìp เก้าสิบ

no, not DET mâi mii ไม่มี (used with nouns. NOTE: there are many ways of expressing 'no' – this being dependent on the form of the question asked), e.g. 'to have no friends' mâi mii phûean ไม่มีเพื่อน

no, not ADV mâi ไม่ (used with verbs and adjectives), e.g. 'it's not hot' mâi ráwn ไม่ร้อน (NOTE: 'not' may be expressed in other ways depending on the form of question asked, or nature of statement being made)

nobody N (as in 'there is nobody here') mâi mii khrai ไม่มีใคร

noise, a sound N sĭang เสียง

noisy, loud noise ADJ sĭang dang เสียงดัง

nominate V tàeng tang แต่งตั้ง

none PRON mâi mii ไม่มี

nonsense N (to be meaningless) rái săa rá ไร้สาระ, or lĕow-lăi เหลวไหล

nonstop ADJ mâi yùt ไม่หยุด

noodles N (rice noodles) kŭai tĭao ก๋วยเตี๋ยว, or (egg noodles) bà-mìi บะหมี่

noon N tawn thîang ตอนเที่ยง

normal ADJ pà-kà-tì ปกติ

normally ADV dohy pà-kà-tì โดยปกติ

north N nŭea เหนือ

north-east N tàwan àwk chĭang nŭea ตะวันออกเฉียงเหนือ (NOTE: in Thailand the north-east region of the country is referred to as iisăn – this is written in English in various ways: Isarn/Isan/Isaan – อีสาน)

north-west N tà-wan tòk chĭang nŭea ตะวันตกเฉียงเหนือ

nose N jà-mùuk จมูก; (COLLOQUIAL) 'mucous' khîi mûuk (literally, 'excrement' - shortened word for 'nose') ขี้มูก

nostril N ruu jà-mùuk รูจมูก

notable ADJ dèhn เด่น

note N (i.e. banknote) (COLLOQUIAL) (from the English 'bank') báeng แบงค์

notebook N sà-mùt สมุด

note down V jòt nóht จดโน้ต, or (MORE COLLOQUIALLY – the equivalent to) 'jot it down' jòt wái จดไว้

nothing N (as in 'nothing is going on') mâi mii arai ไม่มีอะไร (NOTE: in certain instances, e.g. in response to the question 'What did you say?' to answer 'Nothing!' the word plàaw เปล่า [which also means 'empty/vacant/plain/bare'] is commonly used)

notice V (to notice something) săngkèht สังเกต

notify V (e.g. the police) jâehng khwaam แจ้งความ

notorious ADJ sĭa chûeh เสียชื่อ

novel N ná-wá ní-yaai นวนิยาย, or simply ní-yaai นิยาย

November N phrúet-sà-jì-kaa-yon พฤศจิกายน

noun N (part of speech) kham-naam (pronounced 'narm') คำนาม, or simply naam นาม

nourish V bam-rung บำรุง

now ADV dĭao níi เดี๋ยวนี้, or tawn níi ตอนนี้

nowadays/these days ADV sà-mǎi níi สมัยนี้

no way! INTERJ (COLLOQUIAL) (e.g. there is 'no way' to get there, or 'Can I go with you?' – 'No way!') mâi mii thaang ไม่มีทาง

nowhere ADV (as in a sentence such as 'there is nowhere like home') mâi mii thîi nǎi ไม่มีที่ไหน (literally, 'no'-'have'-'where?')

nude ADJ plueai เปลือย, or 'naked body/nude' plueai kaai เปลือยกาย, or (SIMPLE COLLOQUIAL) póh โป๊

nuisance N tham-hâi ram-khaan ทำให้รำคาญ

numb ADJ chaa ชา

number N (from English; most commonly used when asking for a telephone number) boeh เบอร์; (general term for 'number' is) mǎai lêhk หมายเลข

numerous ADJ mâak-maai มากมาย

nurse N phá-yaa-baan พยาบาล

nut N (food, i.e. nuts in general) thùa ถั่ว, (a crazy person) khon bâa คนบ้า

nutrient N sǎan aa-hǎan สารอาหาร

nutrition N phoh-chá-naa-kaan โภชนาการ

nylon N (from English) nai lâwn ไนลอน

O

oar/paddle N mái phaai ไม้พาย

oat N khâao óht ข้าวโอ๊ต

oath N kham sǎa baan คำสาบาน

obese ADJ See 'fat'

obey V **obedient** ADJ chûea fang เชื่อฟัง

object, thing N sìng khǎwng สิ่งของ

object V (to oppose) khát kháan คัดค้าน

oblige V bang kháp บังคับ

obscure ADJ múeht มืด

on

O

ENGLISH–THAI

observe v sang kèet สังเกต
obsess v khrâwp khrawng ครอบครอง
obstacle N ùp-pà-sàk อุปสรรค
obstinate/stubborn ADJ dûeh ดื้อ
obstruct/block v khàt khwǎang ขัด
ขวาง
obtain/get v dâi ráp ได้รับ, or simply
dâi ได้
obvious ADJ chát jehn ชัดเจน
occasion/opportunity N oh-kàat
โอกาส
occasionally ADV pen khráng khraow
เป็นครั้งคราว; once in a while (COLLO-
QUIAL) naan-naan thii นาน ๆ ที
occupation N (profession – term often,
but not always, used to refer to someone with professional qualifications)
aa-chîip อาชีพ; (colloquially the word
for 'work' – ngaan งาน – is used):
'What (work) do you do?' (khun) tham
ngaan àrai ทำงานอะไร
occupy v yúet khrawng ยึดครอง
occur v (for something to happen)
kòeht khêun เกิดขึ้น
ocean N má-hǎa sà-mùt มหาสมุทร
(*also see* 'sea')
o'clock ADV naa lí kaa นาฬิกา (Note:
this word is used in the 24 hour system of telling the time such as in official Thai news broadcasts and more
generally at sea/by aircraft/the military
etc.: e.g. 13 naa lí kaa = 1 p.m.). The
everyday Thai system of telling the
time is somewhat more complex and
cannot be outlined here.
October N tù-laa-khom ตุลาคม
odd ADJ plàek แปลก
odor N (i.e. to smell not so good) mii
klìn มีกลิ่น
of course IDIOM nâeh nawn แน่นอน
off ADV (no longer functioning or operating) pìt ปิด (i.e. turned off the light
'pìt fai' ปิดไฟ)
off ADJ (absent or away from work)
yùt-ngaan หยุดงาน; off to (going to
somewhere) àwk pai ออกไป

offend v (break the law) tham phìt ทำ
ผิด, (to displease someone/to be
offensive) tham hâi mâi phaw jai
ทำให้ไม่พอใจ
offer v sà-nǒeh เสนอ; suggest náe
nam แนะนำ
office N thîi tham ngaan ที่ทำงาน, (also
commonly – from English) áwp-fít
ออฟฟิศ
official(s) N (i.e. government servants,
bureaucrats) khâa râat-chá-kaan ข้า
ราชการ, or jâo nâa thîi เจ้าหน้าที่
official ADJ (having a formal character)
pen thaang kaan เป็นทางการ
often ADV bòi บ่อย; very often bòi-bòi
บ่อยๆ
oil N (general term for 'oil', and common word for petrol/gasoline) náam-
man น้ำมัน
oily/greasy ADJ (food) lîan เลี่ยน: e.g.
greasy food aa-hǎan lîan อาหารเลี่ยน
ointment N (from English 'cream') kriim
ครีม
okay ADJ ADV N tòk-long ตกลง (the
English word OK is also widely used
oh-keh โอเค)
old ADJ (of people) kàeh แก่; an old
person khon kàeh คนแก่; (of things)
kào เก่า
old times N (i.e. 'in the past....') sà-mǎi
kàwn สมัยก่อน
older brother N (or sister) phîi พี่ (NOTE:
an important word in Thai with a far
broader meaning than simply 'older
brother/older sister'; it is used by a
junior or younger person to mean 'you'
when speaking to an older or higher
status person in various, mainly less
formal, contexts. In addition the term
is also commonly used to mean 'he/
she' when talking about another older
or higher status individual)
olive N má-gkàwk มะกอก
omit v tàt-àwk ตัดออก
omniscient ADJ râwp rúu รอบรู้
on PREP (i.e. on top) bon บน; (a particu-

lar date) wan thîi วันที่

on ADJ (operating or in use) pòeht เปิด

on board IDIOM (on a ship, train, or plane) yùu bon… อยู่บน

on fire IDIOM fai mâi ไฟไหม้

on foot ADV (walking, using the feet) doehn เดิน

on the whole/generally ADV dohy thûa pai โดยทั่วไป

on time, punctual ADJ trong weh laa ตรงเวลา

once ADV (at one time in the past) khráng nùeng ครั้งหนึ่ง; a single time khráng diao ครั้งเดียว; once in a while – *see* 'occasionally'

one NUM nùeng หนึ่ง

one-way ticket N tŭa thîao diao (literally, 'ticket'-'trip'-'single') ตั๋วเที่ยวเดียว

one who, the one who (did something etc.) khon thîi… คนที่

oneself PRON tua-ehng ตัวเอง

ongoing ADJ tàw nûeang ต่อเนื่อง

onion N hǎwm yài หอมใหญ่

only ADJ & ADV thâo-nán เท่านั้น

open V pòeht เปิด (same word as 'turn on')

open air N klaang jâeng กลางแจ้ง

operate V tham-ngaan ทำงาน

operation N kaan phàa-tàt การผ่าตัด

opinion N khwaam hěn ความเห็น

opium N fìn ฝิ่น

opportunity/chance N oh-kàat โอกาส

oppose V, **opposed** ADJ tàw tâan ต่อต้าน

opposite PREP (across from) trong khâam ตรงข้าม

opposite ADJ (contrary) khàt yáeng ขัดแย้ง

opposition (opposed to the government) fàai kháan ฝ่ายค้าน

oppress V bang kháp บังคับ

opt V lûeak เลือก

optimal ADJ màw thîi-sùt เหมาะสม ที่สุด

optimistic ADJ mawng lôhk ngâe dii มองโลกแง่ดี

option/alternative N thaang lûeak ทาง เลือก

optional ADJ lûeak dâi เลือกได้

or CONJ rǔeh (commonly pronounced [incorrectly] with an 'l' sound – lǔeh) หรือ

oral ADJ dûai pàak (literally, 'with'-'mouth') ด้วยปาก, or oral sex chái pàak ใช้ปาก (NOTE: for such delicate subject matter the terms given are the least crude and offensive of the possibilities) (fellatio – sucking) om อม, (cunninglis – licking) lia เลีย

orange N (fruit) sôm ส้ม; (color) sǐi sôm สีส้ม

orchard N sǔan สวน

orchid N klûai mái กล้วยไม้

order V (give a command) sàng สั่ง

order N (a command) kham sàng คำสั่ง; (a written form for food, goods, medicine, etc.) bai sàng ใบสั่ง; (sequence) taam lam dàp ตามลำดับ

orderly/well-arranged ADJ pen rá-bìap เป็นระเบียบ

ordinary tham-má-daa ธรรมดา: e.g. 'ordinary person' khon tham-má-daa คนธรรมดา (NOTE: ordinary folk/ householders – both in the city and rural areas – are colloquiallly known by the term chaow bâan ชาวบ้าน)

organ N à-wai-yá-wá อวัยวะ

organization N ong-kaan (pronounced 'ong-garn') องค์การ, or ong-kawn องค์กร

organize/arrange V jàt kaan จัดการ

oriental ADJ tá-wan-àwk ตะวันออก

origin N jùt rôehm tôn จุดเริ่มต้น; source (the source of something, e.g. bootlegged DVDs) làeng แหล่ง

original N (the first and genuine form of something) tua jing ตัวจริง, or khǎwng jing ของจริง; the original of a document is tôn chà-bàp ต้นฉบับ

originate, come from V maa jàak มา จาก: e.g. 'what country do you come from?' khun maa jàak prà-thêht àrai

คุณมาจากประเทศอะไร

ornament N (for the home) khrûeang prà-dàp เครื่องประดับ

orphan N dèk kam-phráa เด็กกำพร้า

orphanage N bâan dèk kam-phráa บ้านเด็กกำพร้า

ostrich N nók krà-jàwk-thêht นก กระจอกเทศ

other ADJ ùehn อื่น: e.g. 'other person' khon ùehn คนอื่น

otherwise ADV mí-chà-nán มิฉะนั้น

ought to, should AUX V khuan ควร

our(s) PRON khǎwng rao ของเรา: e.g. our house bâan khǎwng rao บ้านของ เรา, (colloquial and even simpler) bâan rao บ้านเรา (NOTE: This is a very common idiomatic way in which Thai people refer to their own country or hometown – i.e. 'our home')

oust V lâi àwk ไล่ออก

out ADV (i.e. take something out – 'a plate out of the cupboard') àwk ออก; to take out/withdraw thǎwn ถอน: e.g. take out a tooth/pull a tooth out thǎwn fan ถอนฟัน

outage N (power failure) fai dàp ไฟดับ

out-of-date/outdated/old-fashioned ADJ láa sà-mǎi ล้าสมัย, (COLLOQUIAL) choei เชย

outfit (matching set of clothing) chút ชุด

outgoing, friendly ADJ khâo kàp khon ngâai เข้ากับคนง่าย

outing N (to go out for fun/pleasure) (pai) thîao (ไป)เที่ยว (NOTE: an important Thai word – thîao – is used in a wide range of ways to refer to a pleasant/enjoyable visit somewhere – to a friend's house, the beach, a disco, bar, another country, etc.)

outlook N mum-mawng มุมมอง

output N phǒn-phà-lìt ผลผลิต

outrageous ADJ hòht ráai โหดร้าย

outright ADJ tem thîi เต็มที่

outside PREP khâang nâwk ข้างนอก

outsider N khon nâwk คนนอก

outstanding ADJ dòht dèhn โดดเด่น

oval N (shape) rûup khài รูปไข่

oven N tao òp เตาอบ

over, finished, completed ADJ sèt เสร็จ

over ADV (from an upward position to an inverted position) klàp กลับ (i.e. to turn something over klàp dâan กลับ ด้าน)

overall ADJ dohy ruam โดยรวม

overcast, cloudy mii mêhk มีเมฆ

overcome V ao-chá-ná เอาชนะ

overdose N (of a drug) yaa koen khà-nàat ยาเกินขนาด

overlook V (not to notice) mawng khâam มองข้าม

overpass N (a pedestrian overpass) sà-phaan loi (literally, 'bridge'-'float') สะพานลอย

overseas N tàang prà-thêht ต่าง ประเทศ

overtake/pass V (another vehicle) saeng แซง

over there ADV thîi nôhn ที่โน่น

overturn/capsize V (turn over) lôm ล่ม, khwâm คว่ำ

overturned ADJ (vehicle following an accident – on its roof) ngǎai tháwng หงายท้อง

owe V pen nîi เป็นหนี้

owl N nók hûuk นกฮูก

own, on one's IDIOM (by oneself or alone) khon diao คนเดียว; to come alone/on one's own maa khon diao มาคนเดียว

own, personal ADJ (belonging to one-self) khǎwng sùan tua ของส่วนตัว

own V (owner) pen jâo khǎwng เป็นเจ้า ของ

oxygen N (from English) áwk-sì-jên (jên pronounced like 'gen' in the English word) ออกซิเจน

oyster N (general term) hǒi หอย; a large succulent type of oyster hǒi naang rom หอยนางรม (NOTE: the word hǒi is also a common slang term for a woman's vagina)

P

pace N jang-wà จังหวะ

pack V (luggage) kèp khǎwng เก็บของ

package, parcel N hàw khǎwng ห่อ ของ, or simply hàw ห่อ, or (sent by post) hàw phát-sà-dù ห่อพัสดุ

packet N hàw lék (literally, 'package'- 'small') ห่อเล็ก (a small packet, or sachet, is also referred to as a sawng ซอง)

paddy N khâow plùeak ข้าวเปลือก

paddy field N naa นา

padlock N mâe kun-jae แม่กุญแจ

page N (in a book) nâa หน้า

pagoda/stupa N (spire shaped solid structure with no interior space, not a temple though located in temple grounds) jeh-dii เจดีย์

paid ADJ jàai láew จ่ายแล้ว

pain N /**painful** ADJ jèp เจ็บ; very painful jèp mâak เจ็บมาก

painkiller N yaa kâeh pùat ยาแก้ปวด

paint N sǐi สี (NOTE: sǐi สี is also the word for 'color')

paint V (house, furniture) thaa sǐi ทาสี

painting N phâap wâat ภาพวาด

pair N khûu คู่ (i.e. a pair of' shoes is 'rawng tháo nùeng khûu' รองเท้า หนึ่งคู่)

pair V (to form pairs or a pair) jàp khûu จับคู่

pajamas/pyjamas N chút nawn ชุด นอน

palace N (royal) wang วัง, or (more formally) phrá-râat-chá-wang พระราชวัง

pale ADJ (as in a pale face of someone unwell or in a state of shock) sîit ซีด: e.g. a pale face nâa sîit หน้าซีด

palm N (of hand) See 'sole'

pan N (frying pan/wok) krà-thá กระทะ (NOTE: both syllables are very short)

pancake N phaen-khéhk แพนเค้ก (from English; the word 'pancake' is widely understood)

panda N (animal) mǐi phaen-dâ (literally, 'bear'-'panda') หมีแพนด้า

panic ADJ tòk jai ตกใจ

panorama N phâap kwâang (literally, 'picture'-'wide') ภาพกว้าง

panties N (underpants for women) kaang-kehng nai กางเกงใน

pants/trousers N kaang-kehng กางเกง

papaya N má-lá-kaw มะละกอ

paper N krà-dàat กระดาษ; sandpaper krà-dàat saai (literally, 'paper'-'sand') กระดาษทราย

paper currency, banknote N (FORMAL) thá-ná-bàt ธนบัตร, or simply use báeng แบงค์ (from English)

parade/procession N khà-buan hàeh ขบวนแห่ (NOTE: a common event as part of cultural life, especially in rural Thailand)

paradise/heaven N sà-wǎn สวรรค์

paragraph N yâw nâa ย่อหน้า

parallel ADJ khà-nǎan ขนาน

paralytic/paralyzed N, ADJ am-má- phâat อัมพาต

paraphrase V yâw khwaam ย่อความ

parasite N phá-yâat พยาธิ

pardon me? INTERJ, what did you say? (a most useful expression) àrai ná อะไรนะ

parents N phâw mâeh (literally, 'father'- 'mother') พ่อแม่

park N (a public park/garden) sǔan sǎa-thaa rá-ná สวนสาธารณะ

park V (car) jàwt rót จอดรถ

parliament N rát-thà-sà-phaa รัฐสภา

parrot N nók kâew นกแก้ว; parrot fish (common in southern Thailand) plaa nók kâew ปลานกแก้ว

part N (of something/not the whole) sùan ส่วน; for the most part/the majority sùan mâak ส่วนมาก; a part/one part (of something) sùan nùeng ส่วน หนึ่ง, (spare part of car/machine) à-lài อะไหล่

participate V mii sùan rûam มีส่วนร่วม

particular ADJ, **particularly** ADV especially ADV dohy cha pháw โดยเฉพาะ

partition N (a lightweight wall dividing one room) phà-nǎng-kân ผนังกั้น

partner N (in business) hûn sùan หุ้นส่วน; (spouse) khûu sǒmrót คู่สมรส

party N (birthday party etc.) ngaan งาน (NOTE: the same word also means the opposite – 'work'); (political) phák พรรค (i.e. political party phák kaan mueang พรรคการเมือง)

pass V (of time) phàan ผ่าน, (undergo an exam) sàwp phàan สอบผ่าน (NOTE: to fail an exam is sàwp tòk สอบตก)

pass away, die V taai ตาย

pass out, black out V sà-lòp สลบ

passenger N phûu dohy sǎan ผู้โดยสาร

passion/mood N (with feeling – this term can be used in either a positive or negative sense. NOTE: it also has 'sexual' overtones) aa-rom อารมณ์; passionate mii aa-rom mâak มี อารมณ์มาก

passionfruit N (not particularly common in Thailand) sǎo-wá-rót เสาวรส

passport N nǎngsǔeh doehn thaang (literally, 'book'-'travel') หนังสือเดินทาง, (colloquial) (from English) páat-sà-pàwt พาสปอร์ต

password/pin number N rá-hàt รหัส

past, former ADJ à-dìit อดีต; 'in the past' nai à-dìit ในอดีต

pastime/hobby N ngaan à-dìrèhk งาน อดิเรก

pat, tap V tàe แตะ

path N thaang doehn ทางเดิน

pathetic ADJ nâa song sǎan น่าสงสาร

patient ADJ (the ability to wait/endure)/ to have patience òt thon อดทน

patient N (sick person in hospital) khon khâi คนไข้

patron N (client/customer) lûuk kháa ลูกค้า

pattern, design, style N bàehp แบบ

patterned ADJ (i.e. to have a pattern – material, etc.) mii laai มีลาย

pause V yùt phák หยุดพัก

pavilion N (common in Thailand – an airy, open structure where one can sit and relax) sǎa-laa ศาลา

pawn V jam-nam (pronounced 'jum' as in 'jumble', and 'num' as in 'number') จำนำ; a pawnshop rohng jam-nam โรงจำนำ

pay V jàai จ่าย; to pay a bill jàai bin จ่ายบิล (Note: the word bin บิล is from English as is the word chék เช็ค given below). In higher class restaurants to ask to 'pay the bill' it is usual to say chék bin เช็คบิล. On the other hand when paying for a meal at a street stall, or at an ordinary cheap restaurant it is usual to say kèp tang dûai เก็บตังค์ด้วย

pay attention to/concentrate V (on something) ao jai sài (literally, 'take'-'heart/mind'-'put') เอาใจใส่, tâng-jai ตั้งใจ

pay off V (a debt) chái nîi ใช้หนี้

payment N jàai ngoen จ่ายเงิน

peace N (not war) sǎntì-phâap สันติภาพ

peaceful ADJ sà-ngòp สงบ

peacock N nók yuung นกยูง

peak, summit N yâwt ยอด (NOTE: common colloquial usage – the word yâwt is used when checking the balance of credit on one's mobile/cell phone. The expression for 'the balance' in such a case is yâwt ngoen ยอดเงิน)

peanut N thùa lí-sǒng ถั่วลิสง

pearl N khài múk ไข่มุก

pea(s) N thùa ถั่ว

peasant N (peasant farmer/rice farmer) chaow naa ชาวนา

pedestrian crossing N thaang máa laai ทางม้าลาย (NOTE: máa laai ม้าลาย means 'zebra')

pee/piss/urinate N & V (COLLOQUIAL) yîao เยี่ยว, or chìi ฉี่

peel V (a piece of fruit) pàwk ปอก

pen N pàak-kaa ปากกา

penalize V long thôht ลงโทษ

pencil N din-sǎw ดินสอ

penis N (COLLOQUIAL; extremely vulgar – equivalent of the English 'cock/dick/ prick') khuai ควย, (COLLOQUIAL; but significantly less vulgar – the equiva- lent of something like 'willy') jǔn จู๋ (pronounced similar to the word 'Jew' but with a rising tone)

pension N (government payment to retired workers) bîa bam-naan เบี้ย บำนาญ, or simply bam-naan บำนาญ

people/person N khon คน, (more broadly as in) 'the people/public' prà- chaa-chon ประชาชน

pepper N (i.e. black pepper) phrík thai พริกไทย, (chili pepper) phrík พริก

peppermint N sà-rá-nàe สะระแหน่

perceive V khâo jai เข้าใจ

percent/percentage N (from Engish) poeh-sen เปอร์เซ็นต์

perfect ADJ sǒm-buun สมบูรณ์, or dii lôeht ดีเลิศ

perform V (work/do work) (FORMAL) pàtìbàt ngaan ปฏิบัติงาน (Note: the word 'do' tham is colloquially used – e.g. 'perform work/do work/work' tham ngaan ทำงาน), (present a dramatic or musical work) sà-daeng แสดง

performance N (work) kaan tham ngaan การทำงาน, (dramatic produc- tion) kaan sà-daeng การแสดง

perfume N náam hǎwm (literally, 'wa- ter'-'fragrant') น้ำหอม

perhaps, maybe ADV àat jà อาจจะ, (a common alternative is) baang thii บางที

period N (a full stop) jòp จบ, (menstru- al) prá-jam duean ประจำเดือน, (COLLO- QUIAL) (from English – menstruation) men เมนส์; to be having one's period pen men เป็นเมนส์, (of time) ráyá wehlaa ระยะเวลา

permanent ADJ thǎa-wawn ถาวร

permit, license N bai à-nú-yâat ใบ อนุญาต

permit/allow V à-nú-yâat อนุญาต

person N khon คน

personality N bùk-khá-lík บุคลิก, or simply ní-sǎi นิสัย

perspective N khwaam khít ความคิด

perspire/sweat V ngùea àwk เหงื่อ ออก

persuade V chuan ชวน

pet N (animal) sàt líang สัตว์เลี้ยง

petrol/gasoline N náam man น้ำมัน

petrol station N See 'gasoline/gas'

pharmacy, drugstore, chemist N ráan khǎai yaa ร้านขายยา

phase N (stage) rá-yá ระยะ

phenomenon N praa-kòt-kaan ปรากฏ การณ์

Philippines N fí líp-pin ฟิลิปปินส์

philosophy N pràt-yaa ปรัชญา

phlegm N (mucus) sěm-hà เสมหะ

phobia N khwaam klua ความกลัว

phone N See 'telephone'

photocopy N sǎm-nao สำเนา

photocopy V thǎai sǎm-nao ถ่ายสำเนา

photograph N rûup thàai รูปถ่าย, or simply rûup รูป

photograph V thàai rûup ถ่ายรูป

pick, choose V lûeak เลือก

pick up V (e.g. to pick someone up from the airport) ráp รับ

pickpocket N khà-mohy lúang krà-pǎo ขโมยล้วงกระเป๋า

pickpocket V lúang krà-pǎo ล้วง กระเป๋า

picky ADJ See 'fussy'

picture N (general term used for both photographic and non-photographic images) rûup phâap รูปภาพ, (movie) nǎng หนัง

piece, portion, section N tawn ตอน (NOTE: commonly used in 'time expres- sions': e.g. tawn cháo ตอนเช้า '[in] the morning', tawn yen ตอนเย็น '[in] the evening')

piece N (a piece or item) chín ชิ้น

pierce, penetrate V jàw เจาะ

pig N mǔu หมู

pigeon N nók phí-râap นกพิราบ

pigtail N (hairstyle) hǎang pia หางเปีย; ponytail hǎang máa (literally, 'tail'-'horse') หางม้า

pile N (e.g. a pile of rubbish) kawng กอง

pill(s) N yaa mét (literally, 'pill'-'medicine/drug') ยาเม็ด

pillar N sǎo เสา

pillion ADV (seated behind the rider on a motorcycle) (COLLOQUIAL) sáwn tháai ซ้อนท้าย

pillow/cushion N mǎwn หมอน

pimp, procurer N (SLANG) maehng-daa แมงดา

pimple(s) N See 'acne'

pin number/PIN N See 'password'

pinch V (e.g. to pinch someone on the arm) yìk หยิก

pineapple N sap-pà-rót สับปะรด

pink N sǐi chomphuu สีชมพู

pipe N thâw ท่อ

pistol N puen phók ปืนพก

pit N lǔum หลุม

pitcher, jug N yùeak เหือก

pity V (to feel pity/sympathy) song sǎan สงสาร

pitiful ADJ nâa song sǎan น่าสงสาร

place N thîi ที่ (used in conjunction with the name of a particular place, e.g.) at home thîi bâan ที่บ้าน; at a/the store thîi ráan ที่ร้าน. (Or it can be used as follows: 'He has a place' [this could refer to a home/a piece of land, etc.] khǎo mii thîi เขามีที่)

place/put (on) V waang วาง

placid ADJ ngîap เงียบ

plain ADJ (not complicated or not fancy) rîap เรียบ, (flat) thîi râap ที่ราบ

plan N (from English) phǎehn แผน

plan V waang phǎehn วางแผน

plane N khrûeang bin เครื่องบิน

planet N daow khráw ดาวเคราะห์

plant N (general term covering everything from a small plant to a large tree) tôn mái ต้นไม้

plant V plùuk ปลูก

plastic N (from English; pronounced either) pláat-sàtìk or pláastìk พลาสติก

plastic or cosmetic surgery N sǎn-lá-yá-kam ศัลยกรรม (in colloquial speech often pronounced sǎn-yá-kam)

plate N jaan (pronounced 'jarn') จาน

plateau N thîi râap ที่ราบ

platform N (at a bus/railway station) chaan chaa laa ชานชาลา

play V lên เล่น

playful ADJ khîi lên ขี้เล่น

plead V (beg) âwn wawn อ้อนวอน, (advocate (a case) in a court of law) hâi kaan ให้การ

pleasant ADJ (in the sense of a 'pleasant atmosphere' – somewhere where one feels 'relaxed and comfortable') sà-baai jai สบายใจ

please ADV (go ahead – 'come in', 'sit down' etc.) choehn (pronounced similar to the word 'churn') เชิญ, (request for help) chûai ช่วย, (request for something) khǎw ขอ

please V (to please someone/attend to someone's needs/wishes) ao jai sài (literally, 'take'-'heart'-'put') เอาใจใส่, or simply ao jai เอาใจ

pleased ADJ dii jai ดีใจ

pleasing ADJ (to hit the spot) thùuk jai ถูกใจ; (COLLOQUIAL; to be pleasing in the sense of) meeting all one's 'requirements', or 'specifications' thùuk sà-pék ถูกสเป็ก (NOTE: the word here sà-pék สเป็ก is from English)

pleasure N khwaam sùk ความสุข

plenty N (a lot) mâak maai มากมาย

plow/plough V thǎi ไถ

plug N (bath) plák ปลั๊ก, (electric) plák fai ปลั๊กไฟ

plus CONJ (as in '2 plus 2', or 'the price of the ticket, plus the hotel, plus the rental car') bùak บวก

pocket N (also the word for 'bag' as in 'suitcase' or 'overnight travel bag', etc.) krà-pǎo กระเป๋า

poem N klawn กลอน

poet N kà-wii กวี

point/dot N jùt จุด

point (out) V chíi ชี้

point of view N khwaam hěhn ความเห็น

poison N yaa phít ยาพิษ

poisonous ADJ mii phít มีพิษ; a poisonous snake nguu mii phít งูมีพิษ

pole N sǎo เสา

police N tam-rùat ตำรวจ, (SLANG) chà-lǎam bòk (literally, 'shark'-'land' or 'land shark') ฉลามบก

police station N sà-thǎa-nii tamrùat สถานีตำรวจ, (COLLOQUIAL) rohng phák โรงพัก

policy N (i.e. government policy, the policy of a company) ná-yoh-baai นโยบาย

polish V khàt ngao ขัดเงา, or simply khàt ขัด (pronounced like the English word 'cut', but with a low tone)

politics N kaan mueang การเมือง; to be involved in politics lên kaan mueang (literally, 'play'-'politics') เล่นการเมือง; a politician nák kaan mueang นักการเมือง

polite ADJ sù-phâap สุภาพ

pollution N mon-lá-phaa-wá มลภาวะ

pool N sá สระ (i.e. swimmimg pool is sá wâai náam สระว่ายน้ำ)

poor ADJ jon จน

ponytail N (hairstyle) See 'pigtail'

popular ADJ pen thîi ní yom เป็นที่นิยม

population N (i.e. 'what is the population of Thailand?') prà-chaakawn ประชากร

porch/verandah N rá-biang ระเบียง

pork N núea mǔu เนื้อหมู or simply mǔu หมู

pornographic ADJ /porno/porn N (abbreviated from English; colloquial) póh โป๊; a pornographic film/DVD etc. nǎng póh หนังโป๊; a pornographic magazine/book, etc. nǎngsǔeh póh หนังสือโป๊ (NOTE: the word póh is also com-

monly used to describe someone who is scantily dressed or revealing more skin/flesh than appropriate in public)

port/wharf/harbor N thâa ruea ท่าเรือ

portable ADJ phók phaa ngâai พกพาง่าย

portion, serve N thîi ที่; (e.g. in a restaurant when ordering) two cups of coffee kaa-faeh sǎwng thîi กาแฟสองที่

pose V (to pose for the camera/strike a pose) waang thâa วางท่า

position N (in an organization) tamnàeng ตำแหน่ง; (position/posture – e.g. yoga posture) thâa ท่า

possess V pen jâo khǎwng เป็นเจ้าของ

possessions N sǒmbàt สมบัติ, (COLLO-QUIAL) khâow khǎwng (literally, 'rice'-'thing(s)') ข้าวของ, or sìng khǎwng สิ่งของ

possible ADJ pen pai dâi เป็นไปได้ (NOTE: 'impossible' is pen pai mâi dâi เป็นไปไม่ได้)

possibly ADV See 'perhaps/maybe'

post, pole, column N sǎo เสา

post, mail N jòt-mǎai จดหมาย

postcard N prai-sà-nii-yá-bàt ไปรษณียบัตร, or (from English) póht-sà-káat โปสการ์ด

post office N prai-sà-nii ไปรษณีย์

postpone V lûean เลื่อน

postponed, delayed ADJ lûean weh-laa เลื่อนเวลา

posture N See 'position'

pot N (for cooking) mâw หม้อ (Note: also used as a slang term for 'vagina')

potato N man fàràng มันฝรั่ง, or simply man มัน

poultry N (i.e. chicken) kài ไก่

pour V (a drink) rin ริน; to pour water or some other liquid over something râat ราด (Note: this word is used, for example, when food, such as curry, is served over/on top of rice – so, rather than having two dishes – one of rice and one of curry/or a stir-fry – there is but one dish [often translated in a menu!) as râat khâow ราดข้าว)

poverty N (also see 'hardship') khwaam yâak jon ความยากจน

powder N (as certain cosmetics) pâeng แป้ง, (tiny loose particles) phǒng ผง

power, authority N am-nâat อำนาจ

powerful ADJ mii am-nâat มีอำนาจ

practice V fùek hàt ฝึกหัด, or simply just fùek ฝึก

praise V (COLLOQUIAL) chom ชม (the same word is also translated as 'admire'), or (formal) yók yâwng ยกย่อง

pram/stroller N (for a baby/young child) rót khěn dèk รถเข็นเด็ก

prawn/shrimp N kûng กุ้ง

pray V (Buddhist style) sùat mon สวดมนต์, (Christian style) à-thít-thǎan อธิษฐาน

prayer N bòt sùat mon บทสวดมนต์

precious/valuable ADJ mii khâa (literally, 'have'-'value') มีค่า

precise ADJ thùuk tâwng ถูกต้อง

predict V See 'forecast'

prefer V châwp mâak kwàa (literally, 'like'-'more than') ชอบมากกว่า

pregnant ADJ tháwng ท้อง (NOTE: same word as 'stomach')

prejudice N à-khá-tì อคติ, (COLLOQUIAL) 'to look down on someone' duu thùuk ดูถูก

prepare, make ready V triam เตรียม

prepared/ready ADJ (to do something) phráwm พร้อม

prescription N (from a doctor) bai sàng yaa ใบสั่งยา

present N (gift) khǎwng khwǎn ของขวัญ

present V (a formal request, ideas – in a formal context) sà-nǒeh เสนอ

present, at the moment ADJ tawn-ní ตอนนี้

presently, nowadays ADV (formal – for COLLOQUIAL see 'now') pàt-jù-ban-ní ปัจจุบันนี้

preserve V à-nú-rák อนุรักษ์

president N (of a republic) prà-thaa-na thíp-baw-dii ประธานาธิบดี

press V kòt กด

pressure N khwaam kòt dan ความกดดัน Also see 'blood pressure'

prestige N chûeh sǐang ชื่อเสียง

pretend V klâehng แกล้ง (NOTE: this is an interesting Thai word that also means 'to do something to someone else out of spite or malice', 'to annoy or tease')

pretty ADJ (beautiful) sǔai สวย, (cute) nâa rák น่ารัก

prevent, protect V pâwng kan ป้องกัน

previous/before ADV kàwn ก่อน: e.g. to come/arrive before someone else maa kàwn มาก่อน; previously tàeh kàwn แต่ก่อน

prey N yùea เหยื่อ

price N raakhaa ราคา

pride/dignity N sàk-sǐi ศักดิ์ศรี

priest N (Christian) bàat lǔang บาทหลวง

primary school N rohng rian prà-thǒm โรงเรียนประถม; primary (school) education pràthǒm sèuk-sǎa ประถมศึกษา

prime minister N naayók rát-thà-mon-trii นายกรัฐมนตรี

prince N jâo chaai เจ้าชาย

princess N jâo yǐng เจ้าหญิง

principal ADJ sǎm-khan สำคัญ

principle N kòt กฎ

print V phim พิมพ์ (NOTE: the English word 'print' is now widely used — e.g. print a document/photograph etc.) prín ปริ๊นท์

prison N (COLLOQUIAL) khúk คุก; to be imprisoned/jailed tìt khúk (literally, 'stuck'-'prison') ติดคุก

prisoner N nák thôht นักโทษ

private ADJ (not public) sùan tua ส่วนตัว

privilege N à-phí-sìt อภิสิทธิ์

prize/reward N raang-wan รางวัล

probably ADV See 'perhaps'

problem N pan-hǎa ปัญหา, (COLLOQUIAL) 'no problem(s)/no worries' mâi mii pan-hǎa ไม่มีปัญหา

procedure, process N khán tawn ขั้น
ตอน

procession N *See* 'parade'

proclaim V prá-kàat ประกาศ

procrastinate V phlàt wan ผลัดวัน

produce/manufacture V phà-lìt ผลิต

product N phà-lìt-tà-phan ผลิตภัณฑ์

profession, occupation N aa-chîip
อาชีพ; a professional mueh aa-chîip
มืออาชีพ

professor N sàat-traa-jaan
ศาสตราจารย์

profile N prà-wàt ประวัติ

profit N (financial gain from business)
kam-rai กำไร

profound ADJ (to have a deep meaning)
léuk-séung ลึกซึ้ง, or (more colloquially simply) séung ซึ้ง

program N (e.g. television progam, list
of items – *also see* 'menu') raai-kaan
รายการ

prohibit V *See* 'forbid', 'forbidden'

project N khrohng-kaan โครงการ

promise V & N sǎnyaa สัญญา (NOTE: as
a noun this word means a 'contract')

promote V sòng-sǒehm ส่งเสริม

pronounce V àwk sǐang ออกเสียง

proof/evidence N làk-thǎan หลักฐาน

propaganda V *See* 'advertise'

proper, appropriate ADJ màw-sǒm
เหมาะสม

property N sáp-sǐn ทรัพย์สิน *Also see*
'possessions'

propose V (offer for consideration)
sà-nǒeh เสนอ, (ask someone to marry) khǎw tàeng-ngaan ขอแต่งงาน

prosper V (develop) jà-roehn เจริญ;
progress (in the sense of development
to more complex, advanced society)
khwaam jà-roehn ความเจริญ; (to do
well) râm-ruai (râm pronounced like
the English word 'rum') ร่ำรวย

prostitute N sǒh-pheh-nii โสเภณี; *also
see* 'hooker'

protest V prà-thúang (NOTE: the syllable
prà is very short) ประท้วง; a 'protest

march' is doehn prà-thúang (literally,
'walk'-'protest') เดินประท้วง

proud ADJ phuum-jai ภูมิใจ

prove V phí-sùut พิสูจน์

proverb N sù-phaa-sìt สุภาษิต

provide V (afford) hâi ให้

province N (administrative unit; there
are presently 76 provinces in Thailand
outside the Bangkok area) jang-wàt
จังหวัด

prude N prudish ADJ – a 'fuddy-duddy'
(i.e. to be opposed to liberal social
ideas/behavior) châo rá-bìap เจ้า
ระเบียบ

psychiatrist N jìt-tà-phâet (literally,
'mind/spirit'-'doctor') จิตแพทย์

pub N (from English) phàp (pronounced
similar to the English word 'pup') ผับ

pubic hair/pubes N (VULGAR) mǒi หมอย

public ADJ sǎa-thaa rá-ná สาธารณะ; a
public place thîi sǎa-thaa rá-ná ที่
สาธารณะ

public relations N prà-chaa sǎm-phan
ประชาสัมพันธ์ (NOTE: the same term
is used for both an 'information booth/
tourist information' and 'reception' in
a hotel)

publish V tii-phim ตีพิมพ์

puke, vomit V aa-jian อาเจียน, or (COL-
LOQUIAL) ûak อ้วก

pull V dueng ดึง

pump V sùup สูบ; a pump N khrûeang
sùup เครื่องสูบ (Note: the word sùup
is also used to mean 'smoke' as in
'smoke a cigarette' sùup bùrìi สูบ
บุหรี่)

pumpkin N fák thawng ฟักทอง

punch V (as in to 'punch' someone) tòi
ต่อย, or chók ชก

punctual/on time ADJ trong weh-laa
ตรงเวลา

punish V long thôht ลงโทษ

pupil/student N nák rian นักเรียน

puppet N hùn krà-bàwk หุ่นกระบอก

puppy N lûuk mǎa ลูกหมา

purchase, buy V súeh ซื้อ

pure/innocent ADJ bawrí-sùt บริสุทธิ์

purple N sĭi mûang สีม่วง

purpose N (i.e. 'the purpose is to increase literacy') jùt mûng măai จุดมุ่งหมาย

purse N (for money) krà-păo ngoehn กระเป๋าเงิน

pus N (in a wound) năwng หนอง

push V phlàk ผลัก, or dan (pronounced like the word 'done') ดัน

put, place V (i.e. put the books on the table) waang วาง

put off, delay, postpone V lûean เลื่อน

put on (clothes) sài ใส่

puzzled/confused ADJ ngong งง

Q

quake V sàn สั่น

qualification N khun-ná-sŏmbàt คุณสมบัติ

quality N (as in 'good quality merchandise') khun-ná-phâap คุณภาพ: e.g. good quality khun-ná-phâap dii คุณภาพดี

quantity N jam-nuan จำนวน

quarrel V See 'argue'

quarter N (¼) sèht nùeng sùan sìi เศษหนึ่งส่วนสี่

queen N prá raa-chí-nii พระราชินี, or simply raa chí-nii ราชินี

queer N (gay/homosexual) keh เกย์ (from English), ADJ (brightly colored) sòt-săi สดใส

question N,V kham thăam คำถาม

queue N (from English) khiu คิว; to line up in a queue khâo khiu (literally, 'enter'-'queue') เข้าคิว

quick ADJ **quickly** ADV rew เร็ว

quicken V rêhng เร่ง

quiet ADJ ngîap เงียบ

quit V (resign) laa àwk ลาออก; (discontinue, i.e 'quit smoking') lôehk เลิก

quite ADV (really) thii diao ทีเดียว (COLLOQUIAL); (rather) khâwn khâang ค่อนข้าง

quiz V, N thòt sàwp ทดสอบ

R

rabbit N krà-tàai กระต่าย

race N (i.e. race of people – Caucasian, Asian, etc.) chúeah châat เชื้อชาติ; (competition) kaan khàeng khăn การแข่งขัน

racism N lát-thí yìat phĭu (literally, 'ism/doctrine'-'despise'-'skin') ลัทธิเหยียดผิว

radiation N rang sĭi รังสี

radio N wít-thá-yú วิทยุ

raft N (also 'houseboat') phaeh แพ

rail N (i.e. travelled by rail/train) dohy rótfai โดยรถไฟ

railroad, railway N thaang rótfai ทางรถไฟ

rain N fŏn ฝน

rain V fŏn tòk ฝนตก

raincoat N sûea kan fŏn เสื้อกันฝน

raise, lift V yók ยก

raise V (bring up children) líang เลี้ยง, (increase in amount, e.g. wages) khûen ขึ้น

rambutan N ngáw เงาะ

rancid ADJ (foul smelling) mĕhn hŭehn เหม็นหืน

random ADJ sùm สุ่ม

Rangoon (largest city in Burma) yâang kûng ย่างกุ้ง

rank N (an official position, e.g. military, police) yót ยศ

rape V khòm khŭen ข่มขืน

rapid ADJ (very quick) rûat rew รวดเร็ว or simply 'rew' เร็ว

rare ADJ (uncommon) hăa yâak หายาก; (uncooked) dìp ดิบ

rarely, seldom, not often ADV mâi bòi ไม่บ่อย

rash N (skin eruption) phùen ผื่น (NOTE: 'to have a rash' is pen phùen เป็นผื่น)

rat/mouse N nŭu หนู

rate of exchange N (for foreign currency) àt-traa lâehk plìan อัตราแลกเปลี่ยน

rather ADV (i.e. 'rather big', 'rather expensive') khâwn khâang.... ค่อนข้างง

rational ADJ (scientific; reason as opposed to superstition) mii hèht mii phŏn มีเหตุมีผล, or simply mii hèht phŏn มีเหตุผล

rattan N (i.e. rattan furniture) wăai หวาย

raven V plôn ปล้น

raw, uncooked ADJ dìp ดิบ

razor N (for shaving) mîit kohn มีดโกน (kohn pronounced like 'own' with a 'g' in front); a razor blade bai mîit kohn ใบมีดโกน

reach/arrive V thŭeng ถึง

react V (to react to something) mii pàtì-kì-rí-yaa มีปฏิกิริยา; reaction, response pàtì-kì-rí-yaa ปฏิกิริยา

read V àan อ่าน

ready ADJ phráwm พร้อม, to get ready triam tua เตรียมตัว, to make ready tham hâi phráwm ทำให้พร้อม

realize, become aware of V rúu tua รู้ตัว

real ADJ (to be genuine, not an imitation) tháech แท้; real (not imaginary) khăwng jing ของจริง

reality N khwaam pen jing ความเป็นจริง

really ADV (in fact) thîi jing ที่จริง

really! (it's true) jing-jing จริง ๆ

really? INTERJ (is that so?) jing rŭeh จริงหรือ

rear ADJ (of the bus/plane/shop, etc.) khâang lăng ข้างหลัง, or dâan lăng ด้านหลัง

reason N (as in a reason for doing something) hèht phŏn เหตุผล

reasonable/fair ADJ (price) phaw sŏm khuan พอสมควร, appropriate máw-sŏm เหมาะสม

recall V (an incident that occurred/ where some missing object may be found) núek àwk นึกออก

receipt N bai sèt ใบเสร็จ

receive V ráp รับ

recent ADJ recently ADV mûea rew-rew níi เมื่อเร็ว ๆ นี้

recess N phák พัก

recipe N sùut aà-hăan สูตรอาหาร; recipe or cookbook tam-raa aà-hăan ตำราอาหาร

recite V thâwng jam ท่องจำ

reckless ADJ sà-phráo สะเพร่า

recognize/remember V jam dâi จำได้

recommend V náenam แนะนำ

reconcile V prawng dawng ปรองดอง

record N ban-thúek บันทึก

record V àt-sĭang อัดเสียง

recover V (to recover something) ao klàp kheun เอากลับคืน

recovered ADJ (to be cured) hăi láew (literally, 'disappear'-'already') หาย แล้ว

red N sĭi daeng สีแดง

Red Cross, the (humanitarian organization) sà-phaa kaa-châat สภากาชาด

reduce V (speed, weight, etc.) lót ลด

redundant ADJ (superfluous) mâak koehn pai มากเกินไป, (overlapping) sám-sáwn ซ้ำซ้อน

reef N hĭn pà-kaa-rang หินปะการัง

refer V âang-thŭeng อ้างถึง

refill V toehm เติม

reflect V (e.g. for light to reflect off the water) sà-tháwn สะท้อน

reform V pràp-prung ปรับปรุง

refreshment N (i.e. a drink) khrûeang dùehm เครื่องดื่ม

refrigerator N tûu yen (literally, 'cup-board'-'cold') ตู้เย็น

refugee N phûu lí-phai ผู้ลี้ภัย

refuse/reject/deny V pàtì-sèht ปฏิเสธ; refusal kaan pàtì-sèht การปฏิเสธ

regarding/concerning PREP kìao kàp เกี่ยวกับ

region N (of a country – general geographic term) phuumí-phâak ภูมิภาค (NOTE: Thailand has four major regions – the center, the north, the north-east, and the south.) The word used to refer to 'region' is phâak ภาค, more commonly for the Central Region phâak klaang ภาคกลาง and the Northern Region phâak nŭea ภาคเหนือ. The Northeast Region is commonly referred to as ii-sǎan อีสาน, while Southern Thailand is pàk tâi (literally, 'part'-'south') ปักษ์ใต้.

register v (a marriage etc.) jòt thá-bian จดทะเบียน

registered post N (i.e. registered letter) jòtmǎai long thá-bian จดหมายลงทะเบียน

regret v (to feel sorry) sĭa jai เสียใจ, or sĭa daai เสียดาย

regrettably ADV (what a pity!) nâa sĭa daai น่าเสียดาย

regular, normal ADJ pàkàtì ปกติ

relatives N (family) yâat ญาติ

relax/rest v phák phàwn พักผ่อน

release v (let go/set free) plòi ปล่อย

reliable ADJ (trustworthy) wái waang-jai ไว้วางใจ

religion N sàat-sà-nǎa ศาสนา

remainder N (that which is left over) thîi lǔea ที่เหลือ

remarkable ADJ dòht-dèhn โดดเด่น

remedy N wí-thii rák-sǎa (literally, 'method'-'treat') วิธีรักษา

remember v jam (pronounce like 'jum' in 'jumble') จำ

remind v tuean เตือน (also the word for 'to warn')

remove v (take something out of…) aw àwk (literally, 'take'-'out') เอาออก

rent v châo เช่า, rent out v hâi châo ให้เช่า

repair v (a car, etc.) sâwm ซ่อม

repeat v tham sám (sám pronounced similar to the English word 'sum') ทำ ซ้ำ; repeatedly ADV sám-sám ซ้ำ ๆ

replace, substitute v See 'instead'

reply/answer v tàwp ตอบ

reply v (in writing) khĭan tàwp เขียน ตอบ

report N, v raai ngaan รายงาน

reporter N See 'journalist'

represent v tham thaen ทำแทน

representative N tua thaen ตัวแทน

request v (in the sense of imploring someone to do something etc.) khǎw ráwng ขอร้อง; (to ask for, as in 'May I….?') khǎw ขอ

require/want v (FORMAL) tâwng kaan ต้องการ, (COLLOQUIAL) yàak อยาก (i.e. want to eat 'yàak kin' อยากกิน)

rescue/help v chûai lǔea ช่วยเหลือ

research N ngaan-wí-jai งานวิจัย

research v tham wí-jai ทำวิจัย

resemble, similar ADJ (COLLOQUIAL) duu khláai ดูคล้าย, also duu mǔean ดูเหมือน

reserve v (a room in a hotel) jawng จอง

resident, inhabitant N phûu aa-sǎi ผู้อาศัย

resign v See 'quit'

resist v tàw-tâan ต่อต้าน, or simply tâan ต้าน

resolve v (a problem) kâeh pan hǎa แก้ปัญหา

respect N khwaam khao-róp ความ เคารพ

respect v (somebody) khao-róp เคารพ, or náp-thǔeh นับถือ

respond v (FORMAL) tàwp sà-nǎwng ตอบสนอง

response N kham tàwp คำตอบ

responsible ADJ ráp phìt châwp รับผิด ชอบ; responsibility N khwaam ráp phìt châwp ความรับผิดชอบ

rest N (i.e. remainder/what's left over) thîi lǔeah ที่เหลือ

rest/relax v phák phàwn พักผ่อน

restaurant N ráan aa-hǎan ร้านอาหาร

restless/agitated ADJ (COLLOQUIAL) yùu mâi sùk อยู่ไม่สุข

restrain v dueng ao wái ดึงเอาไว้

restrict v (limit availability/to be limited – time, etc.) jam-kàt จำกัด

restroom N (bathroom) hâwng náam ห้องน้ำ

result N (e.g. of a test, etc.) phǒn ผล

resulting from, as a result CONJ pen phǒn maa jàak… เป็นผลมาจาก

retail ADJ (the sale of goods in small quantities) khǎai plìik ขายปลีก

retarded ADJ (to be mentally retarded) panyaa àwn (literally, 'intellect'-'weak/soft') ปัญญาอ่อน

retired ADJ kà-sǐan-aa-yú เกษียณอายุ, or (MORE COLLOQUIALLY) kà-sǐan เกษียณ

return V (go back) klàp กลับ (e.g. return home is klàp bâan กลับบ้าน); (give back) khuehn คืน

return ticket N (round trip ticket) tǔa pai klàp (literally, 'ticket'-'go'-'return') ตั๋วไปกลับ

reveal V (make known/to be open – not keeping secrets) pòeht phǒei เปิดเผย

reverse, back up V thǒi lǎng ถอยหลัง, or simply thǒi ถอย

reversed, backwards, inside out V klàp khâang กลับข้าง

review V thóp thuan ทบทวน

revise V trùat kâe ตรวจแก้

revolt/rebellion/coup d'état N pàtìwát ปฏิวัติ

revolting/disgusting ADJ nâa rang-kìat น่ารังเกียจ, or khà-yà khà-yǎehng ขยะแขยง

reward/prize N raang-wan รางวัล

rhythm N See 'tempo'

rice N (cooked) khâow sǔai ข้าวสวย; (uncooked) khâow sǎan ข้าวสาร; (food) khâow ข้าว

rice fields N (irrigated) naa นา

rich/wealthy ADJ ruai รวย

rid: get rid of/eliminate V (pests, termites etc.) kamjàt กำจัด

ride N (in car) nâng rót นั่งรถ

ride V (on a bicycle, an animal) khìi ขี่

ridiculous ADJ (meaningless) rái sǎará ไร้สาระ

right/correct ADJ thùuk ถูก, or thùuk tâwng ถูกต้อง

right N (right-hand side) khwǎa ขวา; to be right-handed thànàt mueh khwǎa ถนัดมือขวา

rights N sìt-thí สิทธิ (often pronounced as simply sìt สิทธิ์)

right now ADV dǐao níi เดี๋ยวนี้

rind/peel N (i.e. orange peel) plùek เปลือก, (also the general word for) bark on a tree, e.g. plùek mái เปลือกไม้

ring N (jewelry) wǎehn แหวน; (boxing ring) weh-thii เวที (also means 'stage for performances')

ring V (to ring someone on the phone) thoh pai โทรไป; (to sound a doorbell) kòt krìng กดกริ่ง

rinse/wash V (plates, hands, etc.) láang ล้าง: e.g. wash your face láang nâa ล้างหน้า

riot N jà-laajon จลาจล

rip/tear V chìik ฉีก

ripe ADJ (of fruit) sùk สุก

rise V (ascend) khûen ขึ้น; (increase) phôehm khûen เพิ่มขึ้น

risk/risky ADJ sìang เสี่ยง

ritual/ceremony N phí-thii พิธี

rival N khûu khàeng คู่แข่ง

river N mâeh náam (literally, 'mother'-'water') แม่น้ำ

road/street N (major thoroughfare) thà-nǒn ถนน

roar V kham raam คำราม

roast V (cook in an oven) òp อบ, (grill, BBQ) yâang ย่าง, (toast) pîng ปิ้ง

rob V (a bank) plôn ปล้น; to rob (a person/to hold someone up) jîi จี้

robot N hùn yon หุ่นยนต์

rock N hǐn หิน

rocket N jà-rùat จรวด

role N (a role in a movie, the role of the press, etc.) bòt bàat บทบาท

roll V (to roll over) klîng กลิ้ง

roll N (as in a roll of toilet paper) múan ม้วน; to roll/make a cigarette muan bùrìi มวนบุหรี่

roof N lǎng khaa หลังคา

room N (in house/hotel, etc.) hâwng ห้อง; (to have some free/extra space) thîi wâang ที่ว่าง

oot N (of plant or a tooth) râak ราก

ope/string N chûeak เชือก

ose (flower) kù-làap กุหลาบ

otate v mǔn wian หมุน เวียน

otten ADJ nâo เน่า

ough ADJ (as in a rough road/an un-shaven face) khrù khrà ขรุขระ

oughly, approximately ADV prà-maan ประมาณ

ound ADJ (shape) klom กลม

ound, around, surrounding ADV râwp-râwp รอบ ๆ

outine N ngaan prà-jam (literally, 'work'-'regular') งานประจำ

ub v (also 'scrub') thǔu ถู

ubber N yaang ยาง

ubber band N (COLLOQUIAL) nǎng yaang หนังยาง

ubbish N khà-yà ขยะ; rubbish bin thǎng khà-yà ถังขยะ

uby N tháp-thim ทับทิม (the word also means 'pomegranate'). NOTE: mét tháp-thim เม็ดทับทิม is slang for 'clitoris' (literally, 'seed'-'ruby')

ude/crude/coarse ADJ (speech/behav-ior) yàap khaai หยาบคาย, also mâi sù-phâap ไม่สุภาพ

ules N kòt กฎ

umor N khàaw lueh ข่าวลือ

un v wîng วิ่ง

un away v (i.e. to flee) wîng nǐi วิ่งหนี

ural ADJ (the countryside) chon-nabòt ชนบท, (COLLOQUIAL) bâan nâwk บ้านนอก

ush v rîip รีบ

ust N sà-nǐm สนิม; rust v sà-nǐm khûen สนิมขึ้น

uthless ADJ thaa run ทารุณ

S

sabotage v tham laai ทำลาย

sack v (to dismiss an employee) See 'fire'

sack N (bag – e.g. sack of rice) krà-sàwp กระสอบ

sacred/sacrosanct ADJ sàk-sìt ศักดิ์สิทธิ์

sacrifice v sǐa sàlà เสียสละ; sacrifice kaan sǐa sàlà การเสียสละ

sad ADJ sâo เศร้า

safe ADJ plàwt-phai ปลอดภัย; safety khwaam plàwt-phai ความปลอดภัย

safe N (for keeping valuables – from English) tûu sép ตู้เซฟ

sago N (food) sǎa-khuu สาคู

sail v (a yacht) lâen ruea แล่นเรือ

salad N (from English) sà-làt สลัด; also see 'lettuce'

salary, wage N ngoen duean เงินเดือน

sale (for) IDIOM (available to customers) khǎai ขาย (also 'sell')

sale (on) IDIOM (reduced prices) lót raa-khaa ลดราคา

sales assistant N phá-nák-ngaan khǎai พนักงานขาย

saline N náam kluea น้ำเกลือ

saliva N (spittle) náam laai น้ำลาย

salt N kluea เกลือ

salt-water N (sea water) náam khem น้ำเค็ม

salty ADJ (taste) khem เค็ม

same PRON (i.e. the same) mǔean เหมือน

sample/example N tua yàang ตัวอย่าง

sand N saai ทราย

sandals N rawng tháo tàe รองเท้าแตะ

sanitation N khwaam sà-àat ความสะอาด

satay N (grilled/BBQ meat/chicken, etc. on a wooden skewer) sà-téh สะเต๊ะ; satay stick(s) mái sà-téh ไม้สะเต๊ะ

satellite N daow thiam ดาวเทียม

satire N sìat sǐi เสียดสี

satisfied ADJ pen thîi phaw jai เป็นที่พอใจ, or simply phaw jai พอใจ; to satisfy someone tham hâi phaw jai ทำให้พอใจ

Saturday N wan sǎo วันเสาร์

sauce N (from English) sáwt ซอส; (dip-ping sauce – spicy, sweet/sour, etc.) nám jîm น้ำจิ้ม

savage v hòht ráai โหดร้าย

save, keep v kèp เก็บ; to save money (to put in the bank) kèp ngoehn เก็บเงิน

savor ADJ (flavor) rót รส, (smell) kiln กลิ่น

saw N (tool) lûeai เลื่อย

say v phûut พูด; say that… phûut wâa… พูดว่า

scales N taa châng ตาชั่ง

scandal N rûeang êuh* chǎow เรื่องอื้อ ฉาว

scanner N (from English) khrûeang sà-kaen เครื่องสแกน

scar N phlǎen pen แผลเป็น

scare v (to scare someone) tham hâi tòk-jai ทำให้ตกใจ

scarce ADV mâi khôi mii ไม่ค่อยมี, or hǎa yâak (literally, 'find'-'difficult') หา ยาก

scared/scary ADJ nâa klua น่ากลัว

scarf N phâa phan khaw (literally, 'cloth'-'wrap around'-'neck') ผ้าพันคอ

scatter v krà-jaai กระจาย

scenery, view N (from English) wiu วิว

scent N kiln hǎwm กลิ่นหอม

sceptical ADJ song-sǎi สงสัย

schedule N kam-nòt กำหนด

scholar N nák wí-chaa-kaan นักวิชาการ

scholarship N (INFORMAL) thun lâo rian ทุนเล่าเรียน, or thun kaan sèuk-sǎa ทุนการศึกษา, (COLLOQUIAL) 'thun' ทุน

school N rohng-rian โรงเรียน

schoolchild N dèk nák-rian เด็ก นักเรียน

science N wít-thá-yaa-sàat วิทยาศาสตร์

scissors N kan-krai กรรไกร

scold/berate v wâa ว่า

scope N khàwp khèt ขอบเขต

score N khá-naen คะแนน

scorn v duu thùuk ดูถูก

Scotland N sà-káwt-laehn สก็อตแลนด์

Scottish, Scots N chaow sà-káwt ชาว สก็อต

scrap N (scrap of food, scrap of paper, something left over, etc.) sèht เศษ:

e.g. scrap of food sèht aa-hǎan เศษ อาหาร

scrape v (e.g. scrape paint off something) khùut ขูด

scratch v (scratch an itch) kao เกา, also (aggressively scratched – by someone with long fingernails, a cat etc.) khùan ข่วน; a scratch (e.g. on a car) roi khùut รอยขูด

scream v ráwng kríit ร้องกรี๊ด

screen N (of computer or television) jaw (pronounced like the English word 'jaw') จอ

screw N (COLLOQUIAL – used with a screwdriver) náwt (pronounced very similar to the word 'not') นอต

screwdriver N khǎi khuang ไขควง

scrub v thǔu ถู, or khàt ขัด

sculpt v pân ปั้น

sculpture N rûup pân รูปปั้น

sea, beach N thá-leh ทะเล

seafood N aa-hǎan thá-leh อาหารทะเล

search for/look for/seek v hǎa หา; to ask 'what are you looking for?' khun hǎa àrai (literally, 'you'-'look for'-'what') คุณหาอะไร

season N rúe-duu ฤดู, or (MORE COLLOQUI-ALLY) nâa หน้า (NOTE: the same word as 'face', 'page of a book', etc.); summer/hot season nâa ráwn (literally, 'season'-'hot') หน้าร้อน (In Thailand the 'high season', in terms of tourist arrivals (Nov-Feb), is colloquially referred to as nâa hai หน้าไฮ)

seat N thîi nâng ที่นั่ง

second N (measure of time) wí-naa-thii วินาที

second ADJ (as in second place) thîi sǎwng ที่สอง

secondhand ADJ (e.g. a used car) mueh sǎwng มือสอง; a used car rót mueh sǎwng (literally, 'car/vehicle'-'hand'-'two') รถมือสอง

secret N khwaam láp ความลับ (i.e. to keep a secret ráksǎa khwaam láp รักษาความลับ)

ecretary N lêh-khǎa nú-kaan เลขานุการ, or (COLLOQUIALLY SIMPLY) leh-khǎa เลขา

ection/segment N (of something) tawn ตอน

ecure/stable ADJ mân-khong มั่นคง

educe V lâw-jai ล่อใจ

ee V hěn เห็น

eed N má-lét เม็ด (although commonly pronounced mét)

eek V See 'search'

eem V (e.g. it might rain) duu mǔean ดู เหมือน

ee you later! INTERJ phóp kan mài พบกันใหม่

eize V yúet ยึด

eldom ADV (or 'not often') mâi bòi ไม่บ่อย

elect/choose V lûeak เลือก

elf N ehng เอง, or tua ehng ตัวเอง

elf-assured ADJ mân-jai tua ehng มั่น ใจตัวเอง

elfish ADJ hěn kàe tua เห็นแก่ตัว

ell V khǎai ขาย

emen/sperm N (medical term) náam à-sù-jì น้ำอสุจิ, also náam kaam น้ำกาม

end V sòng ส่ง

enior ADJ aa-wú-soh อาวุโส

ensible/reasonable ADJ mii hèht phǒn มีเหตุผล

ensitive ADJ (tender feeling – physical) rúu-sùek wai รู้สึกไว

entence N (in written language) prà-yòhk ประโยค

entence V (a final judgment in a criminal case) tàt-sǐn ตัดสิน

eparate V yâehk แยก

September N kan-yaa-yon กันยายน

equence/order N taam lam-dàp ตาม ลำดับ

erious ADJ (i.e. not joking) ao jing เอา จริง; (severe) ráai raeng ร้ายแรง

ervant N khon chái คนใช้

erve V (informal) ráp chái รับใช้, (formal) hâi baw-rí-kaan บริการ

service N bawrí-kaan บริการ

sesame seeds N ngaa งา; sesame oil náam-man ngaa น้ำมันงา

set N (i.e. a set of something – clothes, crockery, etc.) chút ชุด

settle V (resolve) kâe pan-hǎa แก้ปัญหา

settle down V tâng rók-râak ตั้งรกราก

set up V (equipment) tìt-tâng ติดตั้ง; (establish) kàw-tâng ก่อตั้ง

seven NUM jèt เจ็ด

seventeen NUM sìp jèt สิบเจ็ด

seventy NUM jèt sìp เจ็ดสิบ

several/many ADJ lǎai หลาย

severe/violent ADJ run raehng รุนแรง

sew, stitch V yép เย็บ

sex, gender N phêht เพศ

sex, sexual activity V (POLITE) rûam phêht ร่วมเพศ; (COLLOQUIAL) 'to have sex' ao kan เอากัน; 'sleep together' nawn dûai kan (literally, 'lie down'- 'together') นอนด้วยกัน; (slang – vulgar and extremely rude) 'to fuck' yét เย็ด (Note: the English word 'sex' is widely known and pronounced sék เซ็กส์)

sexy ADJ See 'hot'

shack N krà-thâwm กระท่อม

shade N (the shade of a tree) rôm ร่ม

shadow N ngao เงา

shake V (move something up and down) khà-yào เขย่า; (to cause vibration) sàn สั่น

shake hands (in greeting) jàp mueh kan จับมือกัน

shall, will AUX V (indicator of future tense/action) jà จะ: e.g. will/shall go jà pai จะไป

shallow ADJ (opposite of 'deep') tûehn ตื้น

shame N khwaam lá-aai jai ความ ละอายใจ

shame ADJ (as in 'what a shame!') nâa khǎai nâa น่าขายหน้า

shampoo N (hair shampoo) yaa sà phǒm ยาสระผม, or chaem-phuu แชมพู (from English)

shape N (the shape of something) rûup รูป

shapely ADJ (i.e. to have a good figure) hùn dii หุ่นดี

shark N plaa chà-lăam ปลาฉลาม, or simply chà-lăam ฉลาม

sharp ADJ khom คม

sharp-tongued ADJ (vitriolic) (COLLOQUIAL) pàak jàt ปากจัด

shave V kohn โกน

she/her PRON khǎo เขา (NOTE: the same term is also used for 'he/him' and 'they')

sheep N kàe แกะ

sheet N (of paper) phàen krà-dàat แผ่นกระดาษ; (for bed, i.e. bedsheet) phâa puu thîi nawn ผ้าปูที่นอน

shelf/shelves N (for books) chán nǎng-sǔeh ชั้นหนังสือ

shell N plùeak hǒi เปลือกหอย, (COLLO-QUIAL SIMPLY) hǒi หอย

shift N (as in a 'shift at work'/'night shift', etc.) wehn เวร: e.g. the night shift wehn klaang kheun เวรกลางคืน, or (MORE COLLOQUIALLY) a shift (either day or night) kà กะ

shingles N (medical condition) rôhk nguu sà-wàt โรคงูสวัด

shiny ADJ (skin/shoes, etc.) pen man เป็นมัน

ship N ruea เรือ

shirt N sûea chóeht (chóeht from English 'shirt') เสื้อเชิ้ต

shit N See 'excrement'

shiver N tua sàn ตัวสั่น

shock ADJ (to be in a 'state of shock') tòk tàleung ตกตะลึง, or aa-kaan cháwk (cháwk from English 'shock') อาการช็อก

shoe(s) N rawng tháo รองเท้า

shoot V (with a gun) ying ยิง

shop/store N ráan ร้าน

shop, go shopping V pai súeh khǎwng ไปซื้อของ – also very common, particularly with reference to going to a supermarket/department store/mall (from English) cháwp ชอป, or cháwp-pîng ชอปปิ้ง

shopkeeper N jâo khǎwng ráan เจ้าของร้าน

short ADJ (dress/piece of writing, etc.) sân สั้น

short ADJ (not tall) tîa เตี้ย

shortcut N (get somewhere by shortest route) thaang lát ทางลัด

shorts N (short trousers) kaang-kehng khǎa sân กางเกงขาสั้น; (i.e. underpants/boxer shorts) kaang-kehng nai กางเกงใน

shoulder N bàa บ่า

shout V tà-kohn ตะโกน

show V (e.g. one's feeling; to perform in a film/play/live performance etc.) sà-daehng แสดง

show V (live performance) kaan sà-daehng sòt การแสดงสด

shower V (or bath) àap náam อาบน้ำ

showerhead N (in the bathroom) fàk bua ฝักบัว

shrimp/prawn N kûng กุ้ง

shrimp (prawn) paste N kàpì กะปิ

shrine N sǎan jâo ศาลเจ้า

shut/close; closed V pìt ปิด

shut up! V (SLANG) hùp pàak หุบปาก, or ngîap เงียบ

shy/bashful ADJ aai; a very shy person khon khîi aai คนขี้อาย

sibling N (older) phîi พี่ Also see 'older brother/sister'; (younger) náwng น้อง

sick, ill ADJ pùai ป่วย, or simply mâi sàbaai ไม่สบาย

side ADJ khâang ข้าง, also (commonly used) dâan ด้าน

side effect(s) N (of medicine/a drug) phǒn khâang khiang ผลข้างเคียง

sightseeing N pai thát-sá-naa-jawn ไปทัศนาจร, or simply pai thîao ไปเที่ยว

sign/poster/placard N (ranging from small to very large) pâai ป้าย

sign V sen เซ็น; to sign your name sen chûeh เซ็นชื่อ

signal N (radio signal, etc.) sǎn-yaan สัญญาณ

signature N laai sen ลายเซ็น

significant/important ADJ săm-khan สำคัญ

silent ADJ ngîap เงียบ

silk N măi ไหม; silk cloth phâa măi ผ้าไหม

silly ADJ (difficult to readily convey in Thai the sense this word is commonly used in English – arguably, the Thai for 'without reason/irrational' is acceptable, although somewhat formal; the word for 'stupid' would be simply too strong): rái hèht-phŏn ไร้เหตุผล

silver N (metal) ngoehn เงิน (NOTE: the same word as 'money'); silver (the color) sĭi ngoehn สีเงิน

similar ADJ khláai คล้าย, or mŭean เหมือน

simple/easy ADJ ngâai ง่าย

since PREP tâng-tàeh ตั้งแต่

sincere ADJ jing-jai (literally, 'real/true'-'heart/mind') จริงใจ

sing V ráwng phlehng (literally, 'sing'-'song') ร้องเพลง

singer N nák ráwng นักร้อง

Singapore N sĭngkhá-poh สิงคโปร์

single ADJ (not married) sòht โสด

single N (i.e. one person) khon diao คนเดียว; just the one/single (thing) yàang diao อย่างเดียว

singlet/undershirt N See 'vest'

sink/sunk V (also 'drown') jom จม

sink N (for washing up), also 'bathtub' àang náam อ่างน้ำ

sir N (a polite form of address to, or talking about a higher status person – 'you', 'he/she') thân ท่าน

sister N (older) phîi săow พี่สาว; (younger) náwng săow น้องสาว

sister-in-law N (older) phîi sà-phái พี่สะใภ้; (younger) náwng sà-phái น้องสะใภ้

sit V nâng นั่ง; sit down/have a seat V nâng long นั่งลง

situated ADJ tâng yùu ตั้งอยู่

situation N (e.g. political situation, etc.)

sà-thăan-nákaan สถานการณ์

six NUM hòk หก

sixteen NUM sìp hòk สิบหก

sixty NUM hòk sìp หกสิบ

size N khà-nàat ขนาด (NOTE: the English word 'size' is also used in Thai: sái ไซส์)

skewer N mái sìap ไม้เสียบ

ski N (from English – noun/verb) sà-khii สกี; water ski sà-khii náam สกีน้ำ; jet ski jet sà-khii เจ็ตสกี

skilful ADJ mii tháksà มีทักษะ, (COLLOQUIAL) the word for 'clever/adept' – kèng เก่ง

skill N (COLLOQUIAL) fĭi mueh ฝีมือ

skin N phĭu-năng ผิวหนัง, or simply phĭu ผิว

skirt N krà-prohng กระโปรง

skull N hŭa kà-lòhk หัวกะโหลก

sky N fáa ฟ้า

slang N phaa-săa tà-làat (literally, 'language'–'market') ภาษาตลาด (the English word 'slang' is also used sà-laeng สแลง)

slap V tòp ตบ

slash V fan ฟัน

slave N thâat ทาส

sleep V nawn làp นอนหลับ

sleepy ADJ ngûang-nawn ง่วงนอน, or simply ngûang ง่วง

sleeve N khăen sûea แขนเสื้อ

slender ADJ (but shapely) sà-òht sà-ong สะโอดสะอง

slice N (slice/piece of cake, etc.) chín ชิ้น

slide V (slide the door) lûean เลื่อน

slightly, a little bit ADJ nít nòi นิดหน่อย

slim/thin ADJ phăwm ผอม

slip; slippery V, ADJ (surface) lûehn ลื่น

slip N (petticoat, underskirt – from English) sà-líp สลิป

slippers/flip flops/thongs N rawng tháo tàe รองเท้าแตะ

slope N lâat khăo ลาดเขา

sloppy/slovenly ADJ (work) sà-phrâo สะเพร่า

slow ADJ cháa ช้า; (to speak/drive) slowly cháa cháa ช้า ๆ

slum N chum-chon aeh-àt ชุมชน แออัด, (also from English – pronounced similar to the English but with two syllables) sà-lam สลัม

small ADJ (in size) lék เล็ก

smart ADJ chà-làat ฉลาด (NOTE: sometimes used, somewhat ironically, to refer to someone else's 'cleverness' to further their own interests)

smartphone N See 'mobile/cell phone'

smell, to have a bad odor V (also see 'stink') mii klìn มีกลิ่น

smell/sniff V (something) dom ดม

smelling salts N yaa dom (literally, 'medicine/drug'-'smell') ยาดม

smile V yím ยิ้ม

smoke N khwan ควัน

smoke V (tobacco) sùup สูบ (NOTE: the English work 'smoke' pronounced sà-móke สโม้ก is sometimes used to refer to oral sex [i.e. fellatio])

smooth ADJ (to go smoothly) râap rûehn ราบรื่น; (of surfaces) rîap เรียบ

SMS/sms N (texting) (from English) es-em-es เอสเอ็มเอส

smuggle V lák lâwp ลักลอบ

snail N thâak ทาก

snack N khà-nŏm ขนม

snake N nguu งู

snatch V See 'grab'

sneaker N rawng-tháo kii-laa รองเท้า กีฬา

sneeze V jaam จาม

sniff/snort V (a substance) nát นัด

snore V kron กรน

snow N hì-má หิมะ; snow V hì-má tòk หิมะตก

snowpeas N thùa lan-tao ถั่วลันเตา

snuggle V khlaw-khlia คลอเคลีย

so, therefore CONJ dang nán ดังนั้น

soak V jùm จุ่ม, or châeh แช่

soap N sà-bùu สบู่

sober V mâi mao ไม่เมา

soccer N (from English) fút bawn

ฟุตบอล, (COLLOQUIAL) bawn บอล

society N săng-khom สังคม; sociable châwp săng-khom ชอบสังคม

socket N (electric)/powerpoint thîi sìap plák ที่เสียบปลั๊ก

socks N thŭng tháo ถุงเท้า

sofa, couch N (from English) soh-faa โซฟา

soft ADJ (to the touch): (for skin) nîm นิ่ม; (for cloth, etc.) nûm นุ่ม

soft drink N (a fizzy drink, soda pop) náam àt lom น้ำอัดลม

sold ADJ khăai láew (literally, 'sell'-'already') ขายแล้ว

soldier N thá-hăan ทหาร

sold out ADJ khăai mòt láew ขายหมด แล้ว

sole N (of the foot) fàa tháo ฝ่าเท้า (NOTE: palm (of hand) fàa mueh ฝ่ามือ)

solid N khăwng khăeng ของแข็ง

solution N thaang àwk ทางออก (this translation can be used to mean 'an exit')

solve V (a problem) kâeh panhăa แก้ปัญหา

some, partly ADJ bâang บ้าง

somebody, someone PRON baang khon บางคน

something PRON baang yàang บางอย่าง

sometimes ADV baang thii บางที

somewhere (some unspecified place) ADV baang hàeng บางแห่ง, or bang-thîi บางที (literally means 'some-places')

son N lûuk chaai ลูกชาย

son-in-law N lûuk khŏei ลูกเขย

song N phlehng เพลง

soon ADV nai mâi cháa ในไม่ช้า

sore/painful ADJ jèp เจ็บ

sorrow/sad ADJ sâo เศร้า

sorry, regretful ADJ sĭa jai เสียใจ

sorry! INTERJ khăw thôht ขอโทษ

sort, type N chá-nít ชนิด

sort out, deal with, arrange V jàt kaan จัดการ

sound/noise N sĭang เสียง

soul/spirit N win-yaan วิญญาณ

soup N (from English) súp ซุป, (clear soup) náam súp น้ำซุป

sour ADJ (taste) prîao เปรี้ยว (As a slang, this word is also used to describe young women who dress and act with little trace of modesty)

source/cause/reason N (e.g. of/for a problem) săahèht สาเหตุ

south N (direction) tâi ใต้

south-east N tà-wan àwk chĭang tâi ตะวันออกเฉียงใต้

Southeast Asia N eh-chia aa-khá-neh เอเชียอาคเนย์

south-west N tà-wan tòk chĭang tâi ตะวันตกเฉียงใต้

souvenir N khăwng thîi rálúek ของที่ ระลึก

soybean(s) N thùa lŭeang ถั่วเหลือง, or (more commonly – e.g. when referring to tofu) tâo hûu เต้าหู้; soyabean milk náam tâo hûu น้ำเต้าหู้

soy sauce N (salty) sii-íu ซีอิ๊ว; (sweet) sii-íu wăn ซีอิ๊วหวาน

space N (a physical space or gap) châwng wâang ช่องว่าง; (outer) à-wá-kàat อวกาศ

spacious ADJ thîi kwâang ที่กว้าง

spade/shovel N phlûa พลั่ว

sparrow N (ubiquitous small bird) nók krà-jàwk นกกระจอก (NOTE: the word krà-jàwk กระจอก which, by itself, means 'small/petty' is also used as a slang term to mean 'crappy/lousy/ shitty' to describe something of very poor quality)

speak V phûut พูด

special ADJ phí-sèht พิเศษ

specific/in particular ADJ dohy chà pháw โดยเฉพาะ

specimen/example N tua yàang ตัวอย่าง

spectacles/glasses N wâen taa แว่นตา

speech N kham praa-săi คำปราศรัย

speed N khwaam rew ความเร็ว

speedboat N ruea rew เรือเร็ว, (from English) sà-pìit bóht สปีดโบ๊ท

spell V (a word) sà-kòt สะกด

spell N (magical incantation) khaa-thăa คาถา

spend V (as in 'spend money/time') chái ใช้: e.g. spend money chái ngoehn ใช้เงิน

sperm N See 'semen'

spew V See 'vomit'

spices N khrûeang thêht เครื่องเทศ

spicy ADJ phèt เผ็ด

spider N maehng mum แมงมุม; spider web yai maehng mum ใยแมงมุม

spill V (to spill a glass of water) tham hòk ทำหก

spin V pàn ปั่น (e.g. used in making a 'milkshake', 'pedalling a bicycle' etc.) ปั่น; a milkshake/fruit shake/a 'smoothie' náam pàn น้ำปั่น, mŭn (more general term for 'spin'; also means 'dial' for old style telephones) หมุน

spinach N phàk khŏhm ผักโขม

spine N krà-dùuk săn lăng กระดูกสัน หลัง

spirit N See 'soul'

spirit house N (found everywhere in Thailand – to propitiate the local spirits) săan phrá-phuum ศาลพระภูมิ

spirits, hard liquor N lâo เหล้า

splendid ADJ yâwt yîam ยอดเยี่ยม

spoiled ADJ (of food) sĭa เสีย

spokesman/spokeswoman/spokesperson N khoh-sòk โฆษก

sponge N fawng náam ฟองน้ำ

spoon N cháwn ช้อน

sport(s) N kii-laa กีฬา

spot N (small mark) jùt จุด

spotted ADJ (pattern) laai jùt ลายจุด

spouse N (husband or wife) khûu sŏm-rót (literally, 'pair'-'marriage') คู่สมรส

spray N (i.e. to spray something) e.g. mosquito repellent: sà-preh สเปรย์, (from English) chìit sà-preh ฉีดสเปรย์

spread V krá-jaai กระจาย

spring N (metal part) (from English) sà-pring สปริง

spy N nák sùep นักสืบ

squad N klùm กลุ่ม (or 'tiim' ทีม from 'team' in English)

square N (shape) sìi lìam สี่เหลี่ยม; (as in Tiananmen Square) jà-tùrát จัตุรัส

squeeze V (press) bìip บีบ, (extracting liquid, e.g. squeeze an orange) khán คั้น

squid N plaa mùek ปลาหมึก

squirrel N krà-râwk กระรอก

stab V thaeng แทง

stable/secure ADJ mân-khong มั่นคง

staff N (member in a store) phá-nák-ngaan พนักงาน

stage N (for performances, also 'boxing ring') weh-thii เวที

stagger V (e.g. stagger along drunk) doehn soh-seh เดินโซเซ

stain N roi pûean รอยเปื้อน

stairs N ban-dai บันได

stalk V àep-taam แอบตาม

stall N (of vendor) phǎehng khǎai khǎwng แผงขายของ

stamp N (ink) traa pám ตราปั๊ม; (postage – from English) sà-taehm แสตมป์

stand V yuehn ยืน

stand up V lúk khûen ลุกขึ้น

standard N (i.e. commercial/legal standard) mâat-trà-thǎan มาตรฐาน

stapler N (for stapling pieces of paper) (COLLOQUIAL) máek แม็ก

star N (in the heavens) daow ดาว (NOTE: also used in the English sense of a famous person or celebrity)

stare V (to stare at someone) mawng มอง, or jâwng จ้อง

start/begin V rôehm เริ่ม

startle V sà-dûng สะดุ้ง

starve V hǐw mâak หิวมาก

state N rát รัฐ

state V phûut พูด

stationery N khrûeang khǐan เครื่องเขียน

statistics N sà-thì-tì สถิติ

statue N rûup pân รูปปั้น

status N (financial status) thǎa-ná ฐานะ

stay V (somewhere) yùu อยู่, or phák

yùu พักอยู่ (NOTE: 'Where are you staying?' ('you' understood) is phák yùu thîi nǎi พักอยู่ที่ไหน)

stay/remain V yùu kàp thîi อยู่กับที่

stay overnight V kháang khuehn ค้างคืน

steal V khà-mohy ขโมย (NOTE: the same word is also a noun meaning 'a thief/thieves')

steam N ai náam ไอน้ำ

steam V steamed ADJ (e.g. rice) nûeng นึ่ง

steel N lèk เหล็ก

steep ADJ (e.g. a steep hill) chan ชัน

steer V mǔn phuang maa-lai หมุนพวงมาลัย

steering wheel N phuang maa-lai พวงมาลัย

step N (when walking) kâow ก้าว

step V (on something) yìap เหยียบ

steps, stairs N bandai บันได

stepfather N phâw líang พ่อเลี้ยง; stepmother mâeh líang แม่เลี้ยง

sterile V (unable to have children) pen mǎn เป็นหมัน

stick V tìt kàp ติดกับ

stick, branch of tree N gìng mái กิ่งไม้; a walking stick mái tháo ไม้เท้า

stick out V yûehn àwk maa ยื่นออกมา

sticky ADJ nǐao เหนียว

sticky rice N khâow nǐao ข้าวเหนียว

stiff ADJ (as in 'hard'/opposite of 'flexible') khǎeng แข็ง

still, even now ADV yang ยัง: e.g. (he's) 'still in Thailand' yang yùu mueang thai (literally, 'still'-'stay/be located'-'Thailand') ยังอยู่เมืองไทย

sting V (burning/stinging sensation) sàep แสบ

stink V měn เหม็น

stir V (a liquid/when cooking etc.) khon คน, or kuan กวน

stock market N tà-làat hûn (literally, 'market'-'share(s)') ตลาดหุ้น

stomach N tháwng ท้อง (NOTE: also the word for 'pregnant')

stone N (material) hǐn หิน; a stone/rock kâwn hǐn ก้อนหิน

stool N *See* 'excrement'

stop N (i.e. a bus stop) pâai rót-meh ป้ายรถเมล์

stop V (to halt) yùt หยุด; (cease doing something) lôehk เลิก

stop by, pay a visit (pop in and see someone) wáe แวะ

stop it! INTERJ yùt ná หยุดนะ

store V (to collect – e.g. collect stamps) sà-sǒm สะสม

storm N phaa-yú พายุ

story, storey N (of a building) chán ชั้น

story N (tale) rûeang เรื่อง

stout ADJ (plump) oûan อ้วน, (COLLOQUIAL playful) pûm pûi ปุ้มปุ้ย

stove/charcoal cooker N tao เตา

straight ADJ (not crooked) trong ตรง

straight ahead ADJ trong pai (khâang nâa) ตรงไป(ข้างหน้า)

strait(s) N (geographical feature, e.g. Straits of Hormuz) châwng khâehp ช่องแคบ

strange/unusual/weird ADJ plàehk แปลก

stranger N khon plàehk nâa (literally, 'person'-'strange'-'face') คนแปลกหน้า

straw N (for drinking) làwt หลอด

stream N (water course) lam-thaan ลำธาร

street/road N thà-nǒn ถนน

strength, power N kamlang กำลัง

stress N **stressful** ADJ khwaam khrîat ความเครียด, or simply khrîat เครียด

stretch V yûeht ยืด

strict ADJ khrêng khrát เคร่งครัด

strike/protest V prà-thúang ประท้วง

strike, hit V tii ตี

string/rope N chûeak เชือก

strip V (take clothes off) kâeh phâa แก้ผ้า

striped ADJ mii laai มีลาย (more generally, this also means 'to have a pattern/design' on material/surface)

strong ADJ khǎeng raehng แข็งแรง

structure N (e.g. the structure of a building/of society) khrohng sâang โครงสร้าง

stubborn ADJ dûeh ดื้อ

stuck ADJ (i.e. won't move) tìt ติด

student N nák-rian นักเรียน

study/learn V rian เรียน

stuffy ADJ (hot, airless atmosphere) òb âow อบอ้าว

stumble V sà-dùt สะดุด, or lóm ล้ม

stupid ADJ ngôh โง่

style/design N bàehp แบบ (the English word 'style' is also used in various ways – e.g. for clothing and behavior etc. – but pronounced in the Thai way sàty/sàtai สไตล์)

stylish/fashionable/modern ADJ than sà-mǎi ทันสมัย

subject N hǔa khâw หัวข้อ

subject matter N nûea hǎa เนื้อหา

submarine N ruea dam náam เรือดำน้ำ

succeed V sǎmrèt สำเร็จ

success N khwaam sǎmrèt ความสำเร็จ

such as, for example... IDIOM chên... เช่น

suck V dùut ดูด, also om อม (NOTE: this word is also a slang term used to describe female on male oral sex [i.e. fellatio])

sudden ADJ **suddenly** ADV than thii ทันที

sue V (to sue someone; also to 'accuse') fáwng ฟ้อง

suffer V thúk-jai ทุกข์ใจ

suffering ADJ mii-khwaam-thúk มีความทุกข์

sufficient/enough ADJ phaw-phiang พอเพียง, or simply phaw พอ

sugar N náam-taan น้ำตาล

sugarcane N ôi อ้อย

suggest V náenam แนะนำ

suggestion N kham náenam คำแนะนำ

suicide V (to commit suicide) khâa tua taai ฆ่าตัวตาย

suit N (clothes) (from English) sùut สูท

suitable, fitting, appropriate ADJ màw-sǒm เหมาะสม

suitcase N krà-pǎo sûea phâa กระเป๋าเสื้อผ้า

summary N **summarize** V sà-rùp สรุป

summer N nâa ráwn หน้าร้อน

summit N (mountain peak) yâwt ยอด

sun N phrá aathít พระอาทิตย์

sunbathe V àap-dàet อาบแดด

Sunday N wan aa-thít วันอาทิตย์

sunglasses N wâen kan dàeht แว่นกันแดด

sunlight N sǎehng dàeht แสงแดด, or simply dàeht แดด

sunny ADJ dàeht àwk แดดออก

sunrise N phrá aa-thít khûen พระอาทิตย์ขึ้น

sunset N phrá aa-thít tòk din พระอาทิตย์ตกดิน

superficial ADJ (not deep – used figuratively) phǐu phǒen ผิวเผิน

superior/better ADJ dii kwàa ดีกว่า

supermarket N (from English) suu-pôeh-maa-kèt ซูเปอร์มาเก็ต

superstitious ADJ (believing in ghosts, omens, etc.) (COLLOQUIAL) thǔeh phǐi ถือผี

supervise/oversee/control V (work) khûap khum ควบคุม; supervise/look over (e.g. children) duu-laeh ดูแล

supply V (goods/provisions, etc.) jàt hǎa จัดหา

support V (to provide support) sà-nàp sà-nǔn สนับสนุน, also ùt-nǔn อุดหนุน

suppose V sǒm-mút สมมุติ

suppress V (illegal activity) pràap praam ปราบปราม

supreme ADJ sǔung sùt สูงสุด

sure ADJ nâeh jai แน่ใจ

surf V (on a surfboard) lên tôh khlûehn เล่นโต้คลื่น

surface N phǐu phúehn ผิวพื้น

surface mail/ordinary mail N prai-sà-nii tham-má-daa ไปรษณีย์ธรรมดา

surfboard N krà-daan tôh khlûehn กระดานโต้คลื่น

surgery N (medical operation) phàa tàt ผ่าตัด; (operating room) hâwng phàa tàt ห้องผ่าตัด

surname N naam sà-kun นามสกุล

surprised ADJ plàehk jai แปลกใจ

surprising ADJ nâa plàehk jai น่าแปลกใจ

surroundings N sìng wâeht láwm สิ่งแวดล้อม (also the word for the 'environment')

survey V sǎm-rùat สำรวจ

survive V râwt chii-wít รอดชีวิต, (common idiom) to save one's own skin ao tua râwt เอาตัวรอด

suspect V sǒng-sǎi สงสัย

suspicion N khwaam sǒngsǎi ความสงสัย

swallow N kluehn กลืน

swamp/waterhole N bueng บึง

swear V (as in 'I swear it wasn't me') sǎa-baan สาบาน; to swear at someone dàa ด่า

sweat N ngùea เหงื่อ

sweat V ngùea àwk เหงื่อออก

sweep V kwàat กวาด; a broom mái kwàat ไม้กวาด

sweet ADJ wǎan หวาน

sweet/dessert N khǎwng wǎan ของหวาน, also khà-nǒm-wǎan ขนมหวาน (literally means 'sweet-treat')

sweet and sour ADJ prîao wǎan เปรี้ยวหวาน

sweetheart/darling N thîi rák ที่รัก

sweets/candy N khà-nǒm ขนม; a sweet you suck on lûuk om ลูกอม

swim N wâai náam ว่ายน้ำ

swimming costume, swimsuit N chút wâai náam ชุดว่ายน้ำ

swimming pool N sà wâai náam สระว่ายน้ำ

swing V kwàeng แกว่ง

switch N (from English) sà-wít สวิทช์

switch V (change) plìan เปลี่ยน

switch on, turn on V pòeht เปิด

swollen ADJ buam บวม

swoon V *See* 'faint'

sword N dàap ดาบ

symbol N sănyálák สัญลักษณ์

sympathy N **sympathetic** ADJ hĕn òk hĕn jai (literally, 'see'-'chest'-'see'-'heart') เห็นอกเห็นใจ

symptom N aa-kaan อาการ

synthetic ADJ săng-khráw สังเคราะห์

syringe N khĕm chìit yaa (literally, 'needle'-'inject'-'medicine/drug') เข็มฉีดยา

syrup N (cordial/sweet concentrate) náam chûeam น้ำเชื่อม, also (from English) sai-ràp ไซรัป

system N (e.g. of government/of running a business etc.) rá-bòp ระบบ

T

table N tó โต๊ะ (NOTE: at times this word is also used colloquially to refer to chairs)

tablecloth N phâa puu tó ผ้าปูโต๊ะ

tablet(s) N yaa mét ยาเม็ด

tablet PC N (computer) (from English) tháeb-lét phii sii แท็บเล็ทพีซี

tail N (of an animal) hăang หาง

take V ao เอา (NOTE: used in conjunction with other words to express various distinct meanings – e.g. take the book away ao năngsŭeh pai เอาหนังสือไป; bring the book here ao năng-sŭeh maa เอาหนังสือมา)

take care of V duu laeh ดูแล

take off V (clothes/shoes) thàwt ถอด

tale N ní-thaan นิทาน

talk V phûut พูด

talk about V phûut rûeang… พูดเรื่อง

tall ADJ sŭung สูง

tame ADJ (of an animal) chûeang เชื่อง

tampon N ('sanitary napkin') phâa à-naa-mai ผ้าอนามัย

tank N thăng ถัง (same word used for 'bucket'): e.g. petrol tank thăng náam-man ถังน้ำมัน; (military vehicle) rót thăng รถถัง

tap N (i.e. turn on the tap) kók náam ก๊อกน้ำ

tape N (sticky) théhp เทป (from English)

target N (used for shooting practice) pâo เป้า (SLANG/COLLOQUIAL) also refer to the groin region of males

task N ngaan งาน

taste N rót รส, or (more fully) rót châat รสชาติ

taste V (e.g. sample food) chim ชิม

tasty ADJ àròi อร่อย, or mii rót châat (literally, 'have'-'taste') มีรสชาติ

tattoo N sàk สัก

tax N phaa-sĭi ภาษี (NOTE: to pay tax(es) is sĭa phaa-sĭi เสียภาษี. *Also see* 'VAT')

taxi N tháek-sîi แท็กซี่; motorcycle taxi (very common in most areas of Bangkok) maw-toeh-sai ráp jâang มอเตอร์ไซค์รับจ้าง (NOTE: a motorcycle taxi rank is known colloquially as a win วิน)

tea N chaa ชา, or náam chaa น้ำชา (NOTE: some types of tea – usually very sweet – commonly sold in Thailand are as follows: hot tea chaa ráwn ชาร้อน; iced tea chaa yen ชาเย็น; iced black tea chaa dam yen ชาดำเย็น)

teach V săwn สอน

teacher N (from the Sanskrit derived term 'guru') khruu ครู

teak/teakwood N mái sàk ไม้สัก

team N (from English – pronounced very similar to the original) thiim ทีม; group kháná, คณะ

tear/rip V chìik ฉีก

tears N náam-taa (literally, 'water'-'eye{s}') น้ำตา

tease V yàeh แหย่

teaspoon N cháwn chaa (literally, 'spoon'-'tea') ช้อนชา

technician/tradesperson N (general term) châang ช่าง

teenager(s) N wai rûn วัยรุ่น

teeshirt/T-shirt N sûea yûeht เสื้อยืด

teeth/tooth N fan ฟัน

telephone N thoh-rá-sàp โทรศัพท์ (*also see* 'mobile/cell phone')

telephone number N boeh thoh-rá-sàp
เบอร์โทรศัพท์

television N (COLLOQUIAL) thii wii ทีวี,
also (more formally) thoh-rá-thát
โทรทัศน์

tell V (a story) lâo เล่า; to tell someone
bàwk บอก

temperature N ùn-hà-phuum อุณหภูมิ

temple N (Buddhist) wát วัด; an ancient
temple wát boh-raan วัดโบราณ; (Chinese) sǎan jâo ศาลเจ้า

tempo/rhythm N jang-wà จังหวะ

temporary ADJ chûa khraaw ชั่วคราว

ten N sìp สิบ

tender ADJ nûm นุ่ม

tendon N en เอ็น

tennis N (from English) then-nít (pronounced 'ten'-'nit') เทนนิส

tens of, multiples of ten ADJ lǎai sìp
หลายสิบ

tense ADJ (as in 'a tense or strained
muscle') tueng ตึง

tent N (from English) tén เต็นท์

ten thousand NUM mùehn หมื่น

terminal N sà-thǎa-nii สถานี

terminate V jòp จบ

terrible, to be ADJ yâeh แย่

terrify V tham-hâi klua ทำให้กลัว

territory N khèht เขต

terrorist N phûu kàw kaan ráai
ผู้ก่อการร้าย

test V (investigation) trùat sàwp ตรวจ
สอบ; (test for its quality) thót sàwp
ทดสอบ; (test someone's knowledge)
sàwp สอบ

testicles N (medical term) lûuk an-thá
ลูกอัณฑะ, (COLLOQUIAL) khài ไข่ (not
particularly vulgar, but better left unsaid – the word used here means
'egg(s)', the equivalent of the English
'balls/nuts')

Thai N thai ไทย; Thai language phaa-
sǎa thai ภาษาไทย

Thailand N (COLLOQUIAL) mueang thai
เมืองไทย, or (FORMAL) prà-thêht thai
ประเทศไทย

than PREP kwàa กว่า: e.g. more than…
mâak kwàa… มากกว่า; better than…
dii kwàa… ดีกว่า

thank V thank you INTERJ khàwp khun
ขอบคุณ

that PRON nán นั้น; those lào nán เหล่า
นั้น

that, which, the one who CONJ thîi… ที่

theater N (drama) rohng lá-khawn โรง
ละคร

their/theirs ADJ khǎwng khǎo ของเขา

then CONJ (used as a connecting word
when relating a series of events – e.g.
'she went to the beach and then to
see her friends in town and then….')
láew แล้ว

there ADV thîi nân ที่นั้น

therefore CONJ dang nán ดังนั้น

there is, there are PRON (also 'to have')
mii มี

they, them PRON khǎo เขา, or (something like 'that group') phûak khǎo
พวกเขา

thick ADJ (of liquids) khôn ข้น; (not thin)
nǎa หนา

thief N khà-mohy ขโมย (also see 'steal')

thigh N khǎa àwn ขาอ่อน

thin ADJ (skinny) phǎwm ผอม, (of
things) baang บาง

thing N khǎwng ของ, or sìng สิ่ง;
things sìng khǎwng สิ่งของ

think V (ponder) trài trawng ไตร่ตรอง
khít คิด, also commonly néuk นึก:
e.g. 'I can't think of it' néuk mâi àwk
นึกไม่ออก; or 'I've thought of it/I've
got it' néuk àwk láew นึกออกแล้ว

third N (⅓) sèht nùeng sùan sǎam เศษ
หนึ่งส่วนสาม

third… ADJ (the third brother, in third
place, etc.) …thîi sǎam ที่สาม

thirsty ADJ hǐu náam หิวน้ำ

thirteen NUM sìp sǎam สิบสาม

thirty NUM sǎam sìp สามสิบ

this PRON níi นี้; these lào níi เหล่านี้

though, even though CONJ máeh wâa
แม้ว่า

thought(s) N khwaam khít ความคิด

thousand NUM phan พัน

thread N dâai ด้าย

threaten V khùu ขู่

three NUM sǎam สาม

thrill/thrilling/exciting ADJ tùen-tên ตื่น เต้น (NOTE: a word that means 'a thrill' (as in an adrenaline 'rush') is sǐao เสียว. This term is also used, for example, when hearing the sound of someone scratching their nails on a blackboard, or when getting a thrill from doing something dangerous (e.g. bungee jumping). In addition sǐao also refers to the pleasurable tingling sensation when sexually aroused.)

throat N lam khaw ลำคอ, or simply khaw คอ

through PREP (pass through/pass by) phàan ผ่าน

throw V khwâang ขว้าง

throw away, throw out V khwâang thíng ขว้างทิ้ง, or simply thíng ทิ้ง

thunder N fáa ráwng ฟ้าร้อง

Thursday N (full form) wan phá-rúe-hàt sà-baw-dii วันพฤหัสบดี, (normal colloquial term) wan phá-rúe-hàt วัน พฤหัส

thus, so CONJ dang nán ดังนั้น, (MORE COLLOQUIAL) kâw-loei ก็เลย

ticket N (for transport/entertainment, etc.) tǔa ตั๋ว (NOTE: tickets for entertainment/sport, etc. are also referred to as bàt บัตร – pronounced like the word 'but') a fine bai sàng ใบสั่ง

tickle V jîi จี้ (NOTE: *also* slang, meaning 'to rob someone with a weapon')

ticklish ADJ ják-kà jîi จั๊กกะจี้

tidy/neat/well behaved ADJ (in dress/ speech/behavior) rîap rói เรียบร้อย

tie, necktie N (from English) nék-thai เน็คไท

tie V phùuk ผูก

tiger N sǔea เสือ

tight ADJ nâen แน่น (NOTE: the English word 'fit' is commonly used to refer to tight-fitting clothing, fít ฟิต)

till/until PREP jon kwàa จนกว่า, or kwàa jà กว่าจะ

timber/wood N mái ไม้

time N wehlaa เวลา; 'what's the time?' weh-laa thâo rài เวลาเท่าไร, or (more commonly) kìi mohng láew (literally, 'how many'-'hour'-'already') กี่โมง แล้ว

times N (i.e. 4 × 4 = 16) khuun คูณ

timetable N taa-raang wehlaa ตาราง เวลา

tin N (e.g. a tin of beans) krà-pǎwng กระป๋อง

tiny ADJ lék mâak เล็กมาก

tip N (the end of something, e.g. end of one's nose, etc.) plaai ปลาย; (to give someone a tip for their service) (from English) thíp ทิป

tire/tyre N (on a car) yaang rót ยางรถ (NOTE: a flat tire/tyre is yaang baehn ยางแบน)

tired ADJ (sleepy) ngûang ง่วง; (worn out) nùeai เหนื่อย

tissue N (paper) (from English) krà-dàat thít-chûu กระดาษทิชชู

title N (to a piece of land) chànòht thîi din โฉนดที่ดิน

to, toward(s) PREP (a place) pai yang... ไปยัง

tobacco N yaa sùup ยาสูบ, or yaa sên ยาเส้น

today N wan níi วันนี้

toe N níu tháo นิ้วเท้า; toe nail lép tháo เล็บเท้า

tofu/soyabean N tâo hûu เต้าหู้

together N dûai kan ด้วยกัน

toilet N (i.e. bathroom) hâwng náam ห้องน้ำ

toilet paper N krà-dàat cham-rá กระดาษชำระ, (COLLOQUIAL) krà-dàat chét kôn (literally, 'paper'-'wipe'- 'bottom') กระดาษเช็ดก้น

tolerate V òt-thon อดทน

tomato N ma-khǔea thêht มะเขือเทศ

tomorrow ADV, N phrûng níi พรุ่งนี้

tongue N lín ลิ้น

tonight ADV, N khuehn níi คืนนี้

too ADV (also) dûai ด้วย; (excessive) koehn pai เกินไป: too expensive phaehng koehn pai แพงเกินไป, (MORE COLLOQUIAL) phaehng pai แพงไป

too much ADV mâak koehn pai มาก เกินไป

tool, utensil, instrument N khrûeang mueh เครื่องมือ

tooth N fan ฟัน (fan pronounced like the English word 'fun')

toothbrush N praehng sǐi fan แปรงสีฟัน

toothpaste N yaa sǐi fan ยาสีฟัน

toothpick N mái jîm fan ไม้จิ้มฟัน

top ADJ (on top) khâang bon ข้างบน; top/peak (of hill, mountain) yâwt ยอด

topic N (topic in essay, etc.) hǔa khâw หัวข้อ

top secret N khwaam láp sùt yâwt ความลับสุดยอด

torch, flashlight N fai chǎai ไฟฉาย

torn/ripped ADJ (e.g. torn jeans – also refers to worn out clothes etc.) khàat ขาด

torture V thaw-rá-maan ทรมาน

total N, ADJ (the whole lot) tháng mòt ทั้งหมด

touch V tàe แตะ

tough ADJ (chewy – a tough piece of meat) nǐaw เหนียว; (as in strong physically) khǎeng raehng แข็งแรง; tough (as in mentally tough) jai khǎeng ใจแข็ง

tourism N kaan thâwng thîao การท่อง เที่ยว

tourist N nák thâwng thîao นักท่อง เที่ยว

tow V (i.e. to tow a caravan) lâak ลาก

towel N phâa chét tua ผ้าเช็ดตัว, also (MORE COLLOQUIALLY) phâa khǒn nǔn ผ้า ขนหนู

tower N hǎw khoi หอคอย

town N mueang เมือง (also used in certain cases to refer to a country e.g. Thailand mueang thai เมืองไทย, China mueang jiin เมืองจีน)

toxic ADJ (poisonous) pen phít เป็นพิษ

toy N khǎwng lên ของเล่น

trace N râwng-roi ร่องรอย

track V tìt-taam ติดตาม

trade N kaan kháa การค้า

trade V exchange lâehk plìan แลก เปลี่ยน

traditional ADJ dâng doehm ดั้งเดิม

traffic N kaan jà-raa-jawn การจราจร

traffic jam N rót tìt รถติด

train V (someone) fùek ฝึก

train N rót fai รถไฟ

train station N sà-thǎa-nii rót fai สถานี รถไฟ

transfer V (remove from one place to another) yáai ย้าย; (send data/money from one form to another) ohn โอน

transform V plìan เปลี่ยน

translate V plaeh แปล (Note the following useful expression: 'what does it/that mean?' plaeh wâa àrai แปลว่า อะไร)

transparent ADJ (used both in the usual sense of 'clear' and referring to the operations of a company/government etc. – 'transparency') pròhng sǎi โปร่งใส

transport V khǒn sòng ขนส่ง (NOTE: this term is used colloquially to refer to a bus station serving inter-province travel)

transexual ADJ plaeng phêht แปลง เพศ

transvestite N (ladyboy) kà-thoei กะเทย

trap N kàp-dàk กับดัก

trash N khà-yà ขยะ

travel V doehn thaang เดินทาง

travel agency N (COLLOQUIAL) baw-rí-sàt thâwng thîao บริษัทท่องเที่ยว

traveler N nák doehn thaang นักเดิน ทาง, or khon doehn thaang คนเดิน ทาง

tray N thàat ถาด

tread V (walk on) yìap เหยียบ

treasure/wealth N sàp sŏmbàt ทรัพย์สมบัติ

treat V (someone to dinner) líang เลี้ยง; (behave towards) tham tàw ทำต่อ; (give medical aid) rák-sǎa รักษา

tree N tôn mái ต้นไม้

tremble/shake V (with fear) sàn สั่น, or tua sàn ตัวสั่น

trendy ADJ (i.e. the latest something) than sá-mǎi ทันสมัย (NOTE: than pronounced similar to the English word 'ton'; the English word 'trend' has also found its way into Thai – tren เทรนด์)

trespass V (on someone's property) rúk lám รุกล้ำ; (on someone's person, i.e. inappropriate touching) lûang koen ล่วงเกิน

triangle N sǎam lìam สามเหลี่ยม (NOTE: the tri-border area [Thailand, Burma, Laos] the 'Golden Triangle' – sǎam lìam thawng kham สามเหลี่ยม ทองคำ)

tribe N phào เผ่า; hill tribe chaow khǎo ชาวเขา

tricky ADJ (as in a tricky person trying to pull the wool over someone's eyes) mii lêh lìam มีเล่ห์เหลี่ยม

trim V lem เล็ม

trip/journey N kaan doehn thaang การ เดินทาง

tripe/offal N (COLLOQUIAL) phâa khîi ríu ผ้าขี้ริ้ว (NOTE: this term phâa khîi ríu also means 'rag' (for wiping things up))

troops, army N kawng tháp กองทัพ

trouble N (as in 'hardship') khwaam lam-bàak ความลำบาก

troublemaker N khon kàw kuan คนก่อกวน

troublesome ADJ (e.g. for life to be troublesome/difficult) lam-bàak ลำบาก

trousers/pants N kaang-kehng กางเกง

truck N rót ban-thúk รถบรรทุก

true ADJ jing จริง

truly ADV jing-jing จริง ๆ

trust V wái jai ไว้ใจ

truth N khwaam jing ความจริง; to speak the truth phûut khwaam jing พูดความจริง

try V phá-yaa-yaam พยายาม

try on V (clothes) lawng sài ลองใส่

try out V (to try something out) lawng ลอง

Tuesday N wan ang-khaan วันอังคาร

tub N àang อ่าง

tube N thâw ท่อ

tuktuk taxi N rót túk túk รถตุ๊ก ตุ๊ก, or simply túk túk ตุ๊ก ตุ๊ก

tunnel N ù-mohng อุโมงค์

turkey N (fowl) kài nguang ไก่งวง

turn V (change the direction, e.g. turn the car) líao เลี้ยว

turn around V líao klàp เลี้ยวกลับ

turn off V pìt ปิด

turn on V pòeht เปิด

turtle/tortoise N tào เต่า

tutor N khruu-sǎwn-phí-sèht (literally, 'teacher'-'special') ครูสอนพิเศษ

TV N (from English) thii wii ทีวี

tweezers N khiim nìip คีมหนีบ

twelve NUM sìp sǎwng สิบสอง

twenty NUM yîi sìp ยี่สิบ

twice ADV sǎwng khráng สองครั้ง

twin N (as in 'twin bed') pen khûu เป็นคู่

twins N (children/people) fǎa fàet ฝาแฝด (often just the word fàet แฝด is used)

twist V (e.g. as in a 'twisted leg') bìt บิด

two N sǎwng สอง

type, sort N chá-nít ชนิด

type/print V phim พิมพ์

typhoon N tâi-fùn ไต้ฝุ่น

typical ADJ pen tham-má-daa เป็น ธรรมดา

tyre N See 'tire'

U

ugly ADJ (physically ugly) nâa klìat น่า เกลียด (NOTE: in Thai this is commonly expressed as 'not pretty/beautiful' – mâi sǔai ไม่สวย. Furthermore, it should be noted that the term nâa klìat น่าเกลียด is also commonly used to refer to 'unsightly/inappropriate behavior')

umbrella N rôm ร่ม (NOTE: this word also means 'shade')

unable ADJ (not capable of doing something/do not have ability to do something) mâi sǎ-mâat ไม่สามารถ; (MORE COLLOQUIAL) cannot do (something) tham mâi dâi (literally, 'do'-'no'-'can') ทำไม่ได้

unaware ADJ mâi rúu tua ไม่รู้ตัว

unbearable ADJ (to be intolerable – as in 'I can't handle it') thon mâi dâi ทนไม่ได้, or thon mâi wǎi ทนไม่ไหว

uncertainty N khwaam mâi nâeh nawn ความไม่แน่นอน

uncle N (general term – also see 'aunt') lung ลุง (NOTE: this word is pronounced with a very short 'u' – and it does not sound like the English word 'lung'. It is a word that is often used to an unrelated elder male meaning 'you/he')

uncomfortable ADJ (e.g. an uncomfortable place) mâi sà-dùak sà-baai ไม่สะดวกสบาย; uncomfortable (in the sense of feeling uncomfortable about something) mâi sà-baai jai ไม่สบายใจ

unconscious ADJ mâi dâi sà-tì ไม่ได้สติ

uncover/reveal V (e.g. the truth) pòeht phǒei เปิดเผย

under PREP tâi ใต้

undergo/experience V prà-sòp ประสบ, (MORE COLLOQUIAL) joeh-kàp เจอกับ

underpants N kaang-kehng nai กางเกงใน

undershirt N sûea chán nai เสื้อชั้นใน

understand V khâo jai เข้าใจ; to misunderstand V khâo jai phìt เข้าใจผิด

underwear N chút chán nai ชุดชั้นใน

undress/to get undressed V kâeh phâa แก้ผ้า

unemployed ADJ wâang ngaan ว่างงาน

unequal ADJ mâi thâokan ไม่เท่ากัน

unfaithful ADJ (in matters of the heart) nâwk jai (literally, 'outside'-'heart') นอกใจ; for a married person to have a lover mii chúu มีชู้

unfortunate ADJ unfortunately ADV chôhk ráai โชคร้าย

unhappy ADJ mâi mii khwaam sùk (literally, 'no'-'have'-'happiness') ไม่มีความสุข

uniform N (clothing – police/military uniform etc.) khrûeang bàehp เครื่องแบบ

uninteresting ADJ See 'boring'

United Kingdom N (FORMAL TERM) sà-hà râat-chá aa-naa-jàk สหราชอาณาจักร, or simply (UK) yuu kheh ยูเค

United States N (FORMAL TERM) sà-hà-rát à-meh-rí-kaa สหรัฐอเมริกา, or simply à-meh-rí-kaa อเมริกา, or sà-hà-rát สหรัฐฯ

universal ADJ (i.e. occidental – of the 'modern' Western world) sǎa-kon สากล; in general thûa pai ทั่วไป

university N má-hǎawít-thá-yaa-lai มหาวิทยาลัย, (COLLOQUIAL) má-hǎalai มหาลัย

unlawful ADJ phìt kòt mǎai ผิดกฎหมาย

unless CONJ nâwk jàak... นอกจาก

unlimited ADJ mâi jam-kàt ไม่จำกัด

unlock V khǎi kun jae ไขกุญแจ, or pòeht-láwk เปิดล็อค (literally means 'open'-'lock')

unlucky ADJ chôhk ráai โชคร้าย

unnecessary ADJ mâi jam-pen ไม่จำเป็น

unripe ADJ mâi sùk ไม่สุก (it can be used to refer to uncooked food)

unsatisfactory ADJ mâi phaw jai ไม่พอใจ, or mâi dii phaw ไม่ดีพอ, or (not as good as it should be) mâi dii thâo thîi khuan ไม่ดีเท่าที่ควร

until PREP jon krà-thâng จนกระทั่ง, also (MORE COLLOQUIALLY) jon kwàa... จนกว่า, or simply kwàa กว่า

unwrap v kâeh àwk แก้ออก

up, upward ADV khûen ขึ้น

update v, N (from English, with essentially the same meaning and pronunciation) àp dèht อัพเดท

upgrade v yók-rá-dàp ยกระดับ

uphold v yók-khûen ยกขึ้น

upset, unhappy ADJ mâi sà-baai jai ไม่สบายใจ

upside down ADV (e.g. a car on its roof) ngâai thǎwng หงายท้อง

upstairs ADJ, ADV khâang bon ข้างบน

urban N nai mueang ในเมือง

urge, to push for v (e.g. equal rights) rîak ráwng เรียกร้อง

urgent ADJ rêng dùan เร่งด่วน, or simply dùan ด่วน

urinate v (medical/formal term) pàt-sǎa-wá ปัสสาวะ, (COLLOQUIAL – whereas in English one might say 'piss' – in Thai this is not a vulgar word) chìi ฉี่, or (mildly vulgar) yîao เยี่ยว

use, utilize v chái ใช้

used to ADJ (to be used to) chin ชิน; to be accustomed to... khún khoei kàp... คุ้นเคยกับ; (do something) khoei เคย (NOTE: for fuller description of how the word khoei เคย is used – see 'have')

useful ADJ mii prà-yòht มีประโยชน์

useless ADJ mâi mii prà-yòht ไม่มีประโยชน์, (COLLOQUIAL – as in a 'useless person') mâi dâi rûeang ไม่ได้เรื่อง

usual ADJ pà-kà-tì ปกติ

usually ADV taam pà-kà-tì ตามปกติ, or (MORE SIMPLY COLLOQUIAL) pà-kà-tì ปกติ

uterus/womb N mót lûuk มดลูก

utmost ADJ thîi-sùt ที่สุด

V

vacant ADJ wâang ว่าง: e.g. (at a hotel) 'do you have any vacant rooms?' mii hâwng wâang mǎi (literally, 'have'-'room'-'vacant'-'question marker') มีห้องว่างไหม

vacation/holiday N wan yùt phák phàwn (literally, 'day'-'stop'-'rest') วันหยุดพักผ่อน

vaccination N chìit wák-siin ฉีดวัคซีน

vacuum N sǔn-yaa-kàat สุญญากาศ

vagabond/vagrant/homeless person N (FORMAL) khon phá-neh-jawn คนพเนจร, or (COLLOQUIAL) khon rêh-rôn คนเร่ร่อน

vagina N (colloquial – not too vulgar) jĭm จิ๋ม, also (VERY COLLOQUIAL) pî ปี๋, (colloquial and extremely vulgar, the equivalent of the English word 'cunt') hǐi หี

vague ADJ khlum khruea คลุมเครือ

vain ADJ (self-important) thǔeh tua ถือตัว, or yìng หยิ่ง

valid/usable ADJ chái dâi ใช้ได้

valley N hùp khǎo หุบเขา

valuable ADJ mii khun khâa มีคุณค่า

value N (cost/price) raa-khaa ราคา

value v (to estimate a price) tii khâa ตีค่า

van N (vehicle) rót tûu รถตู้

vanish v hǎai pai หายไป

various ADJ lǎai หลาย

varnish v khlûeap เคลือบ

vase N jaeh-kan แจกัน

vast ADJ yài-toh ใหญ่โต

VAT N (value added tax – Thailand does have one) phaa-sǐi mun-lá-khâa pôehm ภาษีมูลค่าเพิ่ม

venereal disease/VD N (general term for STDs) kaam-má-rôhk กามโรค

vegetable(s) N phàk ผัก

vegetarian N mang-sà-wí-rát มังสวิรัติ

vegetarian ADJ kin jeh กินเจ

vehicle N (general term for wheeled vehicles) rót รถ

vein N (in the body) sên lûeat เส้นเลือด

verandah N See 'porch'

vernacular/colloquial/spoken language N phaa-sǎa phûut ภาษาพูด

very, extremely ADV mâak มาก

vest, waistcoat N sûea kák เสื้อกั๊ก

vet N (animal doctor) sàt-tà-wá-phâet สัตวแพทย์

via PREP phàan ผ่าน

vibrant/lively/full of life ADJ mii chii-wít chii-waa มีชีวิตชีวา, or râa roehng ร่าเริง

Vientiane N (the capital of Laos) wiang-jan เวียงจันทน์ (pronounced something like wiang-jahn)

Vietnam N wîat-naam เวียดนาม

Vietnamese N (people) chaow wîat-naam ชาวเวียดนาม

view, panorama N (from English) wiu วิว

view, look at V chom wiu ชมวิว

village N mùu bâan หมู่บ้าน

villager N (also more generally 'ordinary folk' – both in the country and the city) chaow bâan ชาวบ้าน

vinegar N nám sôm น้ำส้ม (Thai vinegar is not quite the same as 'western vinegar'. It is something which one adds to such things as noodle soup, etc. to enhance the flavor)

violent ADJ run raehng รุนแรง; violence khwaam run raehng ความรุนแรง

virus N (from English) chúea wai-rát เชื้อไวรัส, or simply wai-rát ไวรัส

visa N (from English) wii-sâa วีซ่า

visit V yîam เยี่ยม; make a visit pai yîam ไปเยี่ยม

visitor N (guest in one's home) khàek แขก

vitamin(s) N (from English) wí-taa-min วิตามิน

vivid ADJ sòt-sǎi สดใส

vocabulary N (words) sàp ศัพท์ (pronounced very similar to the English word 'sup' – from 'supper')

voice/sound N sǐang เสียง (also the colloquial word for 'a vote' in an election)

voicemail N (from English) wois-mehl วอยซ์เมล์

volcano N phuu khǎo fai ภูเขาไฟ

volume N (quantity) pà-rí-maan ปริมาณ; volume (sound level) rá-dàp sǐang ระดับเสียง

volunteer V aa-sǎa อาสา, N (a person who performs voluntary service) aa-sǎa-sà-màk อาสาสมัคร

vomit V (POLITE) aa-jian อาเจียน, (colloquial – though less polite) spew/chuck/throw up ûak อ้วก

voodoo, black magic N sǎi-yá-sàat ไสยศาสตร์

vote V (from English) wòht โหวต, also àwk sǐang ออกเสียง, or long khá-naehn ลงคะแนน

vulgar/crude/coarse ADJ yàap khaai หยาบคาย

W

wages N khâa jâang ค่าจ้าง *Also see* 'salary'

waist N (of the body) eho เอว

wait (for) V raw รอ

waiter/waitress N (COLLOQUIAL) dèk sòehp เด็กเสิร์ฟ

wake someone up V plùk ปลุก

wake up V tùehn ตื่น

walk V doehn เดิน

walking distance N (within) doehn pai dâi เดินไปได้

wall N (i.e. a stone/solid wall) kam-pha-ehng กำแพง; wall (internal wall of a house) phà-nǎng ผนัง

wallet N krà-pǎo sà-taang กระเป๋าสตางค์, or (MORE COLLOQUIALLY) krà-pǎo tang กระเป๋าตังค์

want V (FORMAL) with the sense of 'need' tâwng kaan ต้องการ, or (COLLOQUIAL) more like the sense of 'wanting' something yàak อยาก

war N sǒng-khraam สงคราม

war, to make V tham sǒng-khraam ทำสงคราม

wardrobe N tûu sûea phâa ตู้เสื้อผ้า

warehouse N koh-dang โกดัง

warm ADJ ùn อุ่น (also for something (e.g. food) to be warm)

warmth N (the feeling of 'warmth') òp ùn อบอุ่น

warn V tuean เตือน

warning N kham tuean คำเตือน

warranty N ráp-prà-kan รับประกัน

wash V (objects – e.g. car, windows, etc. but also to wash the face, hands, feet) láang ล้าง

wash the dishes V láang jaan ล้างจาน; wash clothes sák phâa ซักผ้า; to wash hair sà phŏm สระผม

wart N hùut หูด

waste N khăwng sĭa ของเสีย

wasteful ADJ plueang เปลือง

watch N (wristwatch; also 'clock') naa-lí-kaa นาฬิกา

watch V (show, movie) duu ดู, stare V mawng มอง

watch over, guard V fâo เฝ้า

water N náam น้ำ

water buffalo N khwaai ควาย

waterfall N náam tòk น้ำตก

watermelon N taeng moh แตงโม

waterproof ADJ kan náam กันน้ำ

water-ski N sà-kii náam สกีน้ำ

wave N (in the sea) khlûehn คลื่น

wave V (hand) bòhk mueh โบกมือ

wax N khîi phûeng ขี้ผึ้ง; ear wax khîi hŭn ขี้หู

way N (i.e. the way to get somewhere) thaang ทาง; 'which way do you go?' pai thaang năi (literally, 'go'-'way'-'which') ไปทางไหน; (method of doing something) wí-thii วิธี; (by way of, e.g. bus/train etc.) dohy โดย

way in N thaang khâo ทางเข้า

way out/exit N thaang àwk ทางออก

we, us PRON rao เรา

weak ADJ (lacking physical strength) àwn aeh อ่อนแอ

wealthy ADJ mâng khâng มั่งคั่ง, or simply 'rich' ruai รวย

weapon N aa-wút อาวุธ

wear V sài ใส่

weary ADJ nùeai เหนื่อย

weather N aa-kàat อากาศ

weave V (cloth etc.) thaw (pronounced 'tore') ทอ

weaving N kaan thaw การทอ

website N (from English) wép sái เว็บไซต์

wedding N ngaan tàeng-ngaan งานแต่งงาน

Wednesday N wan phút วันพุธ

weed N (i.e. a weed in the garden) wát-chá-phûet วัชพืช

week N (FORMAL) sàp-daa สัปดาห์, (more commonly) aa-thít อาทิตย์

weekend N wan sùt sàp-daa วันสุดสัปดาห์, (COLLOQUIAL) săo aa-thít เสาร์อาทิตย์

weekly ADV thúk aa-thít ทุกอาทิตย์

weep/cry V ráwng hâi ร้องไห้

weigh V châng ชั่ง; to weigh yourself/ for someone to weigh themselves châng náam-nàk ชั่งน้ำหนัก

weight N náam-nàk น้ำหนัก

weight, to gain V náam-nàk khûen น้ำหนักขึ้น, (COLLOQUIAL) ûan khûen (literally, 'fat'-'increase/go up') อ้วนขึ้น

weight, to lose V lót náam-nàk ลดน้ำหนัก

welcome! INTERJ yin-dii tâwn ráp ยินดีต้อนรับ

welcome V (to welcome someone) tâwn ráp ต้อนรับ

well ADJ (as in 'do something well') dii ดี

well N (for water) bàw náam baa-daan บ่อน้ำบาดาล, or simply bàw náam บ่อน้ำ

well-behaved ADJ tham tua dii ทำตัวดี

well-cooked/well-done ADJ sùk สุก

well done! ADJ dii mâak ดีมาก

well-mannered ADJ maa-rá-yâat dii มารยาทดี

well off/wealthy ADJ ruai รวย

west N (direction) tà-wan tòk ตะวันตก

Westerner N chaow tàwan tòk ชาวตะวันตก

wet ADJ pìak เปียก

whale N plaa waan ปลาวาฬ

what? PRON (or which?) àrai อะไร (NOTE: unlike English, 'what?' in Thai comes at the end of a sentence. For example — 'what's your name' khun chûeh àrai (literally, 'you'-'name'—'what?') คุณชื่ออะไร; 'what color is it?' sĭi àrai (literally, 'color'-'what?') สีอะไร, or 'what's your telephone number?' thoh-rá-sàp boeh àrai (literally, 'telephone'-'number'-'what?') โทรศัพท์เบอร์อะไร

what are you doing? khun tham à-rai คุณทำอะไร

what for? phûea àrai เพื่ออะไร

what is going on?/what's up? (COLLOQUIAL) wâa-ngai ว่าไง

what kind of? chá-nít năi ชนิดไหน, (MORE COLLOQUIAL) bàehp năi แบบไหน

what time is it? kìi mohng láew กี่โมงแล้ว

wheel N láw ล้อ

when? PRON ADV mûea-rài เมื่อไร (usually used at the end of a sentence): e.g. 'when are you going?' khun jà pai mûearài (literally, 'you'-'will'-'go'-'when') คุณจะไปเมื่อไหร่

whenever ADV (as in the expression: 'whenever you like' or, 'any time at all') mûea-rài kâw dâi เมื่อไรก็ได้

where? ADV thîi năi ที่ไหน (usually used at the end of a sentence): e.g. 'where is she?' khăo yùu thîi năi เขาอยู่ที่ไหน

where to? pai thîi năi ไปที่ไหน

which? PRON năi ไหน (usually used at the end of a sentence): e.g. 'which person?' khon năi คนไหน

while/during CONJ nai khà-nà thîi… ในขณะที่

whisper V krà-síp กระซิบ

whistle V phìu pàak ผิวปาก

white N sĭi khăaw สีขาว

who? PRON khrai ใคร

whole, all of N tháng mòt ทั้งหมด

whole ADJ (e.g. a set to be whole/complete) khróp ครบ

wholesale N (price) khăai sòng ขายส่ง (NOTE: retail price is khăai plìik ขายปลีก)

why? ADV tham-mai ทำไม (generally used, in contrast to English, at the end of a sentence)

wicked/evil ADJ ráai ร้าย

wide ADJ kwâang กว้าง

width N khwaam kwâang ความกว้าง

widow N mâeh mâai แม่ม่าย

widowed ADJ pen mâai เป็นม่าย

widower N phâw mâai พ่อม่าย

wife N (FORMAL/POLITE) phan-rá-yaa ภรรยา, (COMMON COLLOQUIAL) mia เมีย

Wifi/wifi N (from English) wai-fai วายฟาย

wig N (from English) wík วิก

wild ADJ (of animals) pàa ป่า: e.g. wild-cat maew pàa แมวป่า

will/shall AUX V (common marker of future tense) jà จะ

win V chá-ná ชนะ; (a/the) winner N phûu chá-ná ผู้ชนะ

wind N (a breeze and stronger) lom ลม

window N (in house) nâa tàang หน้าต่าง

wine N (from English) waai ไวน์

wing N (of a bird) pìik ปีก

wink V kà-phríp taa กะพริบตา

winter N (in Thailand the 'cool season' – Nov-Jan) nâa năow หน้าหนาว

wipe V chét เช็ด

wire N lûat ลวด; an electrical wire săai fai สายไฟ

wise ADJ chà-làat ฉลาด

wish/hope N wăng หวัง; to wish or hope for… wăng wâa… หวังว่า

witch N mâeh mót แม่มด

with PREP kàp กับ

withdraw/take out V (money from a bank/a tooth etc.) thăwn ถอน

with pleasure IDIOM dûai khwaam yin-dii ด้วยความยินดี

within reason/limits IDIOM phaai nai khâw jamkàt (pronounced 'jum-gut') ภายในข้อจำกัด

without PREP pràat-sà-jàak ปราศจาก, or dohy mâi mii โดยไม่มี

witness N phá-yaan พยาน; to witness hĕn pen phá-yaan เห็นเป็นพยาน

wobble V (as in 'to walk with a wobble') soh seh โซเซ

woman N phûu yǐng ผู้หญิง

womanizer N (philanderer, cassanova) jâo chúu เจ้าชู้

wonderful ADJ nâa prà-làat jai น่าประหลาดใจ

wood/timber N mái ไม้

wooden ADJ (i.e. made from wood) tham dûai mái ทำด้วยไม้, or tham jàak mái ทำจากไม้

wool N (from a sheep) khǒn kàe ขนแกะ

word N kham คำ

work/occupation N aa-chîip อาชีพ, (MORE COLLOQUIAL) ngaan งาน

work V tham ngaan ทำงาน

work (e.g. for a piece of machinery, etc. to function) tham ngaan ทำงาน (NOTE: the English word 'work' is also commonly used in this sense but with a slightly 'Thai-ified' pronunciation)

worker on a ship N lôuk-ruea ลูกเรือ

world N lôhk โลก

worm N (general term for 'worm-like' creatures) nǎwn หนอน; earthworm sâi duean ไส้เดือน

worn out, tired ADJ nùeai เหนื่อย; (COLLOQUIAL) to have 'no more energy' mòt raehng หมดแรง

worn out/torn ADJ (clothes etc.) khàat ขาด (NOTE: this term is also used to refer to something that is 'lacking' or 'missing' – from a dish of food/a part from a machine, etc.)

worn out/broken/unrepairable ADJ (machine) phang (similar in sound to 'pung' with the 'ung' sound pronounced as in 'bungle') พัง

worry V (about someone) pen hùang เป็นห่วง; to feel worried, be anxious kang-won กังวล

worse ADJ (e.g. a medical condition) yâeh long แย่ลง

worship V buu-chaa บูชา

worst ADJ yâeh thîi sùt แย่ที่สุด

worth, to have N mii khâa มีค่า

worthless ADJ rái khâa ไร้ค่า

worthwhile/to be worth it ADJ (i.e. value for money) khúm khâa คุ้มค่า, or simply khúm คุ้ม

would like/may I have? khǎw ขอ

wound N bàat phlǎeh บาดแผล, or simply phlǎeh แผล

wrap V hàw ห่อ

wreck V See 'destroy'

wrist N khâw mueh ข้อมือ

write V khǐan เขียน

writer N nák khǐan นักเขียน

wrong ADJ (incorrect) phìt ผิด; (mistaken) khâòjai phìt เข้าใจผิด; (morally) tham phìt ทำผิด

X

x-ray N (from English) ék-sà-reh เอกซเรย์

Y

yatch/sailboat N ruea bai เรือใบ

yank/pull violently/snatch V (as in to have your bag 'snatched') krà-châak กระชาก

yard N (open space) laan ลาน

yawn V hǎaw หาว

yeah ADV (English colloquial form of 'yes') châi ใช่, (MORE COLLOQUIAL) jâ จ้ะ

year N years old ADJ (e.g. 16 years old) pii ปี

yell/shout V tà-kohn ตะโกน

yellow N sǐi lǔeang สีเหลือง

yes INTERJ châi ใช่ (NOTE: there are a number of other ways to say 'yes' in Thai depending on the form of the question asked. But this is the general form used to respond to many simple questions in the affirmative. The opposite to châi ใช่ is mâi châi ไม่ใช่ which means 'no' – again, this being dependent on the form of the question asked. Also see 'no', 'not')

Y

ENGLISH–THAI

yesterday N, ADV mûea waan níi เมื่อ
วานนี้

yet ADV (as in 'not yet') yang ยัง (Note:
the word yang is part of the question
form 'have you/he/they (verb) yet?'
rúe yang หรือยัง: e.g. 'have you eaten
yet?' khun kin khâaw rúe yang คุณ
กินข้าวหรือยัง. If you haven't eaten
yet you would normally answer yang
(not yet). If, on the other hand, you
had eaten you could answer – kin
láew 'I've eaten' กินแล้ว. For another
important meaning of yang *see* 'still')

you PRON (general polite term) khun
คุณ; you (INTIMATE) thoeh เธอ (Note: the
corresponding 'intimate' Thai word for
'I' that thoeh is paired with is chăn
ฉัน. These terms for 'I' and 'you' are
found in the vast majority of Thai popular songs. Try listening for them)

you're welcome! INTERJ mâi pen rai
ไม่เป็นไร

young ADJ (in years) aa-yú nói อา
ยุน้อย

younger brother or sister N (or more
generally meaning 'you' when ad-
dressing a junior person in a store/res-
taurant etc.) náwng น้อง

your PRON khăwng khun ของคุณ

youth, youths N (young people) yao-
wá-chon เยาวชน, (informal) nùm
săow (literally, 'young men'-'young
women') หนุ่มสาว

Z

zebra N máa laai (literally, 'horse'-
'stripe/striped') ม้าลาย

zero N sŭun ศูนย์

zip/zipper N (from English) síp ซิป

zone/area N khèht เขต

zoo N sŭan sàt (literally, 'garden/park'-
'animal') สวนสัตว์